Skip·Beat!

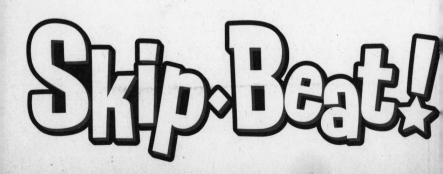

Shojo Beat

Skip·Beat!

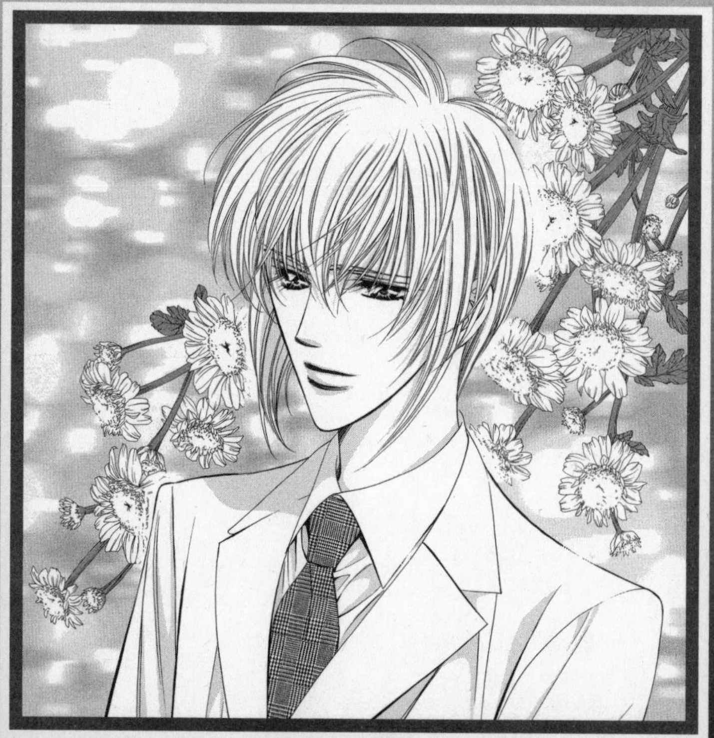

Skip·Beat!

Volume 10

CONTENTS

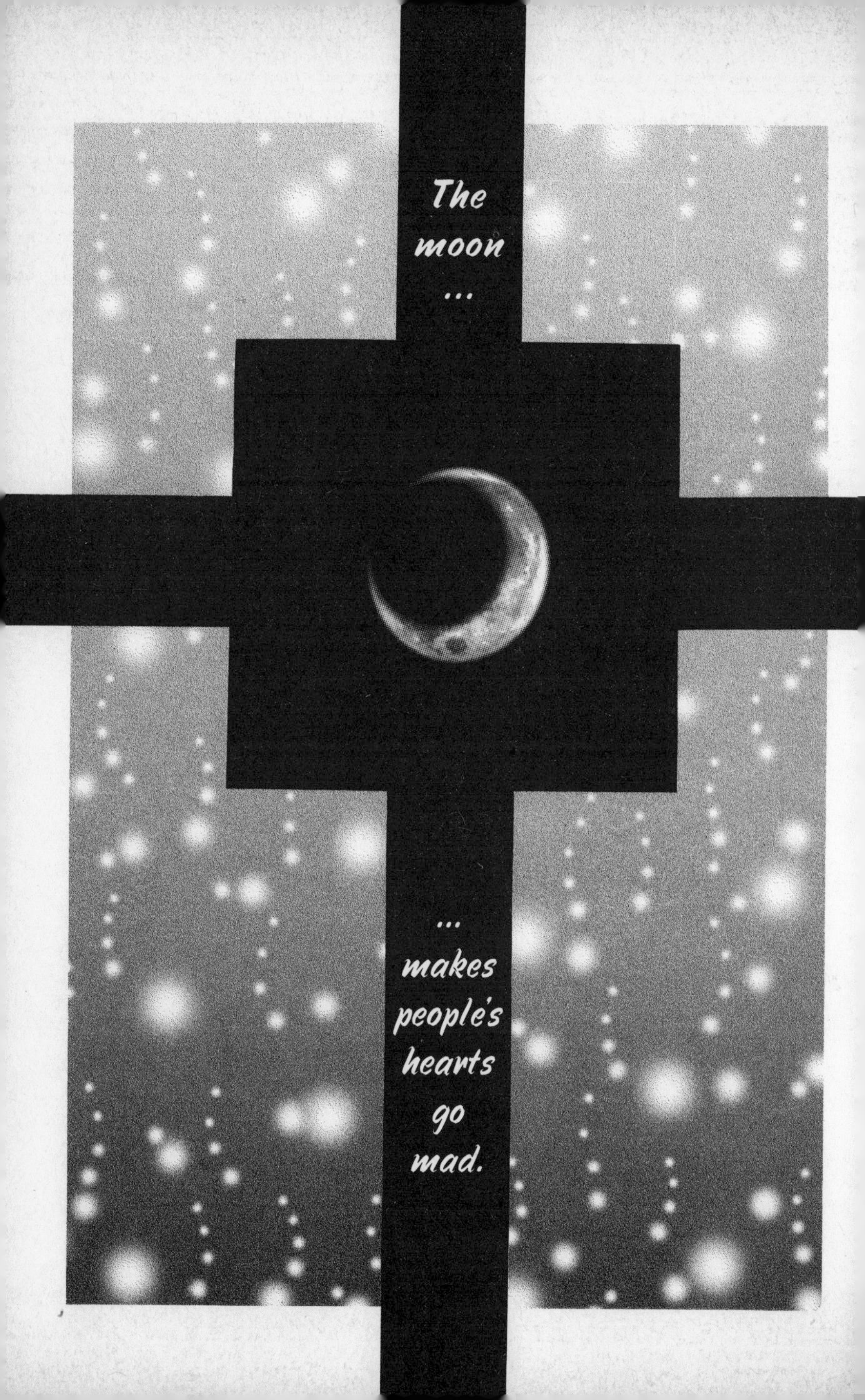
The moon ...
... makes people's hearts go mad.

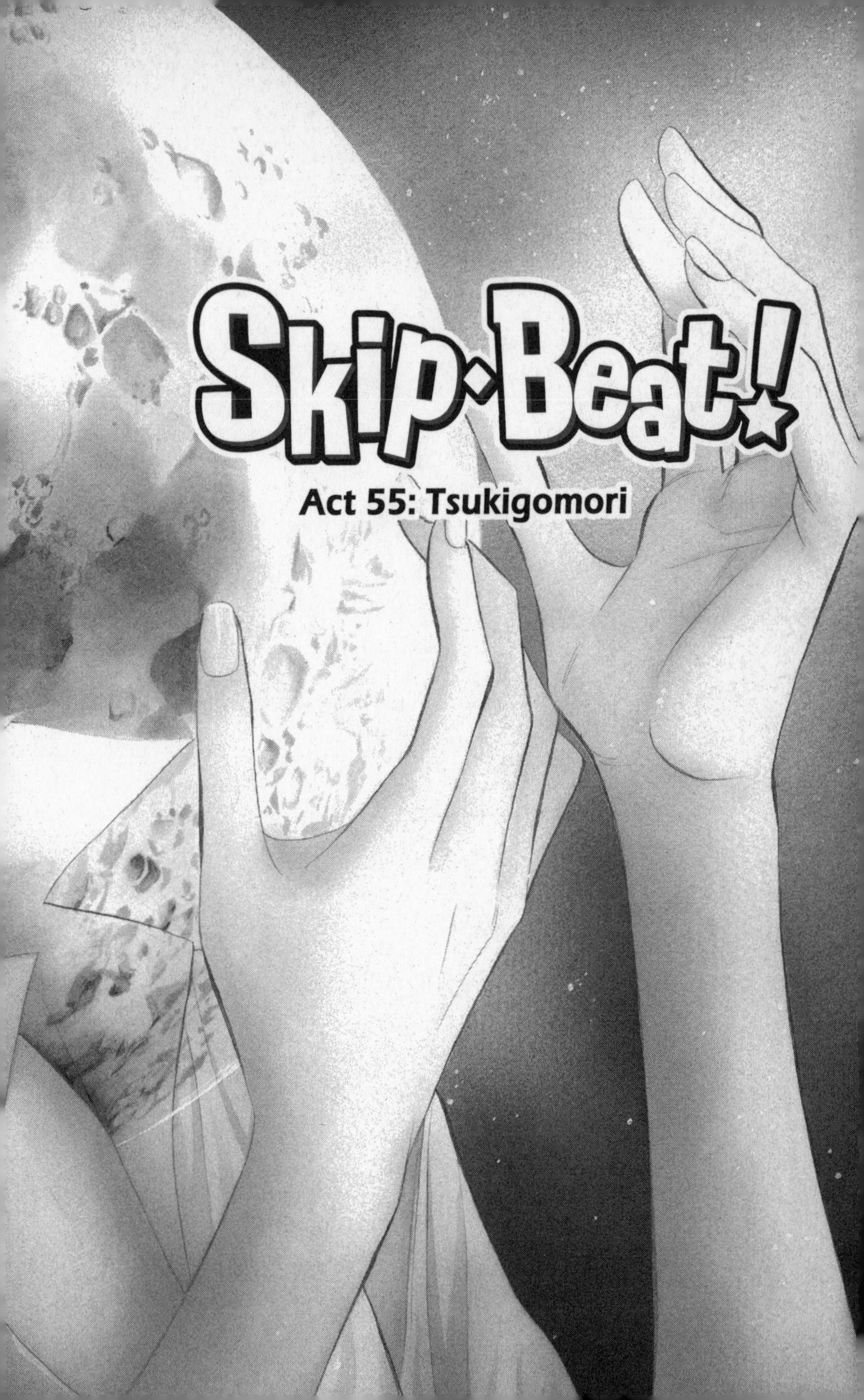
Skip·Beat!
Act 55: Tsukigomori

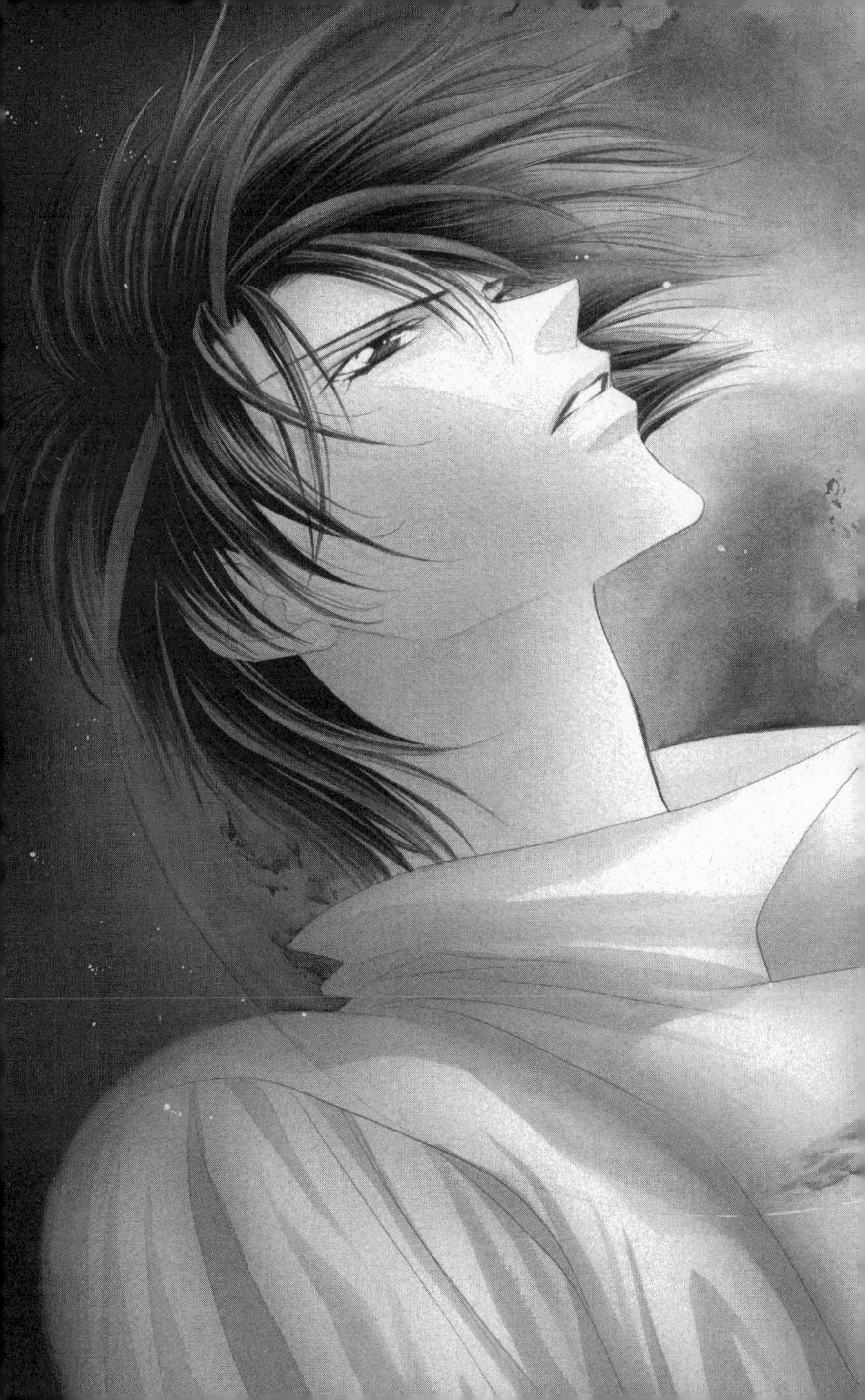

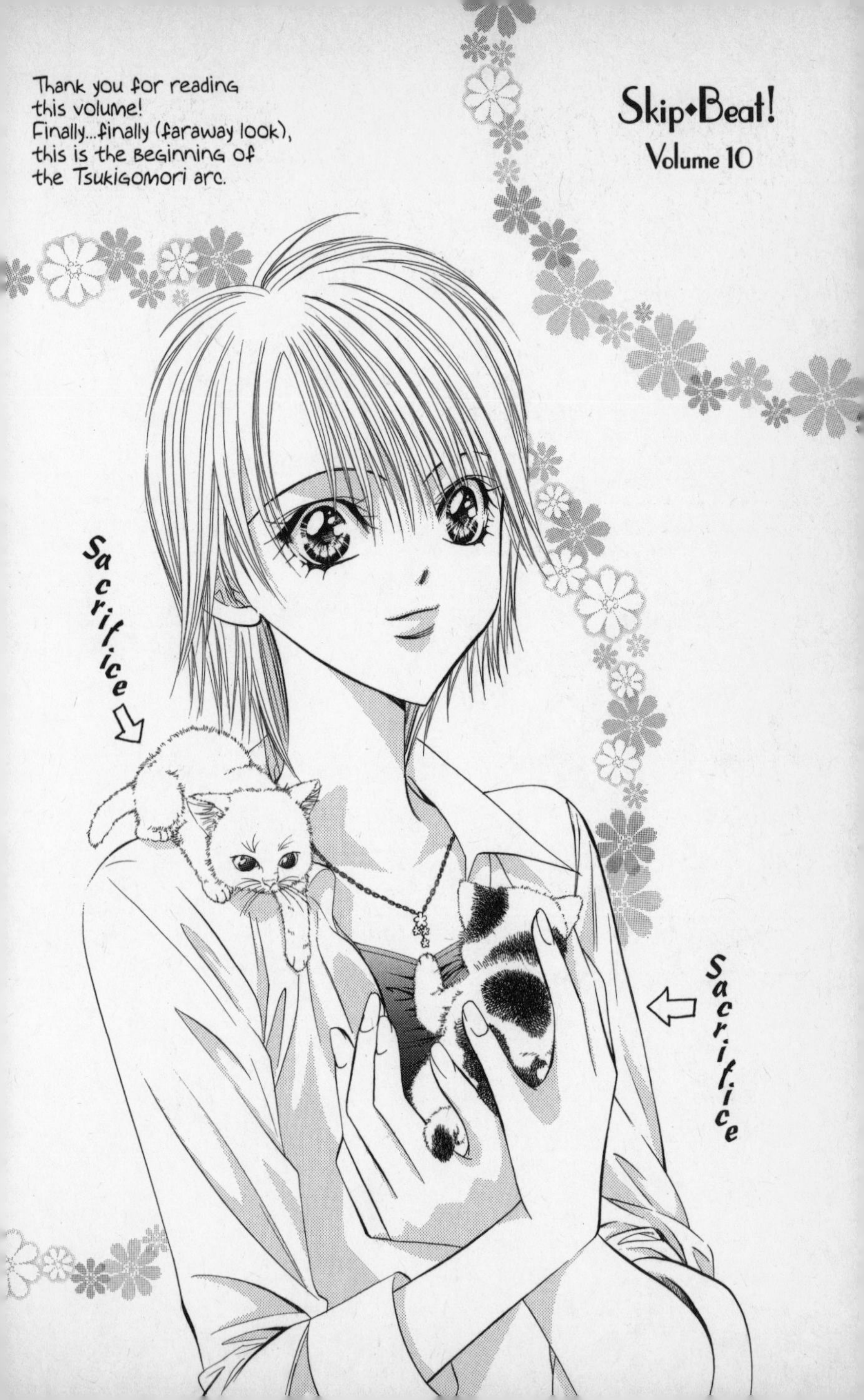
Skip•Beat!
Volume 10
Thank you for reading this volume! Finally...finally (faraway look), this is the beginning of the Tsukigomori arc.
Sacrifice
Sacrifice

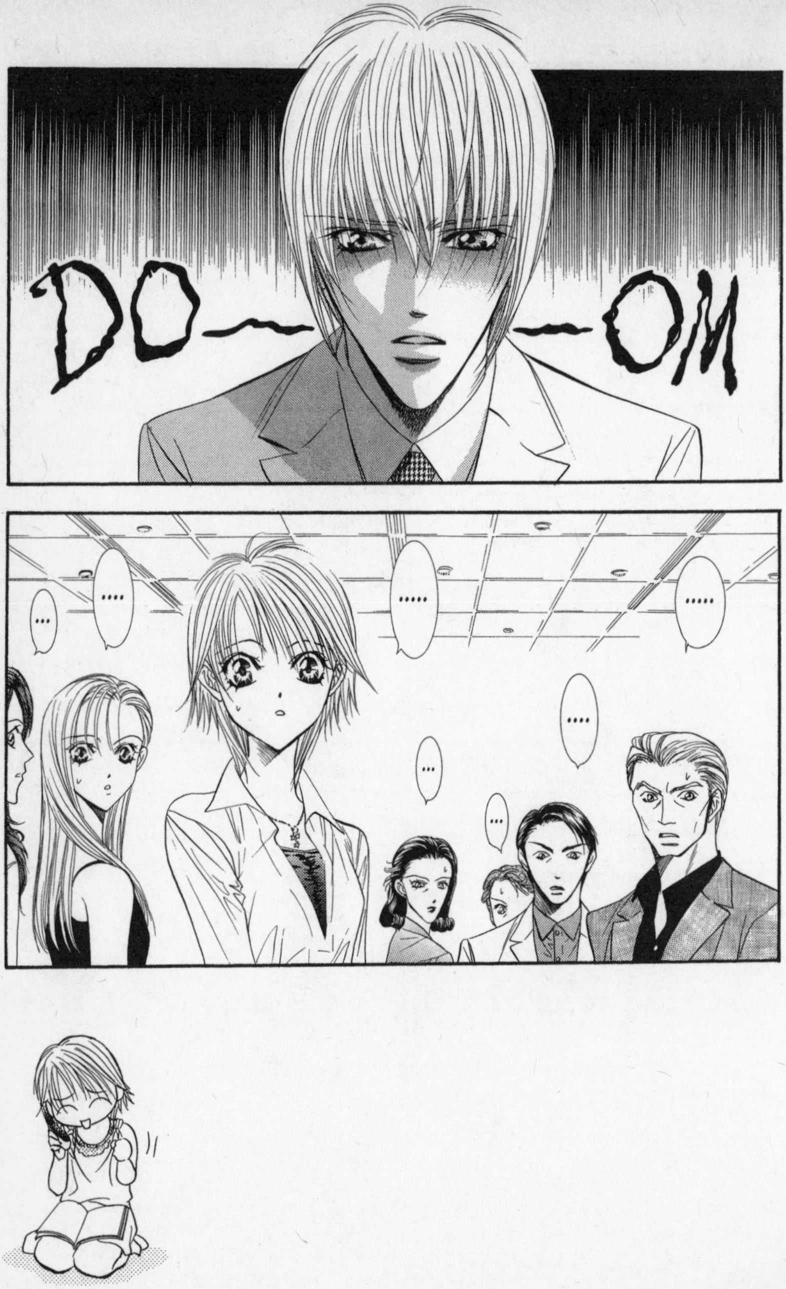
DO—— ——OM
.....
....
.....
...
...
....
...

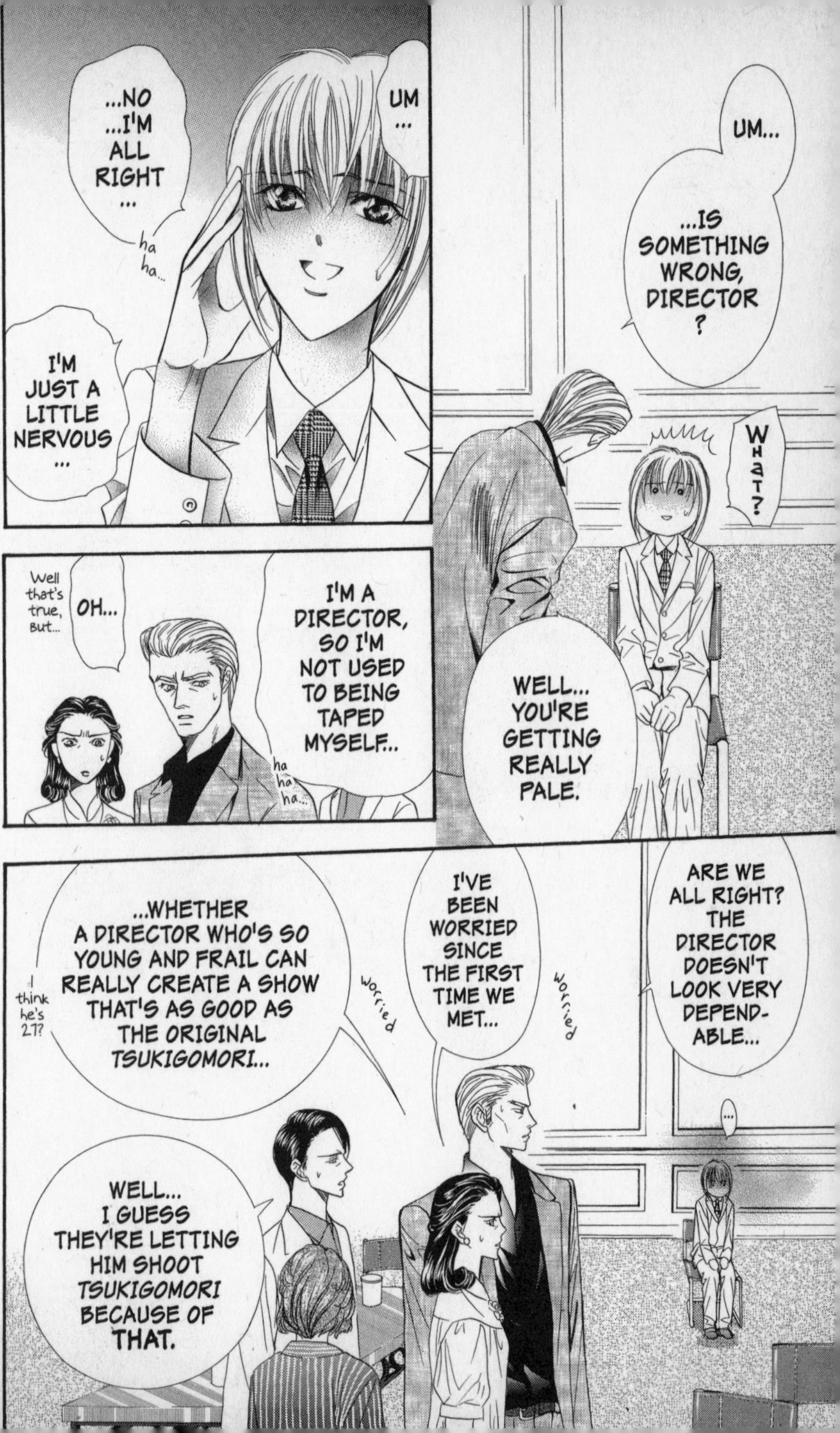
UM...
...IS SOMETHING WRONG, DIRECTOR?
WHAT?
WELL... YOU'RE GETTING REALLY PALE.
UM...
...NO ...I'M ALL RIGHT...
ha ha...
I'M JUST A LITTLE NERVOUS...
I'M A DIRECTOR, SO I'M NOT USED TO BEING TAPED MYSELF...
ha ha ha...
OH...
Well that's true, but...
ARE WE ALL RIGHT? THE DIRECTOR DOESN'T LOOK VERY DEPEND-ABLE...
...
worried
I'VE BEEN WORRIED SINCE THE FIRST TIME WE MET...
worried
...WHETHER A DIRECTOR WHO'S SO YOUNG AND FRAIL CAN REALLY CREATE A SHOW THAT'S AS GOOD AS THE ORIGINAL TSUKIGOMORI...
I think he's 27?
WELL... I GUESS THEY'RE LETTING HIM SHOOT TSUKIGOMORI BECAUSE OF THAT.

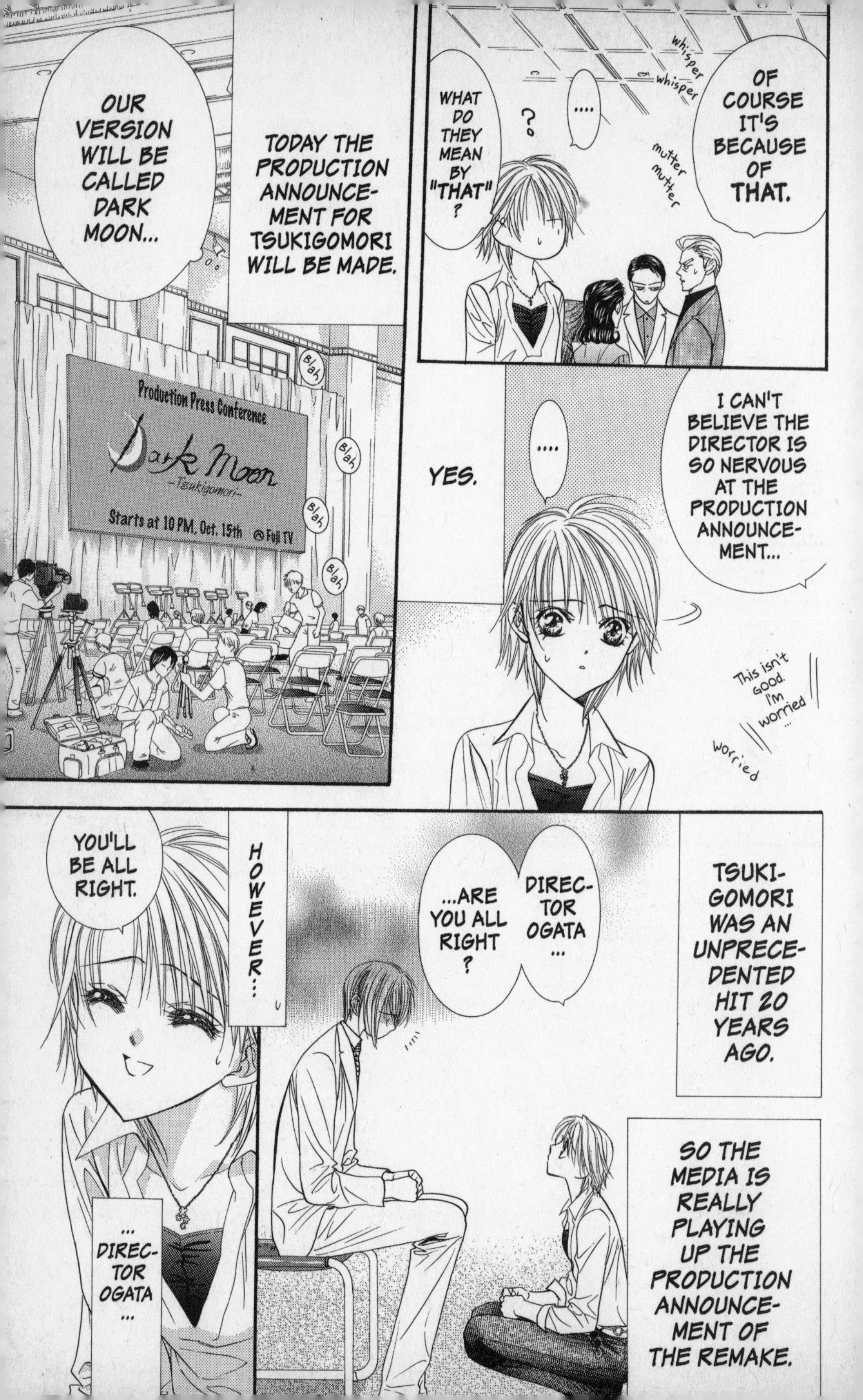
OF COURSE IT'S BECAUSE OF THAT.
whisper whisper
mutter mutter
....
WHAT DO THEY MEAN BY "THAT"?
?
I CAN'T BELIEVE THE DIRECTOR IS SO NERVOUS AT THE PRODUCTION ANNOUNCE-MENT...
....
YES.
This isn't good. I'm worried...
worried
TODAY THE PRODUCTION ANNOUNCE-MENT FOR TSUKIGOMORI WILL BE MADE.
OUR VERSION WILL BE CALLED DARK MOON...
Production Press Conference
Dark Moon
-Tsukigomori-
Starts at 10 PM, Oct. 15th @ Fuji TV
Blah
Blah
Blah
Blah
TSUKI-GOMORI WAS AN UNPRECE-DENTED HIT 20 YEARS AGO.
SO THE MEDIA IS REALLY PLAYING UP THE PRODUCTION ANNOUNCE-MENT OF THE REMAKE.
DIREC-TOR OGATA...
...ARE YOU ALL RIGHT?
HOWEVER...
YOU'LL BE ALL RIGHT.
...DIREC-TOR OGATA...

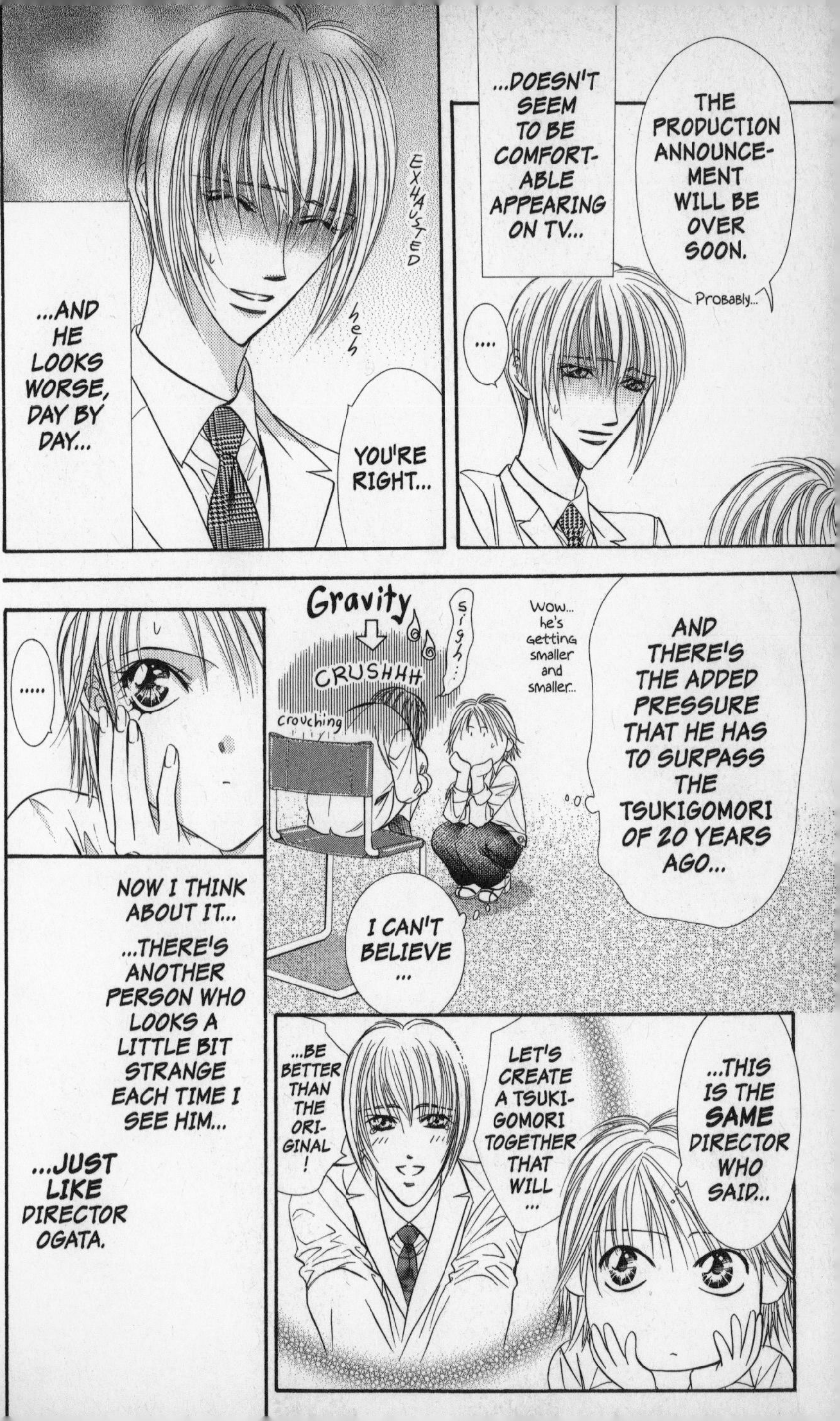
THE PRODUCTION ANNOUNCEMENT WILL BE OVER SOON.
Probably...
...DOESN'T SEEM TO BE COMFORTABLE APPEARING ON TV...
....
EXHAUSTED
heh
YOU'RE RIGHT...
...AND HE LOOKS WORSE, DAY BY DAY...
AND THERE'S THE ADDED PRESSURE THAT HE HAS TO SURPASS THE TSUKIGOMORI OF 20 YEARS AGO...
Wow... he's getting smaller and smaller...
sigh...
Gravity
CRUSHHH
crouching
I CAN'T BELIEVE ...
...THIS IS THE SAME DIRECTOR WHO SAID...
LET'S CREATE A TSUKIGOMORI TOGETHER THAT WILL ...
...BE BETTER THAN THE ORIGINAL!
.....
NOW I THINK ABOUT IT...
...THERE'S ANOTHER PERSON WHO LOOKS A LITTLE BIT STRANGE EACH TIME I SEE HIM...
...JUST LIKE DIRECTOR OGATA.

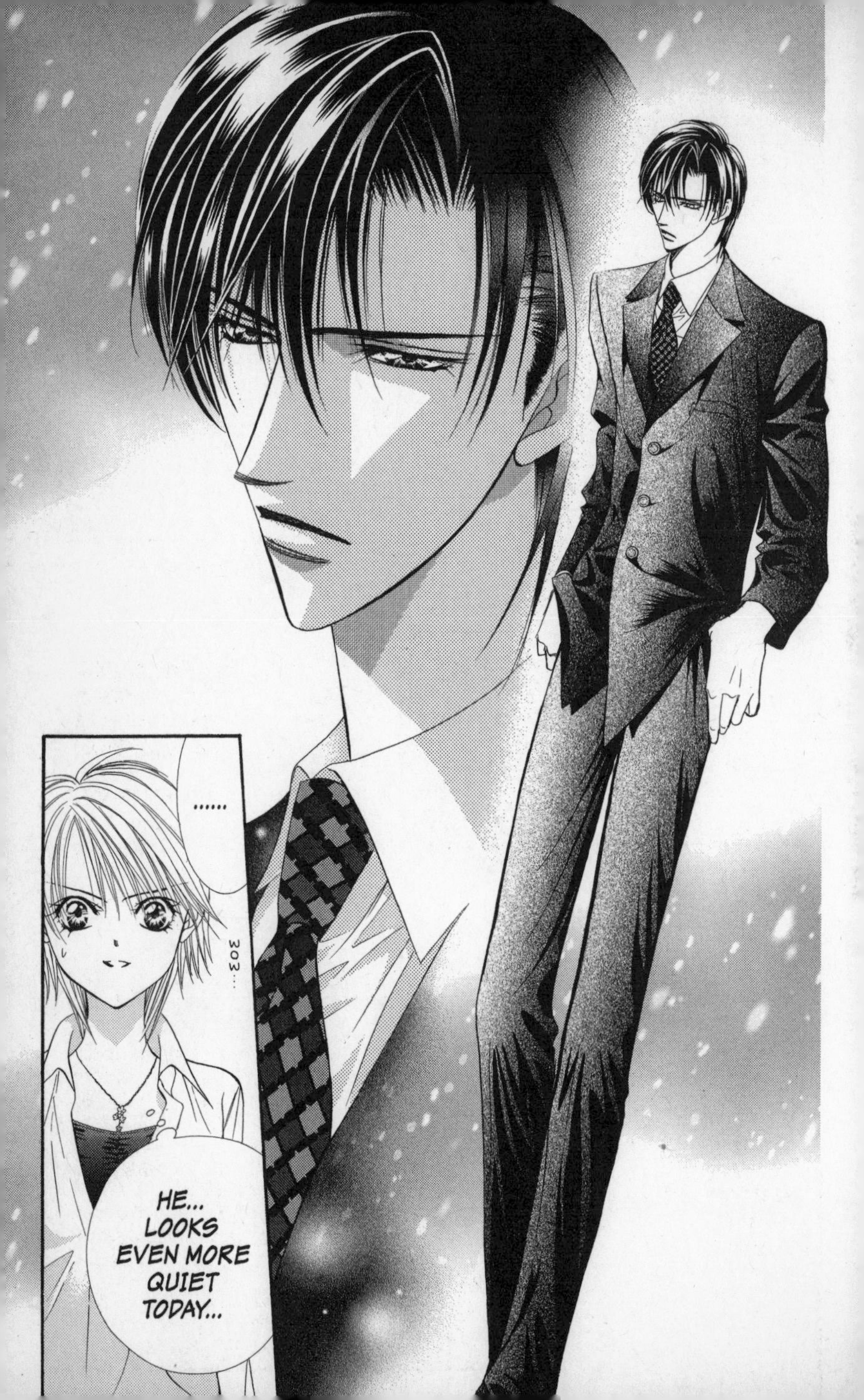
......
WOW...
HE... LOOKS EVEN MORE QUIET TODAY...

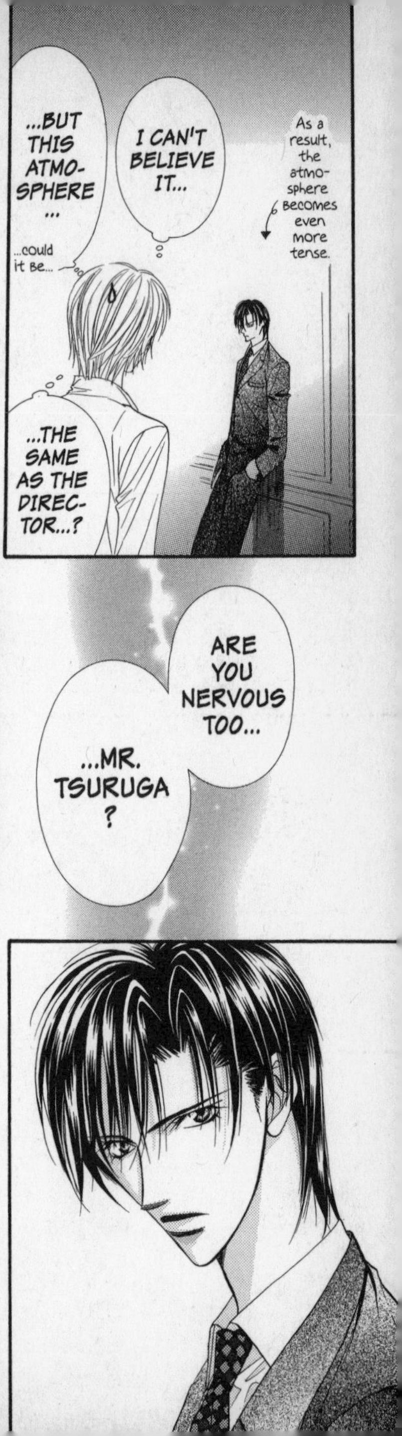
As a result, the atmosphere becomes even more tense.
I CAN'T BELIEVE IT...
...BUT THIS ATMOSPHERE ...
...could it be...
...THE SAME AS THE DIRECTOR...?
ARE YOU NERVOUS TOO...
...MR. TSURUGA?
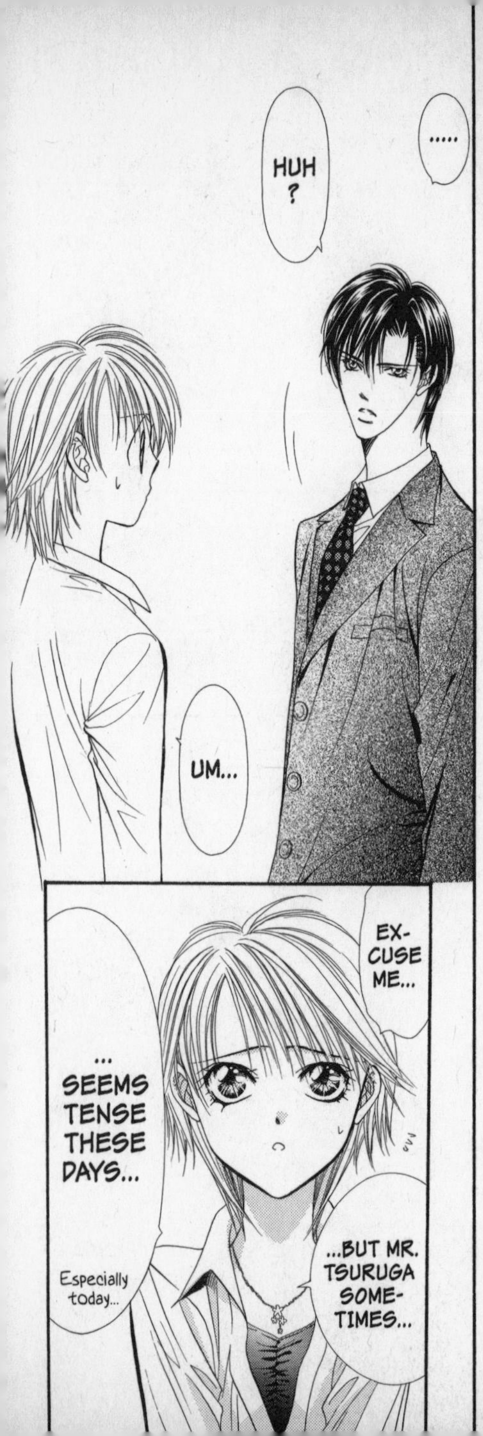
......
HUH?
UM...
EX-CUSE ME...
...BUT MR. TSURUGA SOMETIMES...
...SEEMS TENSE THESE DAYS...
Especially today...

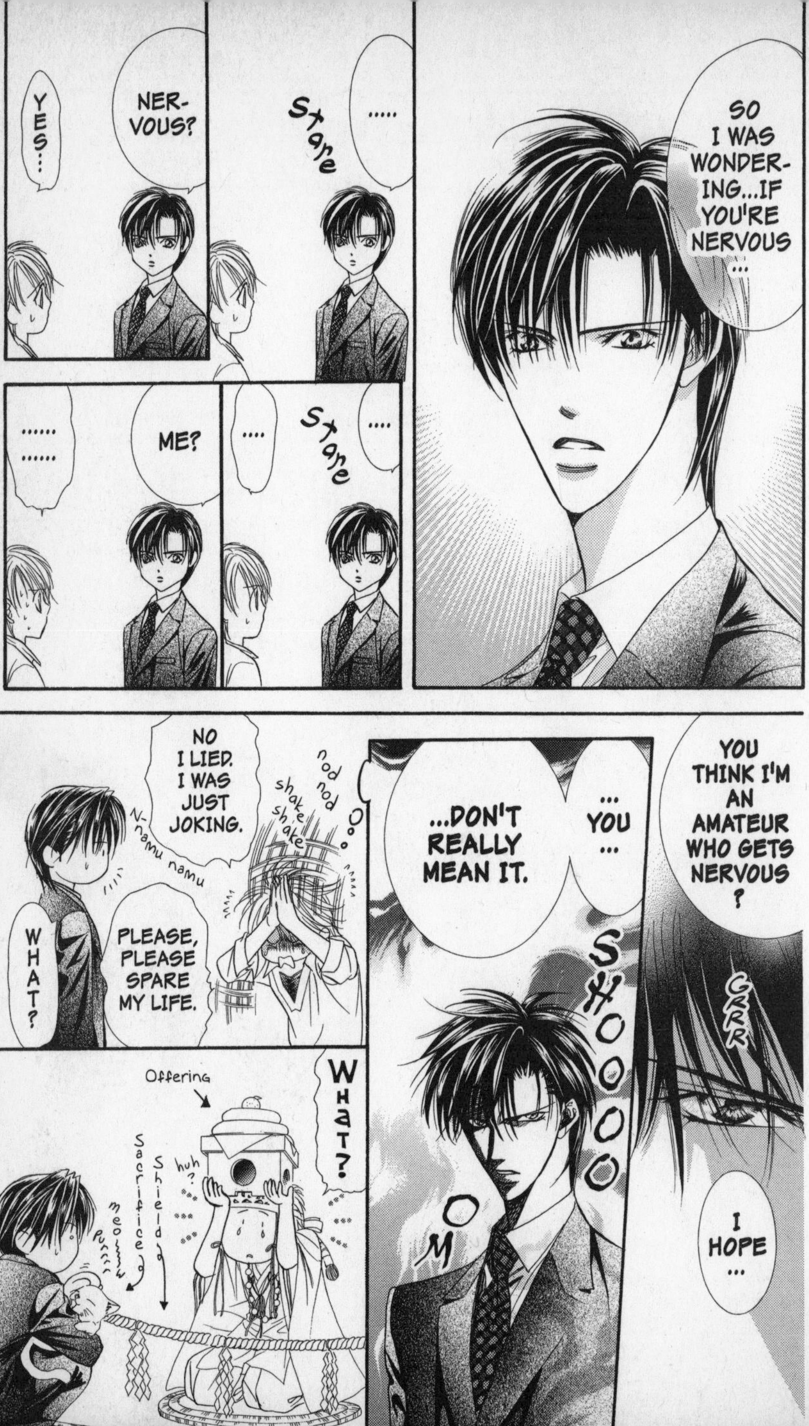
SO I WAS WONDERING...IF YOU'RE NERVOUS...
.....
Stare
NER-VOUS?
YES...
....
Stare
....
ME?
....
YOU THINK I'M AN AMATEUR WHO GETS NERVOUS?
GRRR
... YOU ...
...DON'T REALLY MEAN IT.
SHOOOOO
OM
I HOPE ...
NO I LIED. I WAS JUST JOKING.
nod nod
shake shake
N-namu namu
WHAT?
PLEASE, PLEASE SPARE MY LIFE.
WHAT?
Offering
huh?
Shield
Sacrifice
meow
purrr

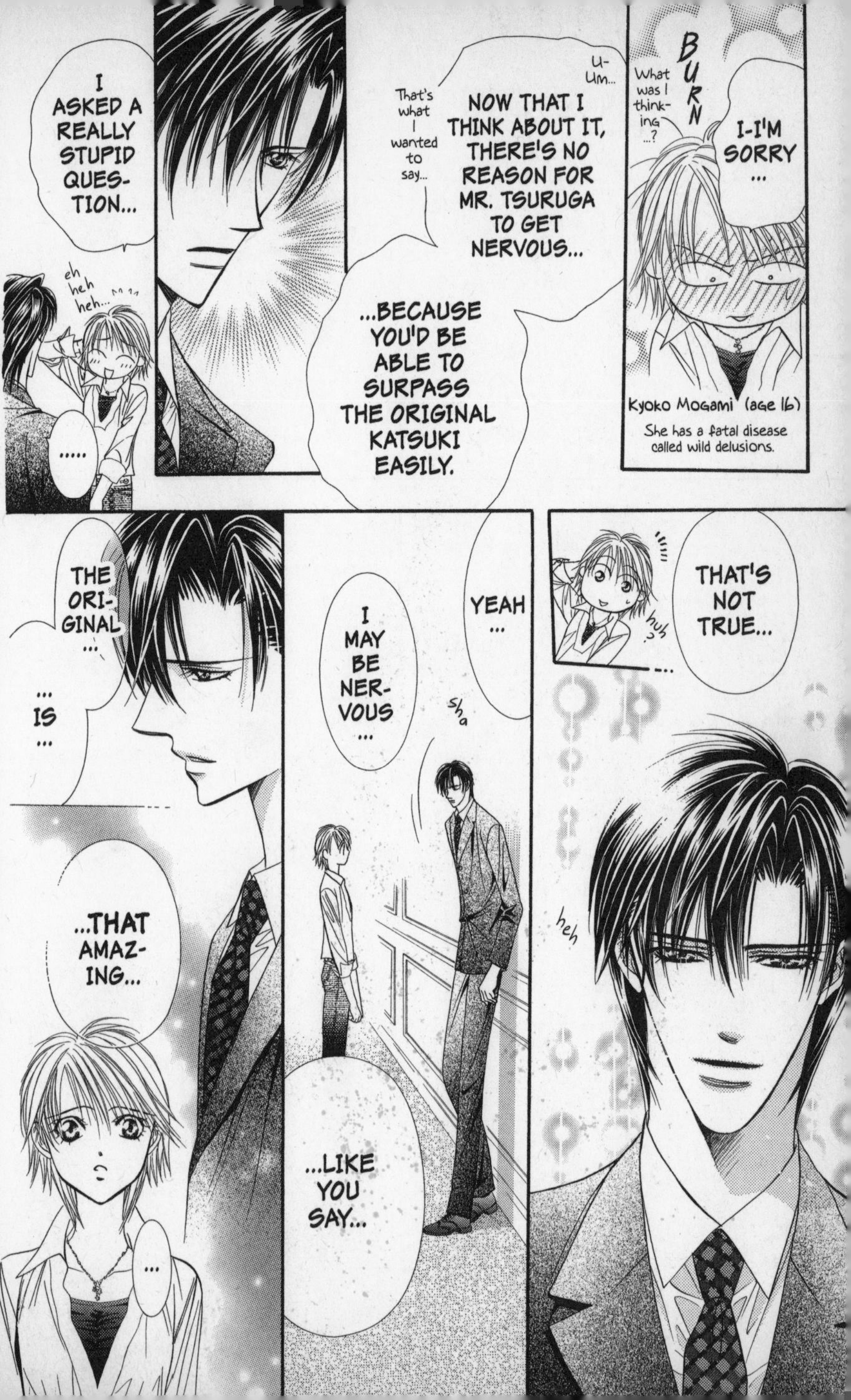
BURN
What was I thinking...?
I-I'M SORRY ...
Kyoko Mogami (age 16)
She has a fatal disease called wild delusions.
U-Um...
NOW THAT I THINK ABOUT IT, THERE'S NO REASON FOR MR. TSURUGA TO GET NERVOUS...
That's what I wanted to say...
...BECAUSE YOU'D BE ABLE TO SURPASS THE ORIGINAL KATSUKI EASILY.
I ASKED A REALLY STUPID QUESTION...
eh heh heh...
......
THAT'S NOT TRUE...
huh?
heh
YEAH ...
I MAY BE NERVOUS ...
sha
...LIKE YOU SAY...
THE ORIGINAL ...
... IS ...
...THAT AMAZING...
...

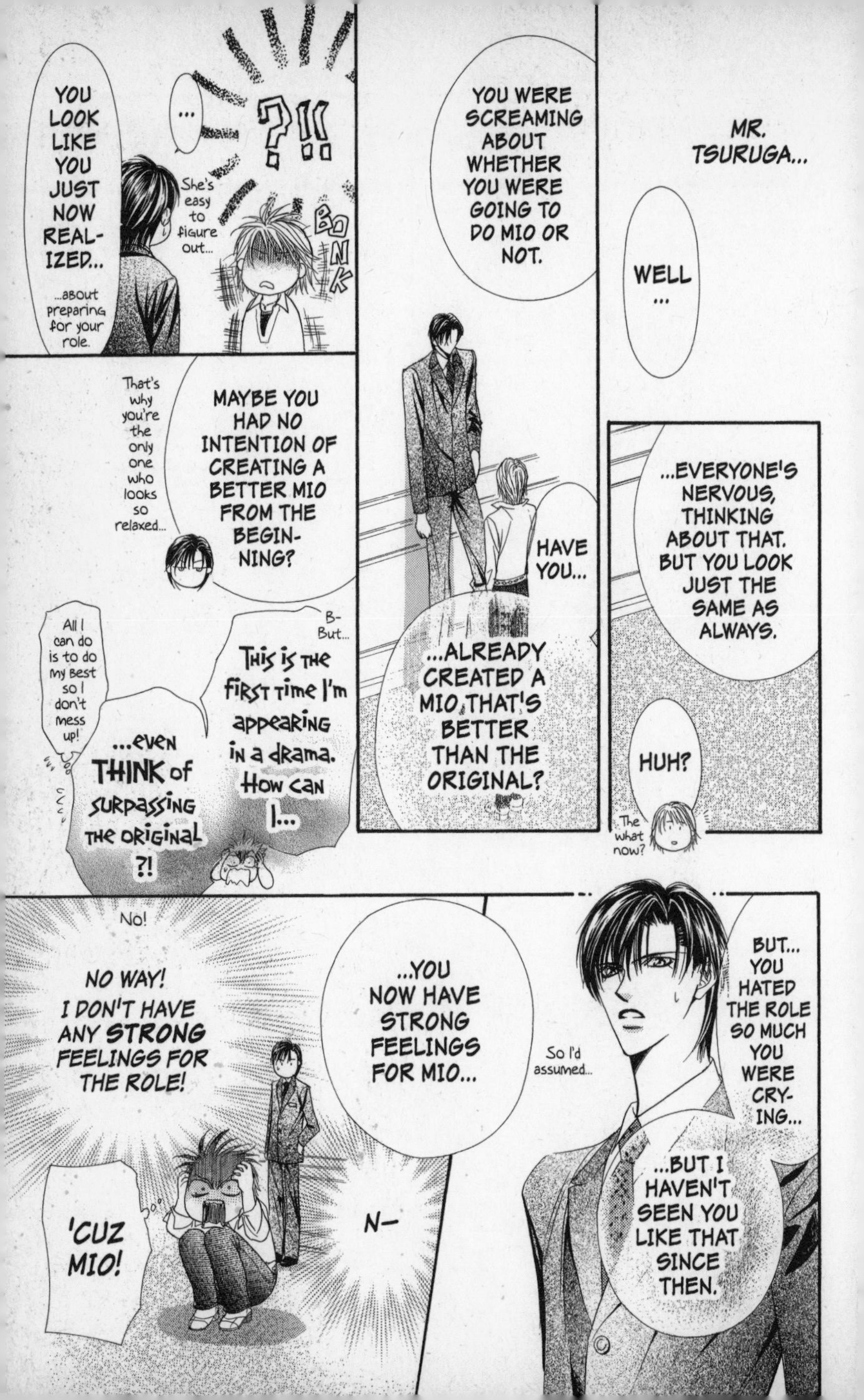

MR. TSURUGA...
WELL...
...EVERYONE'S NERVOUS, THINKING ABOUT THAT. BUT YOU LOOK JUST THE SAME AS ALWAYS.
HUH?
The what now?
YOU WERE SCREAMING ABOUT WHETHER YOU WERE GOING TO DO MIO OR NOT.
HAVE YOU...
...ALREADY CREATED A MIO THAT'S BETTER THAN THE ORIGINAL?
...
?!!
BONK
She's easy to figure out...
YOU LOOK LIKE YOU JUST NOW REAL-IZED...
...about preparing for your role.
MAYBE YOU HAD NO INTENTION OF CREATING A BETTER MIO FROM THE BEGIN-NING?
That's why you're the only one who looks so relaxed...
B-But...
This is the first time I'm appearing in a drama. How can I...
...even THINK of surpassing the original ?!
All I can do is to do my best so I don't mess up!
BUT... YOU HATED THE ROLE SO MUCH YOU WERE CRY-ING...
So I'd assumed...
...BUT I HAVEN'T SEEN YOU LIKE THAT SINCE THEN.
...YOU NOW HAVE STRONG FEELINGS FOR MIO...
N—
No!
NO WAY! I DON'T HAVE ANY STRONG FEELINGS FOR THE ROLE!
'CUZ MIO!

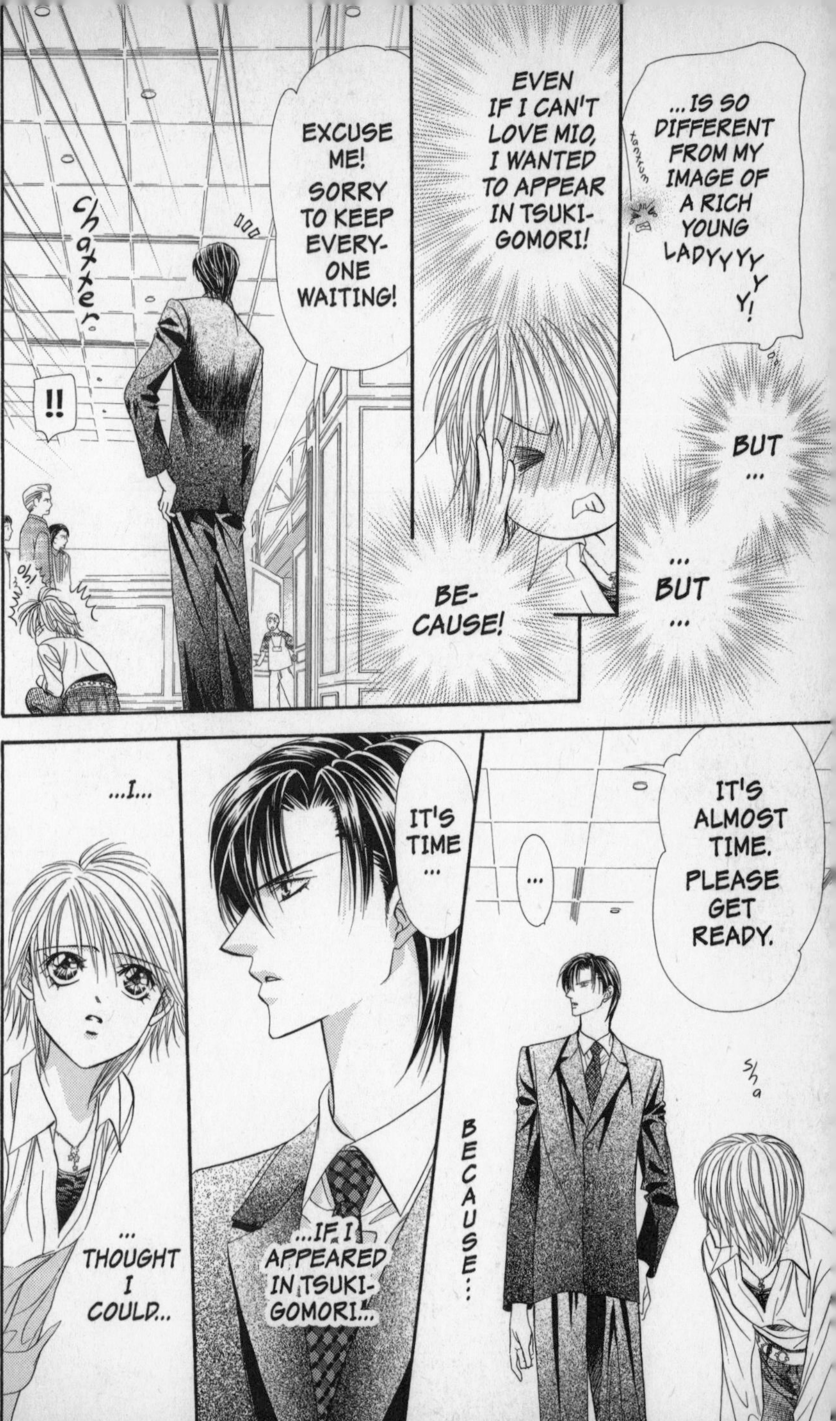
...IS SO DIFFERENT FROM MY IMAGE OF A RICH YOUNG LADYYYYY!
BUT ...
... BUT ...
EVEN IF I CAN'T LOVE MIO, I WANTED TO APPEAR IN TSUKI-GOMORI!
BE-CAUSE!
EXCUSE ME! SORRY TO KEEP EVERY-ONE WAITING!
chatter
!!
Oh!
IT'S ALMOST TIME. PLEASE GET READY.
...
sha
BECAUSE...
IT'S TIME ...
...IF I APPEARED IN TSUKI-GOMORI...
...I...
... THOUGHT I COULD...

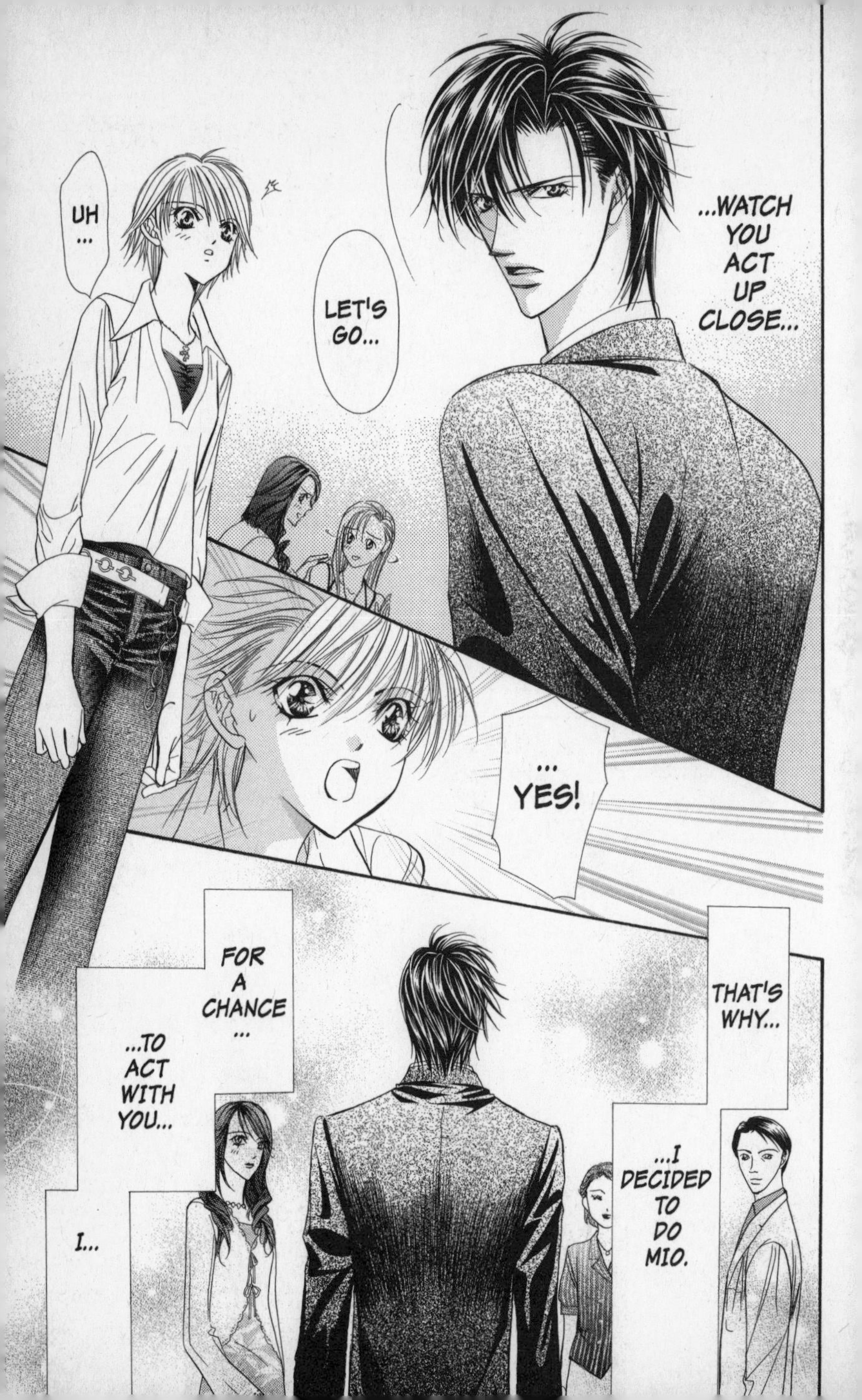
...WATCH YOU ACT UP CLOSE...
LET'S GO...
UH ...
... YES!
THAT'S WHY...
...I DECIDED TO DO MIO.
FOR A CHANCE ...
...TO ACT WITH YOU...
I...

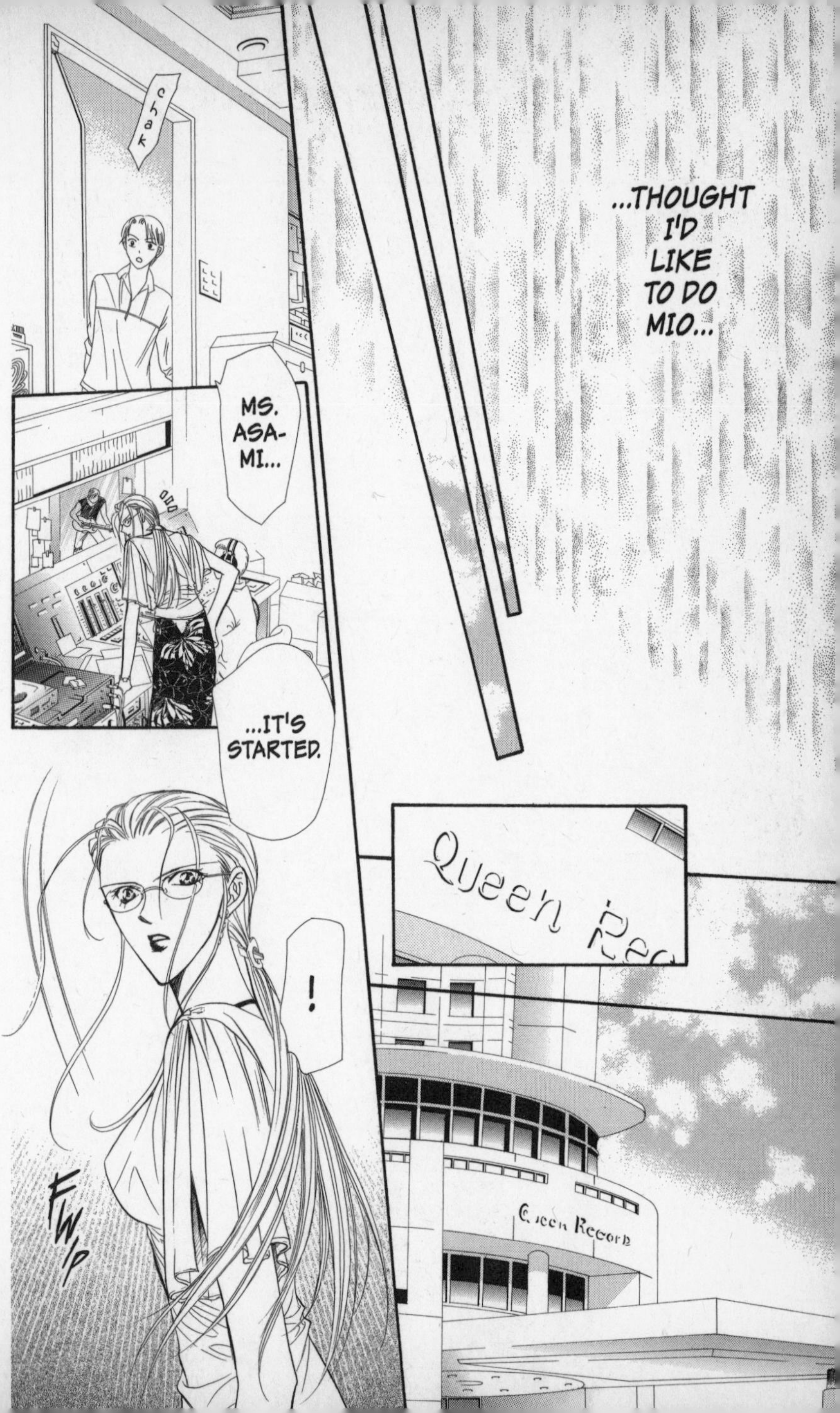
...THOUGHT I'D LIKE TO DO MIO...
Queen Rec
Queen Records
chak
MS. ASAMI...
...IT'S STARTED.
!
FWIP

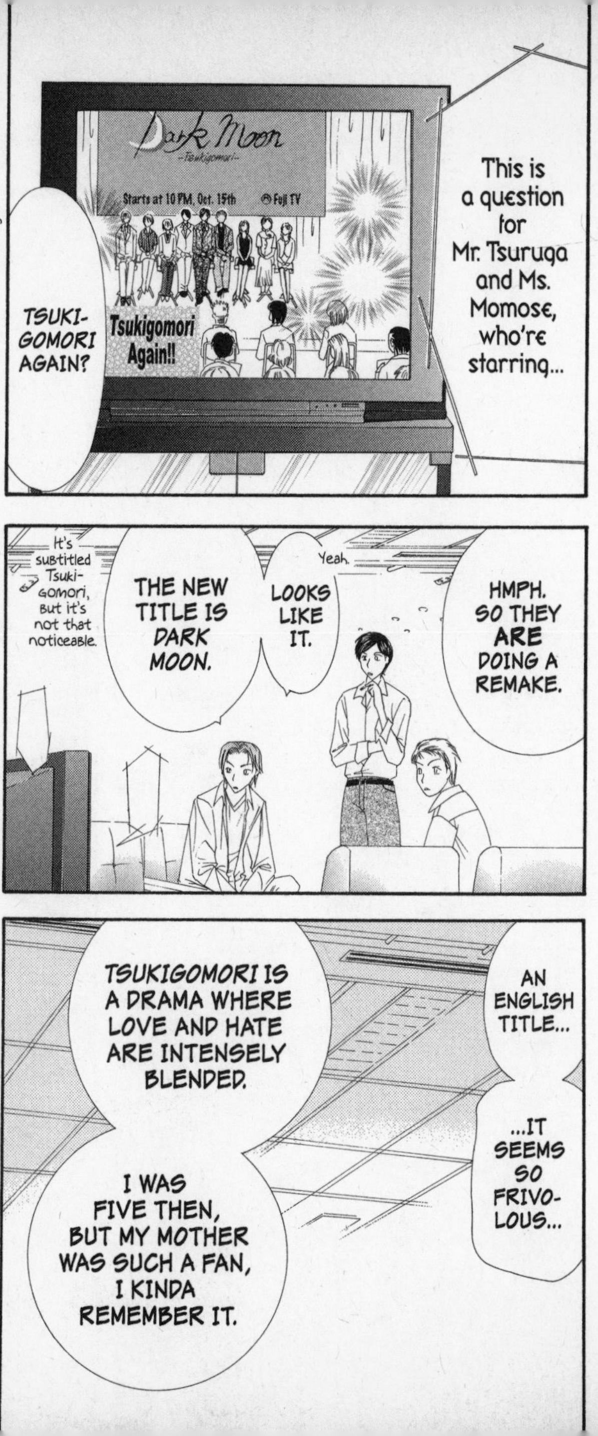
This is a question for Mr. Tsuruga and Ms. Momose, who're starring...
Dark Moon
-Tsukigomori-
Starts at 10 PM, Oct. 15th
Fuji TV
Tsukigomori Again!!
TSUKIGOMORI AGAIN?
HMPH. SO THEY ARE DOING A REMAKE.
Yeah.
LOOKS LIKE IT.
THE NEW TITLE IS DARK MOON.
It's subtitled Tsukigomori, but it's not that noticeable.
AN ENGLISH TITLE...
...IT SEEMS SO FRIVOLOUS...
TSUKIGOMORI IS A DRAMA WHERE LOVE AND HATE ARE INTENSELY BLENDED.
I WAS FIVE THEN, BUT MY MOTHER WAS SUCH A FAN, I KINDA REMEMBER IT.

Hiroaki Ogata

The first time he appeared, my assistants asked "Is he a student?" He doesn't look as if he's older than Ren. He's pale, looks frail (to put it in a good way), and maybe like a boyish man who's 27. I thought that I had to make him different from the directors who'd appeared before (Shingai and Kuroshio)...and this is what happened...

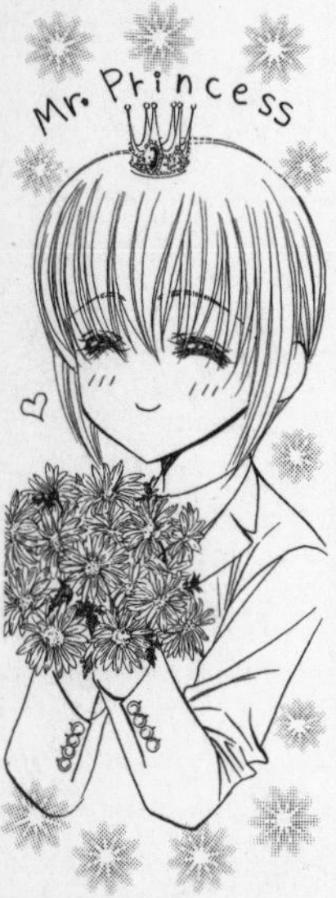
Mr. Princess

Personally, I don't go for guys who weep, but for some reason, the readers like him...and people have various theories about his relationship with Haruki...but...with that Haruki and this Ogata... I wonder if a romantic relationship is possible...

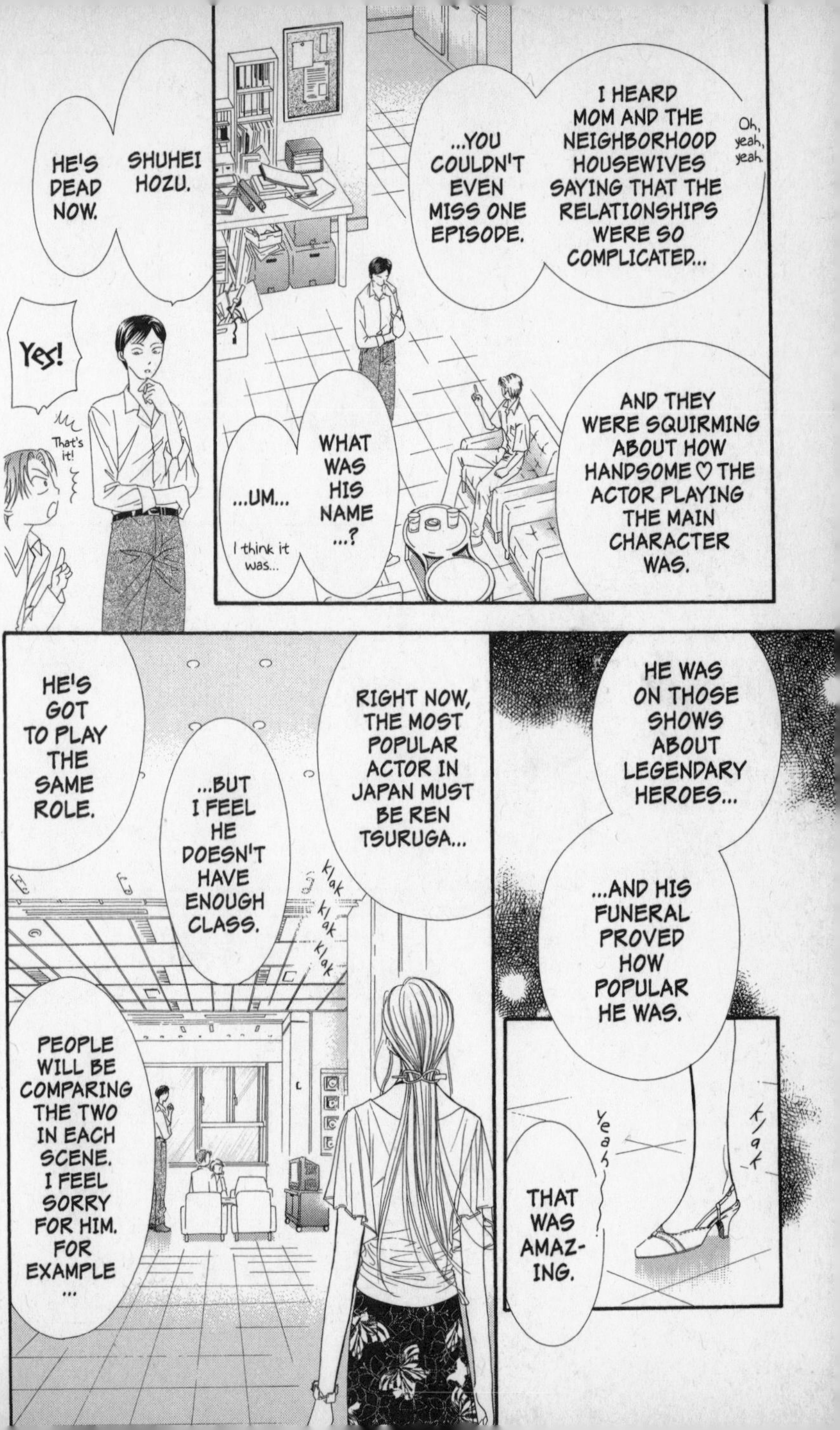
I HEARD MOM AND THE NEIGHBORHOOD HOUSEWIVES SAYING THAT THE RELATIONSHIPS WERE SO COMPLICATED...
Oh, yeah, yeah.
...YOU COULDN'T EVEN MISS ONE EPISODE.
AND THEY WERE SQUIRMING ABOUT HOW HANDSOME ♡ THE ACTOR PLAYING THE MAIN CHARACTER WAS.
WHAT WAS HIS NAME ...?
...UM...
I think it was...
SHUHEI HOZU.
HE'S DEAD NOW.
Yes!
That's it!
HE WAS ON THOSE SHOWS ABOUT LEGENDARY HEROES...
...AND HIS FUNERAL PROVED HOW POPULAR HE WAS.
klak
Yeah
THAT WAS AMAZ-ING.
RIGHT NOW, THE MOST POPULAR ACTOR IN JAPAN MUST BE REN TSURUGA...
...BUT I FEEL HE DOESN'T HAVE ENOUGH CLASS.
klak klak klak
HE'S GOT TO PLAY THE SAME ROLE.
PEOPLE WILL BE COMPARING THE TWO IN EACH SCENE. I FEEL SORRY FOR HIM. FOR EXAMPLE ...

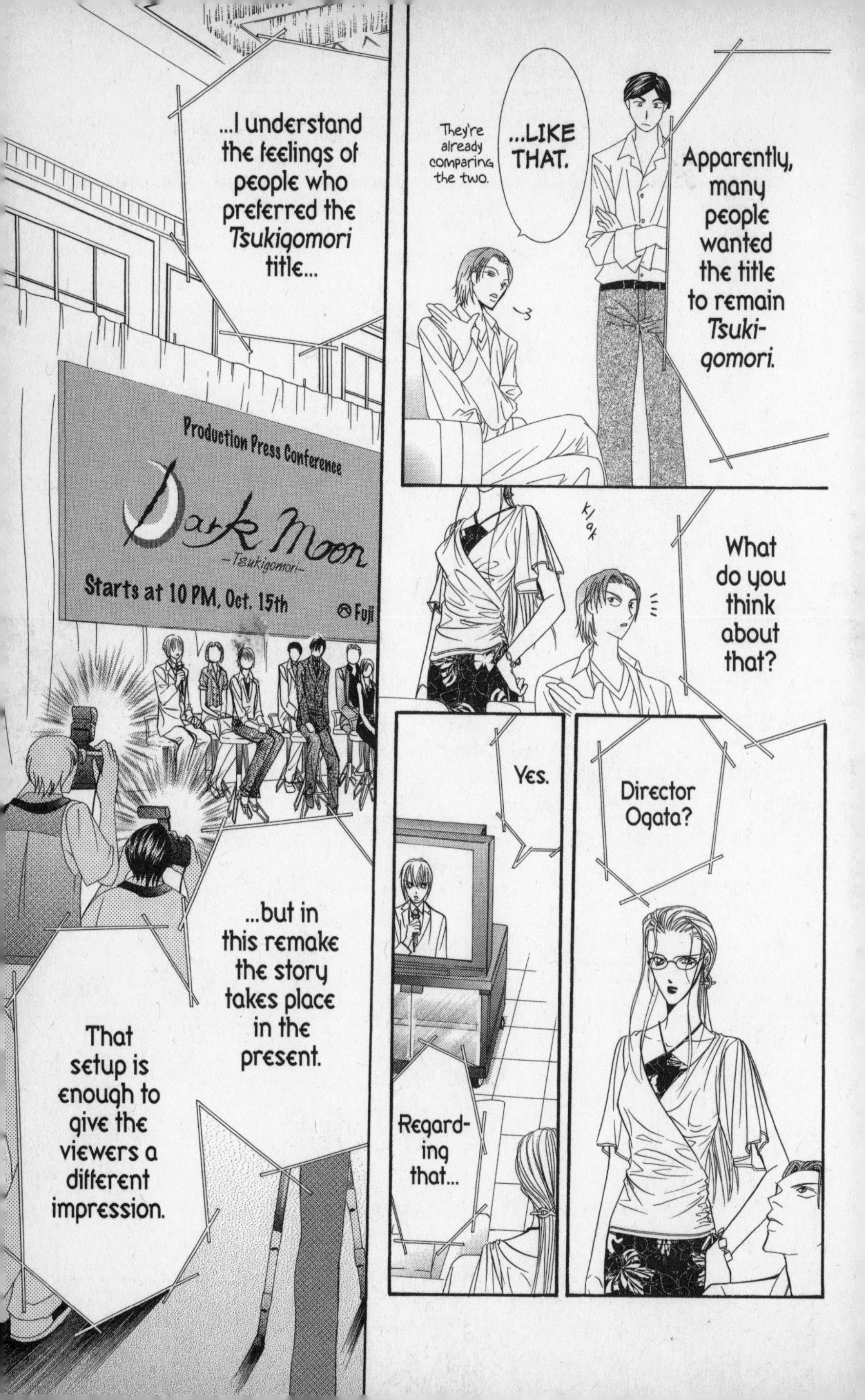
Apparently, many people wanted the title to remain Tsukigomori.
...LIKE THAT.
They're already comparing the two.
What do you think about that?
Director Ogata?
Yes.
Regarding that...
...I understand the feelings of people who preferred the Tsukigomori title...
Production Press Conference
Dark Moon
—Tsukigomori—
Starts at 10 PM, Oct. 15th
Fuji
...but in this remake the story takes place in the present.
That setup is enough to give the viewers a different impression.

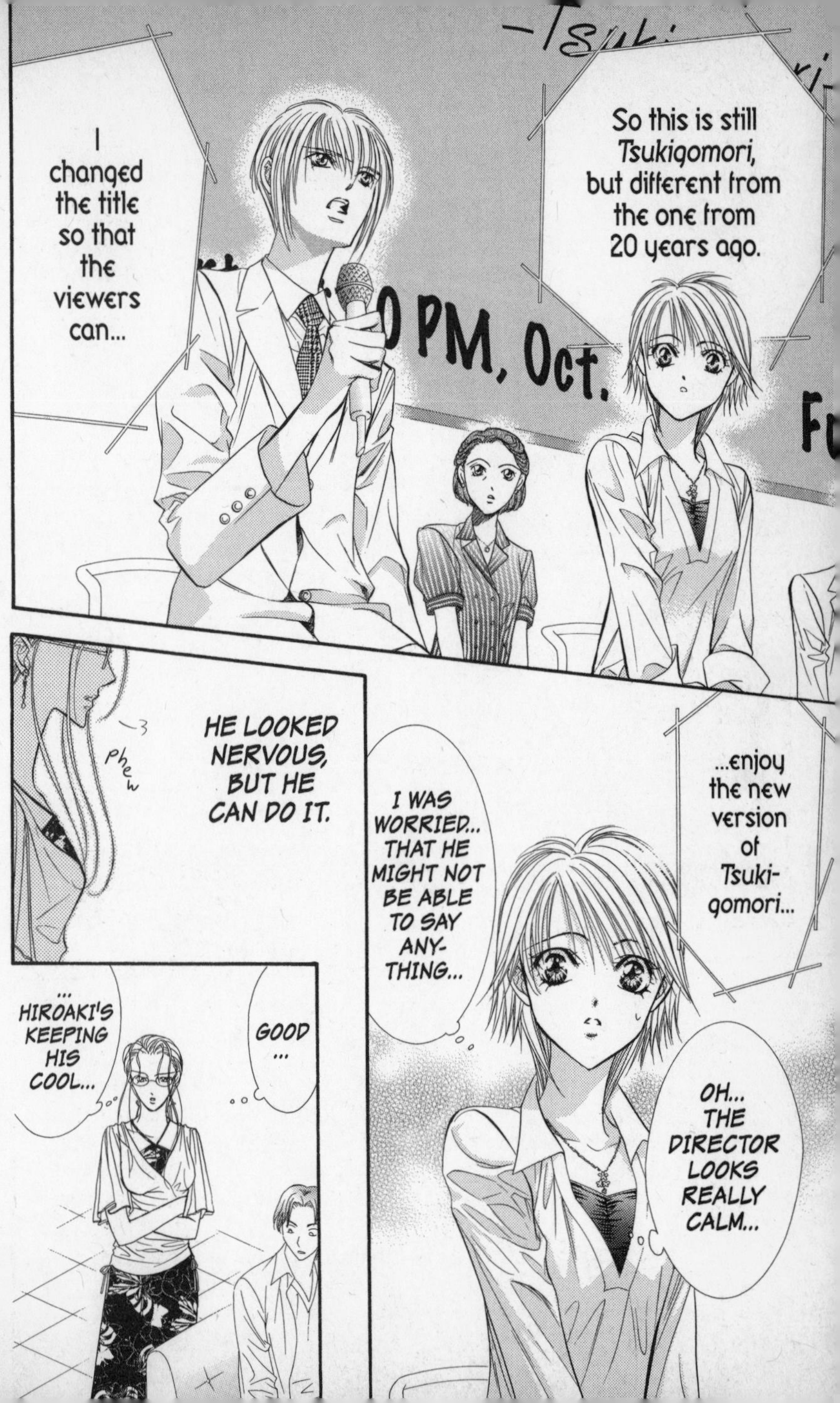
So this is still Tsukigomori, but different from the one from 20 years ago.
I changed the title so that the viewers can...
...enjoy the new version of Tsukigomori...
I WAS WORRIED... THAT HE MIGHT NOT BE ABLE TO SAY ANYTHING...
OH... THE DIRECTOR LOOKS REALLY CALM...
HE LOOKED NERVOUS, BUT HE CAN DO IT.
phew
GOOD ...
... HIROAKI'S KEEPING HIS COOL...

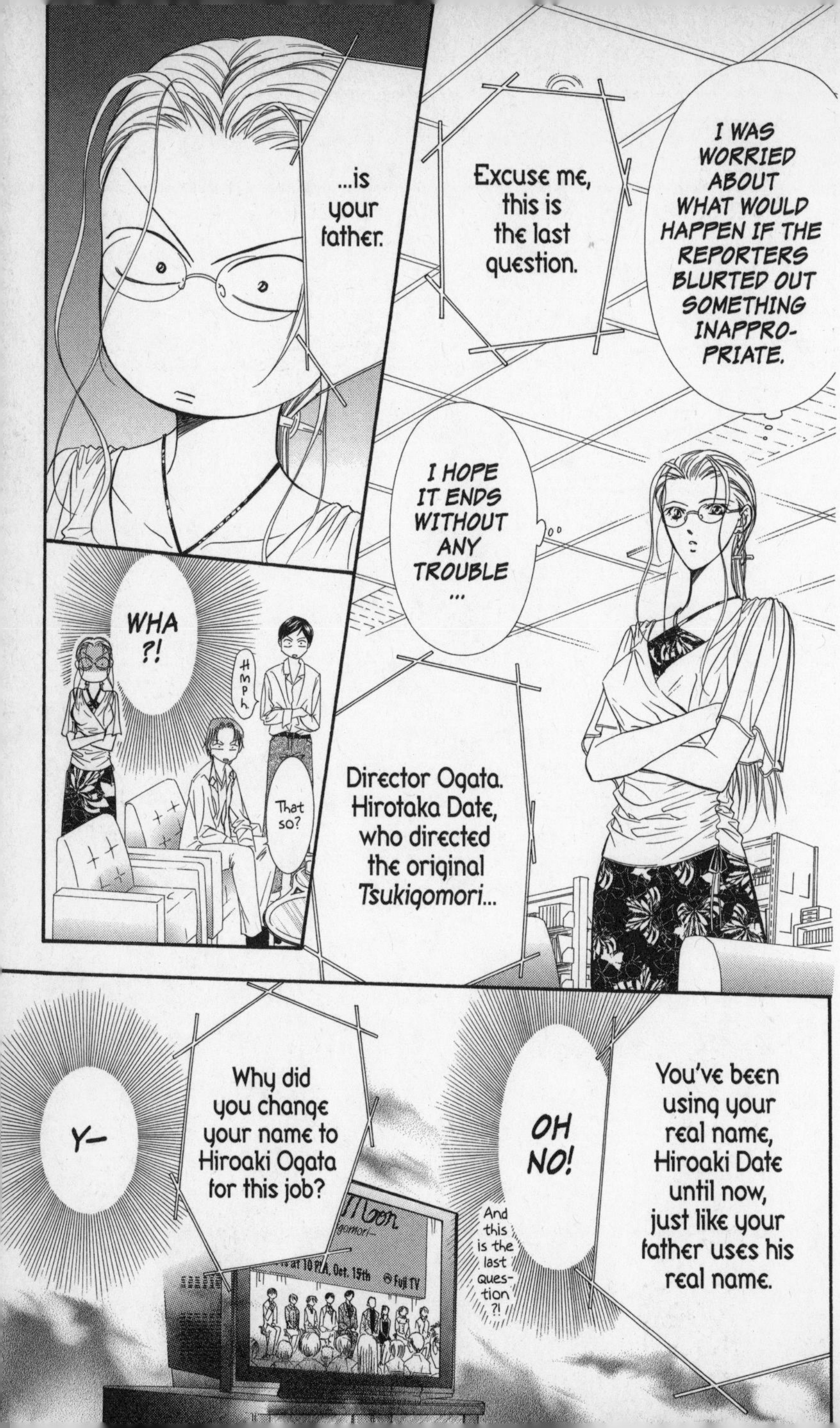

I WAS WORRIED ABOUT WHAT WOULD HAPPEN IF THE REPORTERS BLURTED OUT SOMETHING INAPPROPRIATE.
Excuse me, this is the last question.
I HOPE IT ENDS WITHOUT ANY TROUBLE...
Director Ogata. Hirotaka Date, who directed the original Tsukigomori...
...is your father.
Hmph.
That so?
WHA?!
You've been using your real name, Hiroaki Date until now, just like your father uses his real name.
OH NO!
And this is the last question?!
Why did you change your name to Hiroaki Ogata for this job?
Y—

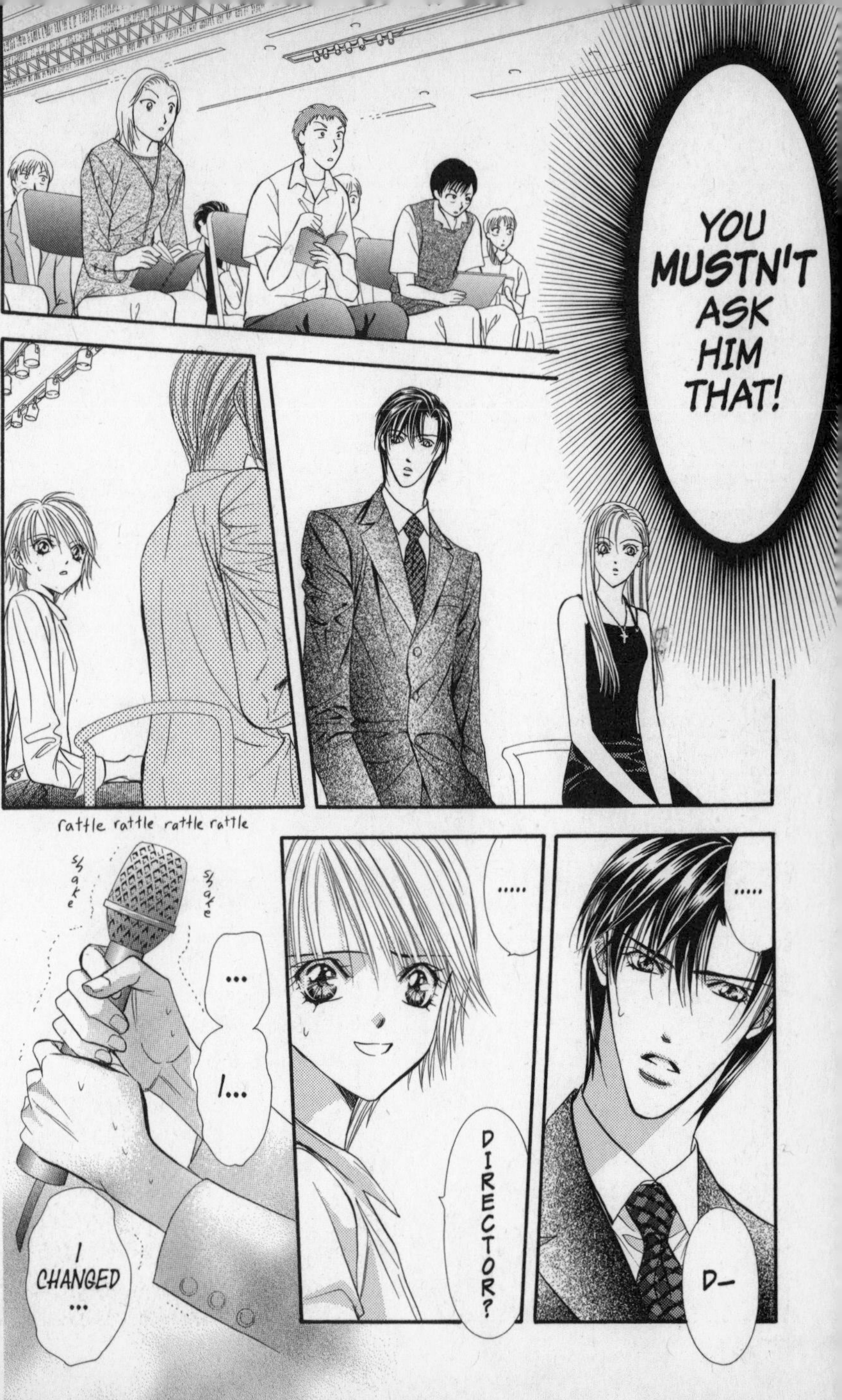
YOU MUSTN'T ASK HIM THAT!
rattle rattle rattle rattle
.....
D—
.....
DIRECTOR?
shake
shake
...
I...
I CHANGED ...

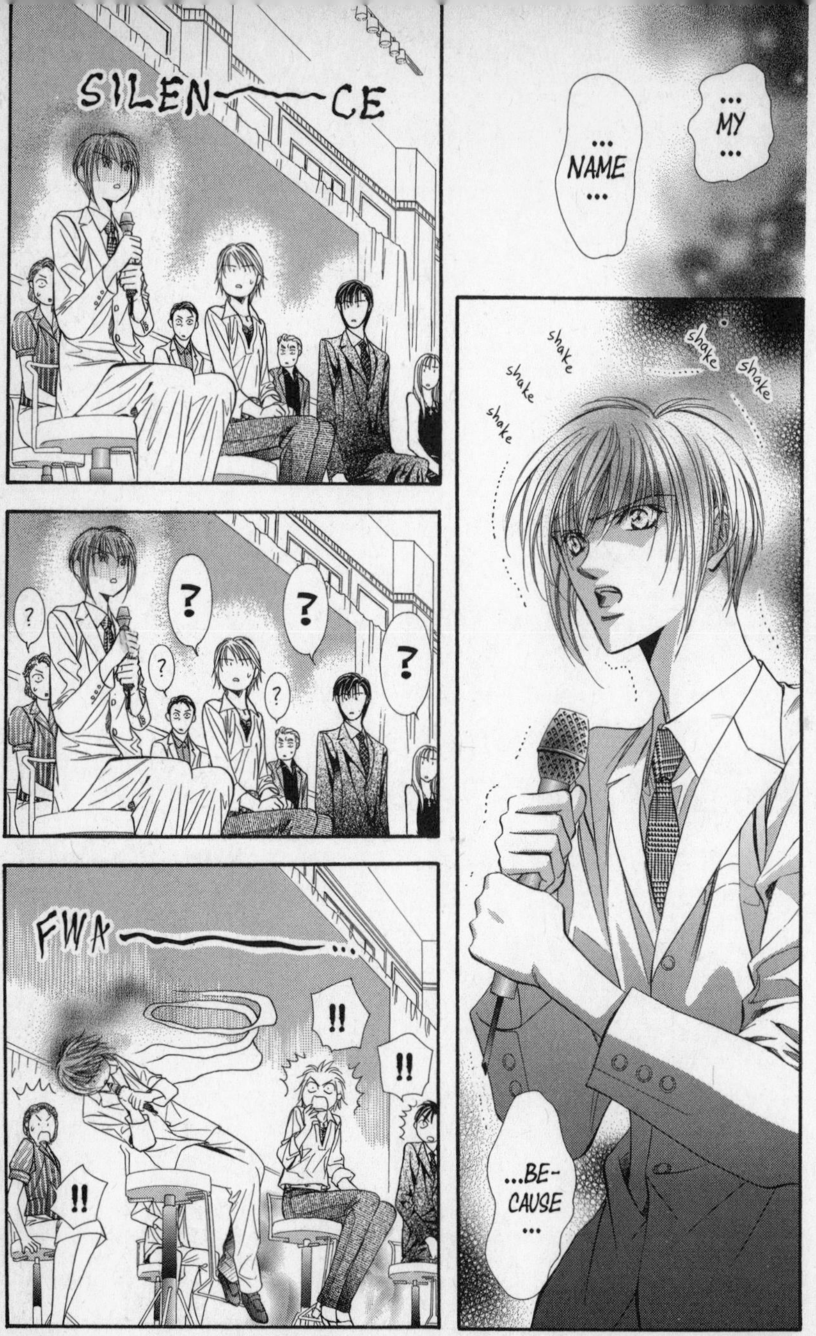
...MY...
...NAME...
shake shake shake shake shake
...BE-CAUSE...
SILEN——CE
?
?
?
?
?
?
FWA——...
!!
!!
!!

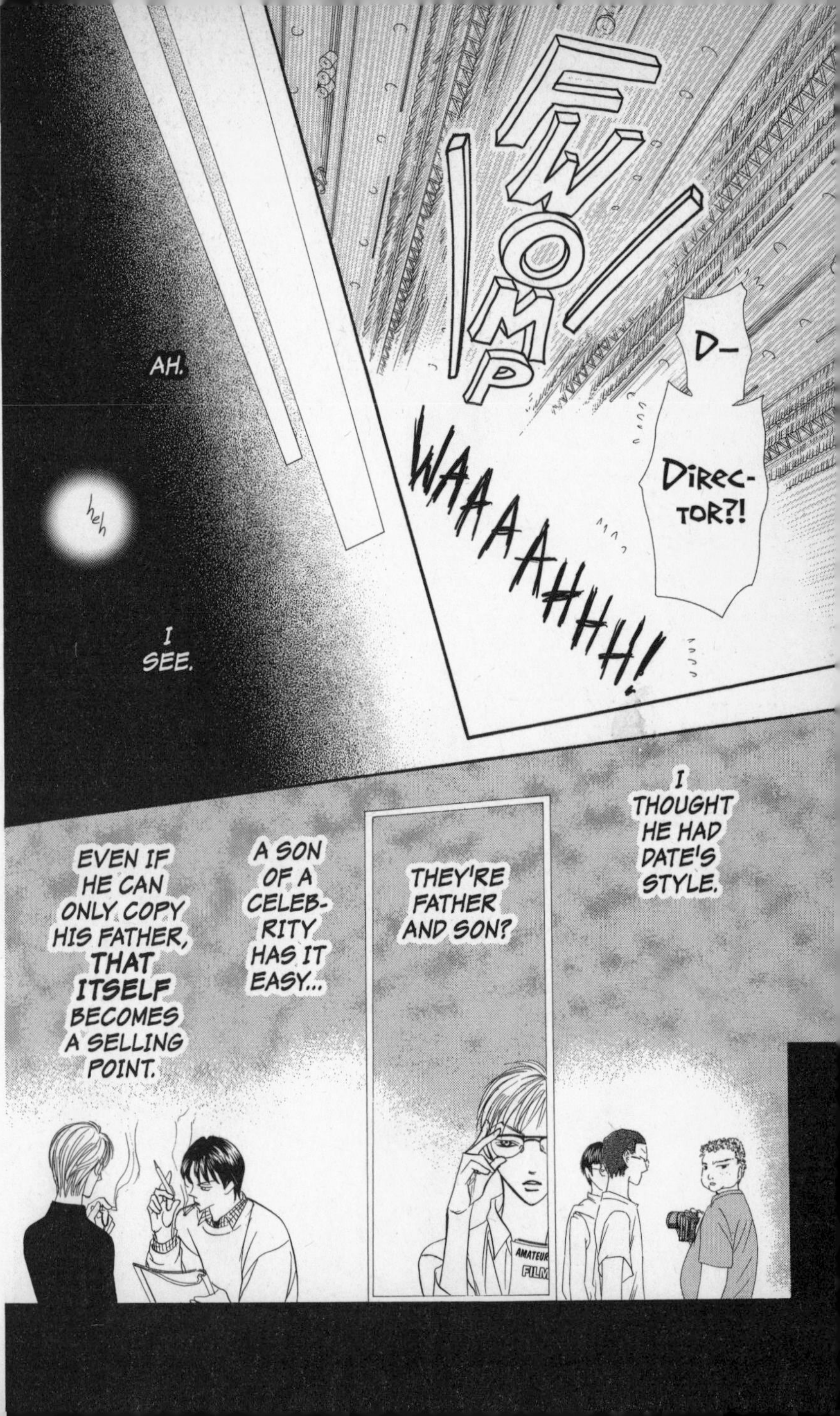
FWOMP
WAAAAHHHH!
D—
DIREC-TOR?!
AH.
heh
I SEE.
I THOUGHT HE HAD DATE'S STYLE.
THEY'RE FATHER AND SON?
A SON OF A CELEB-RITY HAS IT EASY...
EVEN IF HE CAN ONLY COPY HIS FATHER, THAT ITSELF BECOMES A SELLING POINT.
AMATEUR FILM

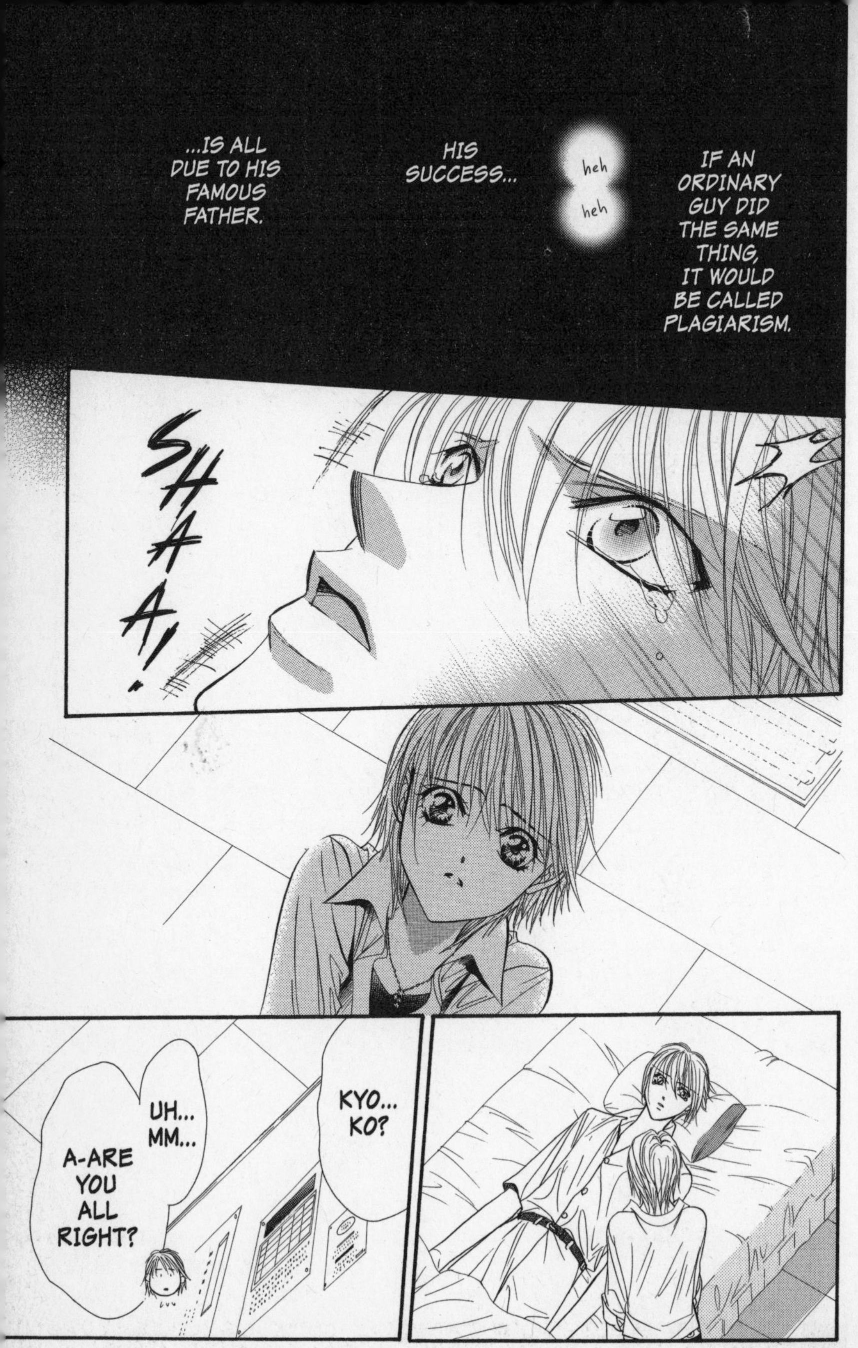
IF AN ORDINARY GUY DID THE SAME THING, IT WOULD BE CALLED PLAGIARISM.
heh heh
HIS SUCCESS...
...IS ALL DUE TO HIS FAMOUS FATHER.
SHAA!!
KYO... KO?
UH... MM... A-ARE YOU ALL RIGHT?

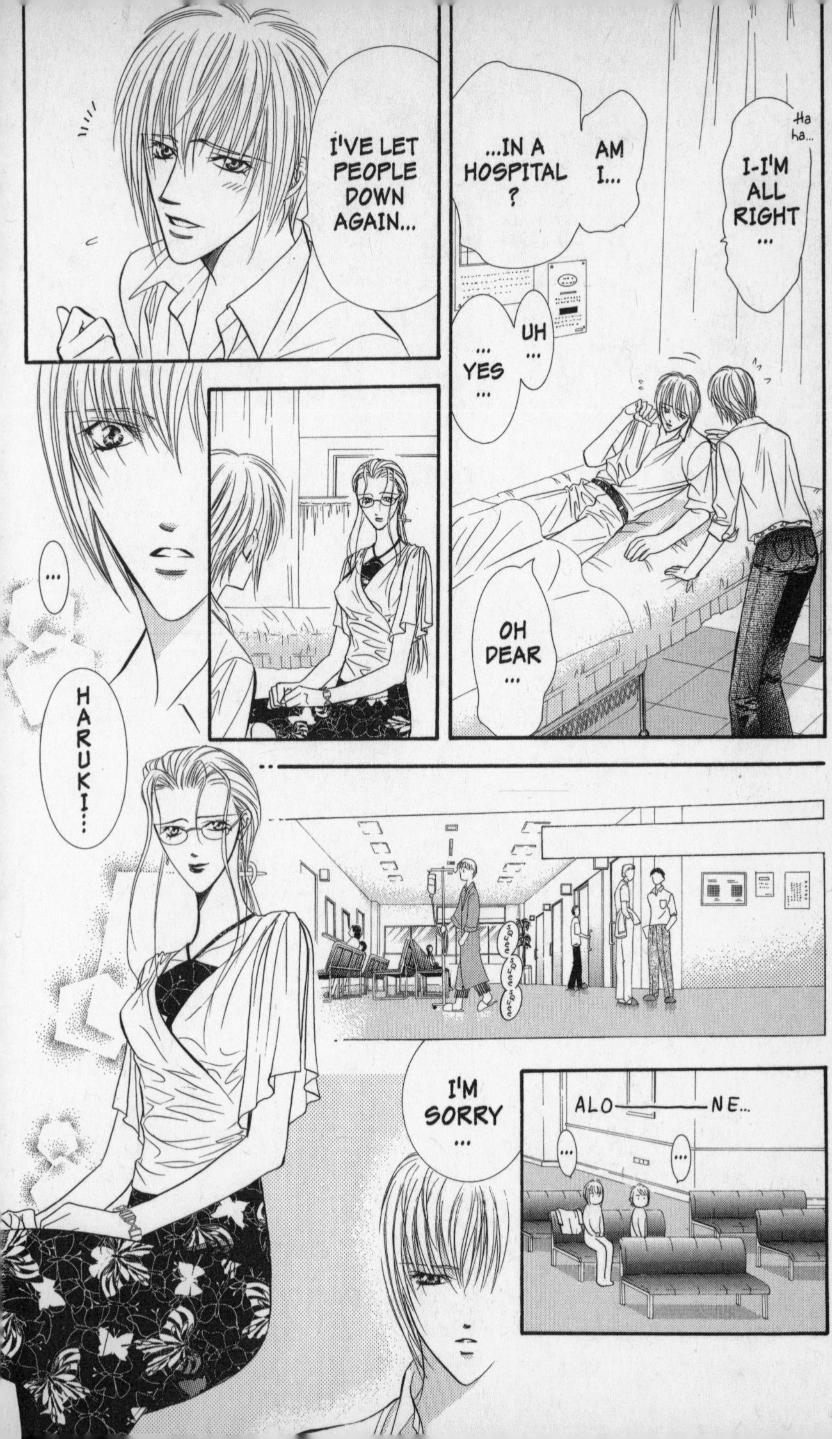

Ha ha...
I-I'M ALL RIGHT...
AM I...
...IN A HOSPITAL?
UH...
...YES...
OH DEAR...
I'VE LET PEOPLE DOWN AGAIN...
...
HARUKI...
SQUEE SQUEE SQUEE
ALO——NE..
...
...
I'M SORRY...

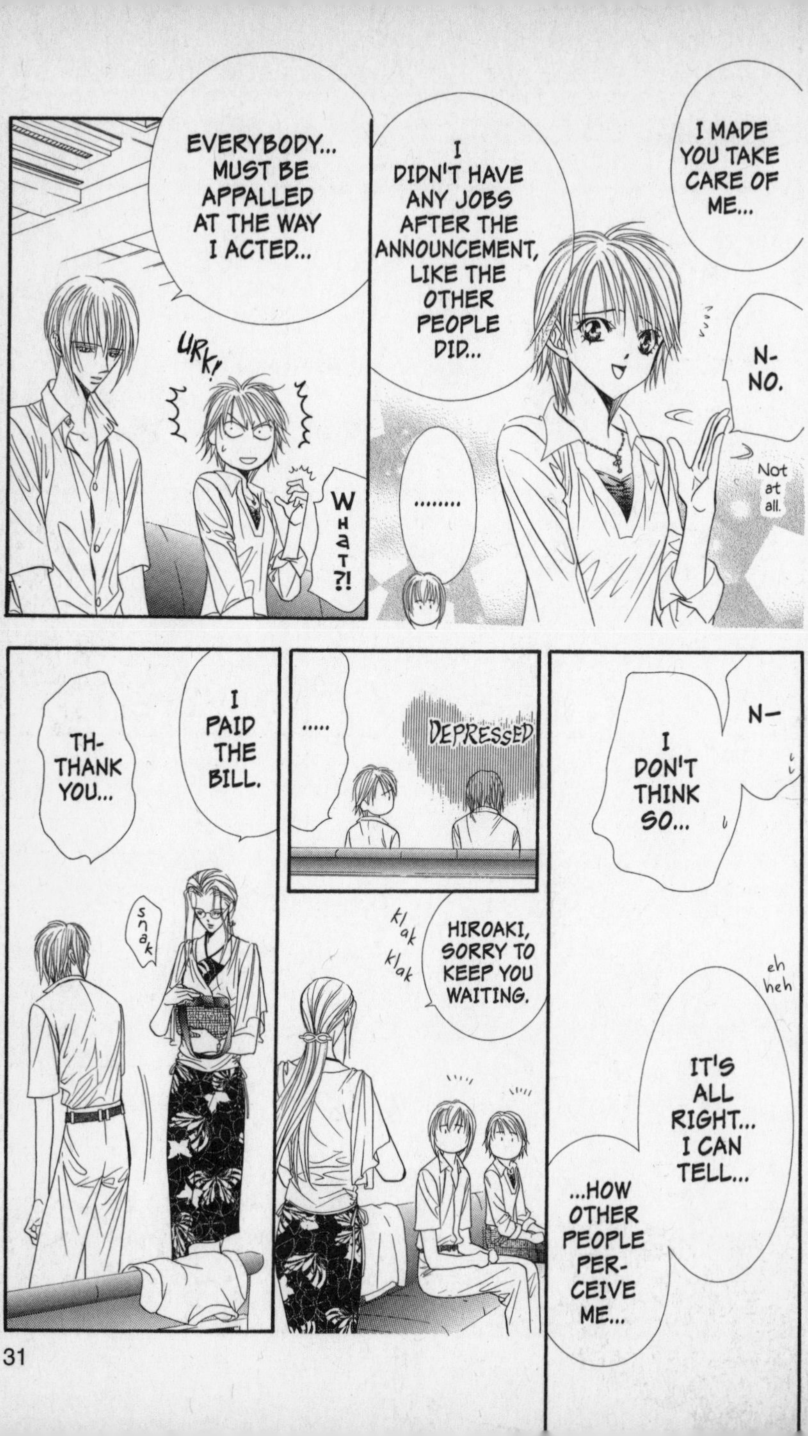
I MADE YOU TAKE CARE OF ME...
N-NO.
Not at all.
I DIDN'T HAVE ANY JOBS AFTER THE ANNOUNCEMENT, LIKE THE OTHER PEOPLE DID...
....
EVERYBODY... MUST BE APPALLED AT THE WAY I ACTED...
URK!
WHAT?!
N—
I DON'T THINK SO...
eh heh
IT'S ALL RIGHT... I CAN TELL...
...HOW OTHER PEOPLE PERCEIVE ME...
.....
DEPRESSED
I PAID THE BILL.
TH-THANK YOU...
snak
klak klak
HIROAKI, SORRY TO KEEP YOU WAITING.

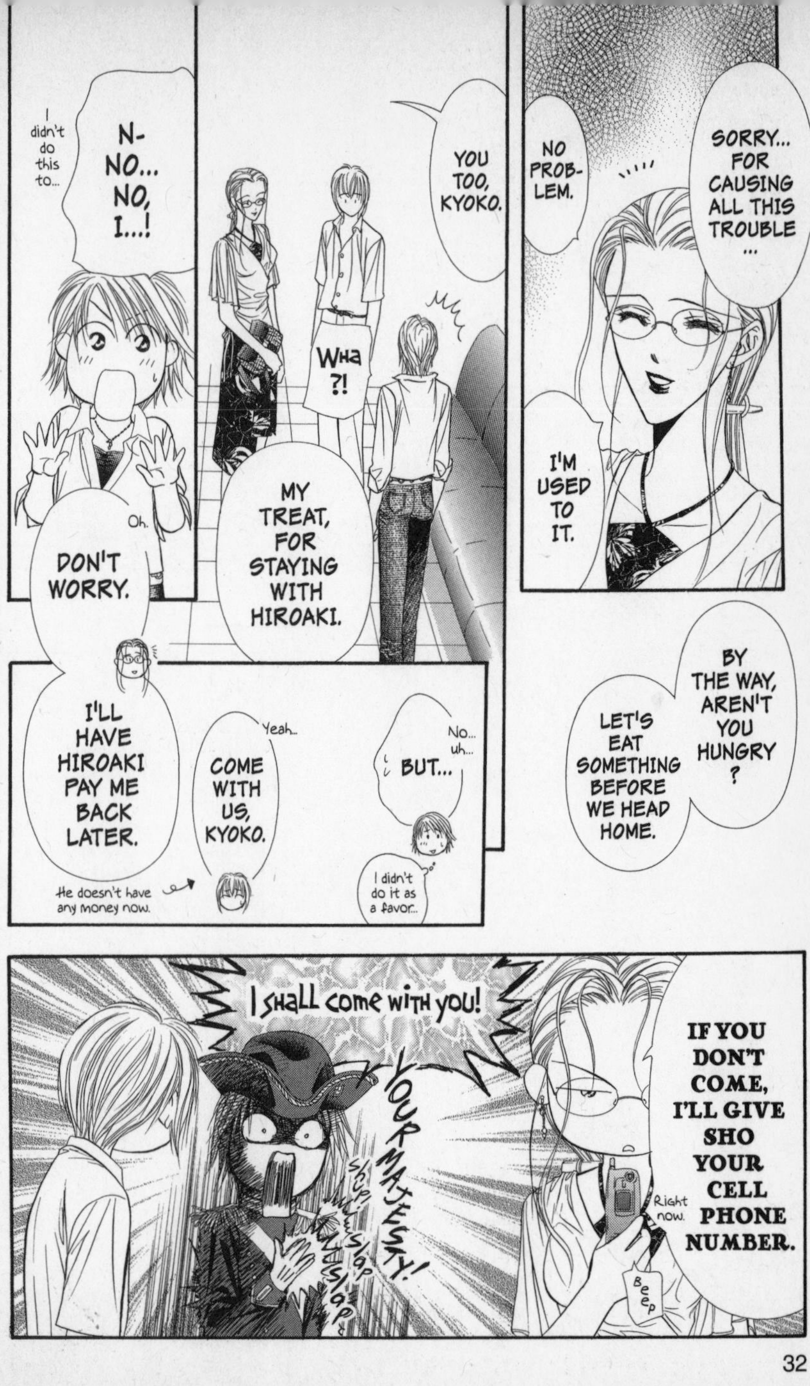
SORRY... FOR CAUSING ALL THIS TROUBLE...
NO PROBLEM.
I'M USED TO IT.
YOU TOO, KYOKO.
WHA?!
MY TREAT, FOR STAYING WITH HIROAKI.
N-NO... NO, I...!
I didn't do this to...
Oh.
DON'T WORRY.
BY THE WAY, AREN'T YOU HUNGRY?
LET'S EAT SOMETHING BEFORE WE HEAD HOME.
No... uh...
BUT...
I didn't do it as a favor...
Yeah...
COME WITH US, KYOKO.
I'LL HAVE HIROAKI PAY ME BACK LATER.
He doesn't have any money now.
IF YOU DON'T COME, I'LL GIVE SHO YOUR CELL PHONE NUMBER.
Right now.
Beep
I shall come with you!
YOUR MAJESTY!
Slurp! slurp! slap slap

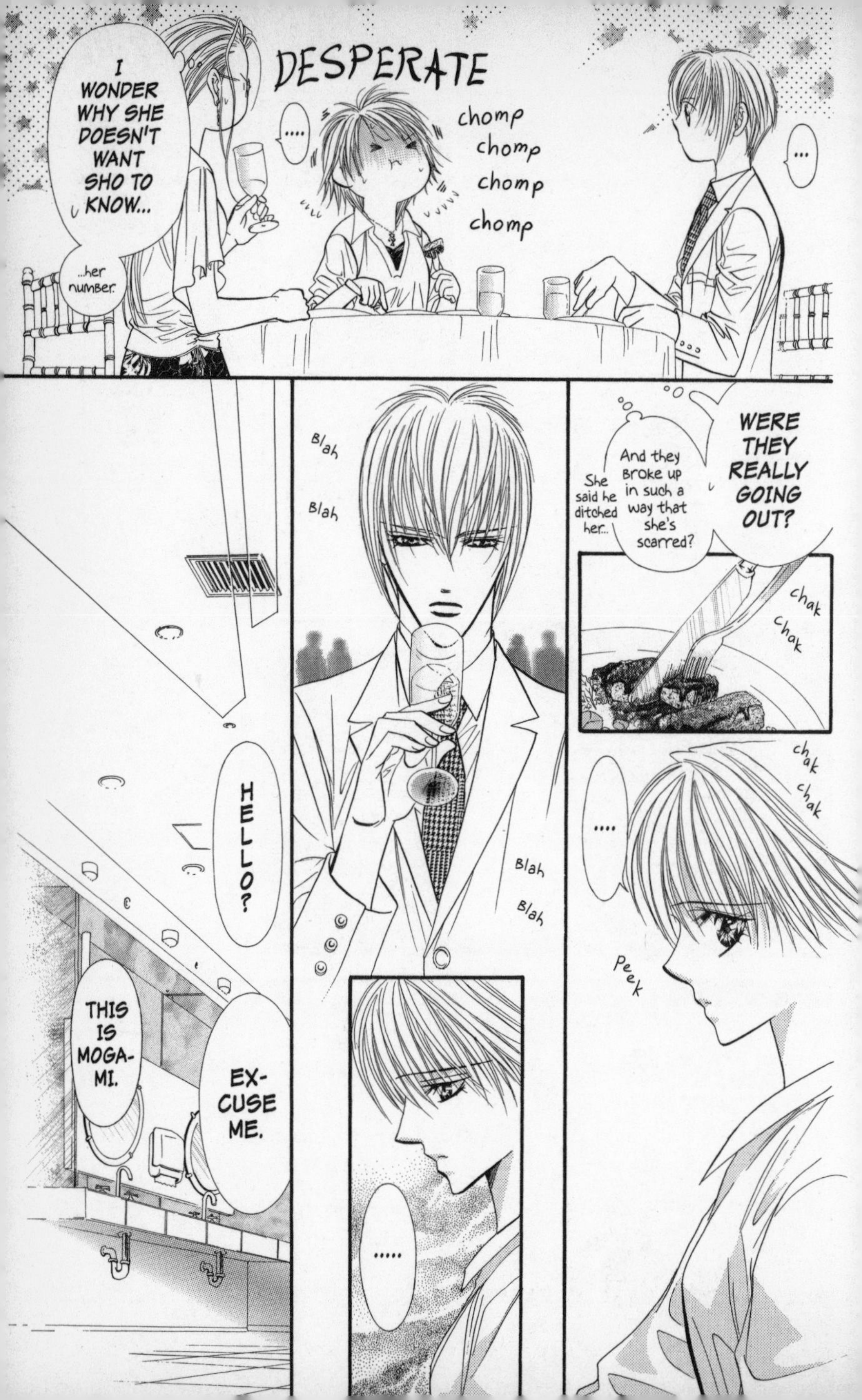
...
DESPERATE
....
chomp chomp chomp chomp
I WONDER WHY SHE DOESN'T WANT SHO TO KNOW...
...her number.
WERE THEY REALLY GOING OUT?
And they broke up in such a way that she's scarred?
She said he ditched her...
chak chak
....
chak chak
Peek
Blah Blah
Blah Blah
.....
HELLO?
THIS IS MOGA-MI.
EX-CUSE ME.

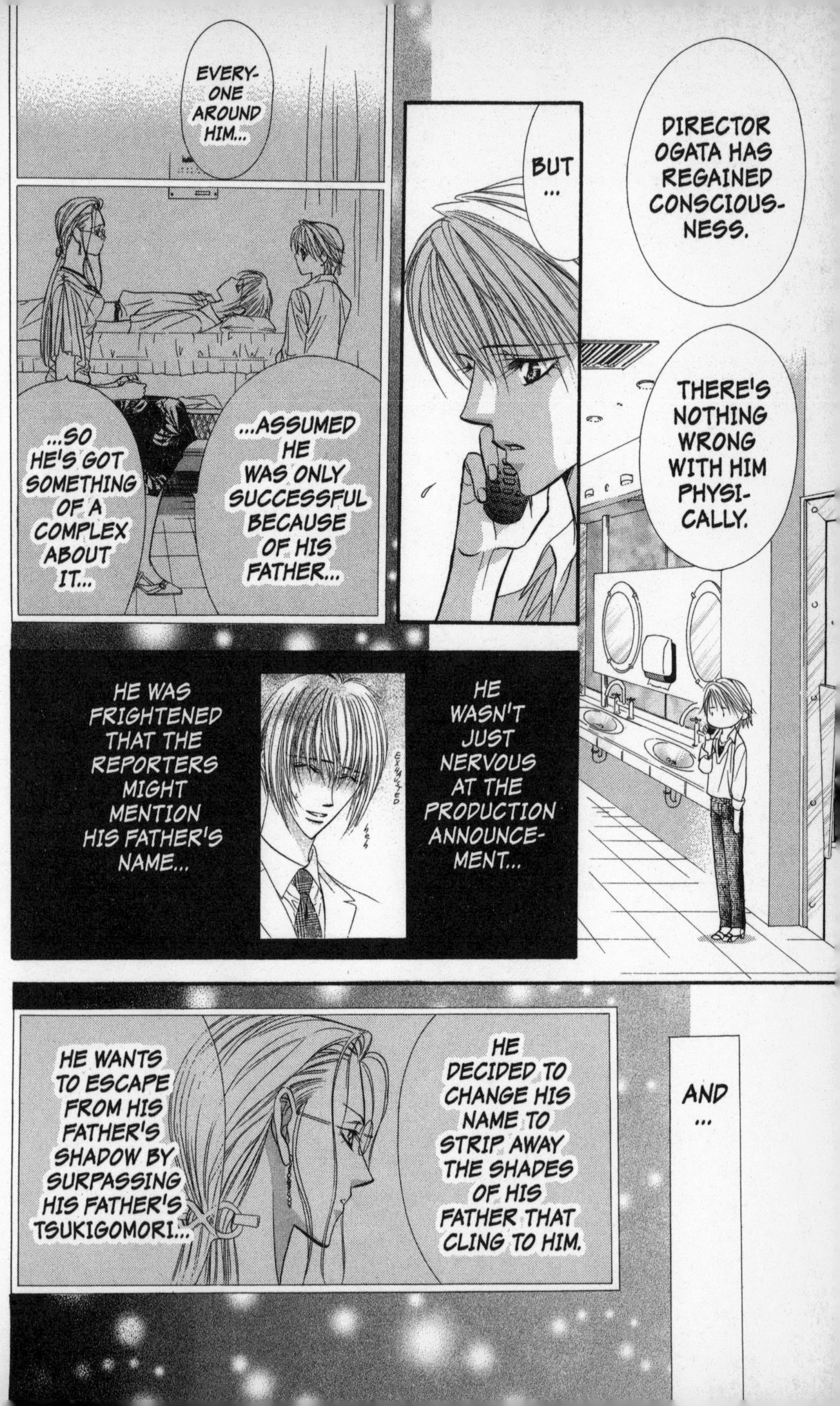
DIRECTOR OGATA HAS REGAINED CONSCIOUS-NESS.
THERE'S NOTHING WRONG WITH HIM PHYSI-CALLY.
BUT ...
EVERY-ONE AROUND HIM...
...ASSUMED HE WAS ONLY SUCCESSFUL BECAUSE OF HIS FATHER...
...SO HE'S GOT SOMETHING OF A COMPLEX ABOUT IT...
HE WASN'T JUST NERVOUS AT THE PRODUCTION ANNOUNCE-MENT...
EXHAUSTED
heh
HE WAS FRIGHTENED THAT THE REPORTERS MIGHT MENTION HIS FATHER'S NAME...
AND ...
HE DECIDED TO CHANGE HIS NAME TO STRIP AWAY THE SHADES OF HIS FATHER THAT CLING TO HIM.
HE WANTS TO ESCAPE FROM HIS FATHER'S SHADOW BY SURPASSING HIS FATHER'S TSUKIGOMORI...

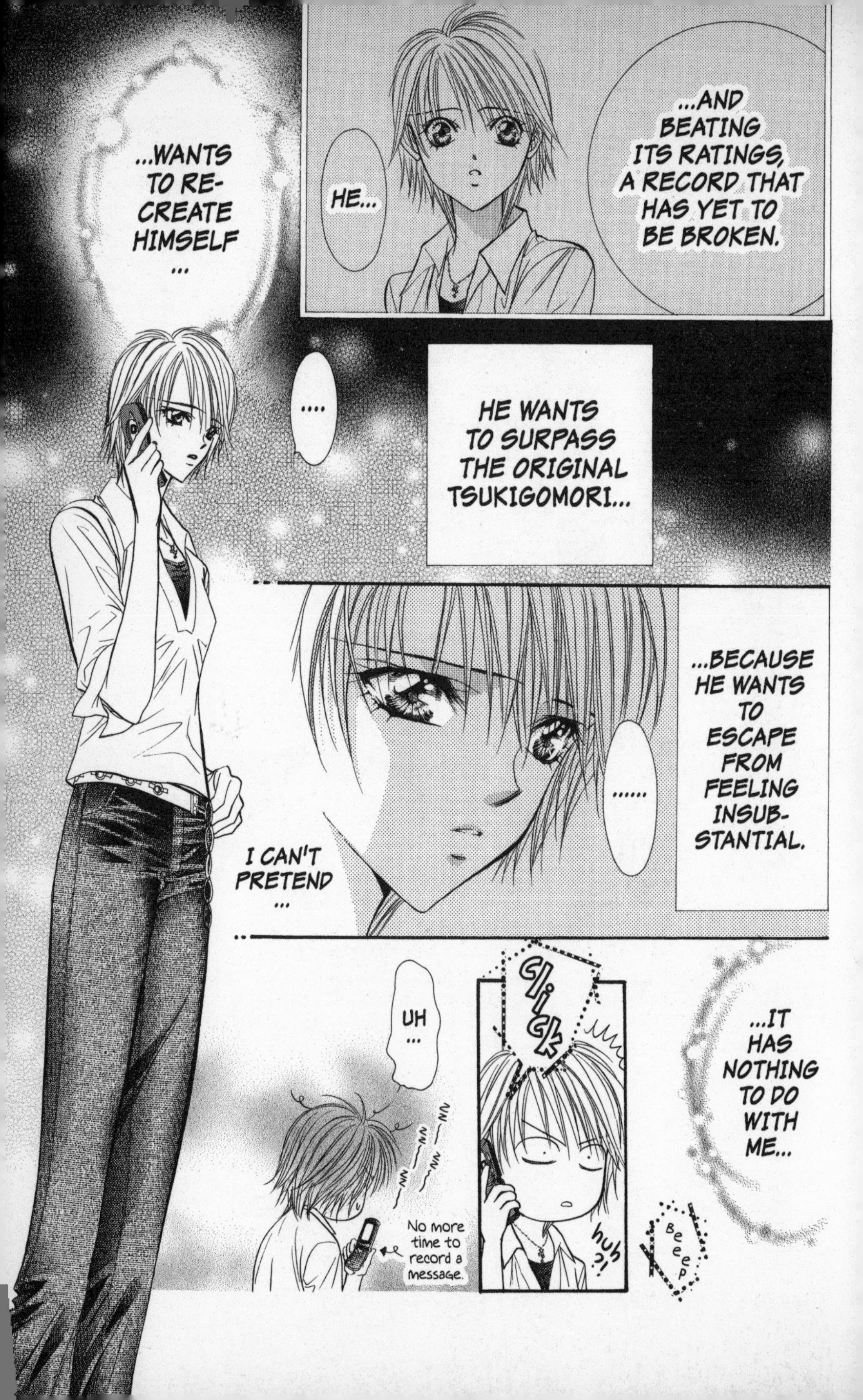
...AND BEATING ITS RATINGS, A RECORD THAT HAS YET TO BE BROKEN.
HE...
...WANTS TO RE-CREATE HIMSELF ...
HE WANTS TO SURPASS THE ORIGINAL TSUKIGOMORI...
....
...BECAUSE HE WANTS TO ESCAPE FROM FEELING INSUBSTANTIAL.
......
I CAN'T PRETEND ...
...IT HAS NOTHING TO DO WITH ME...
Click
huh!?
Beeep
NN— NN— NN— NN—
No more time to record a message.
UH ...

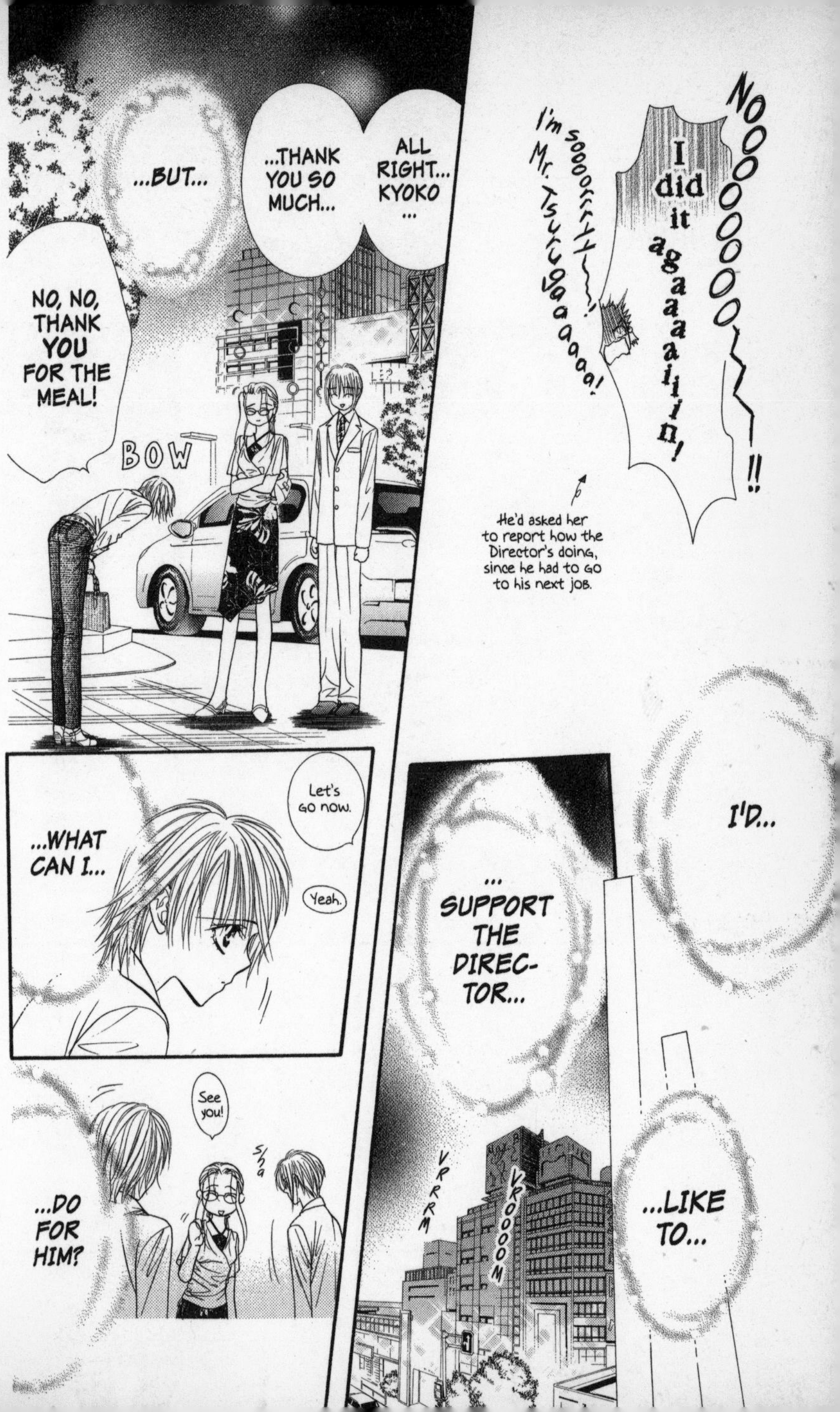
NOOOOOOOOO!!
I did it agaaaaiiin!
I'm sooorryyy! Mr. Tsurugaaaaaa!
He'd asked her to report how the Director's doing, since he had to go to his next job.
ALL RIGHT... KYOKO...
...THANK YOU SO MUCH...
...BUT...
NO, NO, THANK YOU FOR THE MEAL!
BOW
I'D...
...LIKE TO...
...SUPPORT THE DIREC-TOR...
VRRRM
VROOOOM
Let's go now.
...WHAT CAN I...
Yeah.
See you!
Sha
...DO FOR HIM?

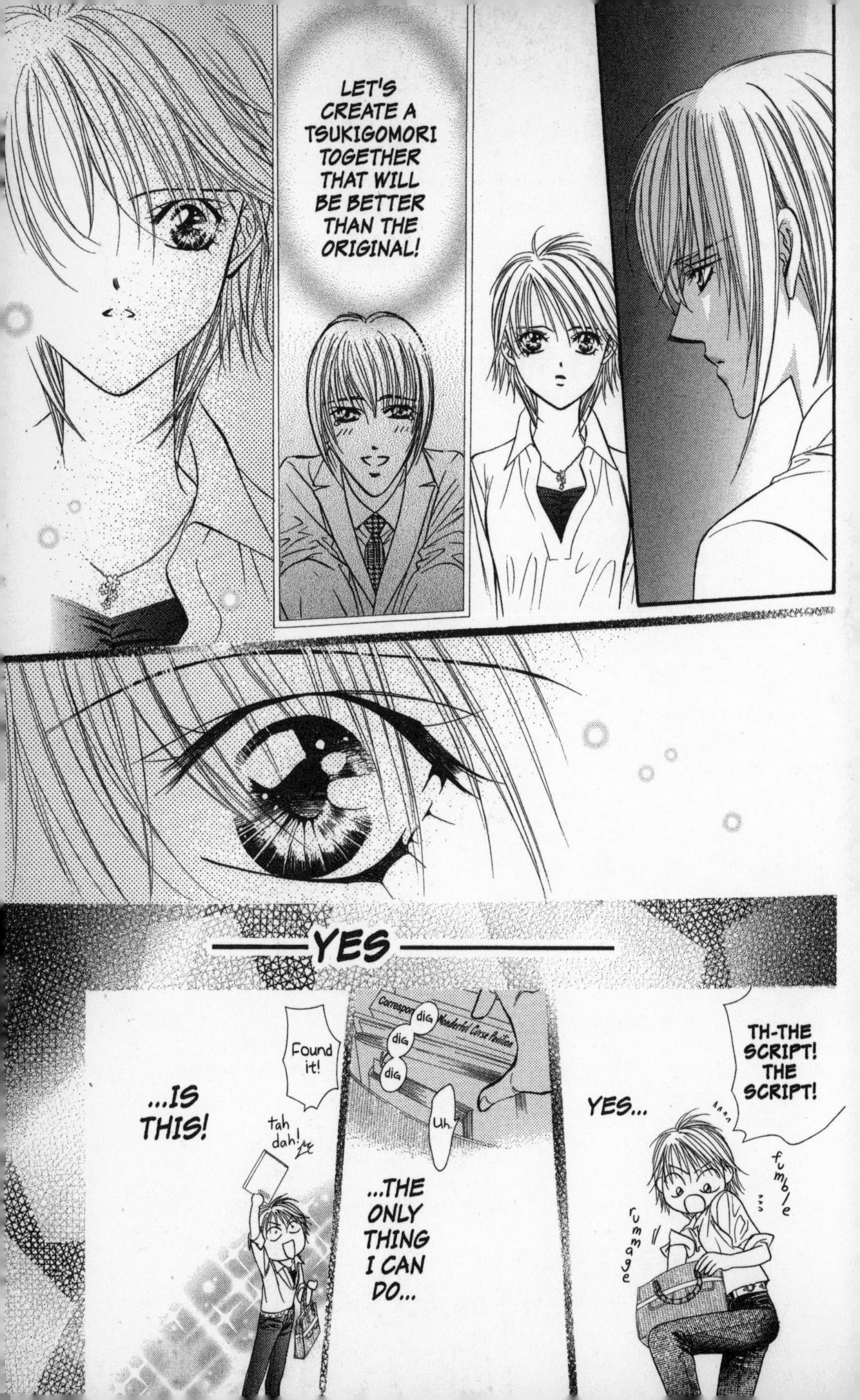
LET'S CREATE A TSUKIGOMORI TOGETHER THAT WILL BE BETTER THAN THE ORIGINAL!
—YES—
TH-THE SCRIPT! THE SCRIPT!
YES...
fumble
rummage
dig
dig
dig
Uh.
...THE ONLY THING I CAN DO...
Found it!
tah dah!
...IS THIS!

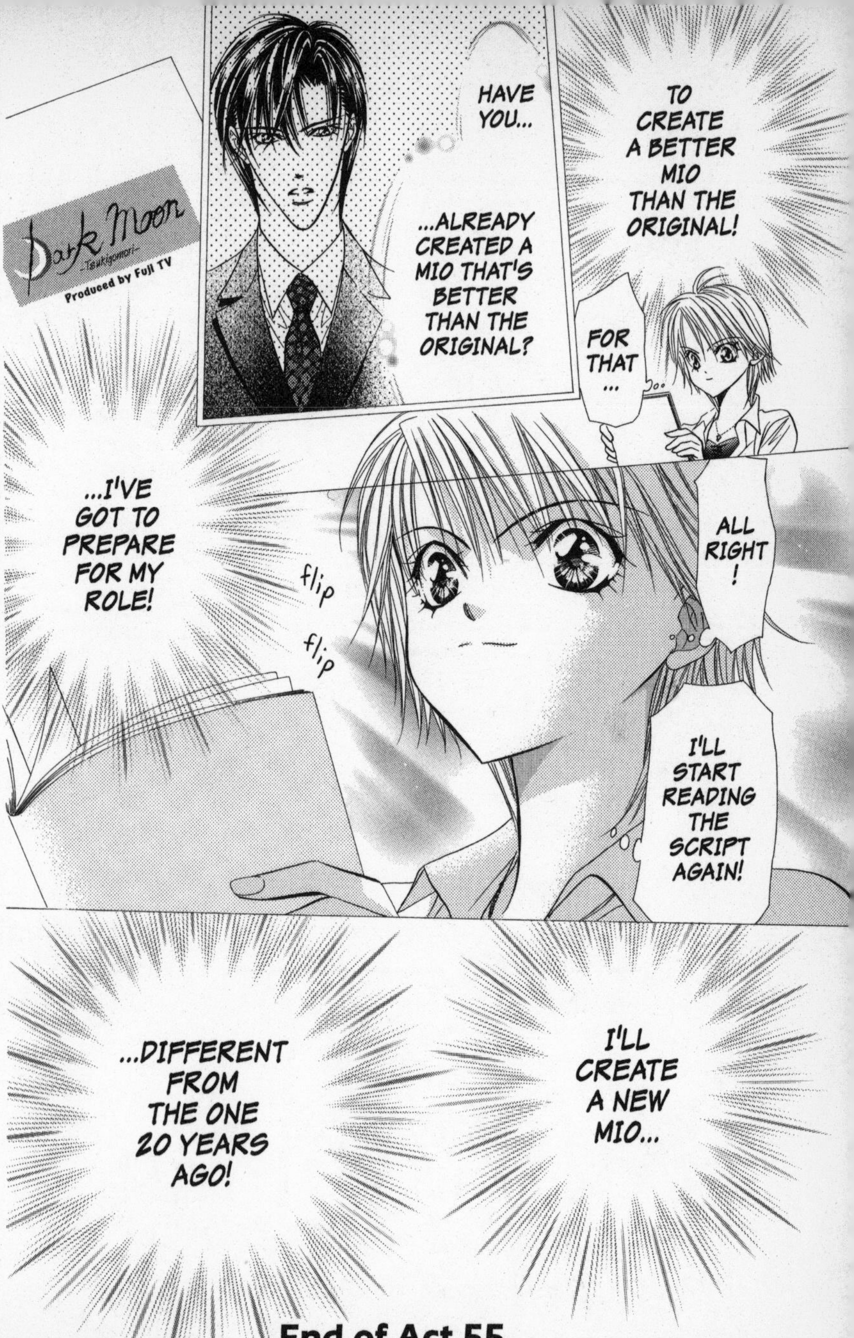
Dark Moon
-Tsukigomori-
Produced by Fuji TV
HAVE YOU...
...ALREADY CREATED A MIO THAT'S BETTER THAN THE ORIGINAL?
TO CREATE A BETTER MIO THAN THE ORIGINAL!
FOR THAT ...
...I'VE GOT TO PREPARE FOR MY ROLE!
ALL RIGHT!
I'LL START READING THE SCRIPT AGAIN!
flip
flip
I'LL CREATE A NEW MIO...
...DIFFERENT FROM THE ONE 20 YEARS AGO!

End of Act 55

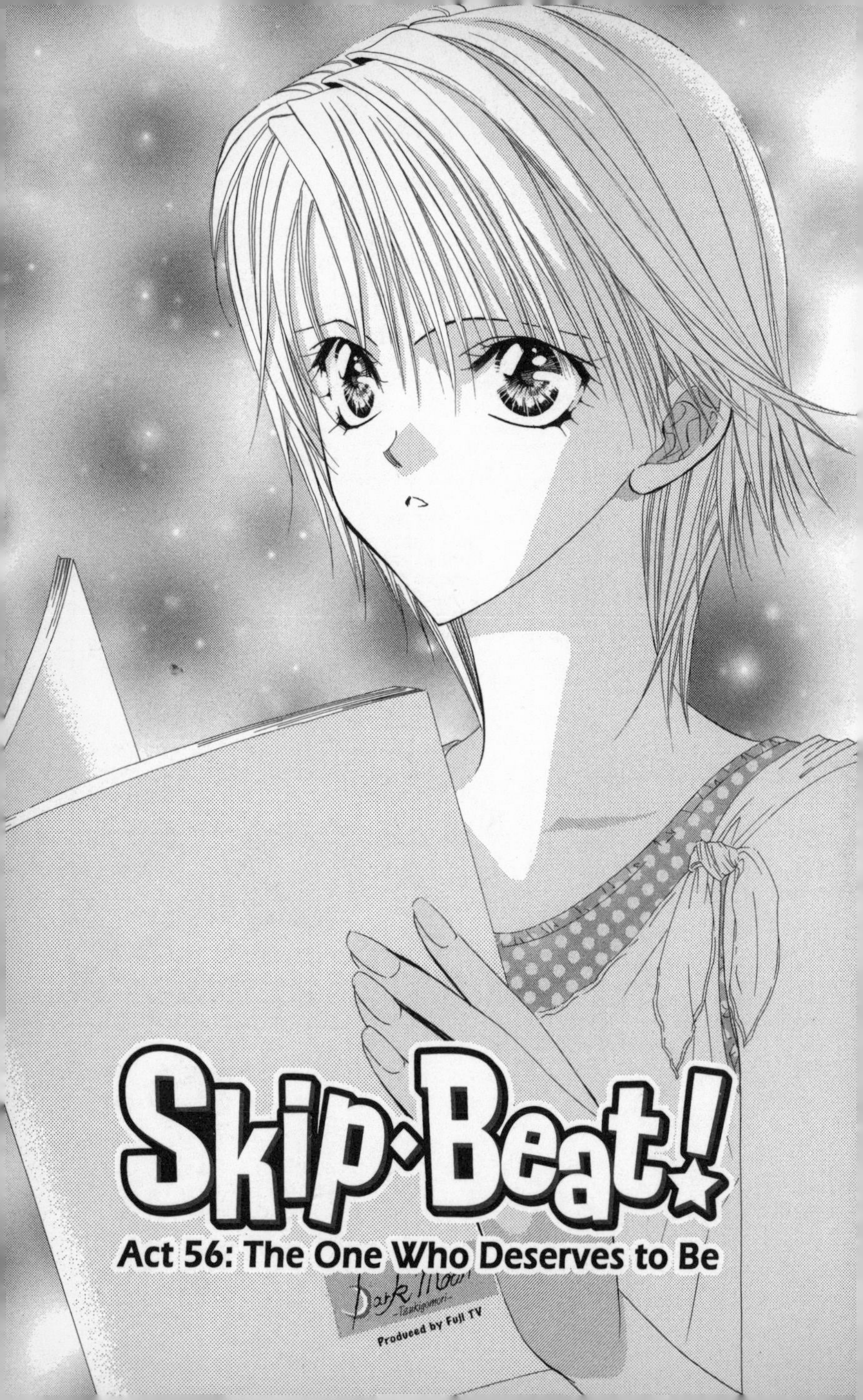
Skip·Beat!
Act 56: The One Who Deserves to Be
Dark Moon
-Tsukigomori-
Produced by Fuji TV

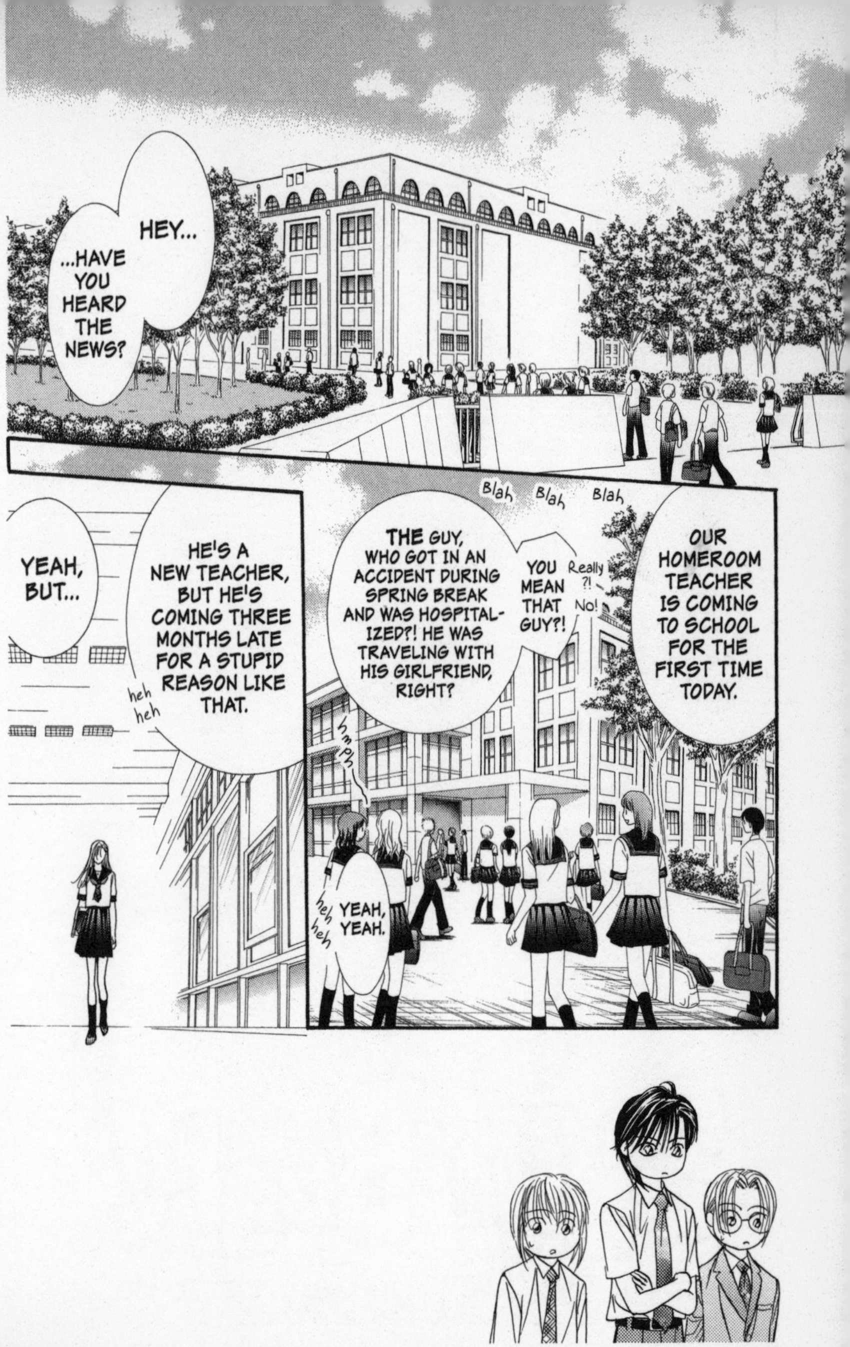
HEY...
...HAVE YOU HEARD THE NEWS?
OUR HOMEROOM TEACHER IS COMING TO SCHOOL FOR THE FIRST TIME TODAY.
Blah Blah Blah
Really ?!
No!
YOU MEAN THAT GUY?!
THE GUY, WHO GOT IN AN ACCIDENT DURING SPRING BREAK AND WAS HOSPITAL-IZED?! HE WAS TRAVELING WITH HIS GIRLFRIEND, RIGHT?
hmph
YEAH, YEAH.
heh heh
HE'S A NEW TEACHER, BUT HE'S COMING THREE MONTHS LATE FOR A STUPID REASON LIKE THAT.
heh heh
YEAH, BUT...

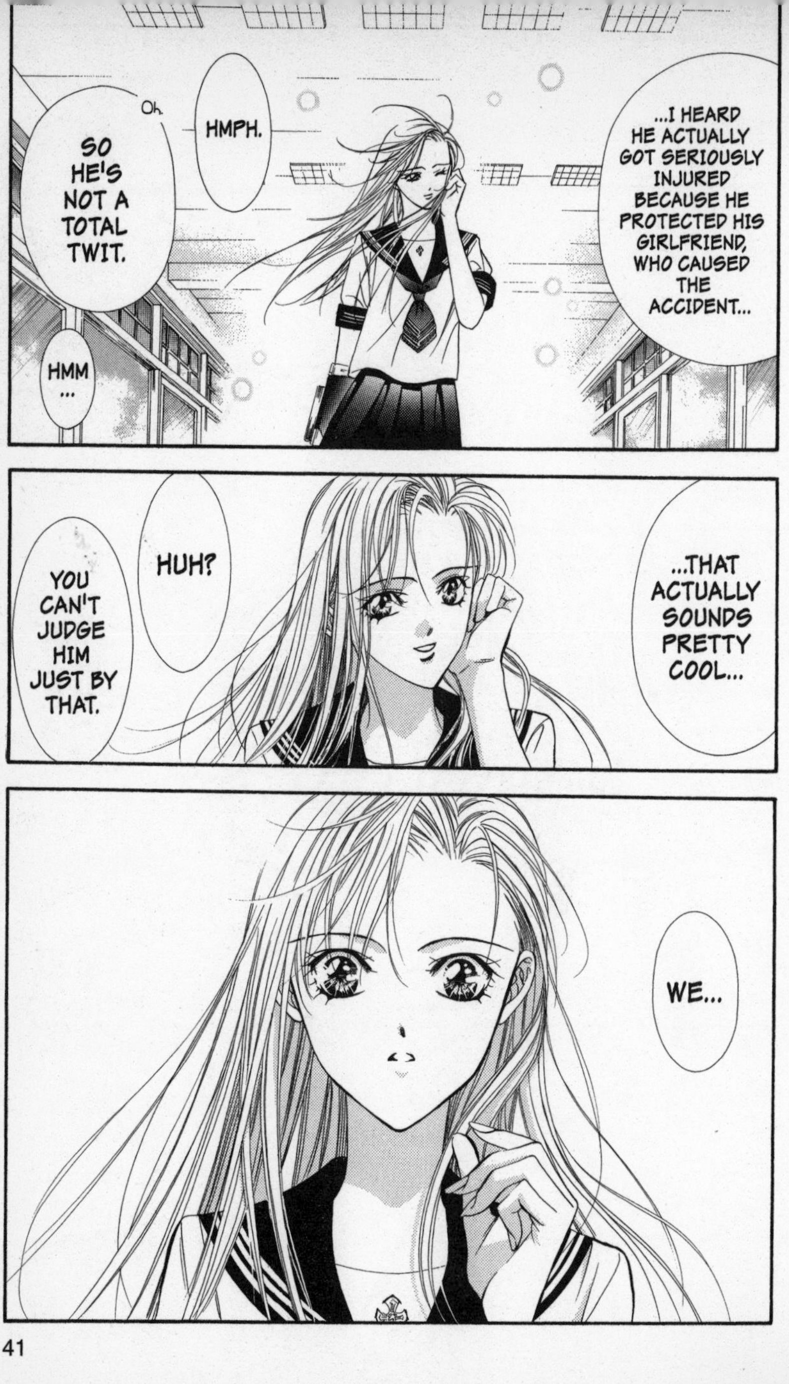
...I HEARD HE ACTUALLY GOT SERIOUSLY INJURED BECAUSE HE PROTECTED HIS GIRLFRIEND, WHO CAUSED THE ACCIDENT...
HMPH.
Oh.
SO HE'S NOT A TOTAL TWIT.
HMM ...
...THAT ACTUALLY SOUNDS PRETTY COOL...
HUH?
YOU CAN'T JUDGE HIM JUST BY THAT.
WE...

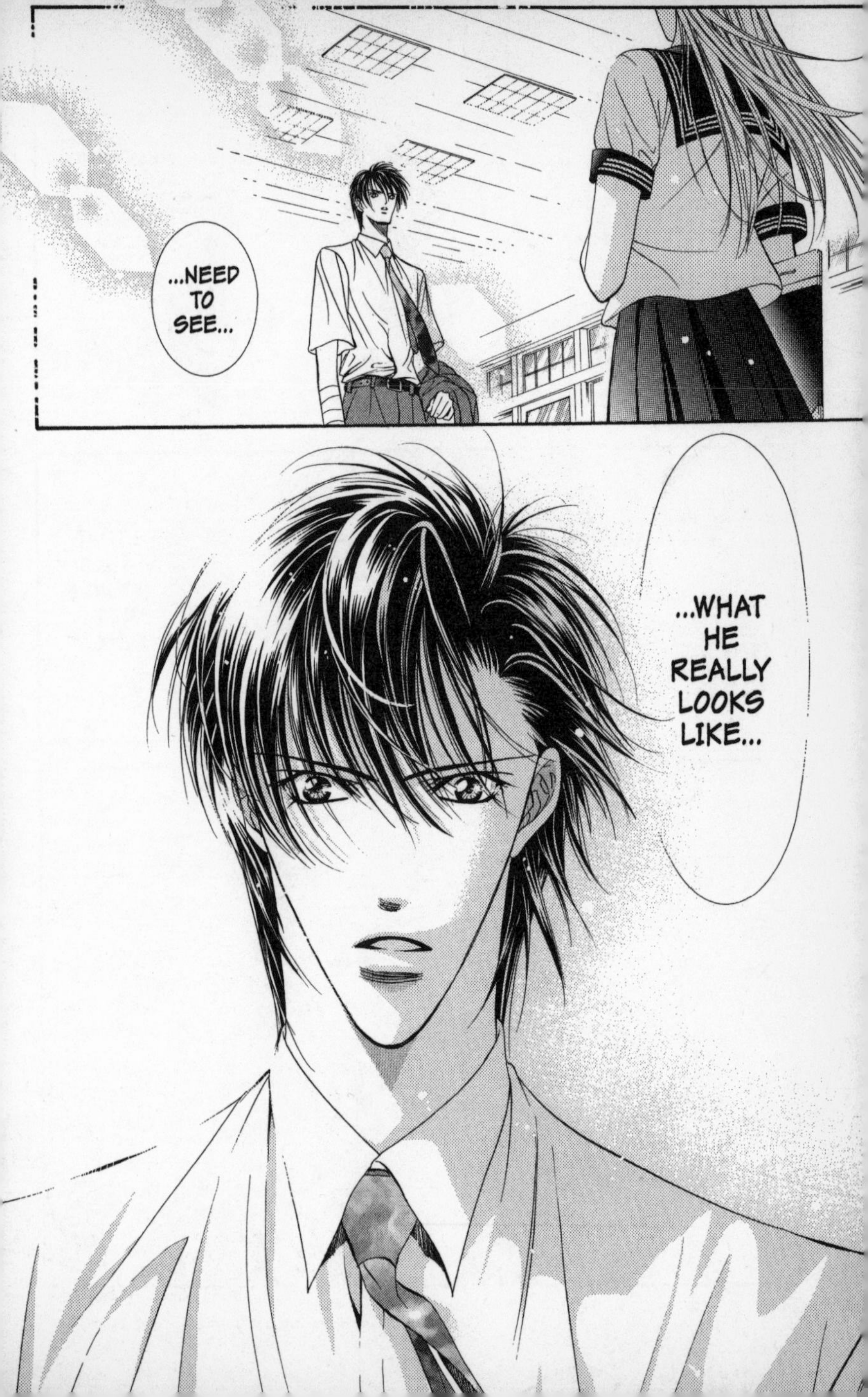
...NEED TO SEE...
...WHAT HE REALLY LOOKS LIKE...

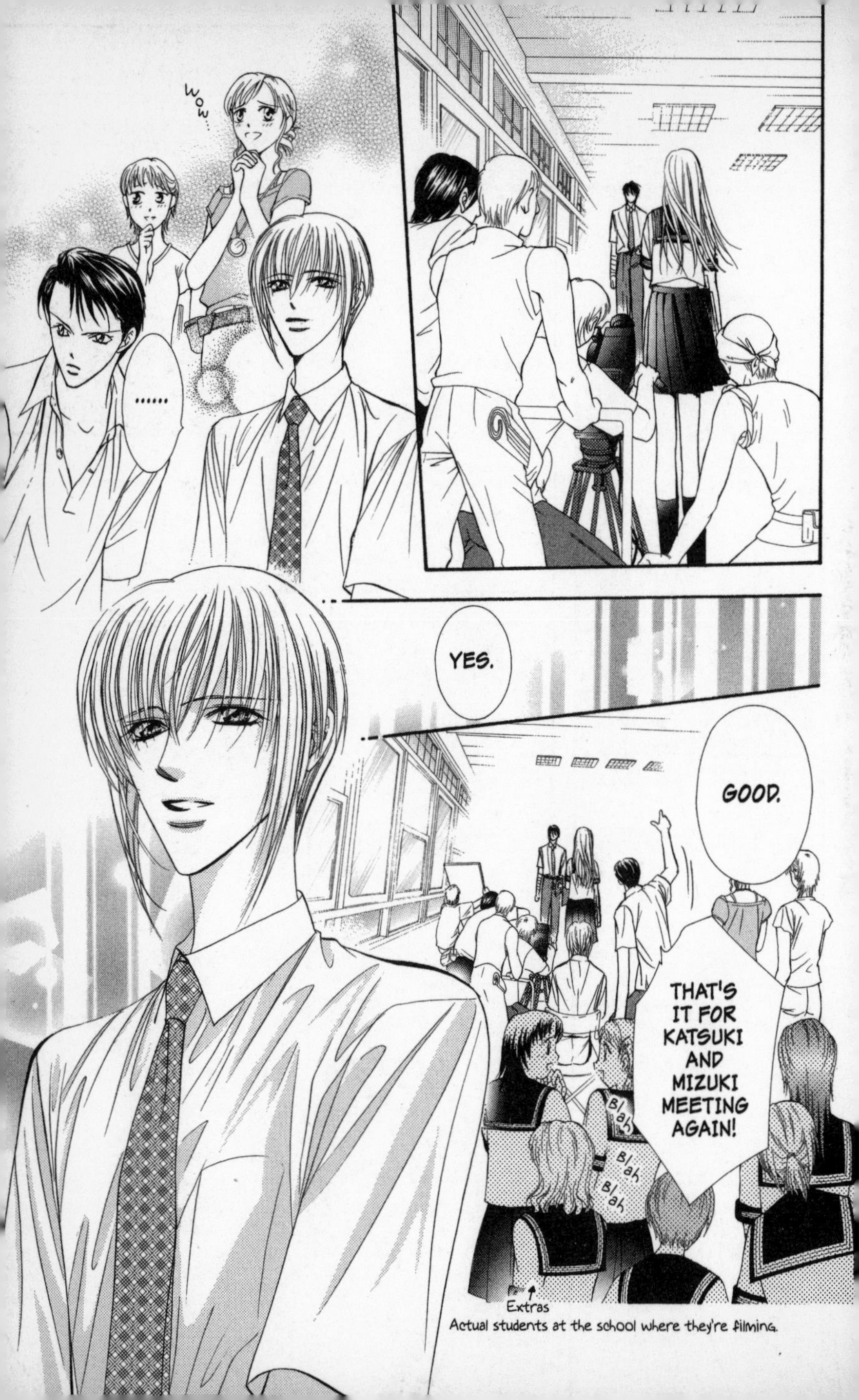
WOW...
......
YES.
GOOD.
THAT'S IT FOR KATSUKI AND MIZUKI MEETING AGAIN!
Blah
Blah
Blah
Extras
Actual students at the school where they're filming.

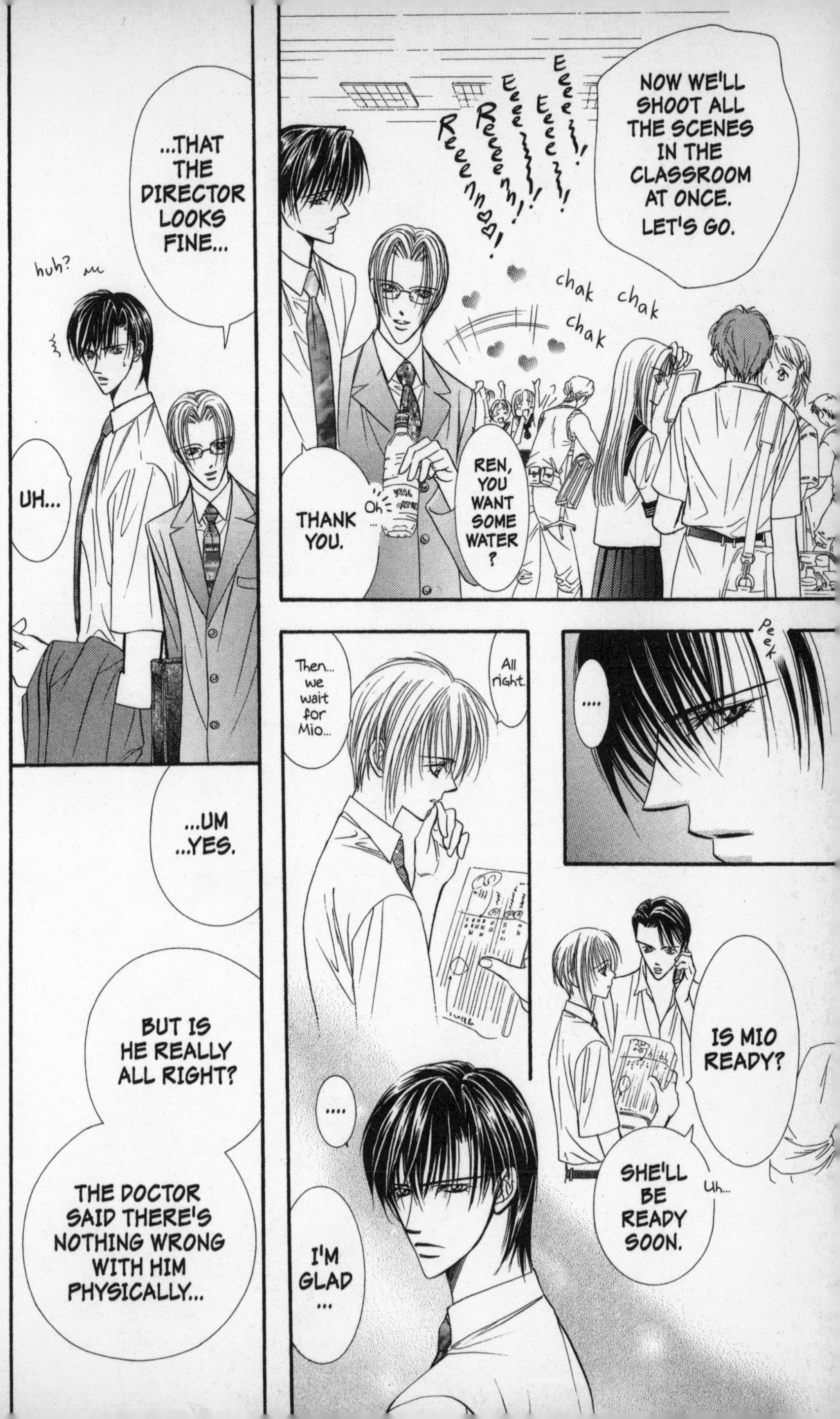
NOW WE'LL SHOOT ALL THE SCENES IN THE CLASSROOM AT ONCE. LET'S GO.
Eeee~!
Eeee~!
Eeee~!
Reeeenn~!
Reeennn♡♡!
chak chak
chak
REN, YOU WANT SOME WATER?
Oh...
THANK YOU.
Peek
....
All right.
Then... we wait for Mio...
IS MIO READY?
Uh...
SHE'LL BE READY SOON.
....
I'M GLAD...
...THAT THE DIRECTOR LOOKS FINE...
huh?
UH...
...UM ...YES.
BUT IS HE REALLY ALL RIGHT?
THE DOCTOR SAID THERE'S NOTHING WRONG WITH HIM PHYSICALLY...

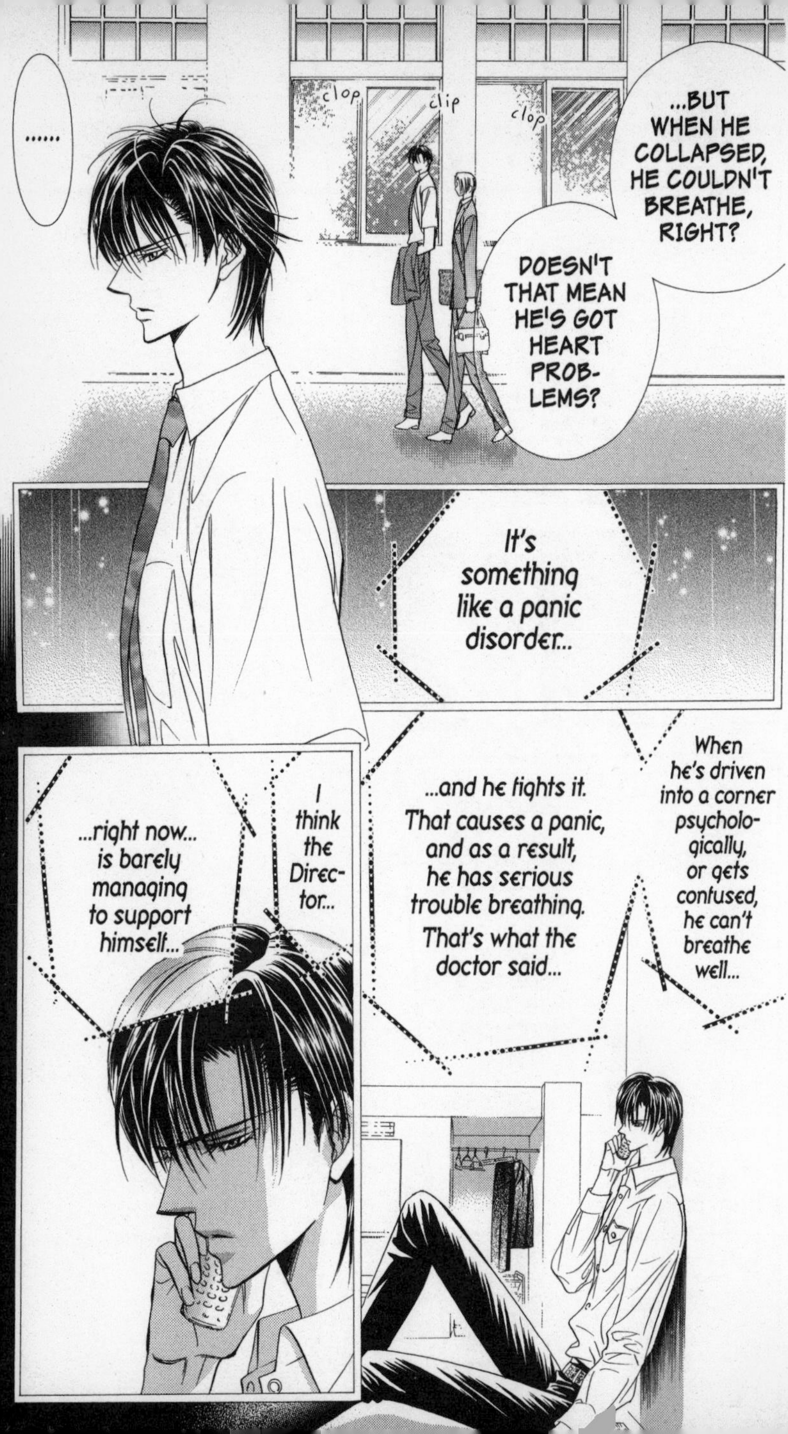

...BUT WHEN HE COLLAPSED, HE COULDN'T BREATHE, RIGHT?
DOESN'T THAT MEAN HE'S GOT HEART PROB-LEMS?
clop
clip
clop
......
It's something like a panic disorder...
When he's driven into a corner psycholo-gically, or gets confused, he can't breathe well...
...and he fights it. That causes a panic, and as a result, he has serious trouble breathing. That's what the doctor said...
I think the Direc-tor...
...right now... is barely managing to support himself...

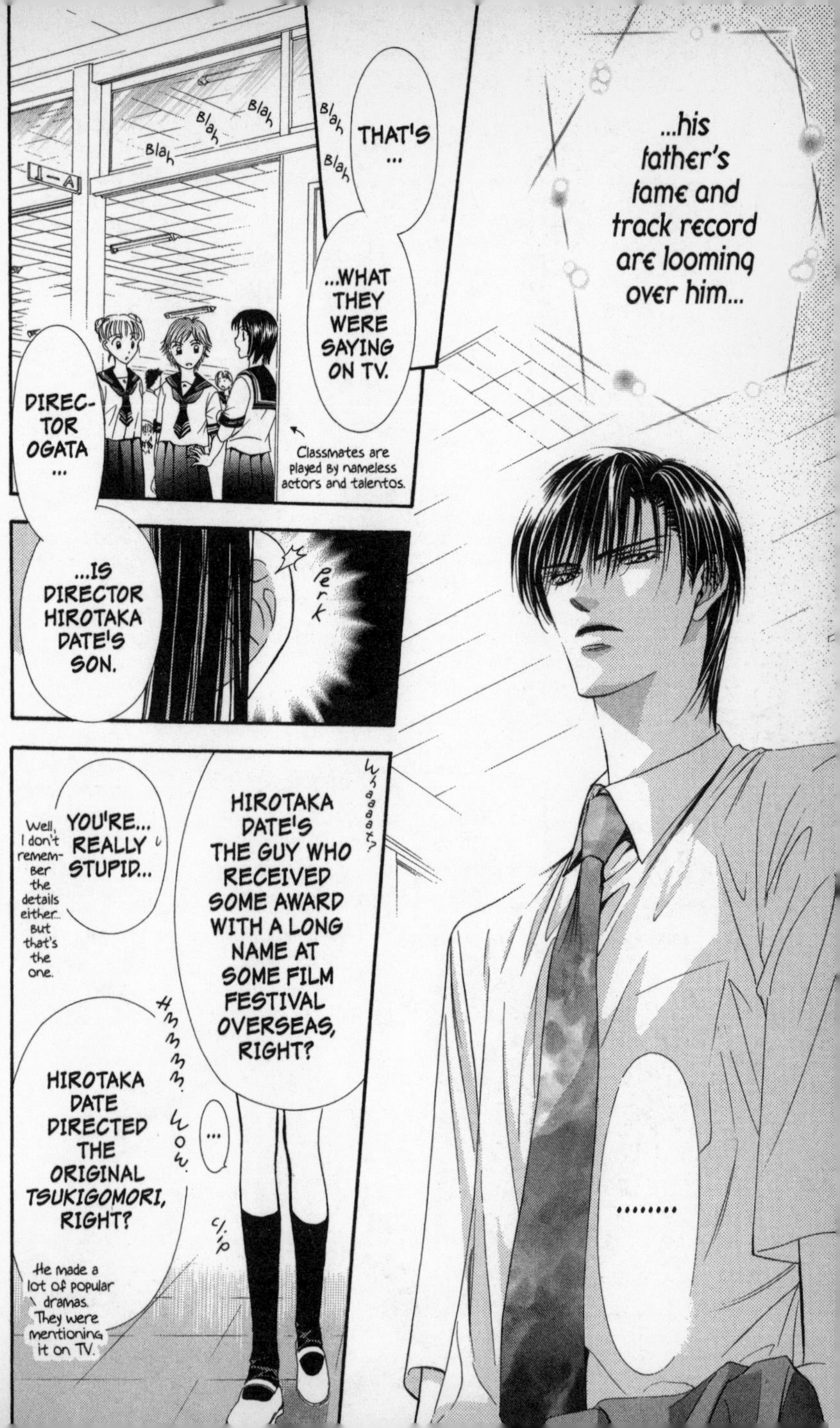

...his father's fame and track record are looming over him...
....
Blah Blah
Blah
Blah
Blah
THAT'S ...
...WHAT THEY WERE SAYING ON TV.
DIRECTOR OGATA ...
Classmates are played by nameless actors and talentos.
I-A
Perk
...IS DIRECTOR HIROTAKA DATE'S SON.
Whaaaat?
HIROTAKA DATE'S THE GUY WHO RECEIVED SOME AWARD WITH A LONG NAME AT SOME FILM FESTIVAL OVERSEAS, RIGHT?
YOU'RE... REALLY STUPID...
Well, I don't remember the details either... But that's the one.
HMMMM. WOW.
...
HIROTAKA DATE DIRECTED THE ORIGINAL TSUKIGOMORI, RIGHT?
clip
He made a lot of popular dramas. They were mentioning it on TV.

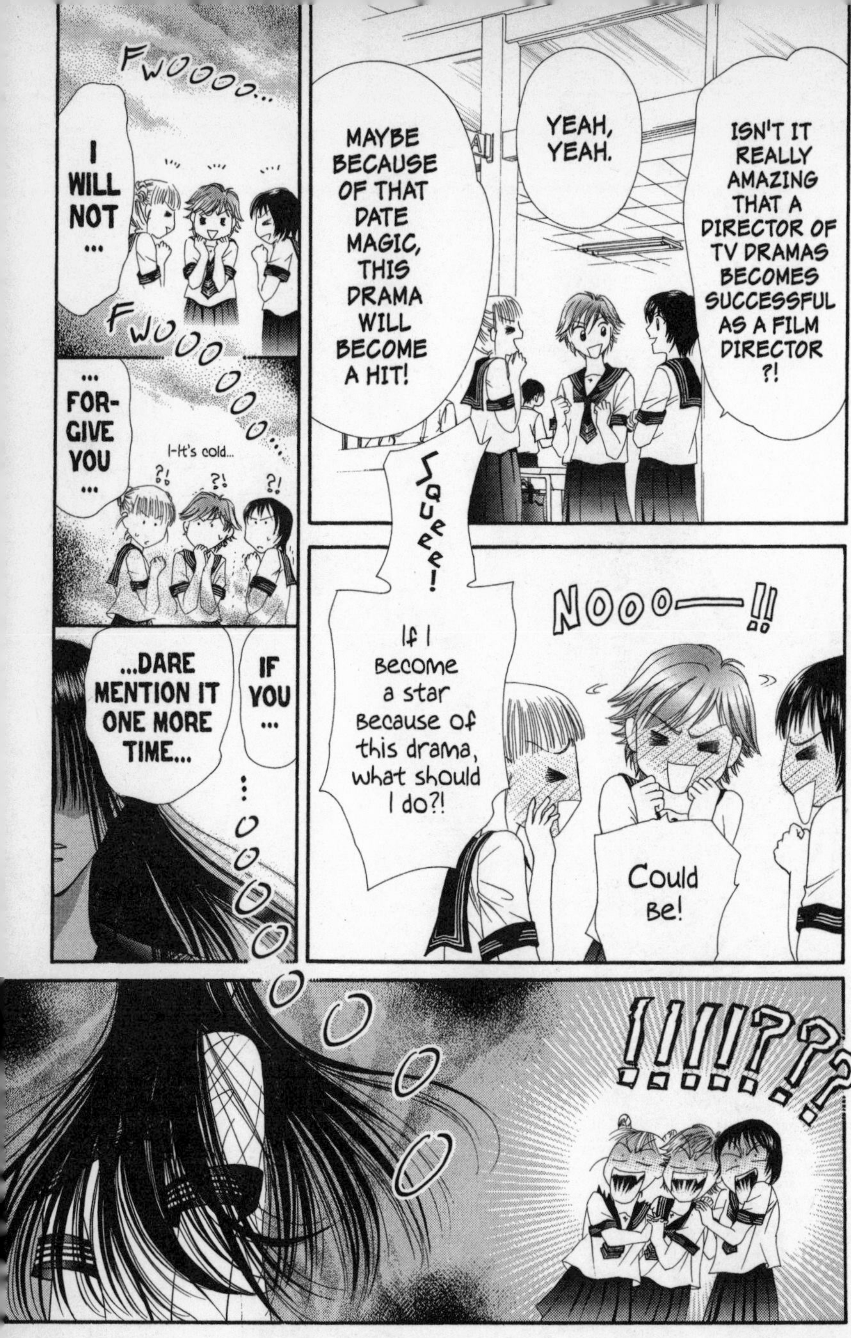
ISN'T IT REALLY AMAZING THAT A DIRECTOR OF TV DRAMAS BECOMES SUCCESSFUL AS A FILM DIRECTOR ?!
YEAH, YEAH.
MAYBE BECAUSE OF THAT DATE MAGIC, THIS DRAMA WILL BECOME A HIT!
Squeeee!
NOOO—!!
If I become a star because of this drama, what should I do?!
Could be!
FWOOOOO...
I WILL NOT ...
FWOOOOOOOOO...
... FOR-GIVE YOU ...
I-It's cold...
?! ?! ?!
IF YOU ...
...DARE MENTION IT ONE MORE TIME...
...OOOOOOOOOO
!!!!???

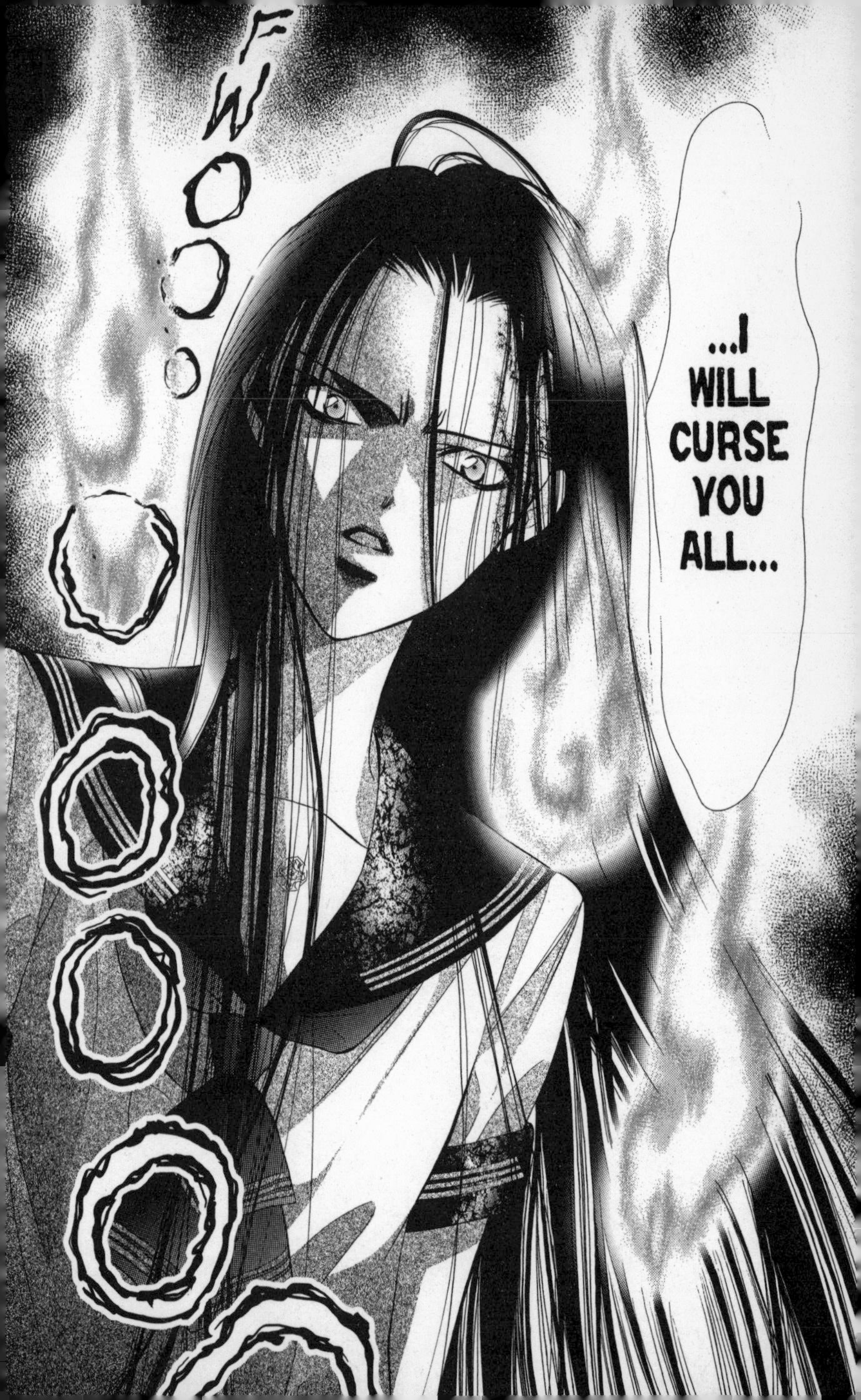
...I WILL CURSE YOU ALL...
FWOOOOOOO

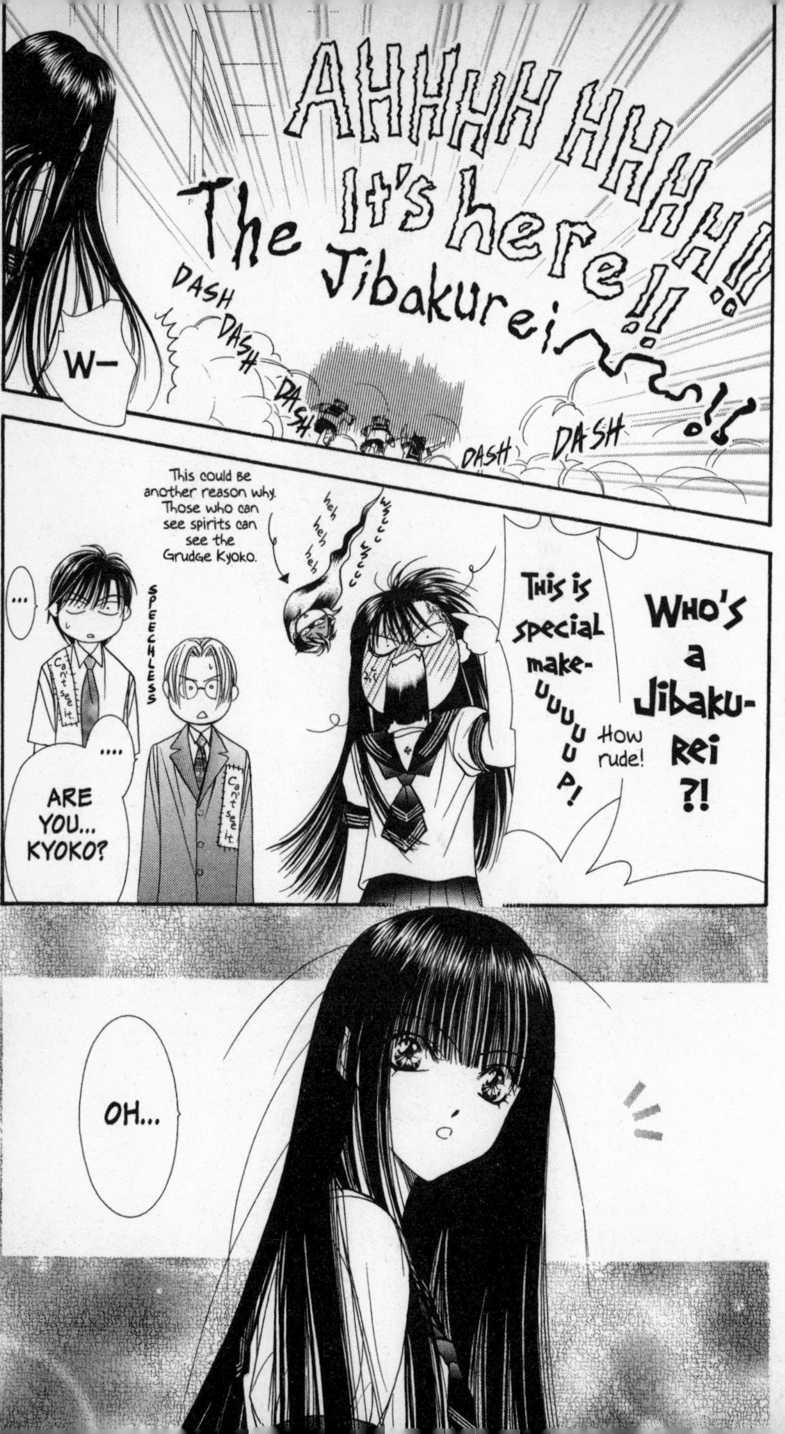
AHHHH HHHHH!!
It's here!!
The Jibakurei~!!
DASH DASH DASH DASH DASH
W—
WHO'S a Jibaku-rei?!
THIS is special make-uuuuup!
How rude!
heh heh heh
This could be another reason why. Those who can see spirits can see the Grudge Kyoko.
SPEECHLESS
Can't see it.
Can't see it.
...
....
ARE YOU... KYOKO?
OH...

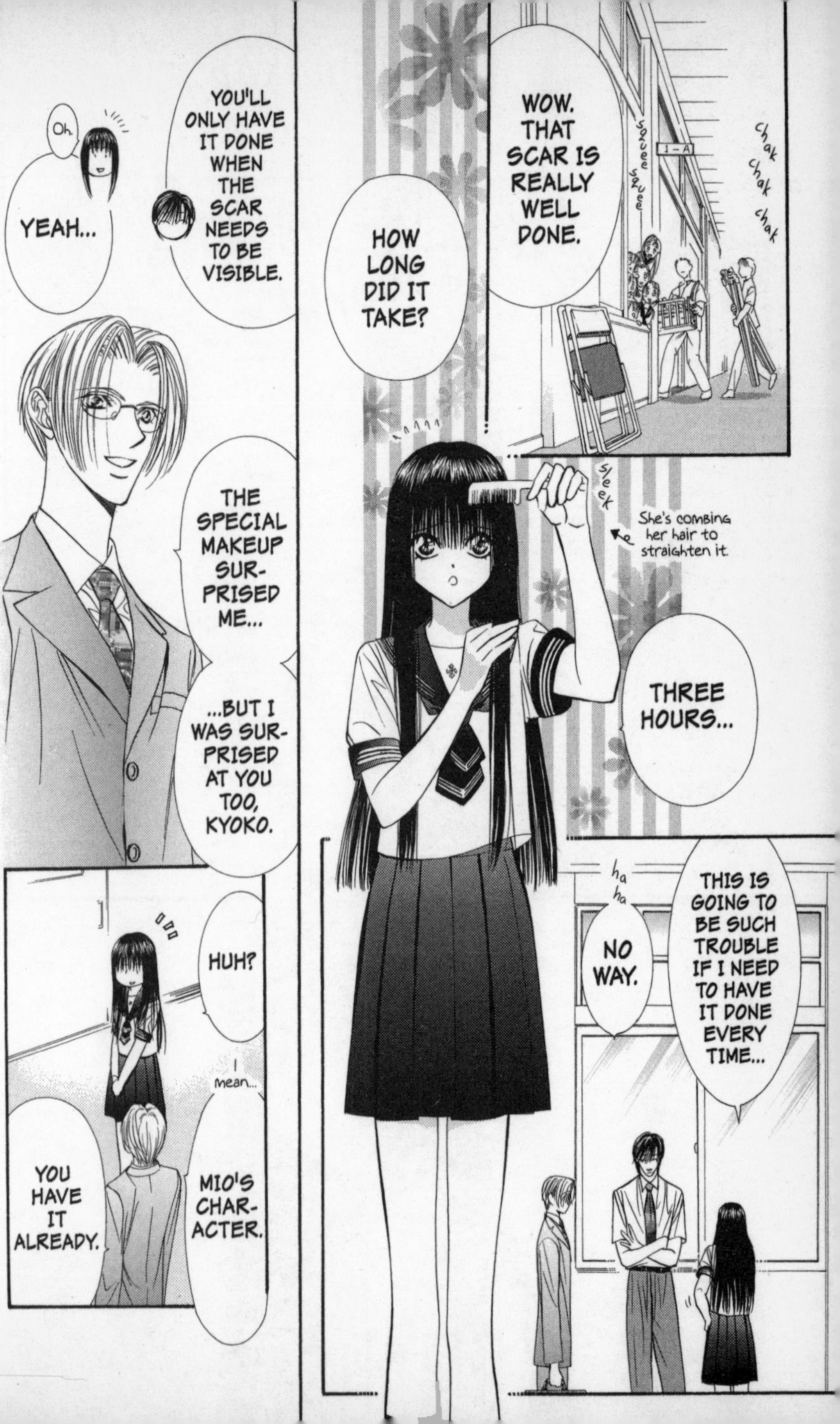
chak chak chak
squee squee
1-A
WOW. THAT SCAR IS REALLY WELL DONE.
HOW LONG DID IT TAKE?
sleek
She's combing her hair to straighten it.
THREE HOURS...
THIS IS GOING TO BE SUCH TROUBLE IF I NEED TO HAVE IT DONE EVERY TIME...
ha ha
NO WAY.
YOU'LL ONLY HAVE IT DONE WHEN THE SCAR NEEDS TO BE VISIBLE.
Oh.
YEAH...
THE SPECIAL MAKEUP SURPRISED ME...
...BUT I WAS SURPRISED AT YOU TOO, KYOKO.
HUH?
I mean...
MIO'S CHARACTER.
YOU HAVE IT ALREADY.

Tsukigomori

The concept was a drama that might have been broadcast in the 80s (sweat) and the sound of the first word in the title. I wanted to put Tsuki (moon) in the title and the candidates were Tsukigomori and another title (also containing Tsuki)...however, the other title lacked the heaviness that implied a love-and-hate drama. Moreover, it sounded as if a story with the same title already exists...so I searched the net and found many works with the same title... ♪no... not just stories, but in various genres, and I was shocked that there were so many... ♪ ...so I searched Tsukigomori... and I found that there weren't too many hits, and there were no signs that somebody was using it as a title for a story (I don't know if my search was thorough enough... ♪) so Tsukigomori was led on all counts, and this became the title.

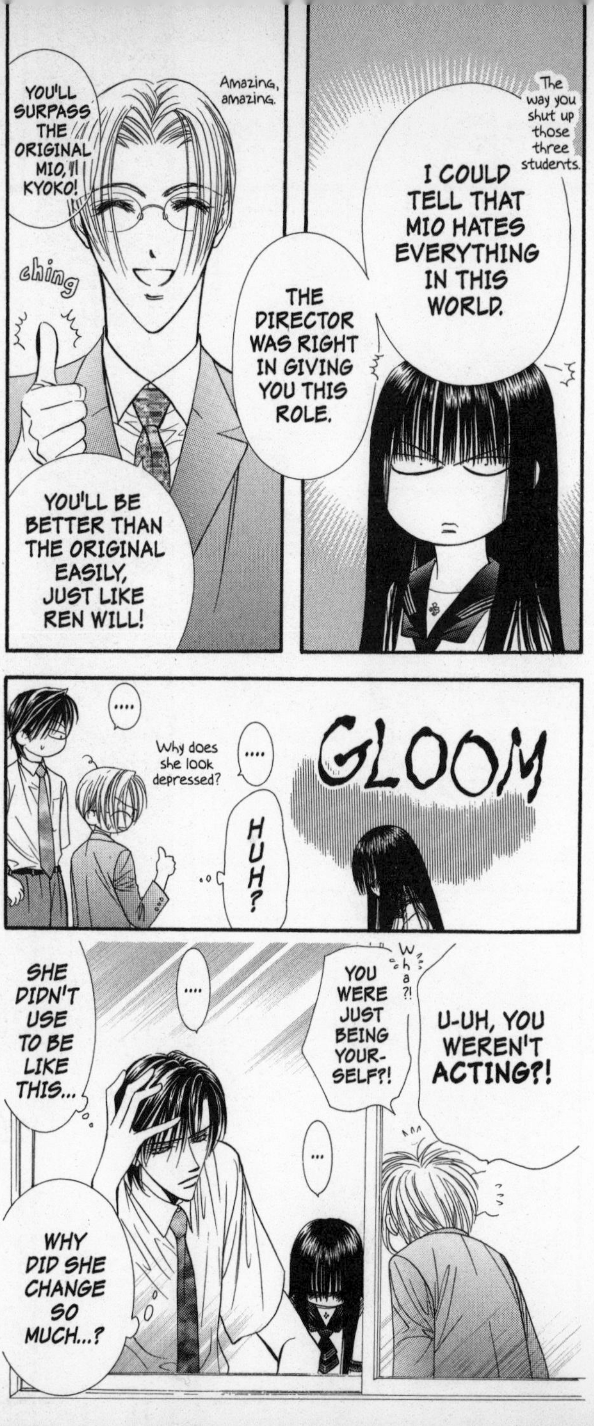
The way you shut up those three students.
I COULD TELL THAT MIO HATES EVERYTHING IN THIS WORLD.
THE DIRECTOR WAS RIGHT IN GIVING YOU THIS ROLE.
Amazing, amazing.
YOU'LL SURPASS THE ORIGINAL MIO, KYOKO!
ching
YOU'LL BE BETTER THAN THE ORIGINAL EASILY, JUST LIKE REN WILL!
GLOOM
HUH?
....
Why does she look depressed?
....
U-UH, YOU WEREN'T ACTING?!
Wha?!
YOU WERE JUST BEING YOURSELF?!
....
SHE DIDN'T USE TO BE LIKE THIS...
...
WHY DID SHE CHANGE SO MUCH...?

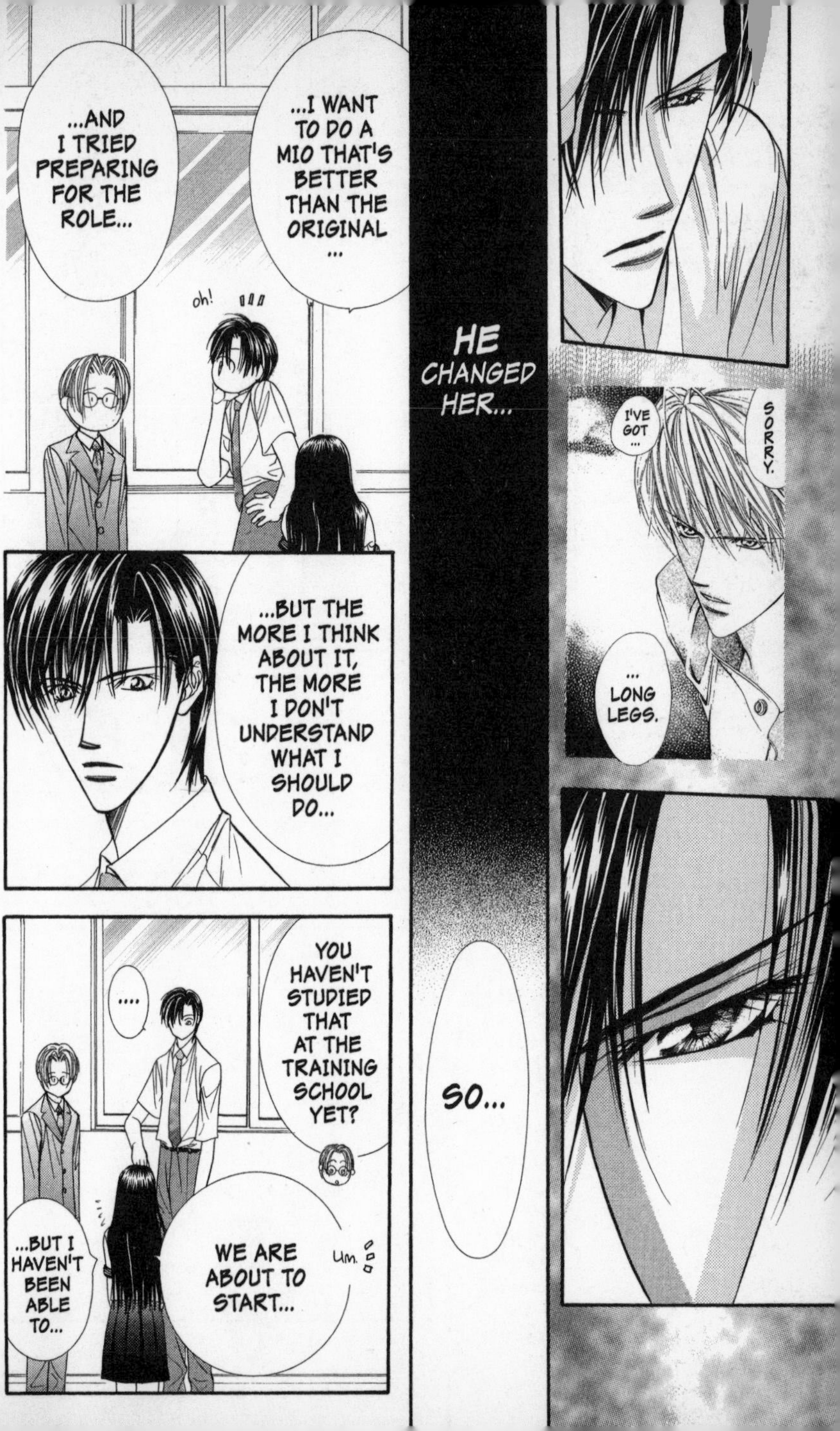
HE CHANGED HER...
SORRY.
I'VE GOT ...
... LONG LEGS.
SO...
...I WANT TO DO A MIO THAT'S BETTER THAN THE ORIGINAL ...
...AND I TRIED PREPARING FOR THE ROLE...
oh!
...BUT THE MORE I THINK ABOUT IT, THE MORE I DON'T UNDERSTAND WHAT I SHOULD DO...
YOU HAVEN'T STUDIED THAT AT THE TRAINING SCHOOL YET?
....
Um.
WE ARE ABOUT TO START...
...BUT I HAVEN'T BEEN ABLE TO...

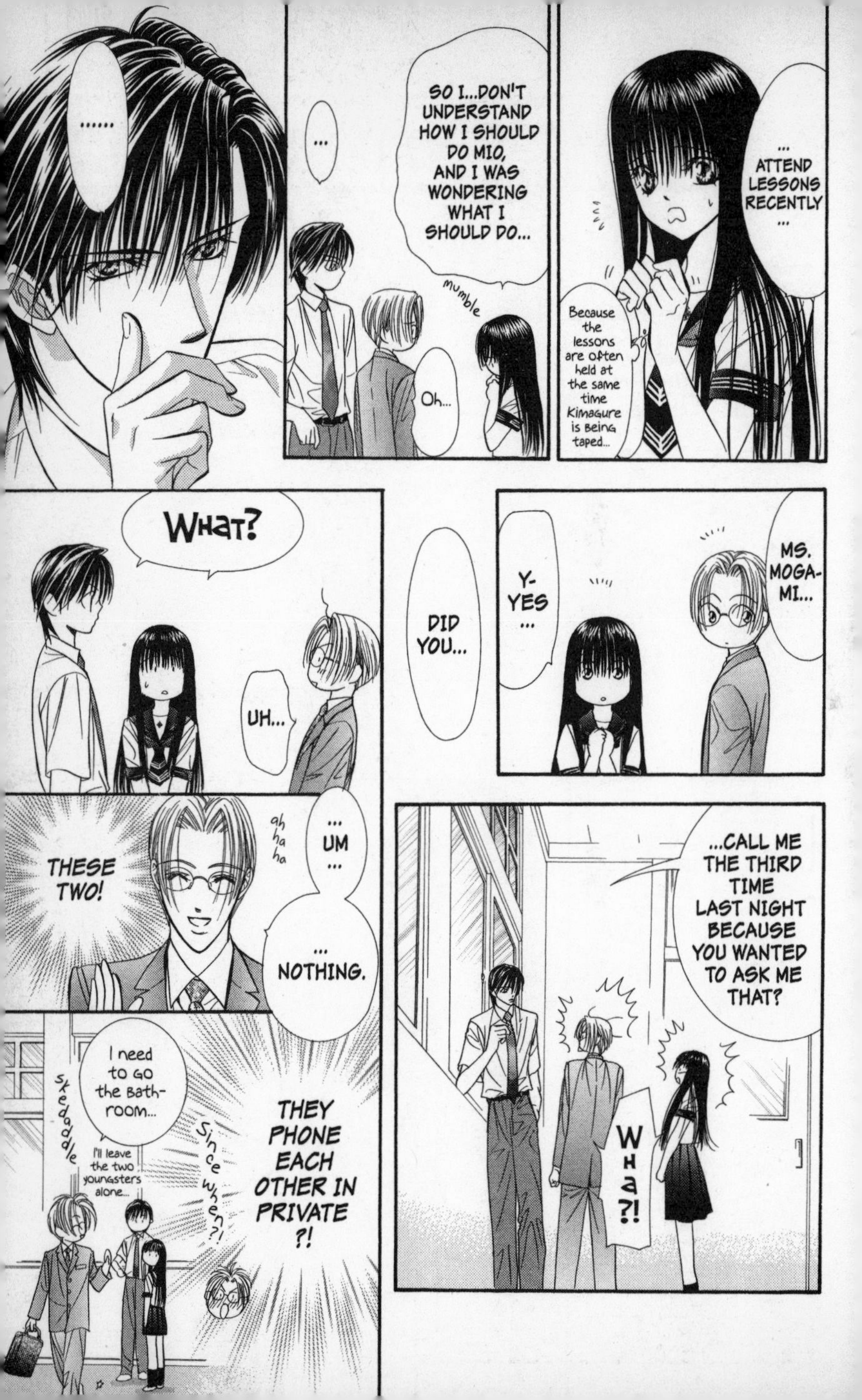

...ATTEND LESSONS RECENTLY...
Because the lessons are often held at the same time Kimagure is being taped...
SO I...DON'T UNDERSTAND HOW I SHOULD DO MIO, AND I WAS WONDERING WHAT I SHOULD DO...
...
mumble
Oh...
......
MS. MOGAMI...
Y-YES...
DID YOU...
WHAT?
UH...
...CALL ME THE THIRD TIME LAST NIGHT BECAUSE YOU WANTED TO ASK ME THAT?
Wha?!
...UM...
...NOTHING.
ah ha ha ha
THESE TWO!
THEY PHONE EACH OTHER IN PRIVATE?!
Since when?!
I need to go the Bath-room...
I'll leave the two youngsters alone...
skedaddle

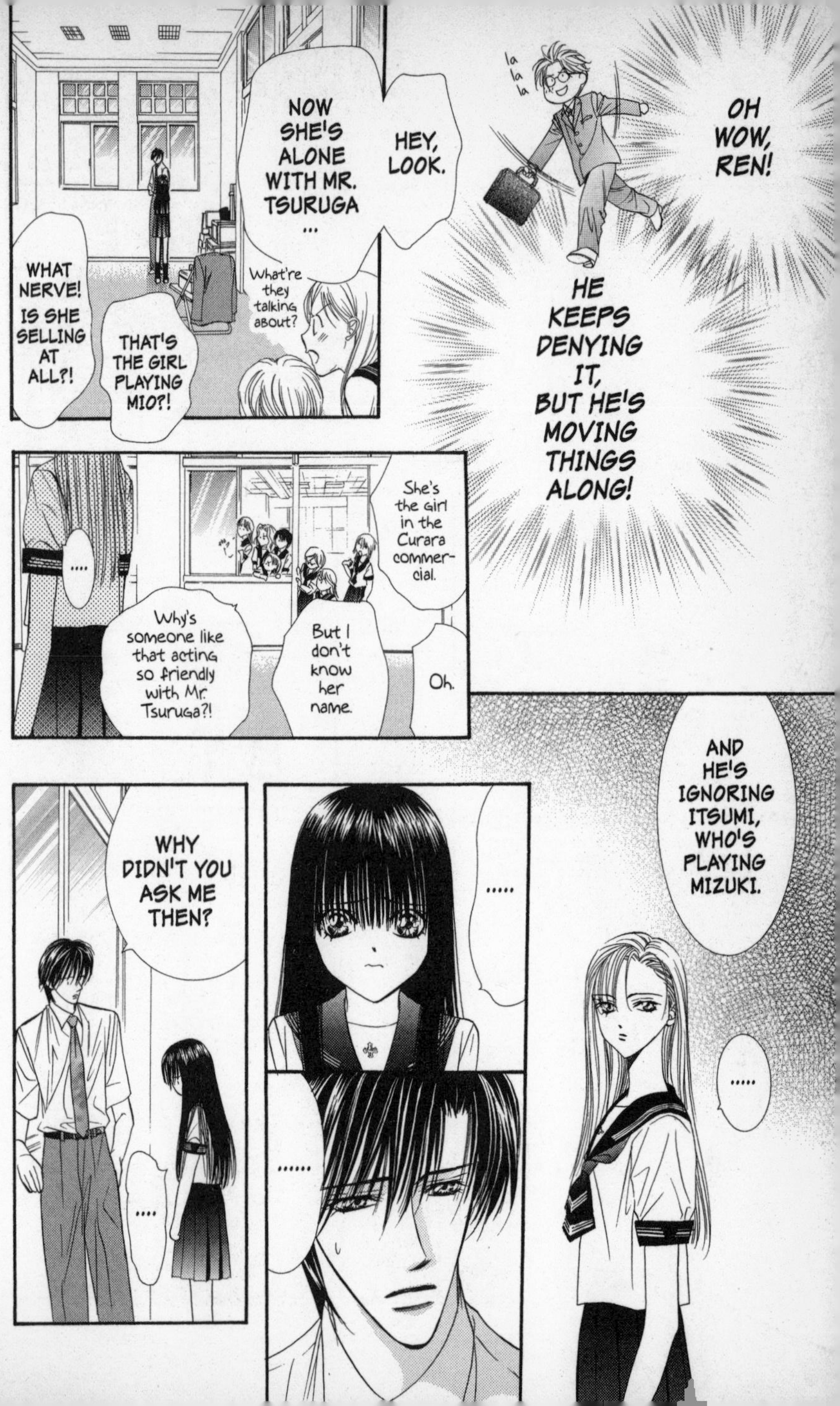
OH WOW, REN!
la la la
HE KEEPS DENYING IT, BUT HE'S MOVING THINGS ALONG!
HEY, LOOK.
NOW SHE'S ALONE WITH MR. TSURUGA...
What're they talking about?
THAT'S THE GIRL PLAYING MIO?!
WHAT NERVE! IS SHE SELLING AT ALL?!
She's the girl in the Curara commercial.
Oh.
But I don't know her name.
Why's someone like that acting so friendly with Mr. Tsuruga?!
....
AND HE'S IGNORING ITSUMI, WHO'S PLAYING MIZUKI.
.....
.....
......
WHY DIDN'T YOU ASK ME THEN?
....

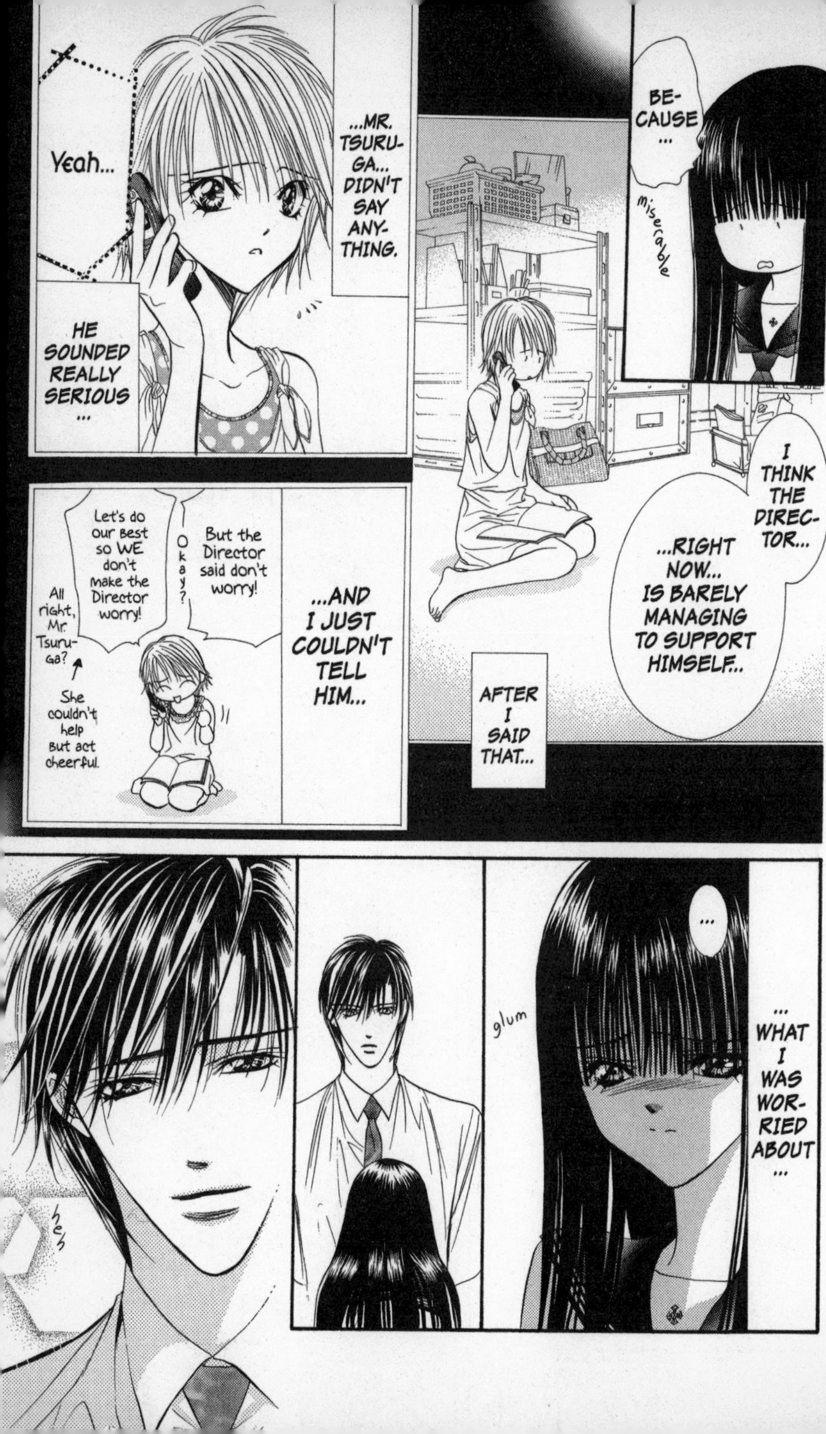
BE-CAUSE...
miserable
I THINK THE DIREC-TOR...
...RIGHT NOW... IS BARELY MANAGING TO SUPPORT HIMSELF..
AFTER I SAID THAT...
...MR. TSURU-GA... DIDN'T SAY ANY-THING.
Yeah...
HE SOUNDED REALLY SERIOUS...
...AND I JUST COULDN'T TELL HIM...
But the Director said don't worry!
Okay?
Let's do our best so WE don't make the Director worry!
All right, Mr. Tsuru-ga?
She couldn't help but act cheerful.
...
...WHAT I WAS WOR-RIED ABOUT...
glum
heh

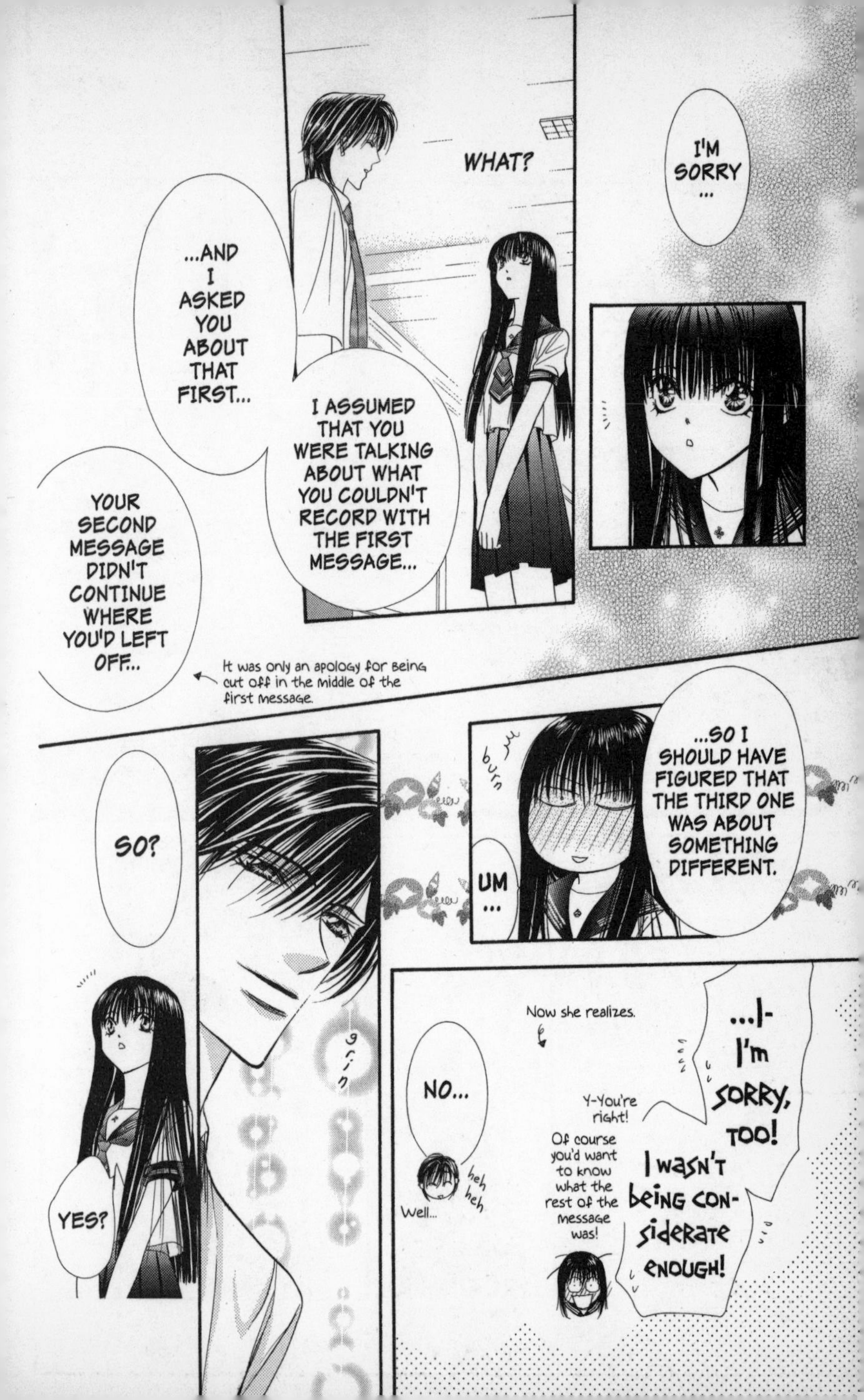
I'M SORRY...
WHAT?
...AND I ASKED YOU ABOUT THAT FIRST...
I ASSUMED THAT YOU WERE TALKING ABOUT WHAT YOU COULDN'T RECORD WITH THE FIRST MESSAGE...
YOUR SECOND MESSAGE DIDN'T CONTINUE WHERE YOU'D LEFT OFF...
It was only an apology for being cut off in the middle of the first message.
...SO I SHOULD HAVE FIGURED THAT THE THIRD ONE WAS ABOUT SOMETHING DIFFERENT.
burn
UM...
...I-I'm SORRY, TOO! I WASN'T being CON-siderate ENOUGH!
Y-You're right! Of course you'd want to know what the rest of the message was!
Now she realizes.
NO...
heh heh
Well...
SO?
grin
YES?

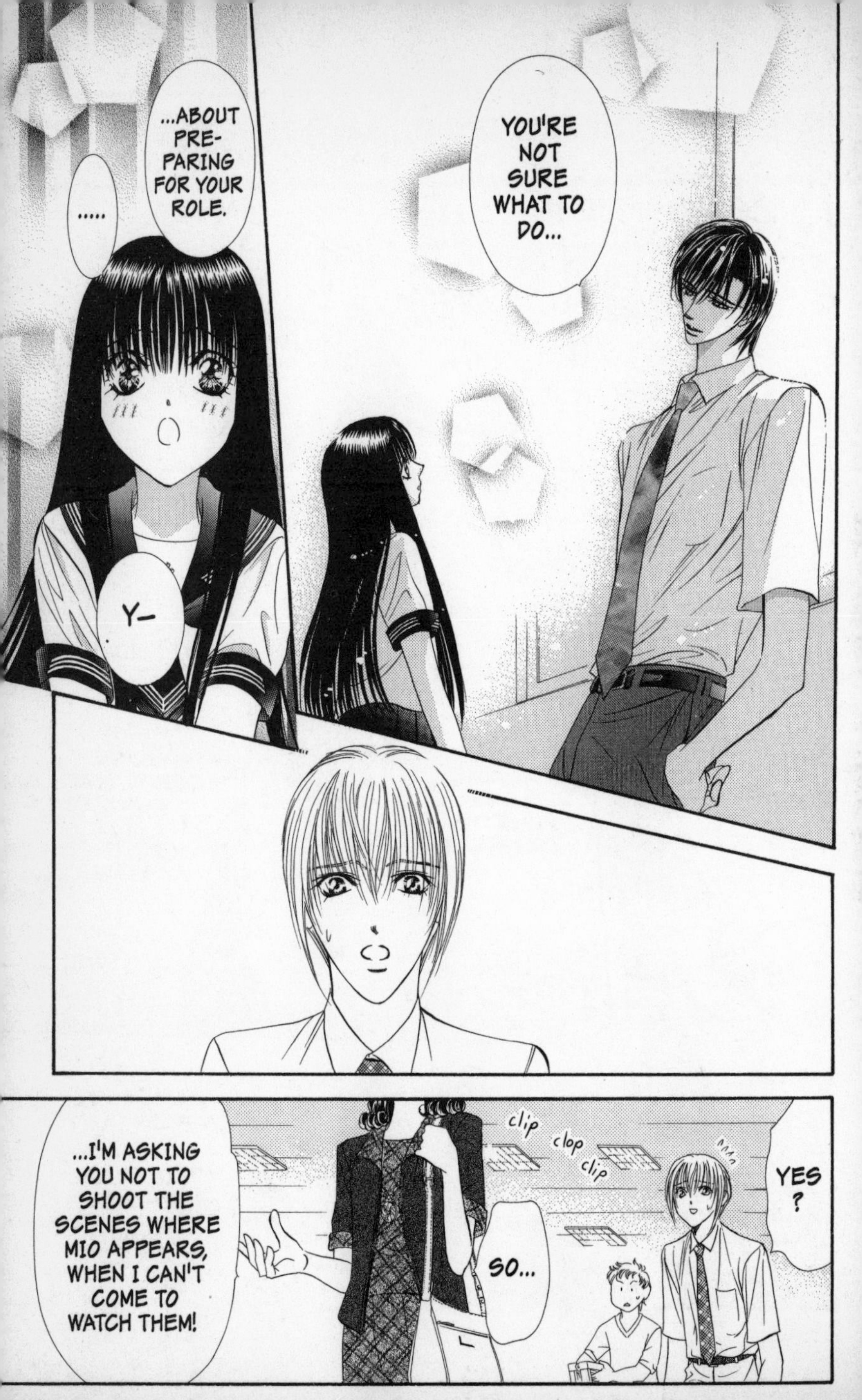
YOU'RE NOT SURE WHAT TO DO...
...ABOUT PRE-PARING FOR YOUR ROLE.
.....
Y–
YES?
clip clop clip
SO...
...I'M ASKING YOU NOT TO SHOOT THE SCENES WHERE MIO APPEARS, WHEN I CAN'T COME TO WATCH THEM!

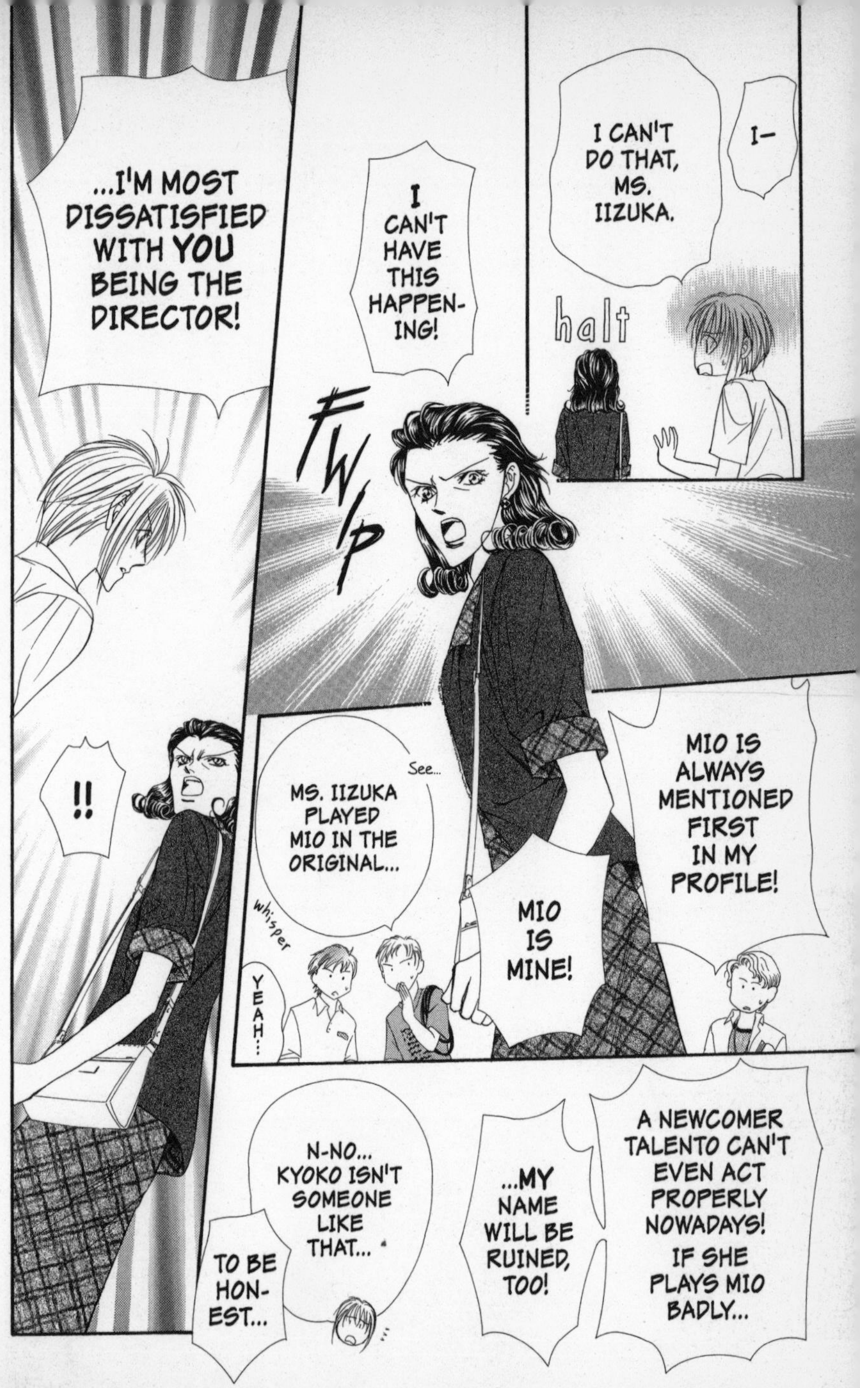
I–
I CAN'T DO THAT, MS. IIZUKA.
halt
I CAN'T HAVE THIS HAPPENING!
FWIP
MIO IS ALWAYS MENTIONED FIRST IN MY PROFILE!
MIO IS MINE!
See...
MS. IIZUKA PLAYED MIO IN THE ORIGINAL...
whisper
YEAH...
A NEWCOMER TALENTO CAN'T EVEN ACT PROPERLY NOWADAYS!
IF SHE PLAYS MIO BADLY...
...MY NAME WILL BE RUINED, TOO!
N-NO... KYOKO ISN'T SOMEONE LIKE THAT...
TO BE HONEST...
...I'M MOST DISSATISFIED WITH YOU BEING THE DIRECTOR!
!!

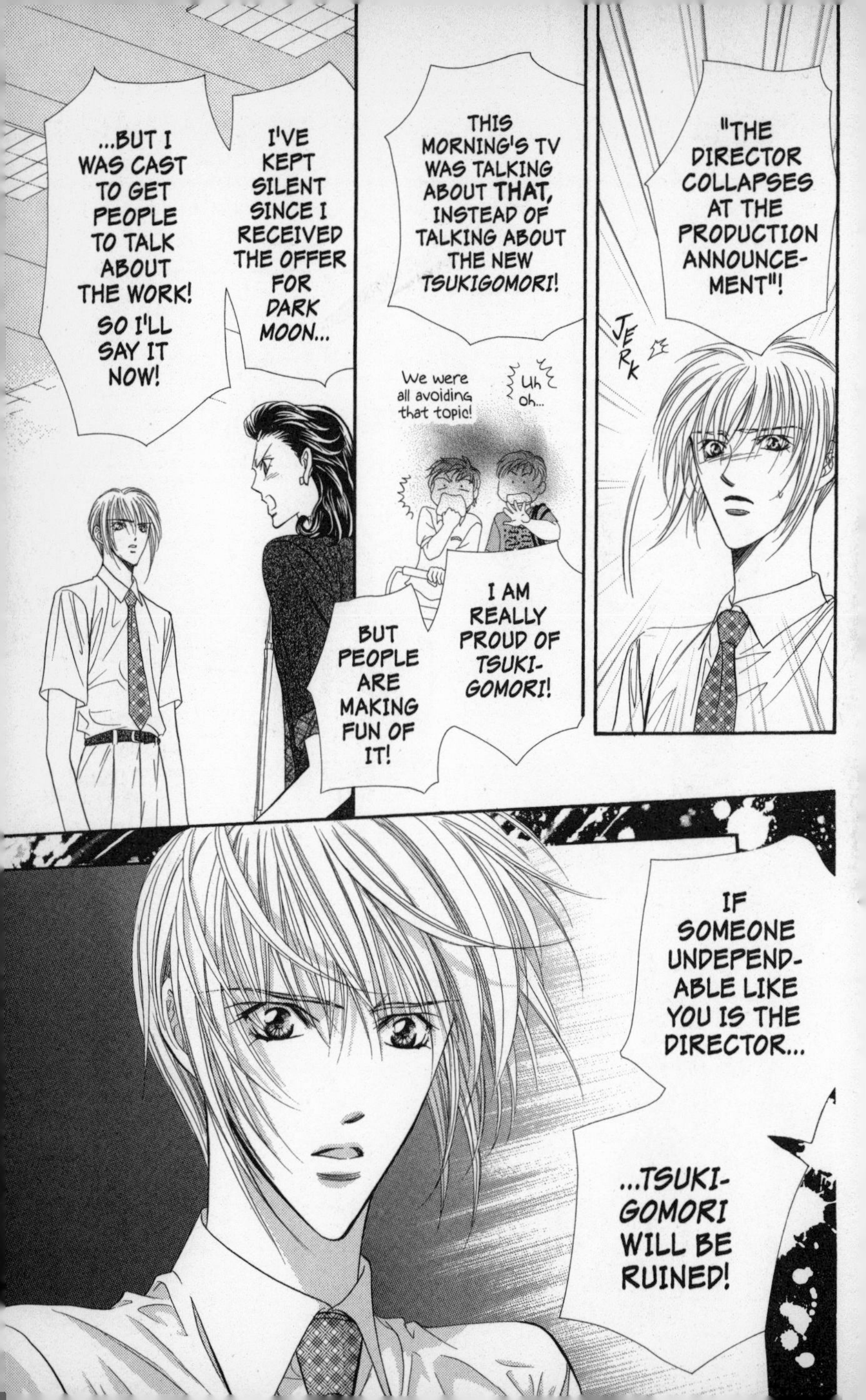
"THE DIRECTOR COLLAPSES AT THE PRODUCTION ANNOUNCEMENT"!
JERK
THIS MORNING'S TV WAS TALKING ABOUT THAT, INSTEAD OF TALKING ABOUT THE NEW TSUKIGOMORI!
Uh oh...
We were all avoiding that topic!
I AM REALLY PROUD OF TSUKI-GOMORI!
BUT PEOPLE ARE MAKING FUN OF IT!
I'VE KEPT SILENT SINCE I RECEIVED THE OFFER FOR DARK MOON...
...BUT I WAS CAST TO GET PEOPLE TO TALK ABOUT THE WORK!
SO I'LL SAY IT NOW!
IF SOMEONE UNDEPEND-ABLE LIKE YOU IS THE DIRECTOR...
...TSUKI-GOMORI WILL BE RUINED!

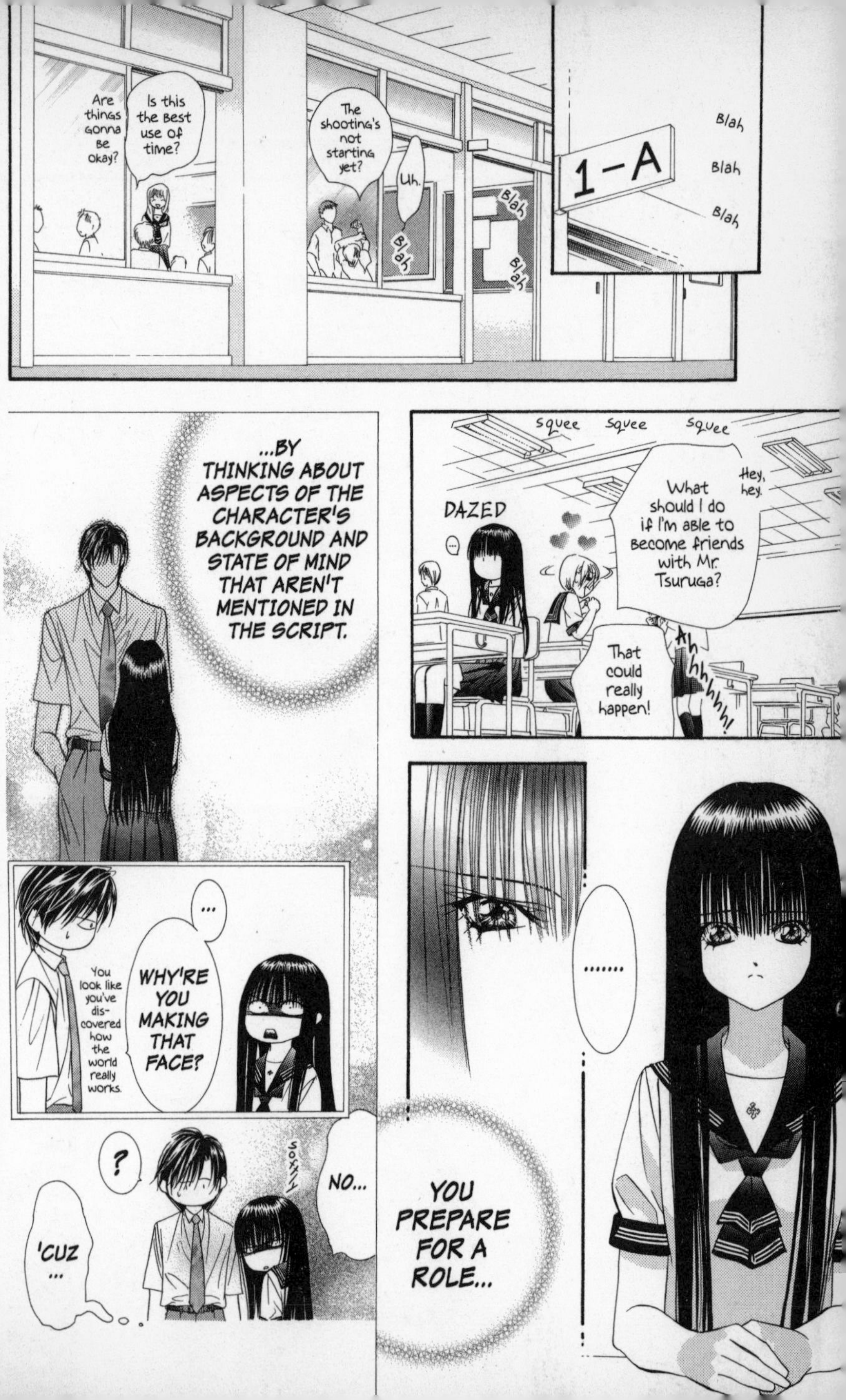
Blah
Blah
Blah
1-A
Blah
Blah
Uh.
The shooting's not starting yet?
Is this the best use of time?
Are things gonna be okay?
squee squee squee
Hey, hey.
What should I do if I'm able to become friends with Mr. Tsuruga?
That could really happen!
Ahhhhhh!
DAZED
...
....
YOU PREPARE FOR A ROLE...
...BY THINKING ABOUT ASPECTS OF THE CHARACTER'S BACKGROUND AND STATE OF MIND THAT AREN'T MENTIONED IN THE SCRIPT.
...
WHY'RE YOU MAKING THAT FACE?
You look like you've dis-covered how the world really works.
NO...
?
'CUZ ...

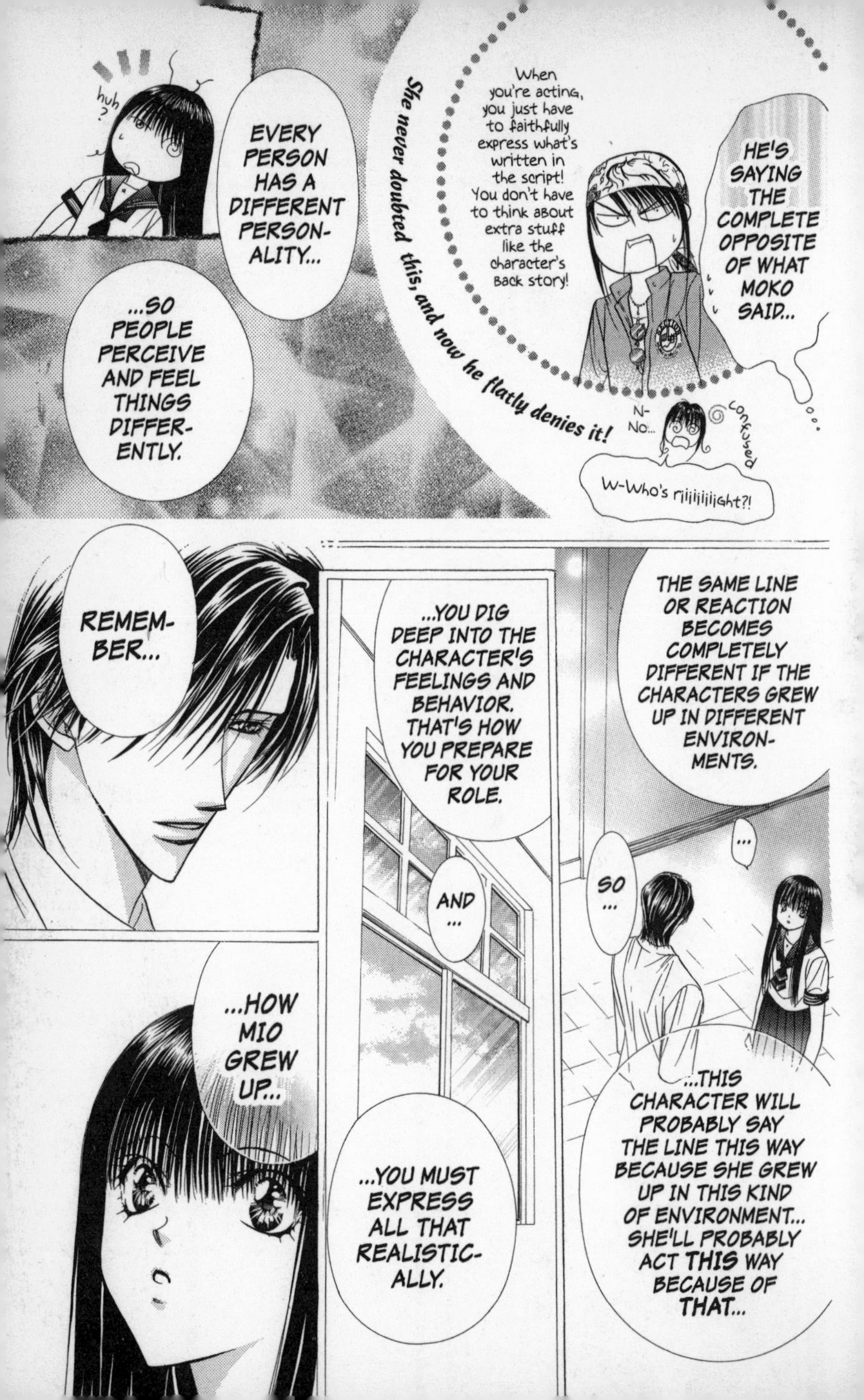
HE'S SAYING THE COMPLETE OPPOSITE OF WHAT MOKO SAID...
When you're acting, you just have to faithfully express what's written in the script! You don't have to think about extra stuff like the character's back story!
She never doubted this, and now he flatly denies it!
N-No...
confused
W-Who's riiiiiiiight?!
huh?
EVERY PERSON HAS A DIFFERENT PERSONALITY...
...SO PEOPLE PERCEIVE AND FEEL THINGS DIFFERENTLY.
THE SAME LINE OR REACTION BECOMES COMPLETELY DIFFERENT IF THE CHARACTERS GREW UP IN DIFFERENT ENVIRONMENTS.
...
SO...
...THIS CHARACTER WILL PROBABLY SAY THE LINE THIS WAY BECAUSE SHE GREW UP IN THIS KIND OF ENVIRONMENT... SHE'LL PROBABLY ACT THIS WAY BECAUSE OF THAT...
...YOU DIG DEEP INTO THE CHARACTER'S FEELINGS AND BEHAVIOR. THAT'S HOW YOU PREPARE FOR YOUR ROLE.
AND...
...YOU MUST EXPRESS ALL THAT REALISTICALLY.
REMEMBER...
...HOW MIO GREW UP...

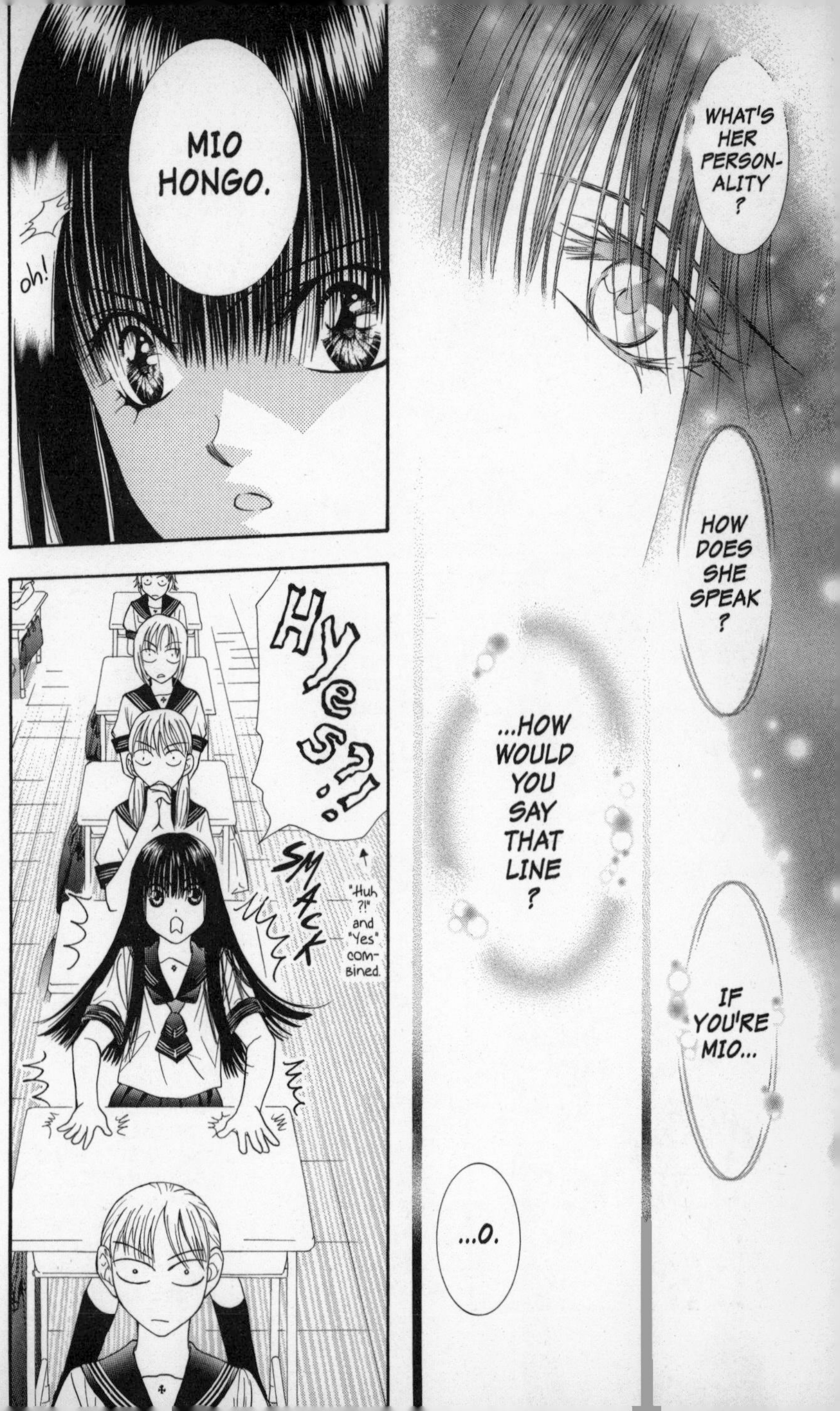
WHAT'S HER PERSONALITY?
HOW DOES SHE SPEAK?
IF YOU'RE MIO...
...HOW WOULD YOU SAY THAT LINE?
...O.
MIO HONGO.
oh!
HYES?!!
SMACK
↑ "Huh?!" and "Yes" combined.

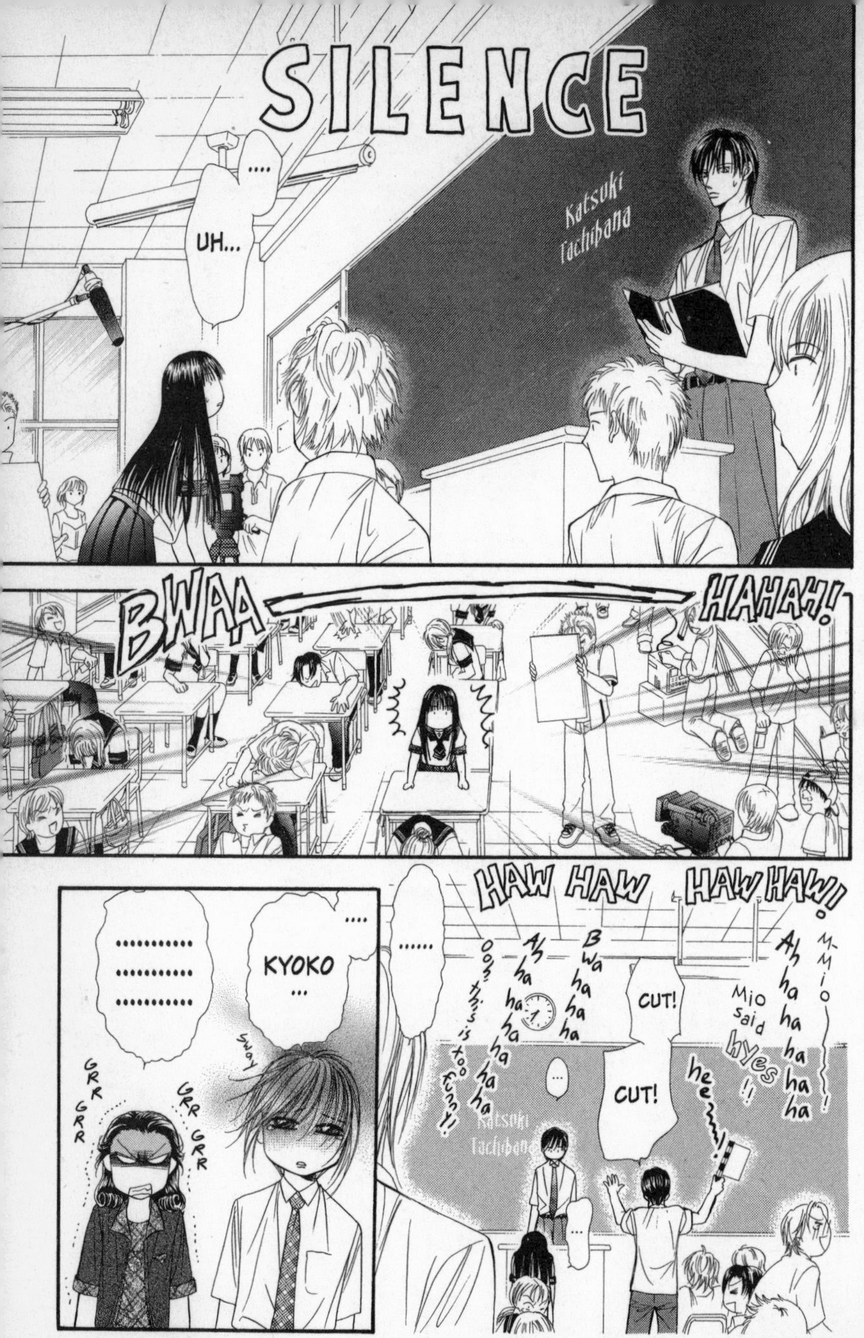
SILENCE
Katsuki Tachibana
....
UH...
BWAA——HAHAH!
HAW HAW HAW HAW!
M-MIO~!
Ah ha ha ha ha ha ha
Mio said hyes!!
hee~!
Bwa ha ha ha ha ha
Ah ha ha ha ha ha ha ha
Ooh! this is too funny!!
CUT!
CUT!
...
......
...
Katsuki Tachibana
....
KYOKO...
....
sway
GRR GRR
GRR GRR

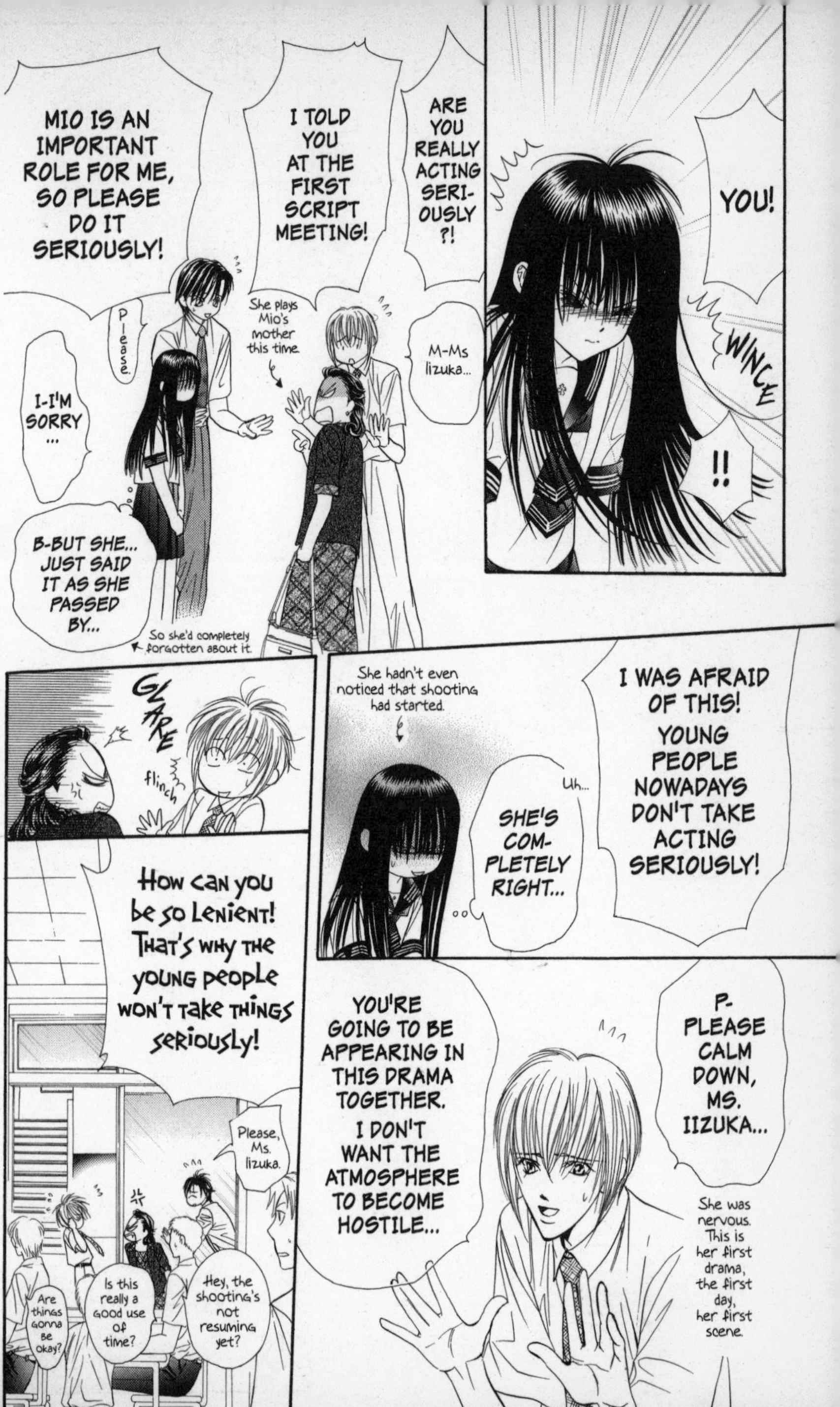
YOU!
WINCE
!!
ARE YOU REALLY ACTING SERI-OUSLY ?!
I TOLD YOU AT THE FIRST SCRIPT MEETING!
MIO IS AN IMPORTANT ROLE FOR ME, SO PLEASE DO IT SERIOUSLY!
M-Ms Iizuka...
She plays Mio's mother this time.
Please.
I-I'M SORRY...
B-BUT SHE... JUST SAID IT AS SHE PASSED BY...
So she'd completely forgotten about it.
I WAS AFRAID OF THIS! YOUNG PEOPLE NOWADAYS DON'T TAKE ACTING SERIOUSLY!
Uh...
SHE'S COM-PLETELY RIGHT...
She hadn't even noticed that shooting had started.
GLARE
flinch
P-PLEASE CALM DOWN, MS. IIZUKA...
YOU'RE GOING TO BE APPEARING IN THIS DRAMA TOGETHER. I DON'T WANT THE ATMOSPHERE TO BECOME HOSTILE...
She was nervous. This is her first drama, the first day, her first scene.
How can you be so lenient! That's why the young people won't take things seriously!
Please, Ms. Iizuka.
Hey, the shooting's not resuming yet?
Is this really a good use of time?
Are things gonna be okay?

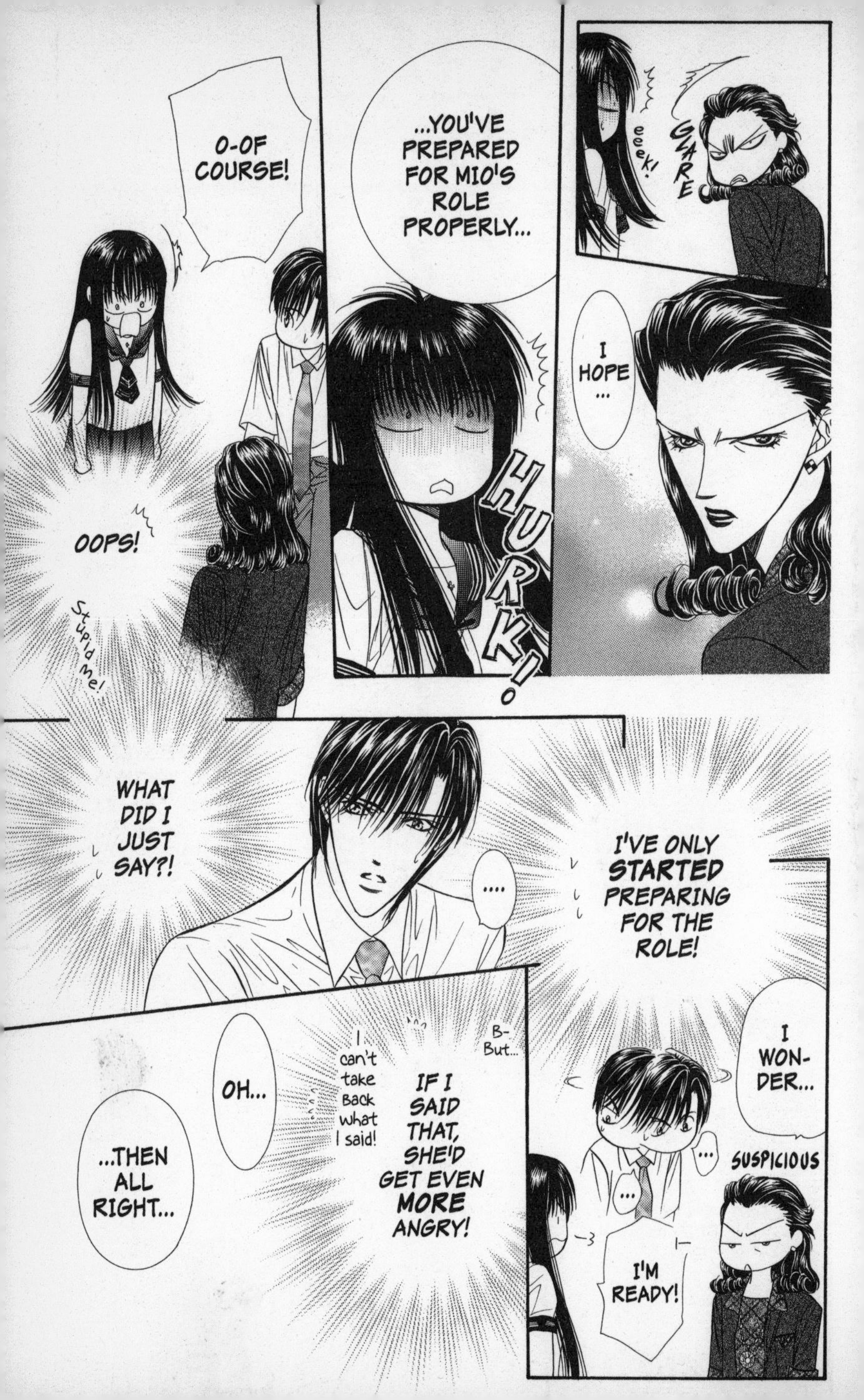
GLARE
eeek!
I HOPE...
...YOU'VE PREPARED FOR MIO'S ROLE PROPERLY...
HURK!
O-OF COURSE!
OOPS!
Stupid me!
I'VE ONLY STARTED PREPARING FOR THE ROLE!
....
WHAT DID I JUST SAY?!
I WONDER...
SUSPICIOUS
...
...
I'M READY!
B-But...
IF I SAID THAT, SHE'D GET EVEN MORE ANGRY!
I can't take back what I said!
OH...
...THEN ALL RIGHT...

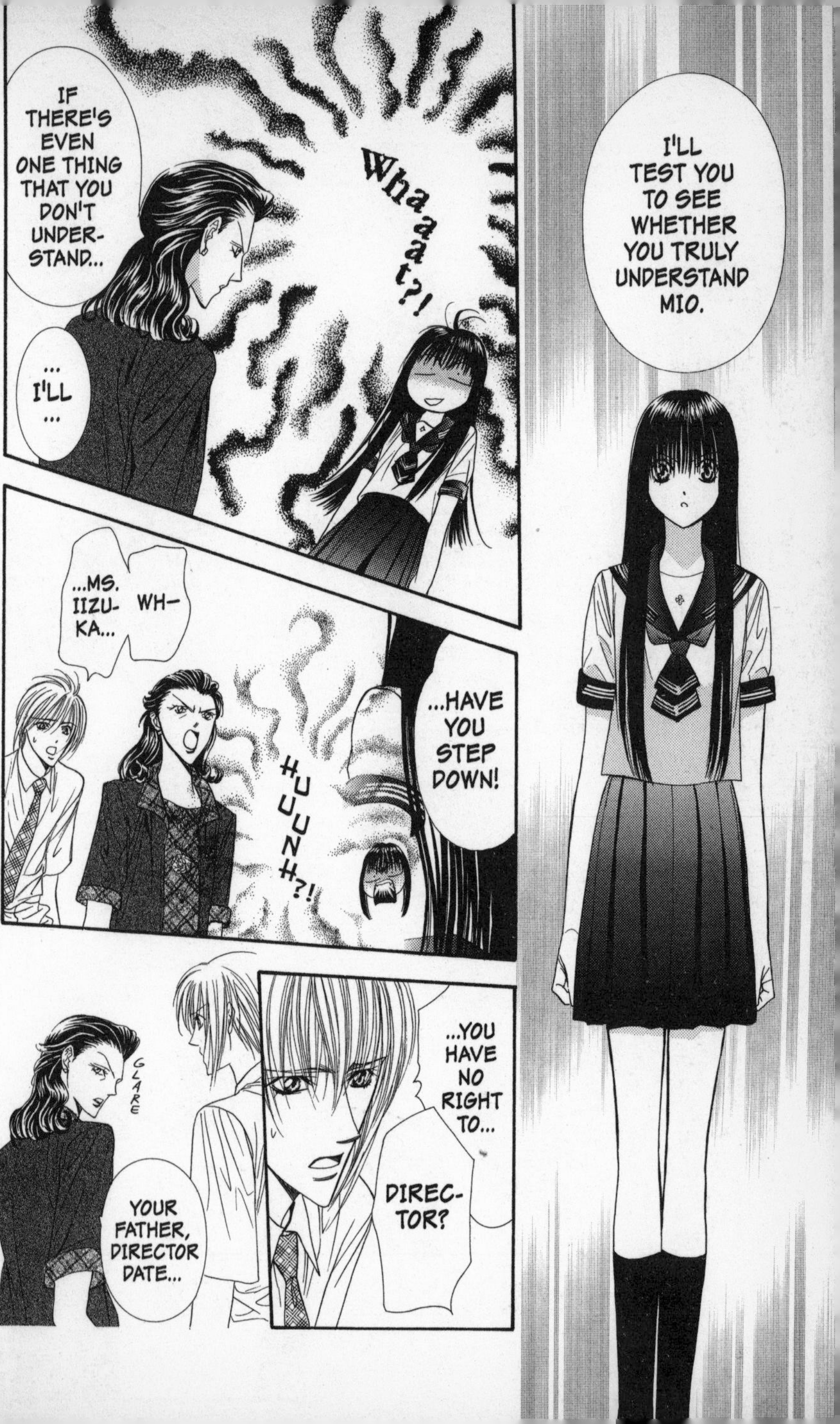
I'LL TEST YOU TO SEE WHETHER YOU TRULY UNDERSTAND MIO.
Whaaat?!
IF THERE'S EVEN ONE THING THAT YOU DON'T UNDER-STAND...
... I'LL ...
...HAVE YOU STEP DOWN!
HUUUNH?!
WH-
...MS. IIZU-KA...
...YOU HAVE NO RIGHT TO...
DIREC-TOR?
GLARE
YOUR FATHER, DIRECTOR DATE...

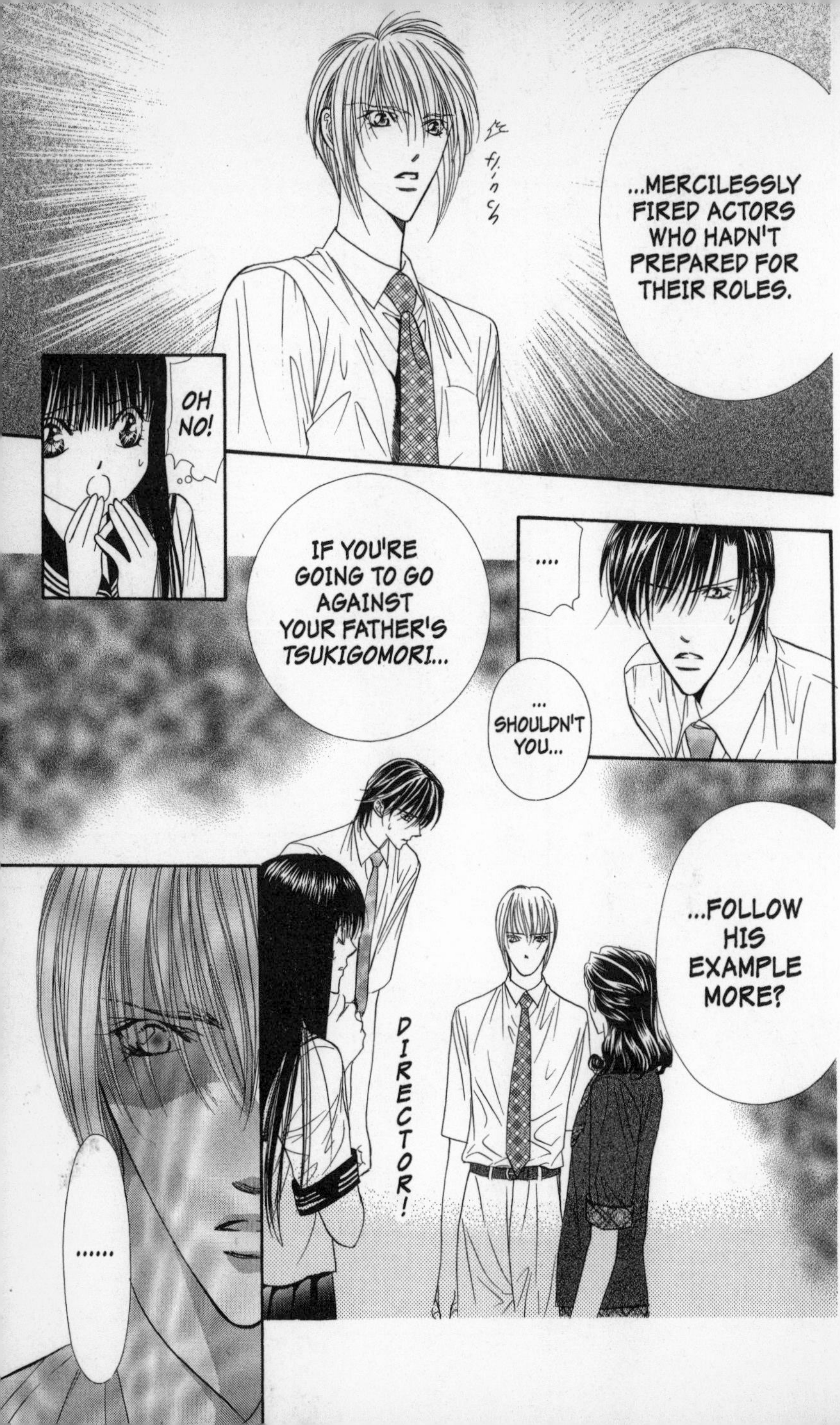
...MERCILESSLY FIRED ACTORS WHO HADN'T PREPARED FOR THEIR ROLES.
flinch
OH NO!
IF YOU'RE GOING TO GO AGAINST YOUR FATHER'S TSUKIGOMORI...
....
... SHOULDN'T YOU...
...FOLLOW HIS EXAMPLE MORE?
DIRECTOR!
......

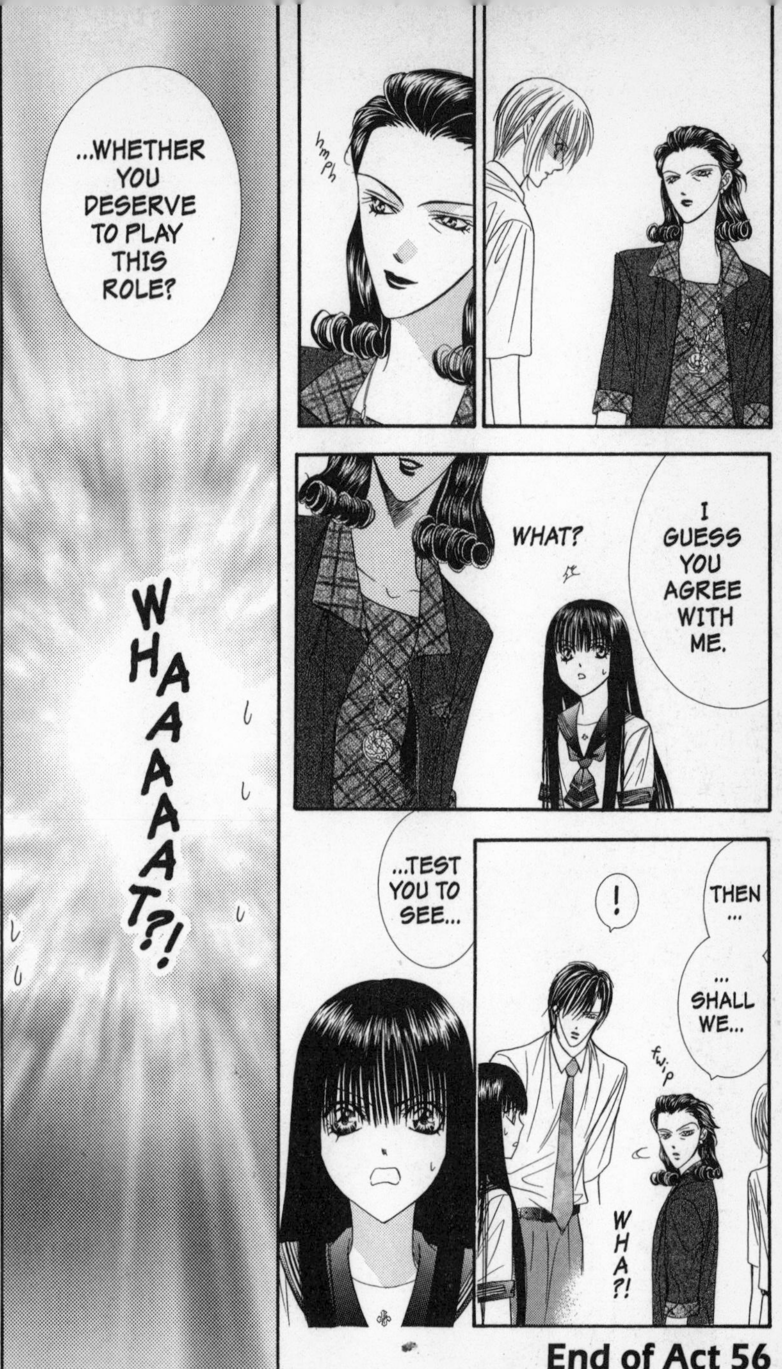
hmph
I GUESS YOU AGREE WITH ME.
WHAT?
THEN...
... SHALL WE...
!
fwip
WHA?!
...TEST YOU TO SEE...
...WHETHER YOU DESERVE TO PLAY THIS ROLE?
WHAAAAAT?!

End of Act 56

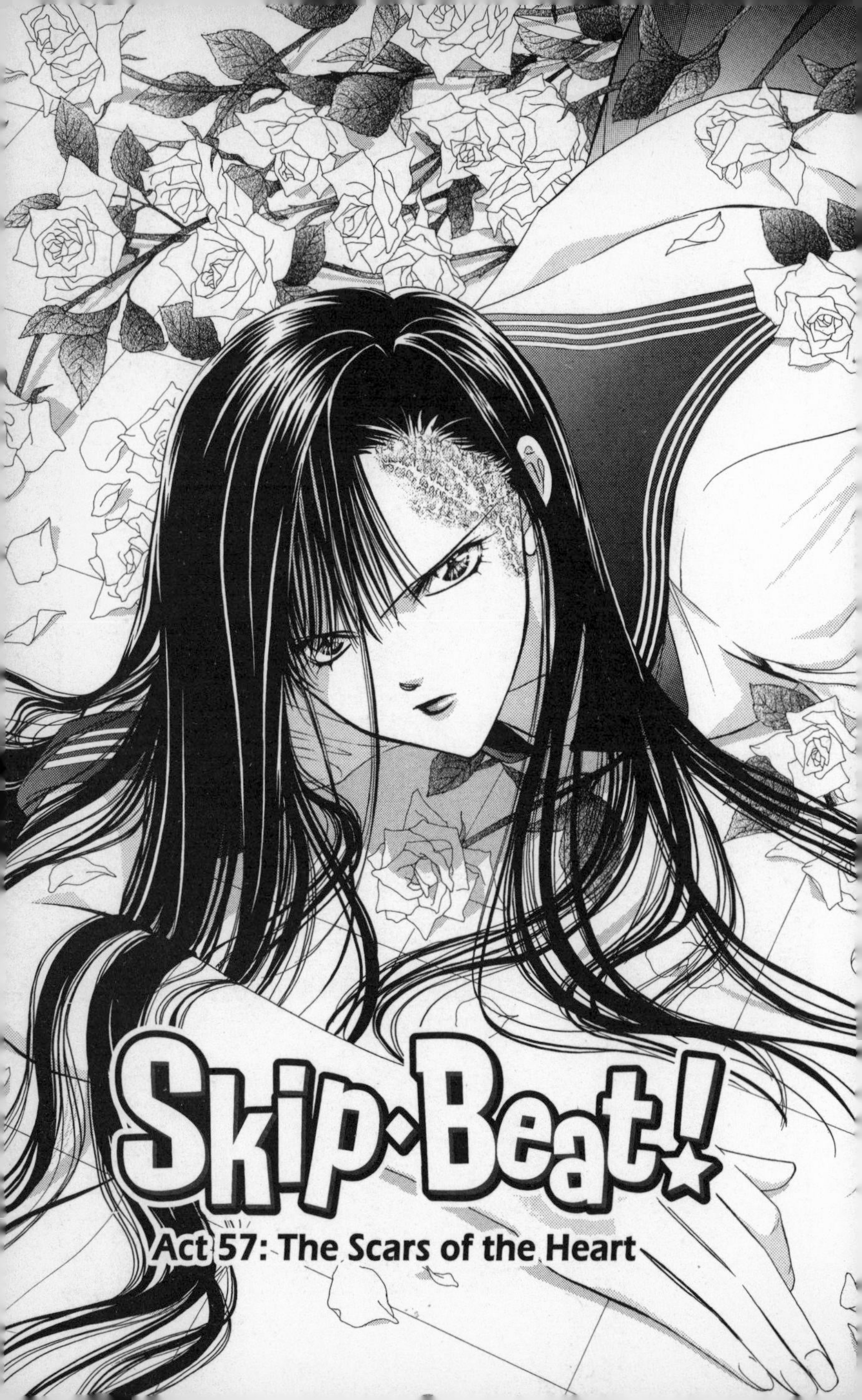
Skip·Beat!
Act 57: The Scars of the Heart

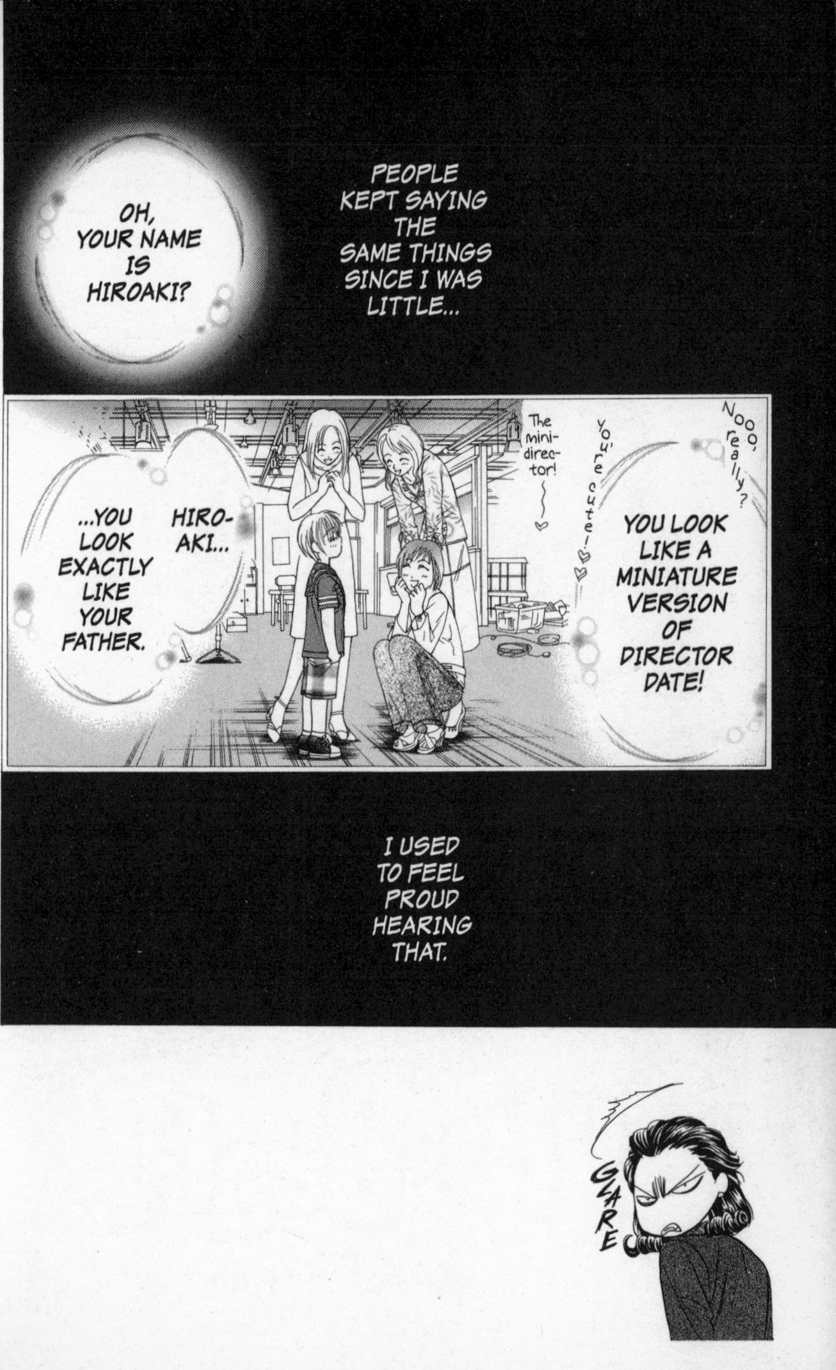
PEOPLE KEPT SAYING THE SAME THINGS SINCE I WAS LITTLE...
OH, YOUR NAME IS HIROAKI?
Nooo, really?
YOU LOOK LIKE A MINIATURE VERSION OF DIRECTOR DATE!
You're cute!
The mini-director!
HIRO-AKI...
...YOU LOOK EXACTLY LIKE YOUR FATHER.
I USED TO FEEL PROUD HEARING THAT.
GLARE

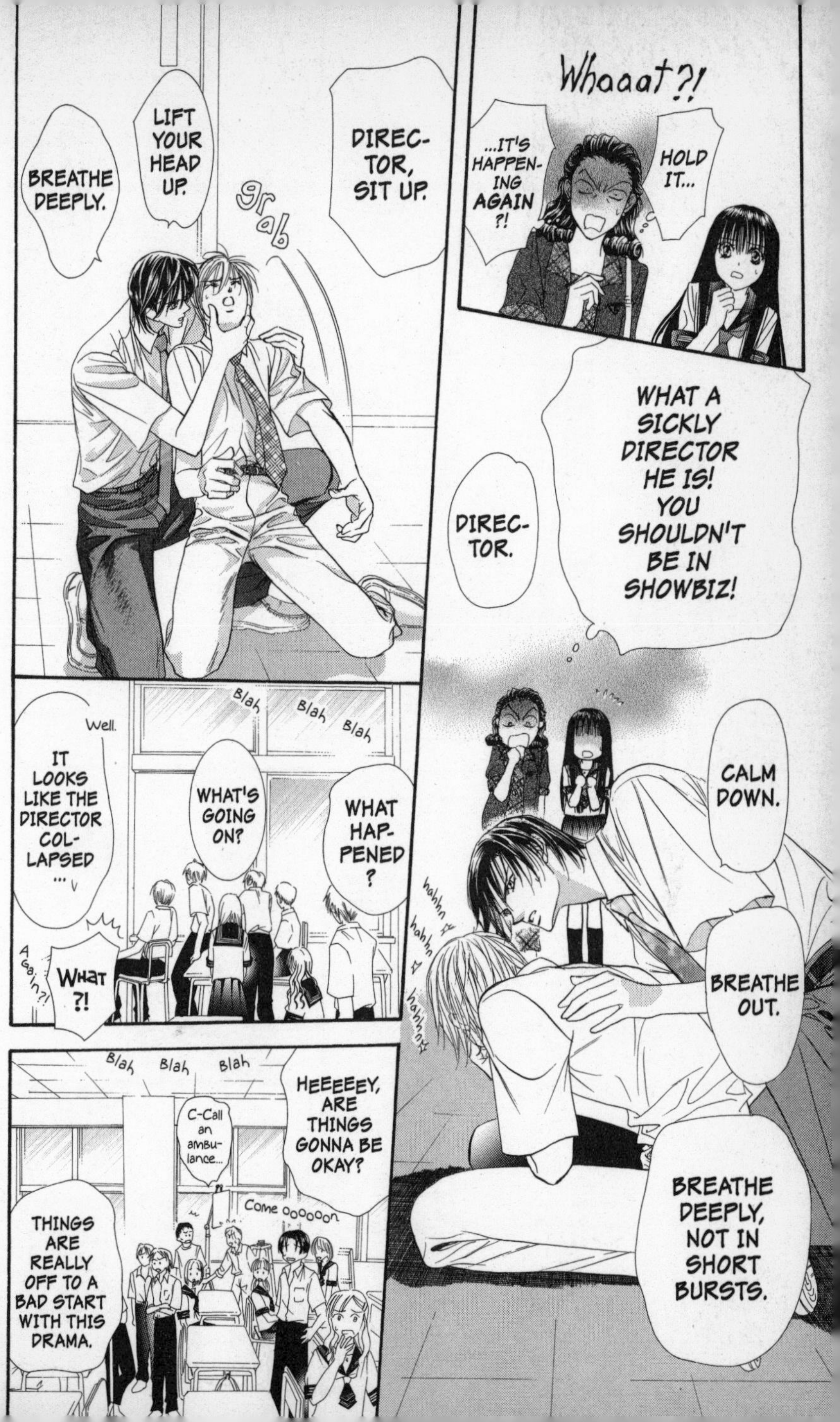
Whaaat?!
HOLD IT...
...IT'S HAPPENING AGAIN?!
WHAT A SICKLY DIRECTOR HE IS! YOU SHOULDN'T BE IN SHOWBIZ!
DIRECTOR.
CALM DOWN.
hahhn
hahhn
BREATHE OUT.
hahhn
BREATHE DEEPLY, NOT IN SHORT BURSTS.
DIRECTOR, SIT UP.
grab
LIFT YOUR HEAD UP.
BREATHE DEEPLY.
Blah Blah Blah
WHAT HAPPENED?
WHAT'S GOING ON?
Well.
IT LOOKS LIKE THE DIRECTOR COLLAPSED...
Again?!
WHAT?!
Blah Blah Blah
HEEEEEY, ARE THINGS GONNA BE OKAY?
C-Call an ambulance...
Come oooooon
THINGS ARE REALLY OFF TO A BAD START WITH THIS DRAMA.

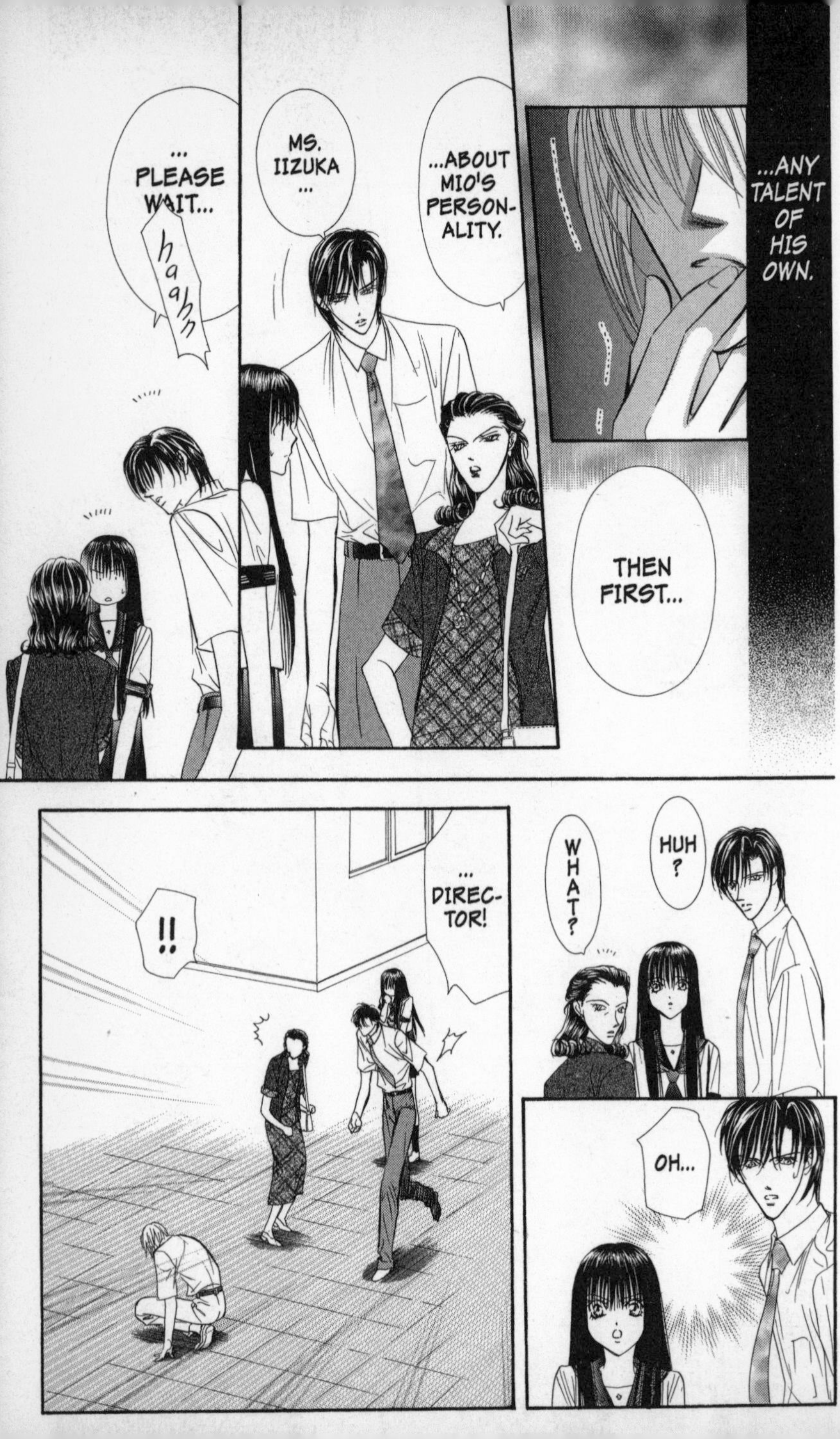
...ANY TALENT OF HIS OWN.
THEN FIRST...
...ABOUT MIO'S PERSON-ALITY.
MS. IIZUKA ...
... PLEASE WAIT...
haahh
HUH?
WHAT?
OH...
... DIREC-TOR!
!!

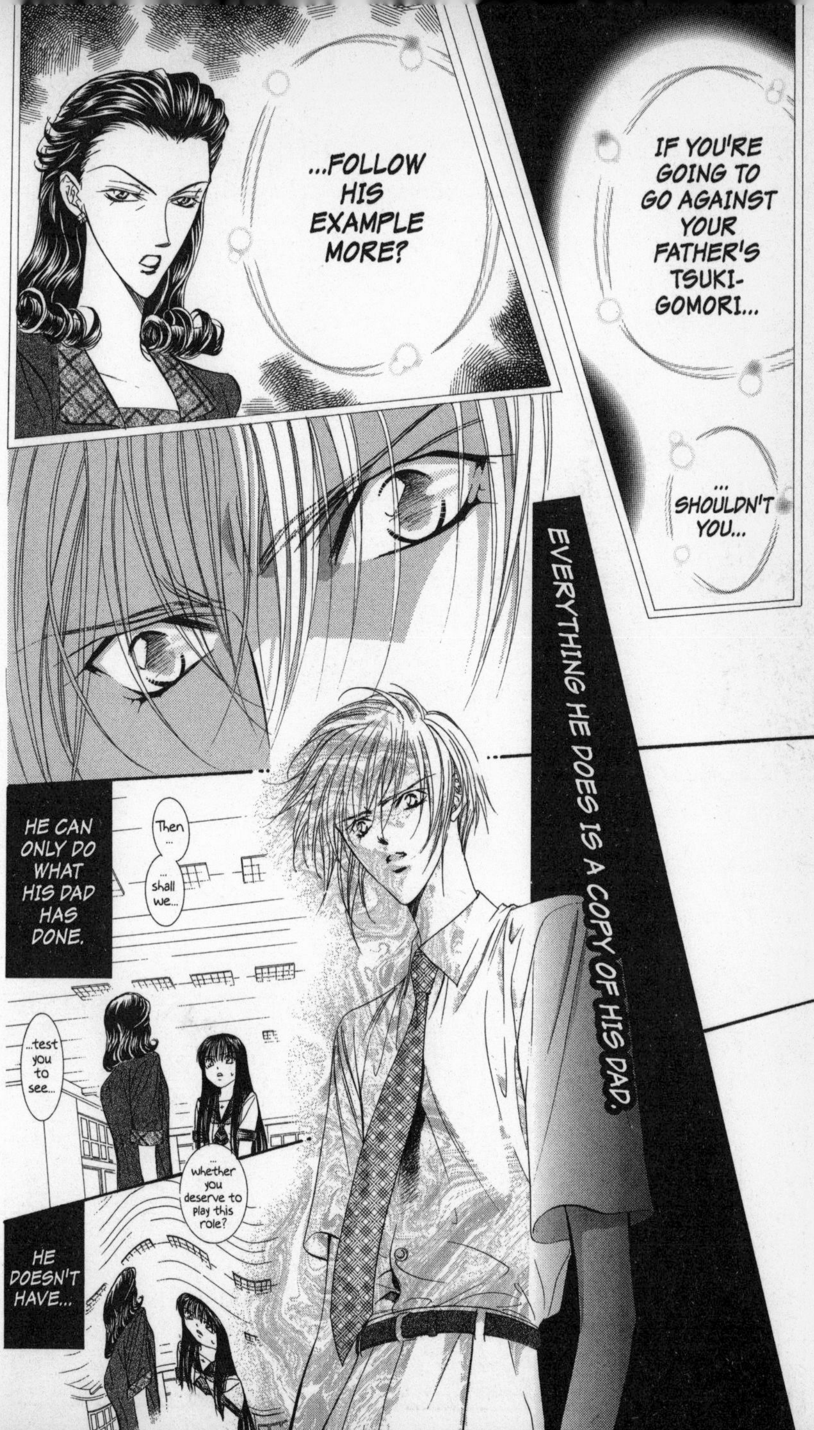
IF YOU'RE GOING TO GO AGAINST YOUR FATHER'S TSUKI-GOMORI...
... SHOULDN'T YOU...
...FOLLOW HIS EXAMPLE MORE?
EVERYTHING HE DOES IS A COPY OF HIS DAD.
Then ...
... shall we...
HE CAN ONLY DO WHAT HIS DAD HAS DONE.
...test you to see...
... whether you deserve to play this role?
HE DOESN'T HAVE...

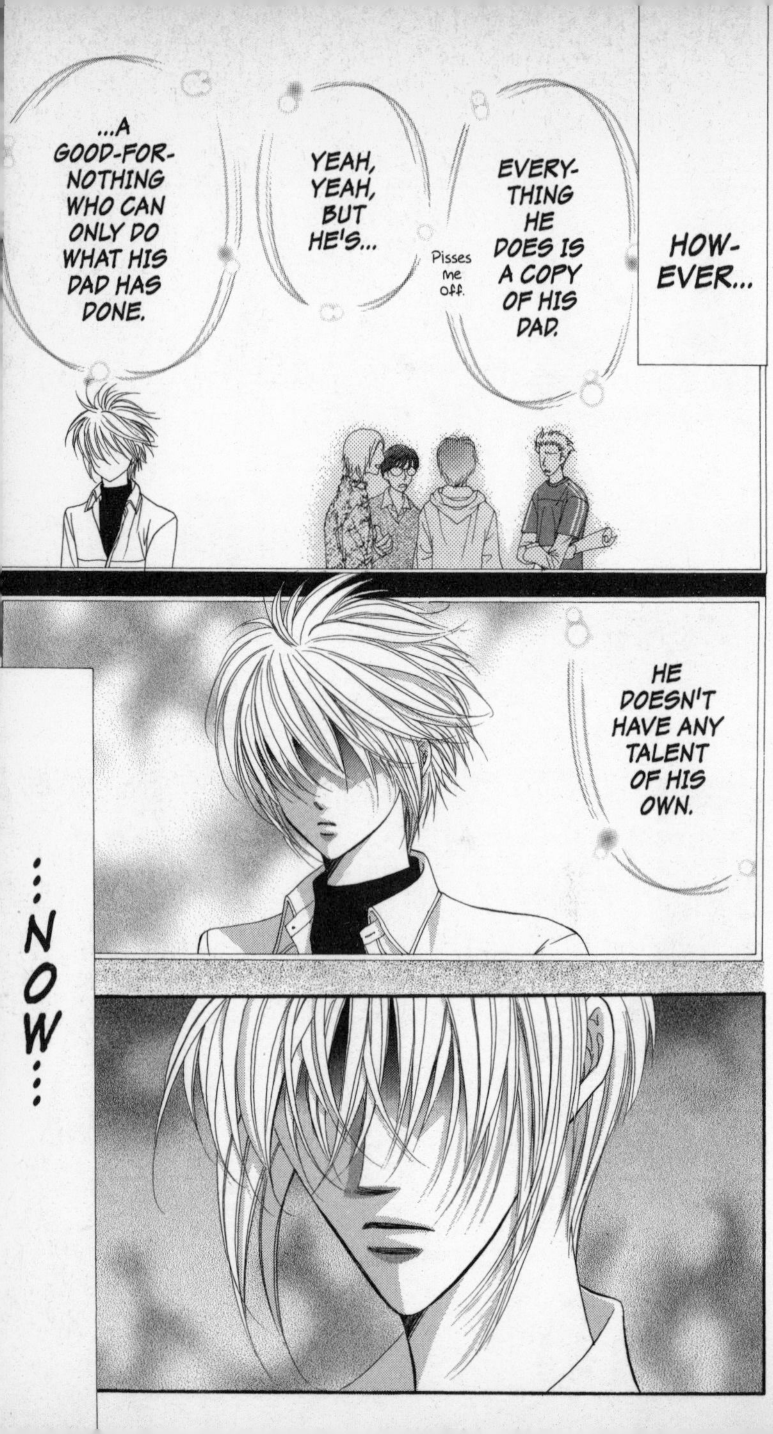
HOW-EVER...
EVERY-THING HE DOES IS A COPY OF HIS DAD.
Pisses me off.
YEAH, YEAH, BUT HE'S...
...A GOOD-FOR-NOTHING WHO CAN ONLY DO WHAT HIS DAD HAS DONE.
HE DOESN'T HAVE ANY TALENT OF HIS OWN.
...NOW...

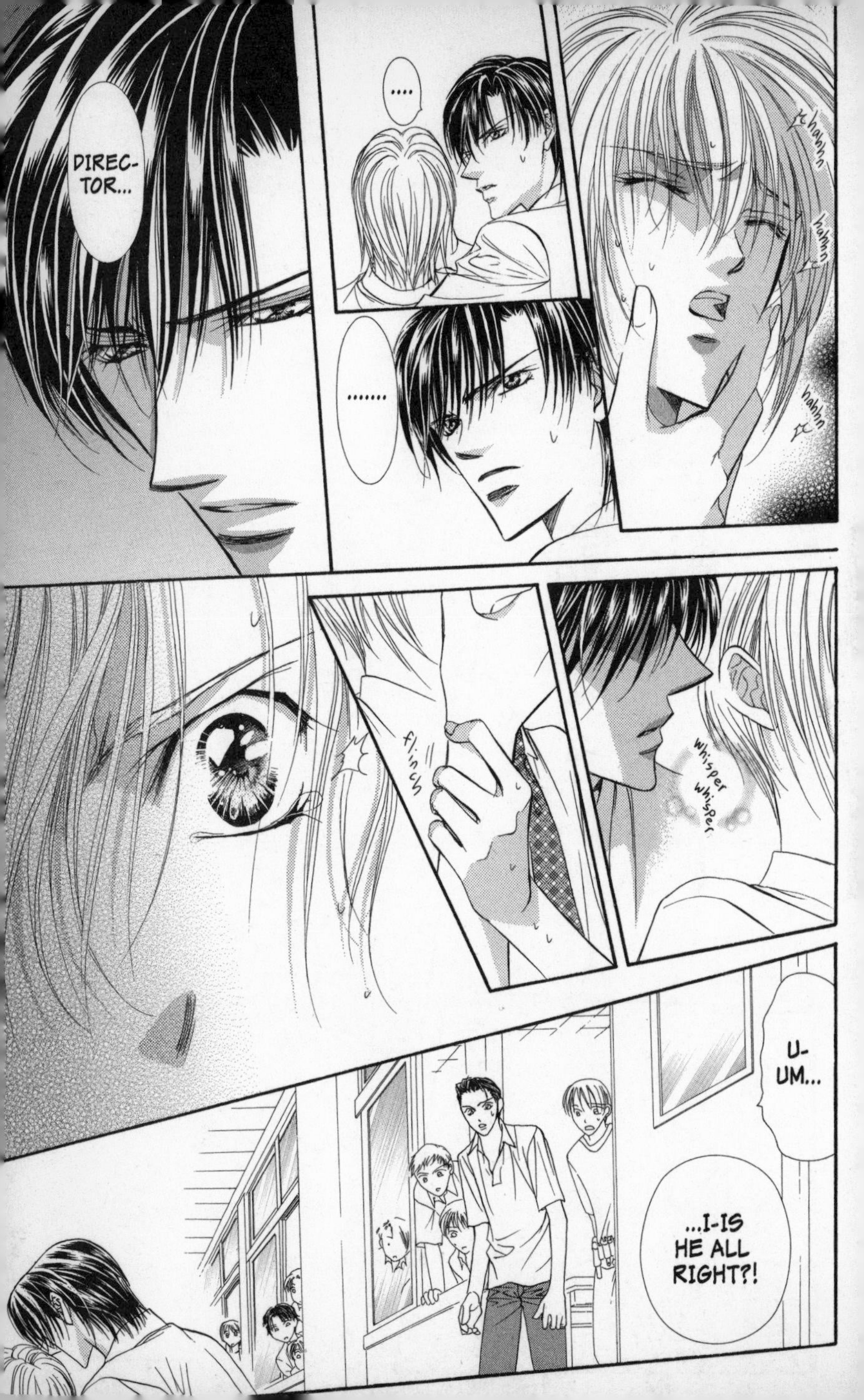
hahhn
hahhn
hahhn
....
....
DIREC-TOR...
whisper whisper
flinch
U-UM...
...I-IS HE ALL RIGHT?!

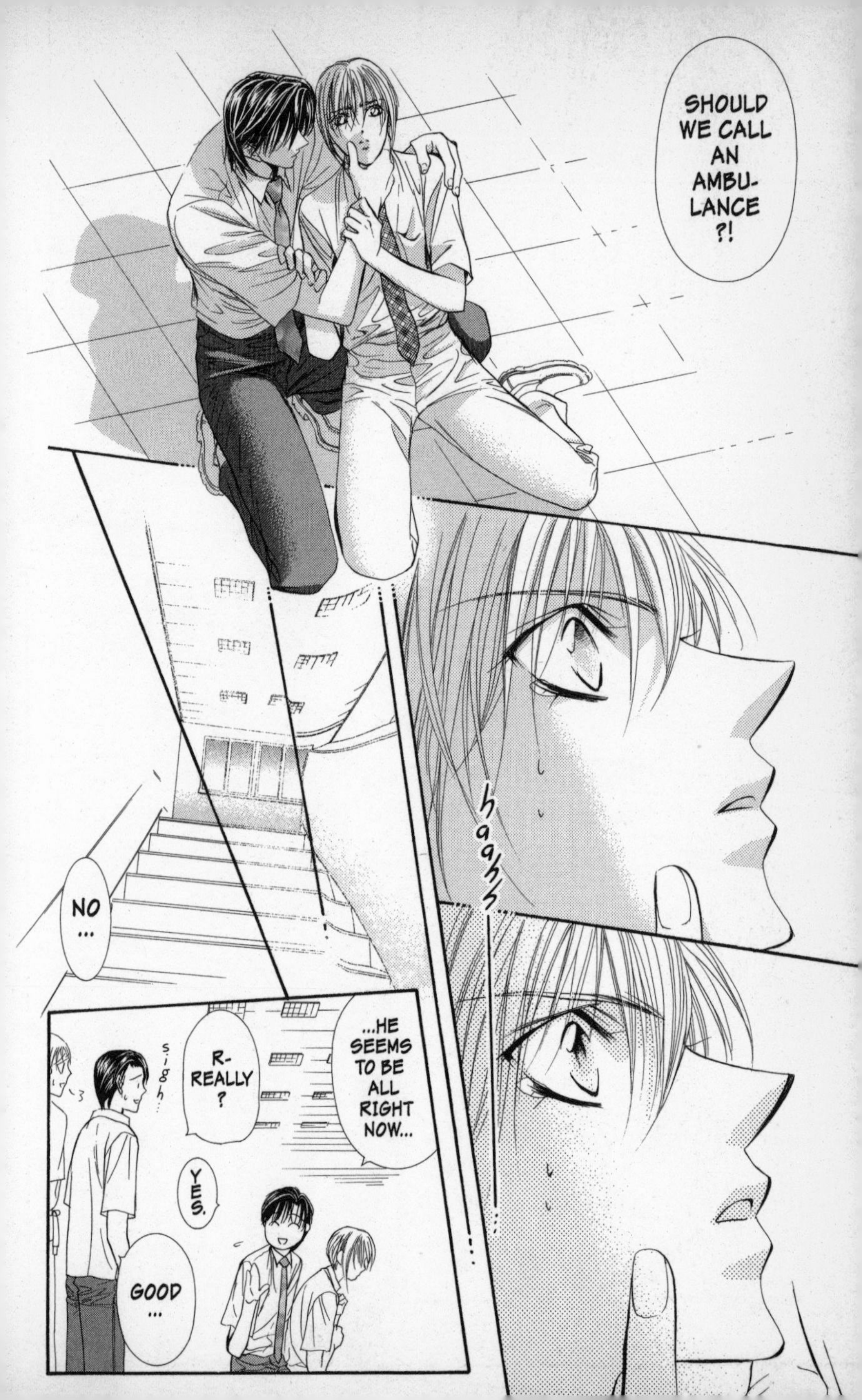
SHOULD WE CALL AN AMBU-LANCE ?!
haahh
NO ...
...HE SEEMS TO BE ALL RIGHT NOW...
R-REALLY ?
sigh...
YES.
GOOD ...

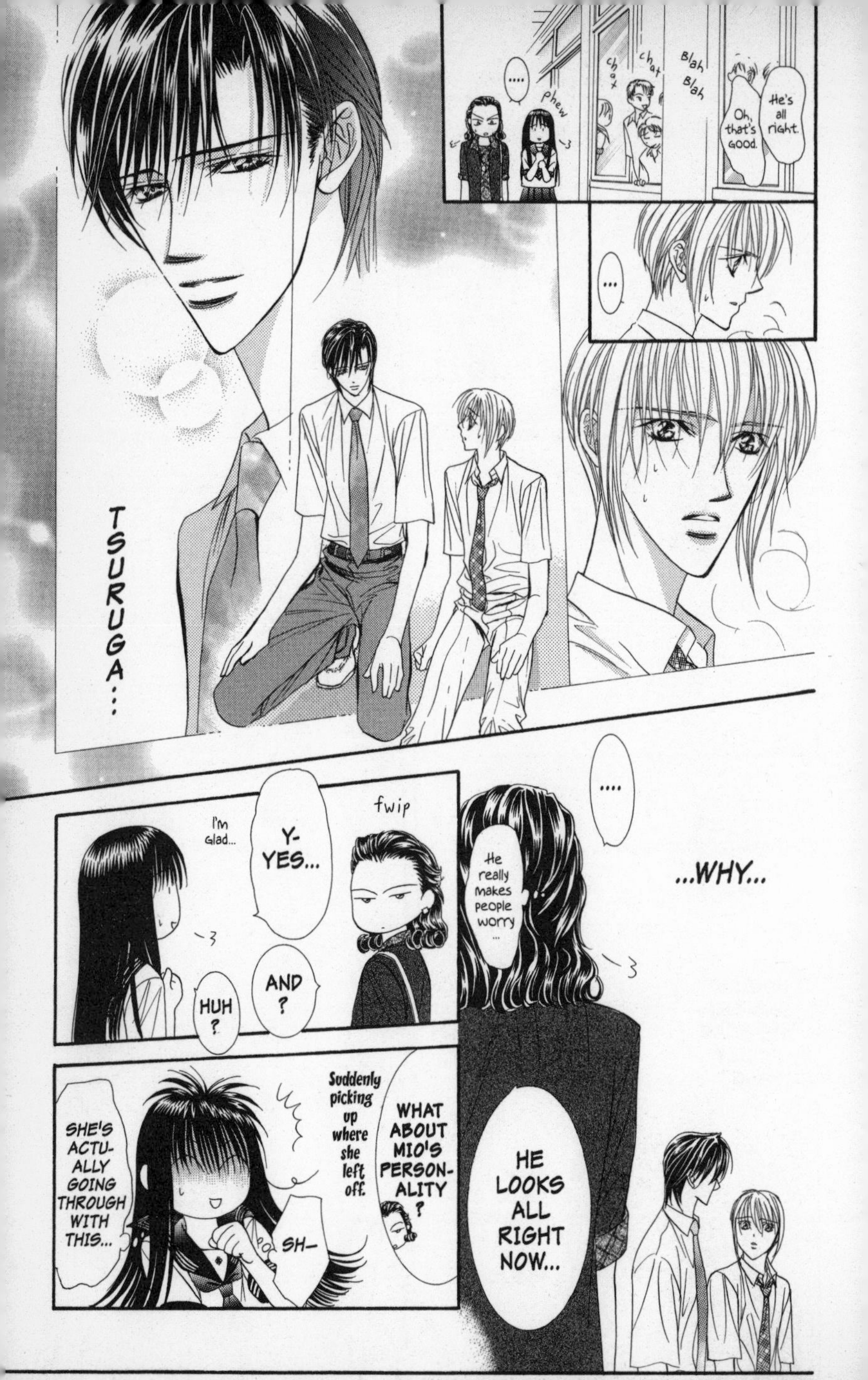
He's all right.
Oh, that's good.
Blah Blah
chat chat
phew
....
...
TSURUGA...
...WHY...
....
He really makes people worry...
HE LOOKS ALL RIGHT NOW...
fwip
Y-YES...
I'm Glad...
AND?
HUH?
WHAT ABOUT MIO'S PERSONALITY?
Suddenly picking up where she left off.
SH—
SHE'S ACTUALLY GOING THROUGH WITH THIS...

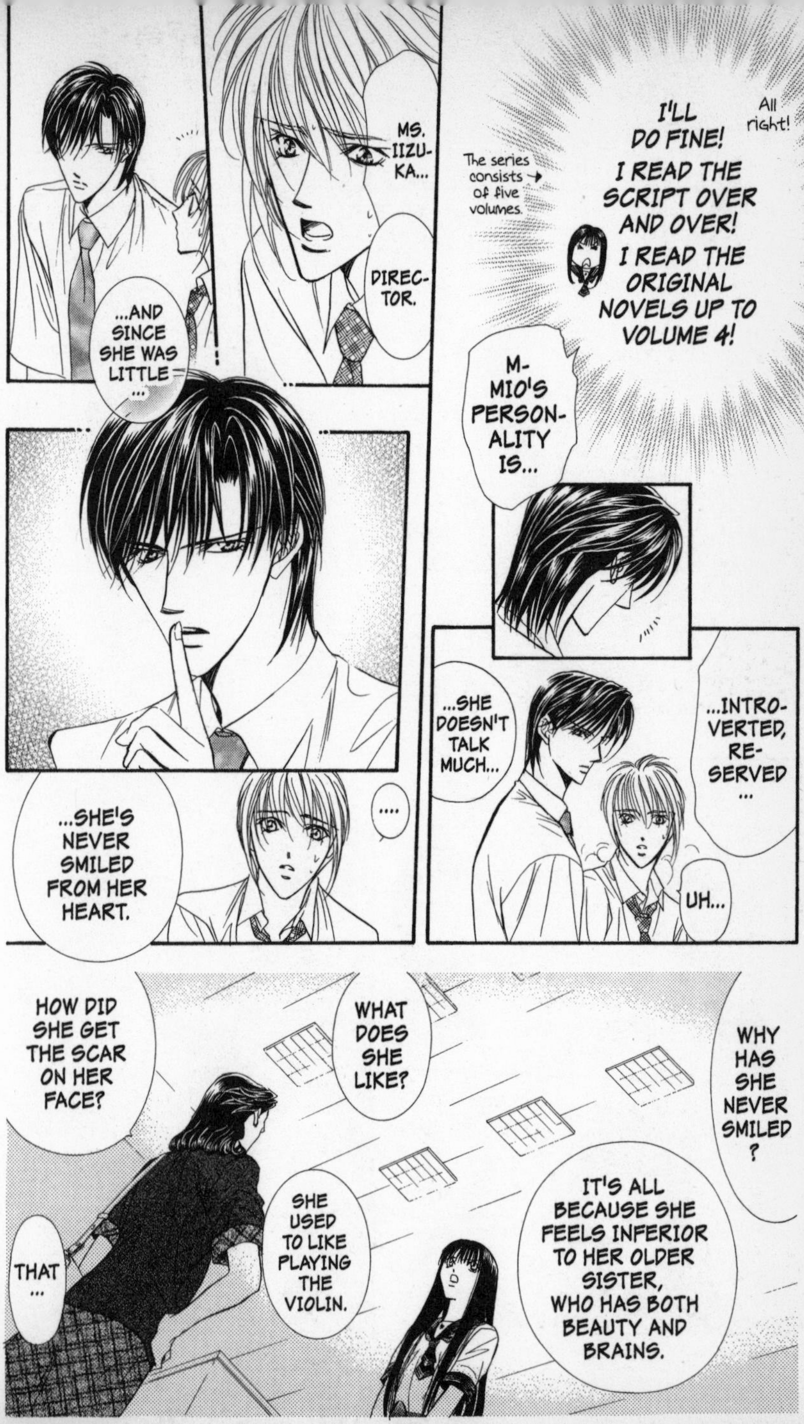
I'LL DO FINE!
All right!
I READ THE SCRIPT OVER AND OVER!
I READ THE ORIGINAL NOVELS UP TO VOLUME 4!
The series consists of five volumes.
M-MIO'S PERSONALITY IS...
...INTROVERTED, RESERVED...
UH...
...SHE DOESN'T TALK MUCH...
MS. IIZUKA...
DIRECTOR.
...AND SINCE SHE WAS LITTLE...
....
...SHE'S NEVER SMILED FROM HER HEART.
WHY HAS SHE NEVER SMILED?
WHAT DOES SHE LIKE?
HOW DID SHE GET THE SCAR ON HER FACE?
IT'S ALL BECAUSE SHE FEELS INFERIOR TO HER OLDER SISTER, WHO HAS BOTH BEAUTY AND BRAINS.
SHE USED TO LIKE PLAYING THE VIOLIN.
THAT...

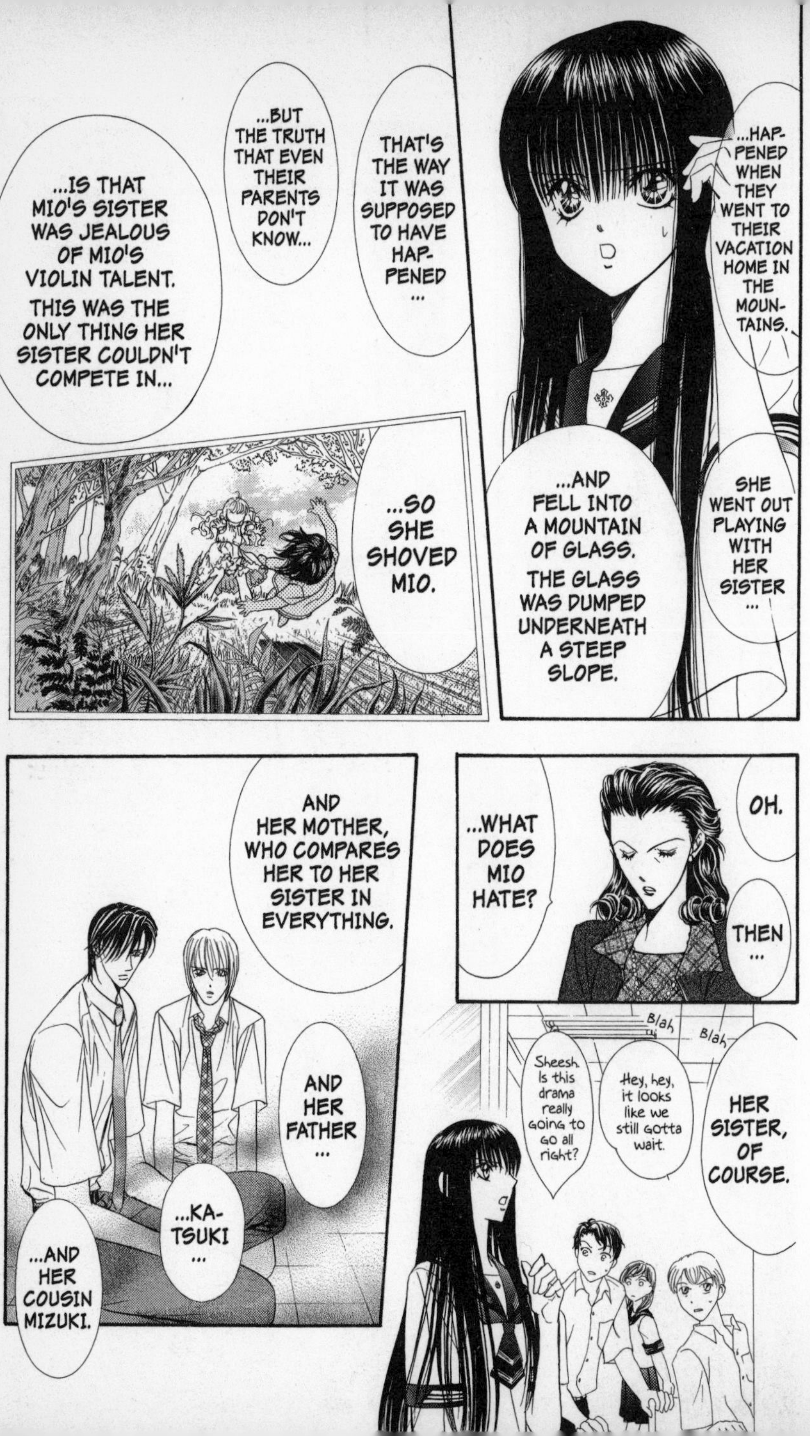
...HAP-PENED WHEN THEY WENT TO THEIR VACATION HOME IN THE MOUNTAINS.
SHE WENT OUT PLAYING WITH HER SISTER...
...AND FELL INTO A MOUNTAIN OF GLASS. THE GLASS WAS DUMPED UNDERNEATH A STEEP SLOPE.
THAT'S THE WAY IT WAS SUPPOSED TO HAVE HAP-PENED...
...BUT THE TRUTH THAT EVEN THEIR PARENTS DON'T KNOW...
...IS THAT MIO'S SISTER WAS JEALOUS OF MIO'S VIOLIN TALENT. THIS WAS THE ONLY THING HER SISTER COULDN'T COMPETE IN...
...SO SHE SHOVED MIO.
OH.
THEN...
...WHAT DOES MIO HATE?
HER SISTER, OF COURSE.
Blah
Blah
Hey, hey, it looks like we still gotta wait.
Sheesh. Is this drama really going to go all right?
AND HER MOTHER, WHO COMPARES HER TO HER SISTER IN EVERYTHING.
AND HER FATHER...
...KA-TSUKI...
...AND HER COUSIN MIZUKI.

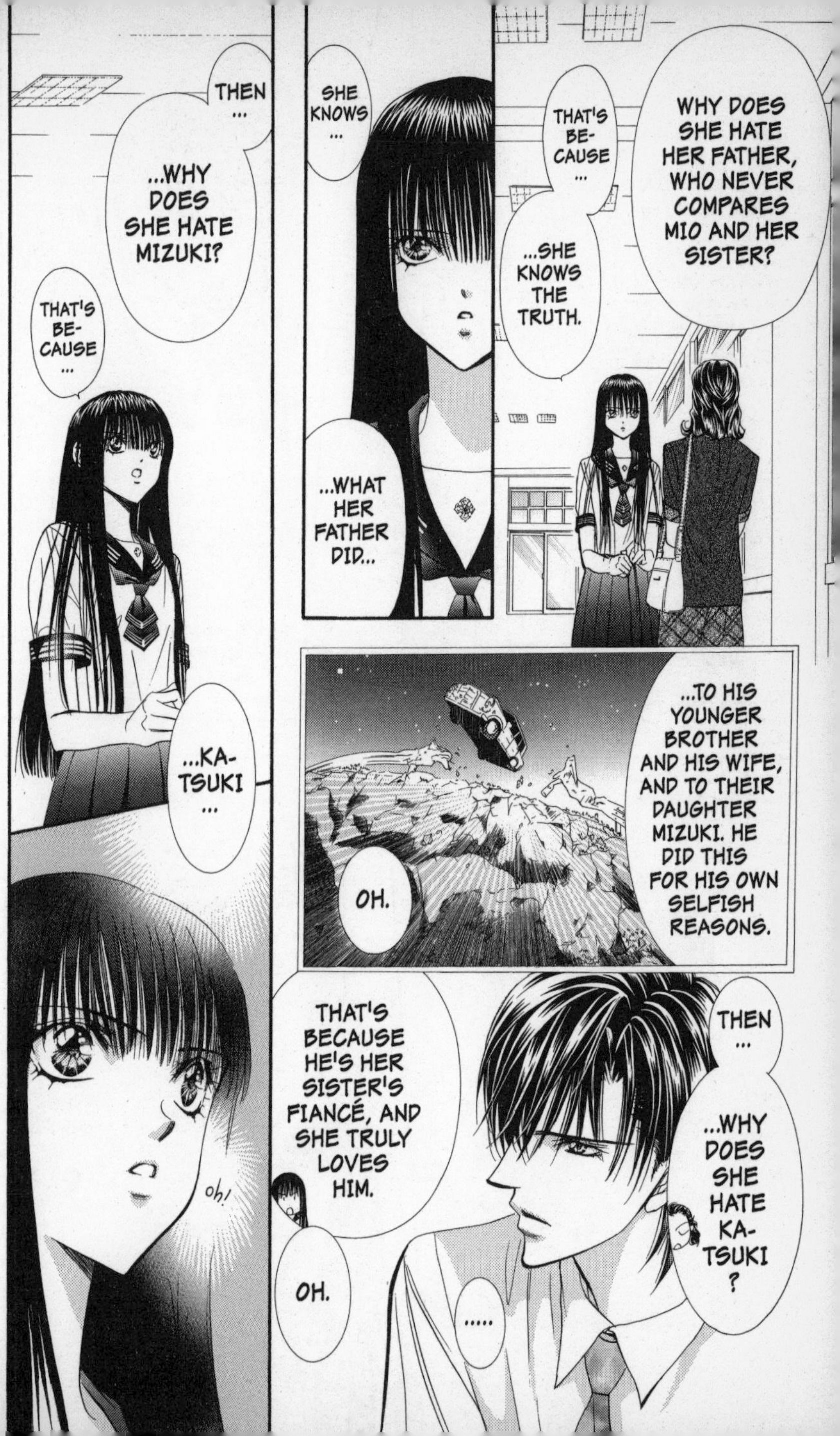
WHY DOES SHE HATE HER FATHER, WHO NEVER COMPARES MIO AND HER SISTER?
THAT'S BE-CAUSE ...
...SHE KNOWS THE TRUTH.
SHE KNOWS ...
...WHAT HER FATHER DID...
...TO HIS YOUNGER BROTHER AND HIS WIFE, AND TO THEIR DAUGHTER MIZUKI. HE DID THIS FOR HIS OWN SELFISH REASONS.
OH.
THEN ...
...WHY DOES SHE HATE MIZUKI?
THAT'S BE-CAUSE ...
...KA-TSUKI ...
THEN ...
...WHY DOES SHE HATE KA-TSUKI ?
THAT'S BECAUSE HE'S HER SISTER'S FIANCÉ, AND SHE TRULY LOVES HIM.
OH.
.....
oh!

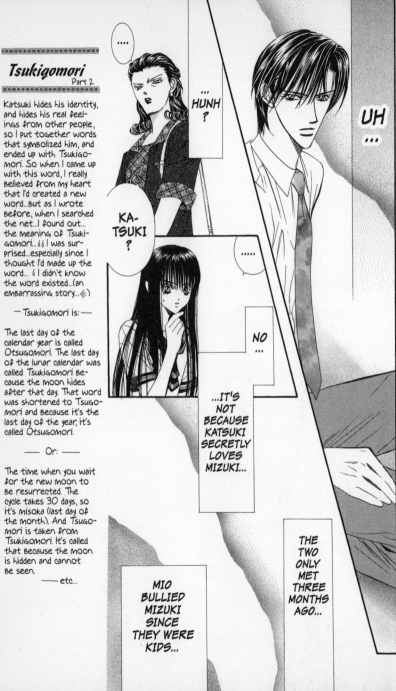

Tsukigomori
Part 2

Katsuki hides his identity, and hides his real feelings from other people, so I put together words that symbolized him, and ended up with Tsukigomori. So when I came up with this word, I really believed from my heart that I'd created a new word...But as I wrote before, when I searched the net...I found out... the meaning of Tsukigomori...'' I was surprised...especially since I thought I'd made up the word... ' I didn't know the word existed...(an embarrassing story...✍)

— Tsukigomori is: —

The last day of the calendar year is called Otsugomori. The last day of the lunar calendar was called Tsukigomori because the moon hides after that day. That word was shortened to Tsugomori and because it's the last day of the year, it's called Otsugomori.

— Or: —

The time when you wait for the new moon to be resurrected. The cycle takes 30 days, so it's misoka (last day of the month). And Tsugomori is taken from Tsukigomori. It's called that because the moon is hidden and cannot be seen.

— etc...

....

...HUNH?

UH...

KA-TSUKI?

.....

NO...

...IT'S NOT BECAUSE KATSUKI SECRETLY LOVES MIZUKI...

THE TWO ONLY MET THREE MONTHS AGO...

MIO BULLIED MIZUKI SINCE THEY WERE KIDS...

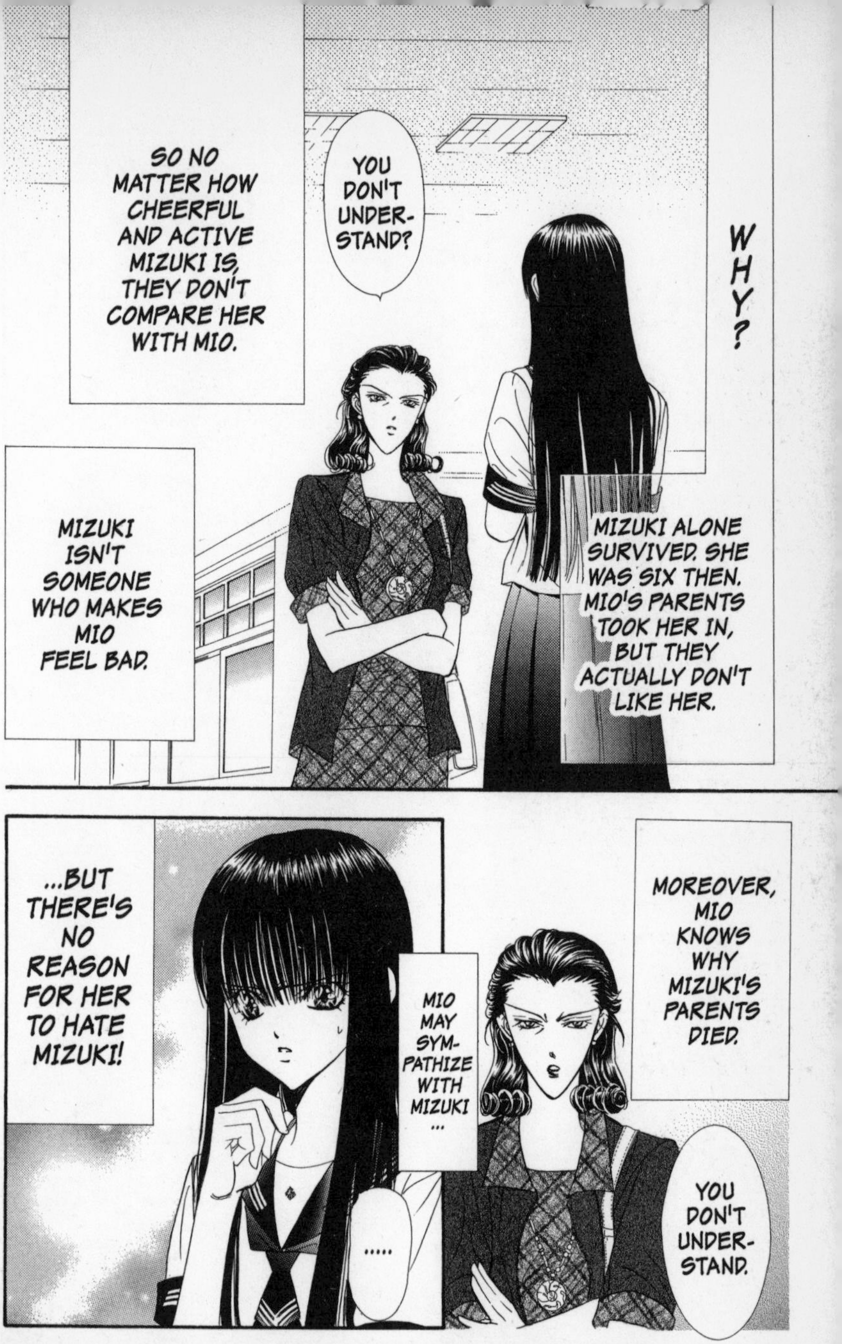
WHY?
YOU DON'T UNDERSTAND?
MIZUKI ALONE SURVIVED. SHE WAS SIX THEN. MIO'S PARENTS TOOK HER IN, BUT THEY ACTUALLY DON'T LIKE HER.
SO NO MATTER HOW CHEERFUL AND ACTIVE MIZUKI IS, THEY DON'T COMPARE HER WITH MIO.
MIZUKI ISN'T SOMEONE WHO MAKES MIO FEEL BAD.
MOREOVER, MIO KNOWS WHY MIZUKI'S PARENTS DIED.
YOU DON'T UNDERSTAND.
MIO MAY SYMPATHIZE WITH MIZUKI...
.....
...BUT THERE'S NO REASON FOR HER TO HATE MIZUKI!

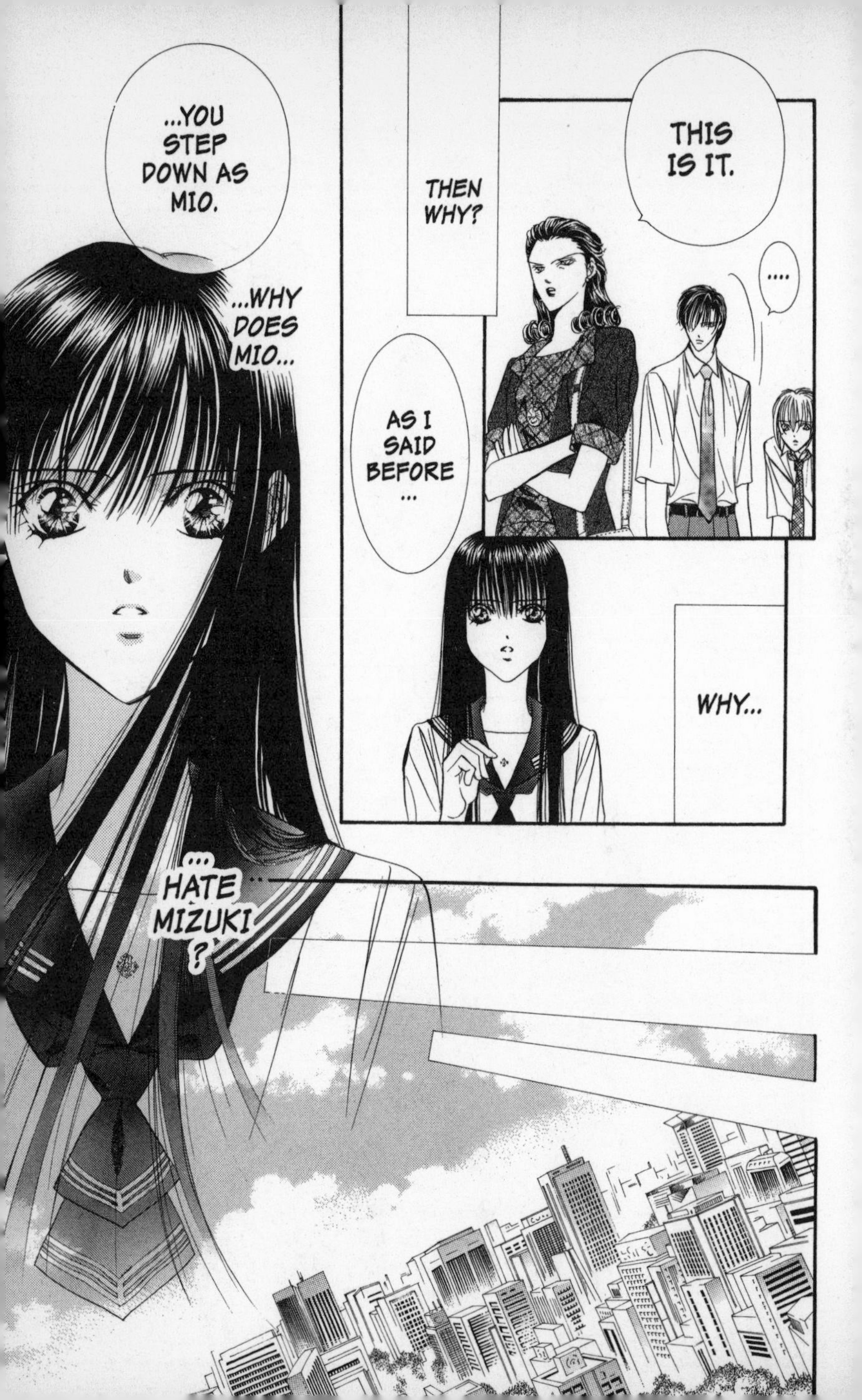
THIS IS IT.
....
THEN WHY?
AS I SAID BEFORE...
...YOU STEP DOWN AS MIO.
WHY...
...WHY DOES MIO...
...HATE MIZUKI?

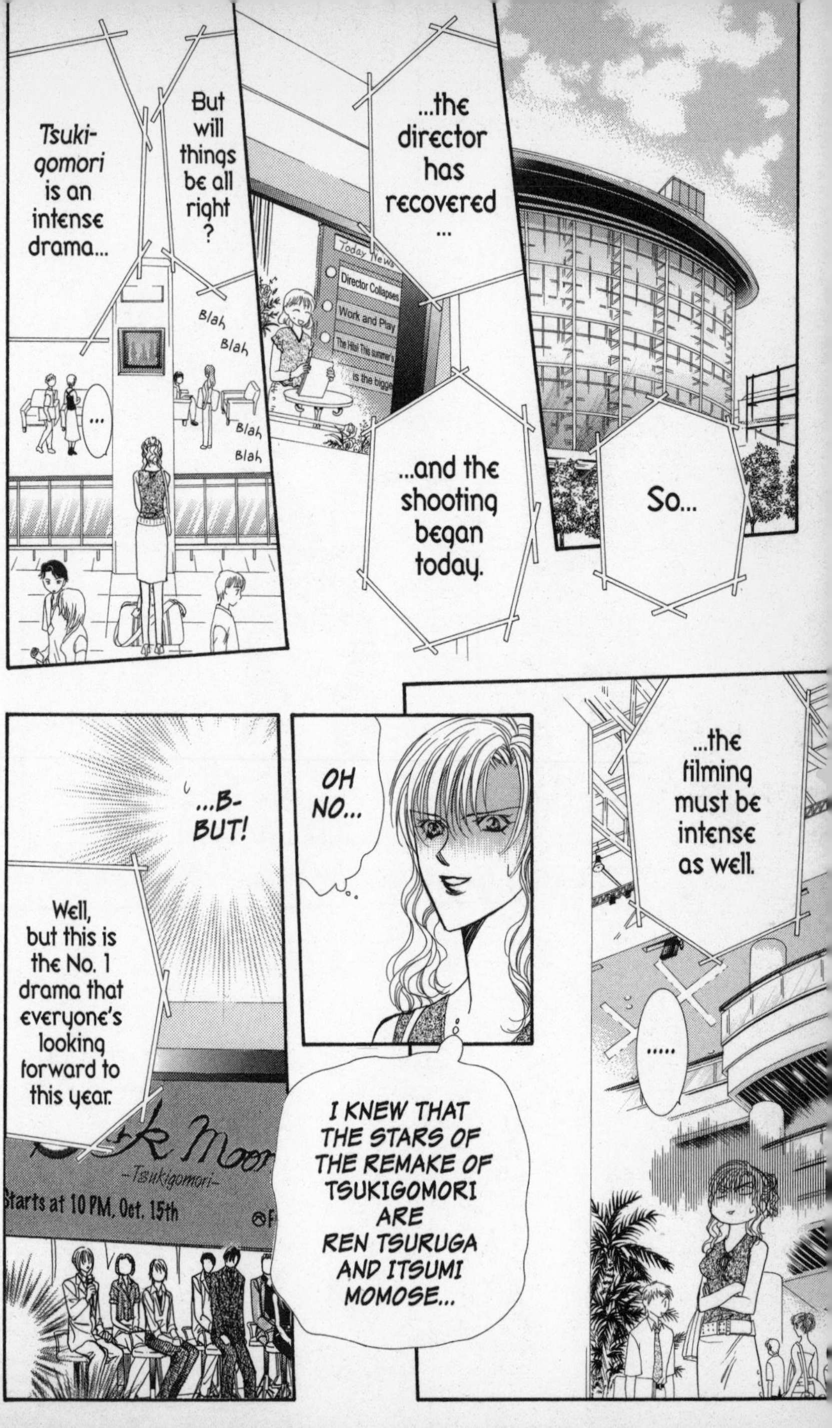
So...
...the director has recovered ...
Today News
Director Collapses
Work and Play
The Hits! This summer's
is the bigg
...and the shooting began today.
But will things be all right?
Tsuki-gomori is an intense drama...
...
Blah
Blah
Blah
Blah
...the filming must be intense as well.
.....
OH NO...
I KNEW THAT THE STARS OF THE REMAKE OF TSUKIGOMORI ARE REN TSURUGA AND ITSUMI MOMOSE...
...B-BUT!
Well, but this is the No. 1 drama that everyone's looking forward to this year.
-Tsukigomori-
Starts at 10 PM, Oct. 15th

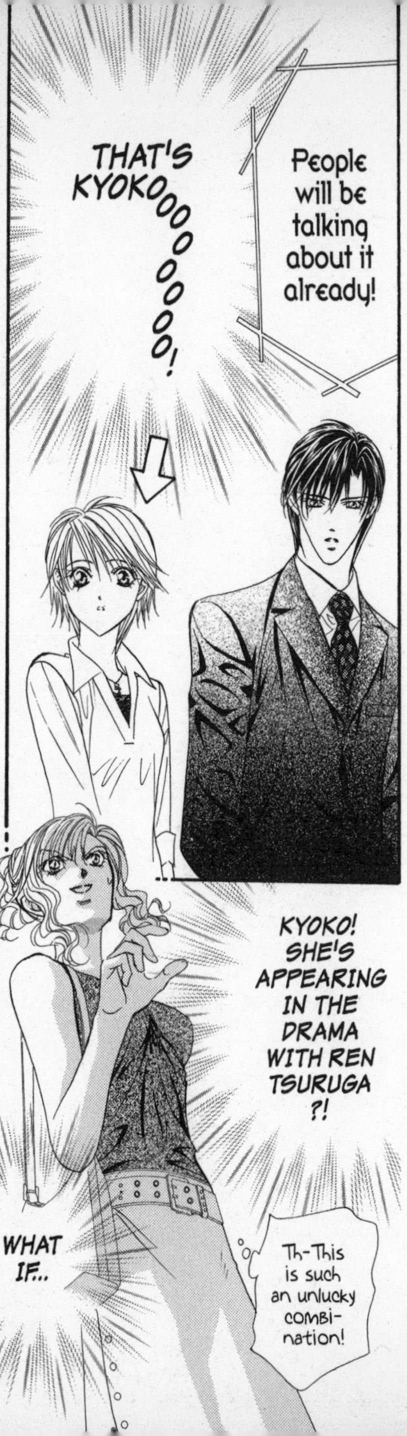
THAT'S KYOKOOOOOOOOOO!
People will be talking about it already!
KYOKO! SHE'S APPEARING IN THE DRAMA WITH REN TSURUGA?!
Th-This is such an unlucky combination!
WHAT IF...
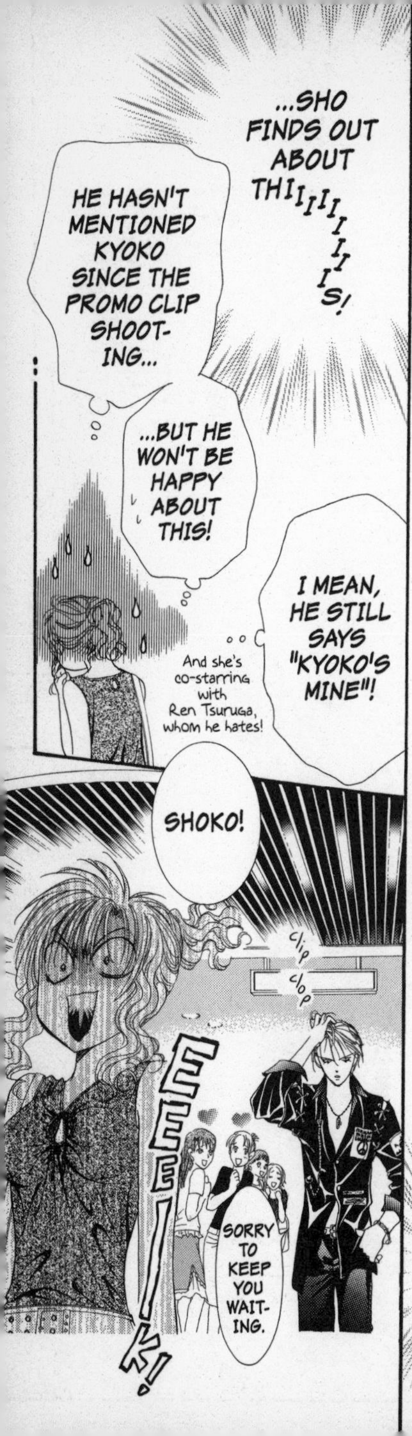
...SHO FINDS OUT ABOUT THIIIIIIIIS!
HE HASN'T MENTIONED KYOKO SINCE THE PROMO CLIP SHOOTING...
...BUT HE WON'T BE HAPPY ABOUT THIS!
I MEAN, HE STILL SAYS "KYOKO'S MINE"!
And she's co-starring with Ren Tsuruga, whom he hates!
SHOKO!
clip clop
EEEEEK!
SORRY TO KEEP YOU WAITING.

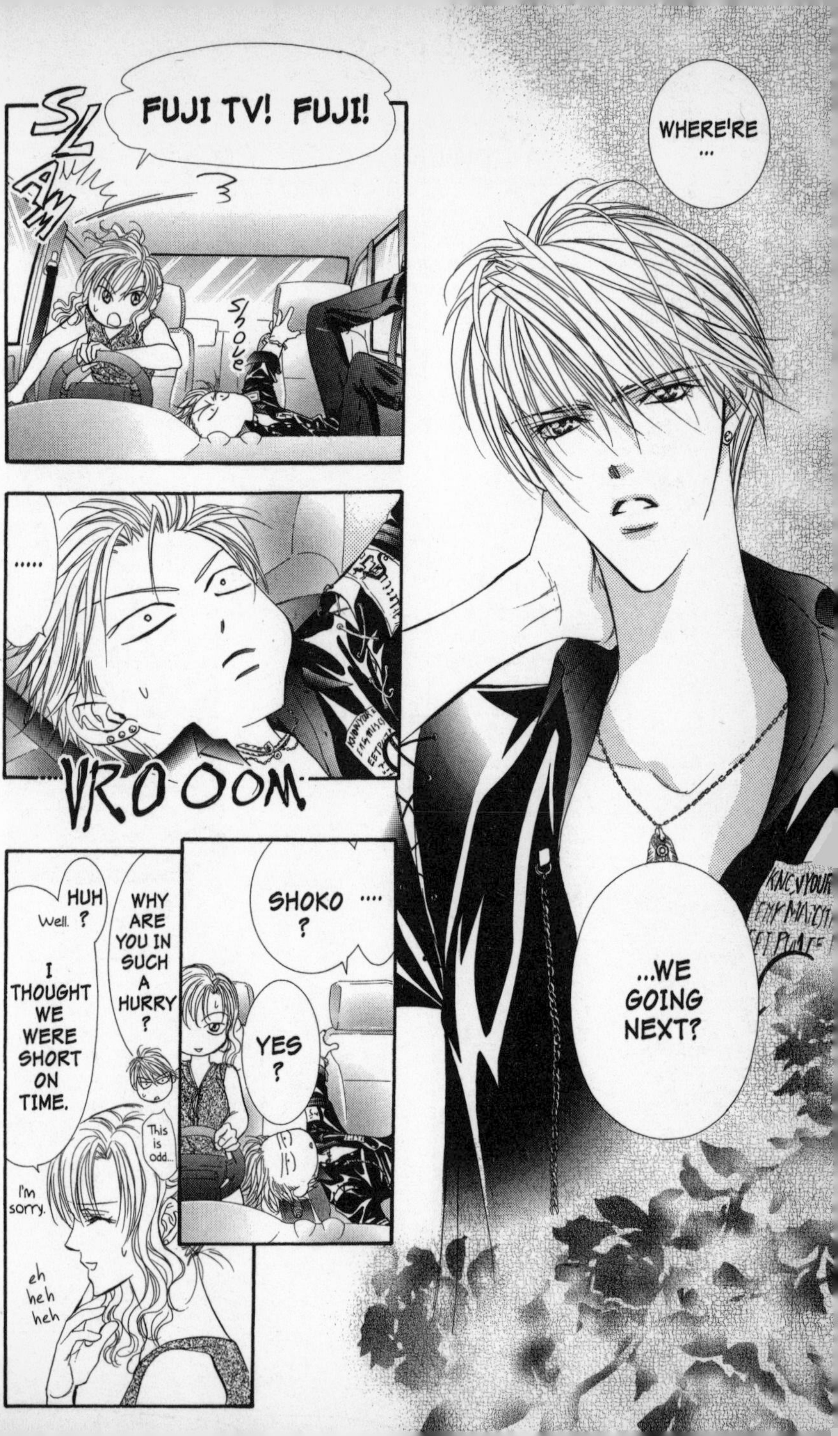
WHERE'RE ...
...WE GOING NEXT?
SLAM
FUJI TV! FUJI!
shove
.....
VROOOM
SHOKO ....?
YES?
This is odd...
WHY ARE YOU IN SUCH A HURRY?
HUH?
Well.
I THOUGHT WE WERE SHORT ON TIME.
I'm sorry.
eh heh heh

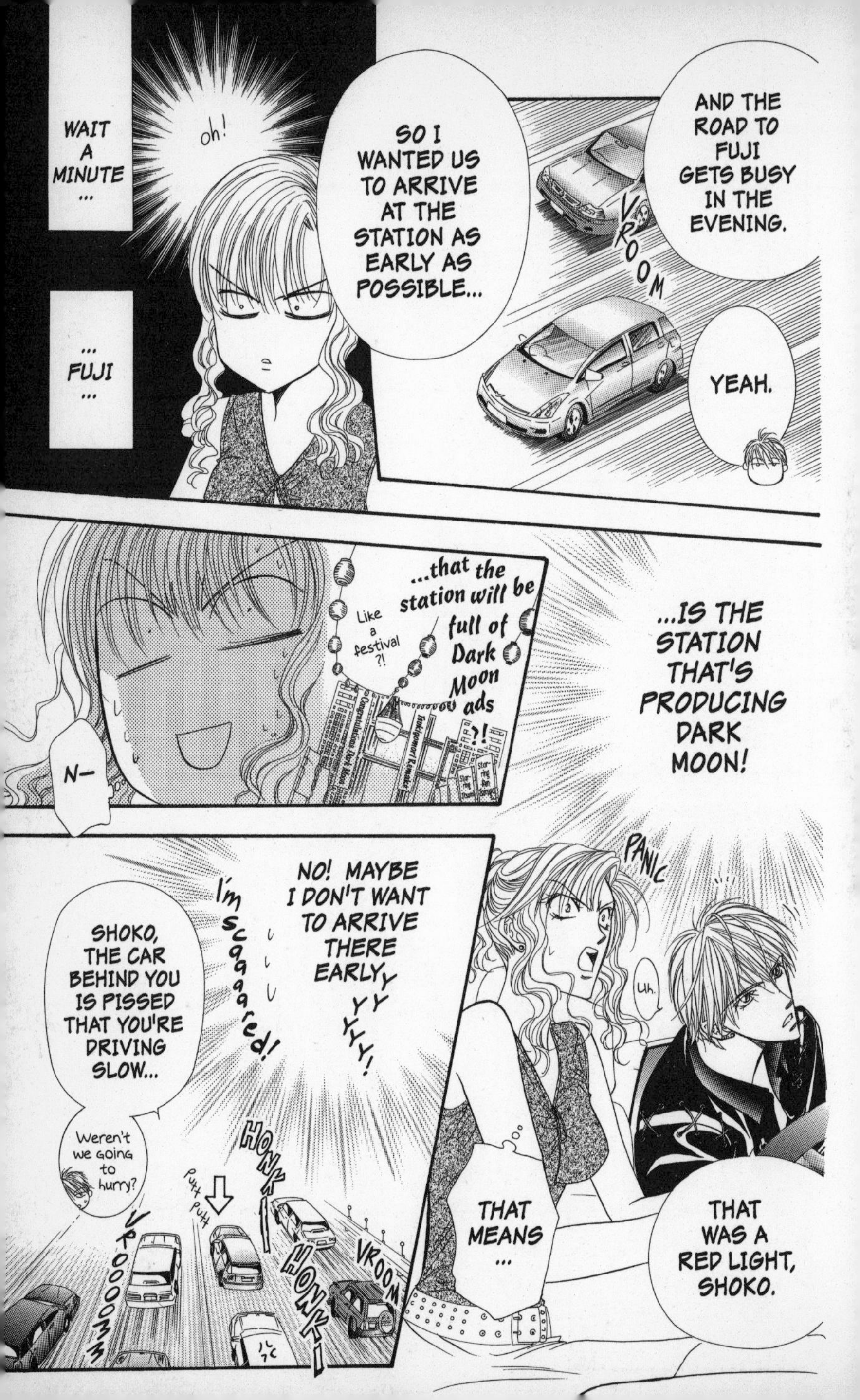
AND THE ROAD TO FUJI GETS BUSY IN THE EVENING.
VROOOM
YEAH.
SO I WANTED US TO ARRIVE AT THE STATION AS EARLY AS POSSIBLE...
oh!
WAIT A MINUTE...
...FUJI...
...IS THE STATION THAT'S PRODUCING DARK MOON!
...that the station will be full of Dark Moon ads ?!
Like a festival ?!
N—
PANIC
Uh.
THAT WAS A RED LIGHT, SHOKO.
THAT MEANS...
NO! MAYBE I DON'T WANT TO ARRIVE THERE EARLYYYYYYY!
I'm scaaaaared!
SHOKO, THE CAR BEHIND YOU IS PISSED THAT YOU'RE DRIVING SLOW...
Weren't we going to hurry?
Putt Putt
HONK!
HONK!
VROOM
VROOOOOMM

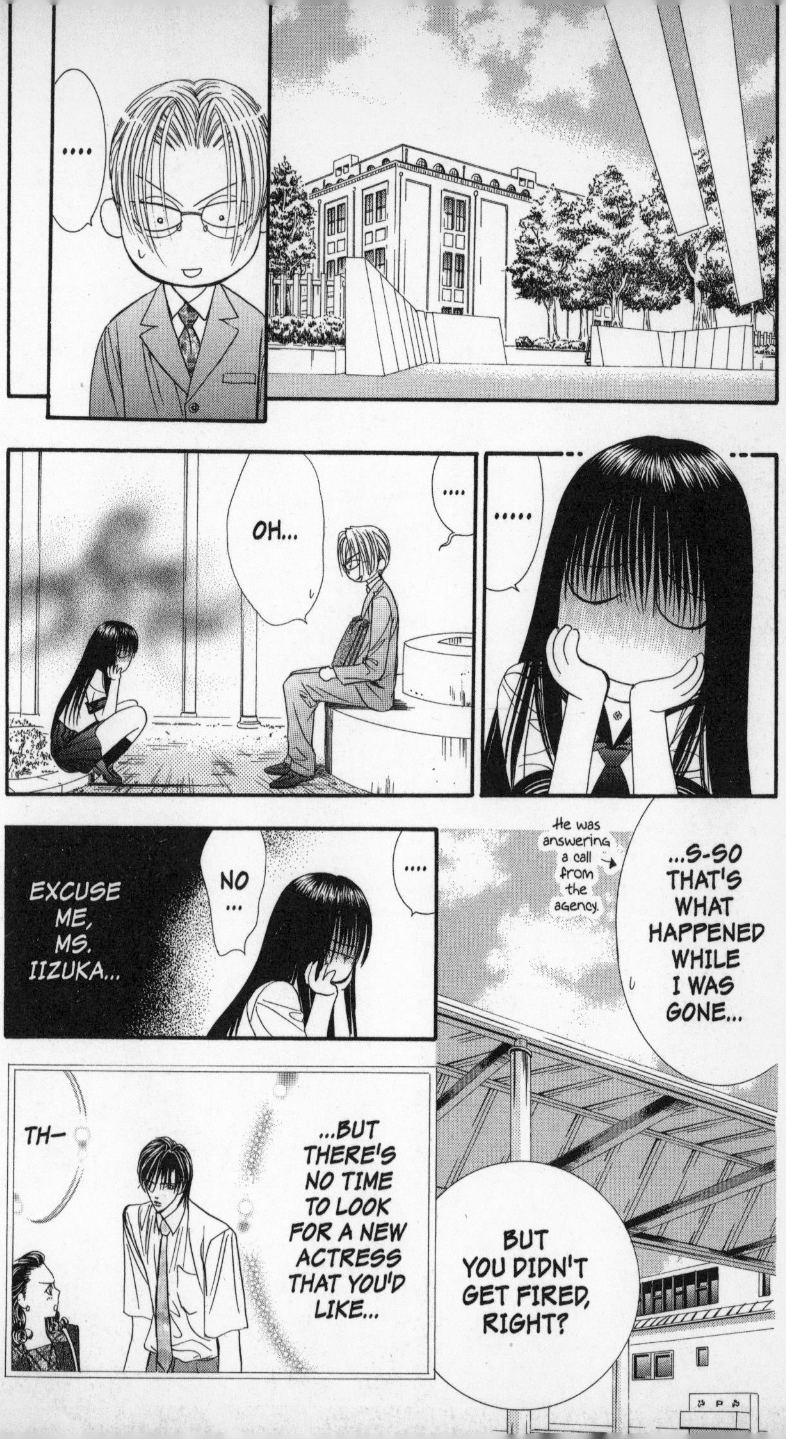
....
.....
....
OH...
...S-SO THAT'S WHAT HAPPENED WHILE I WAS GONE...
He was answering a call from the agency.
BUT YOU DIDN'T GET FIRED, RIGHT?
....
NO ...
EXCUSE ME, MS. IIZUKA...
...BUT THERE'S NO TIME TO LOOK FOR A NEW ACTRESS THAT YOU'D LIKE...
TH-

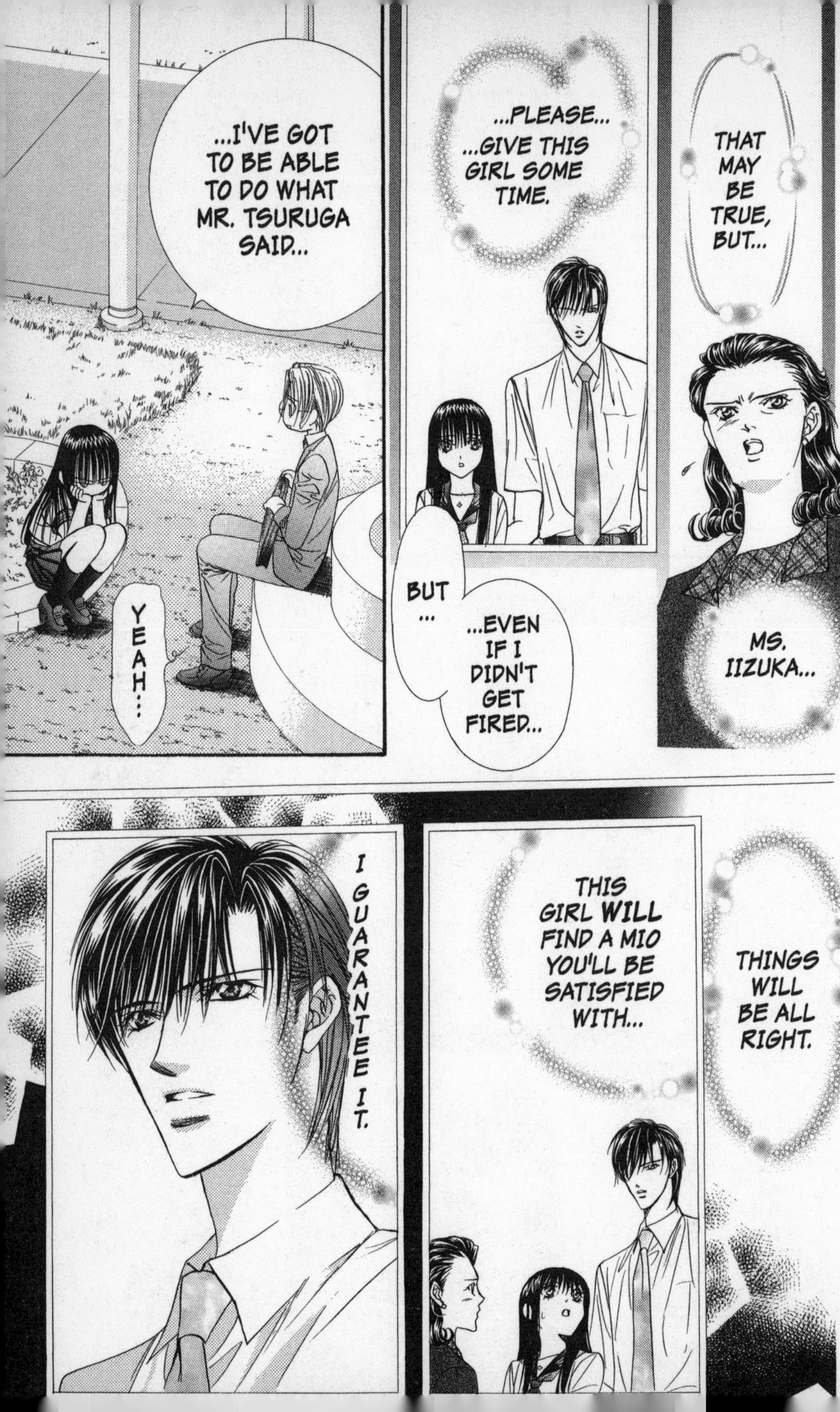
THAT MAY BE TRUE, BUT...
MS. IIZUKA...
...PLEASE... ...GIVE THIS GIRL SOME TIME.
BUT...
...EVEN IF I DIDN'T GET FIRED...
...I'VE GOT TO BE ABLE TO DO WHAT MR. TSURUGA SAID...
YEAH...
THINGS WILL BE ALL RIGHT.
THIS GIRL WILL FIND A MIO YOU'LL BE SATISFIED WITH...
I GUARANTEE IT.

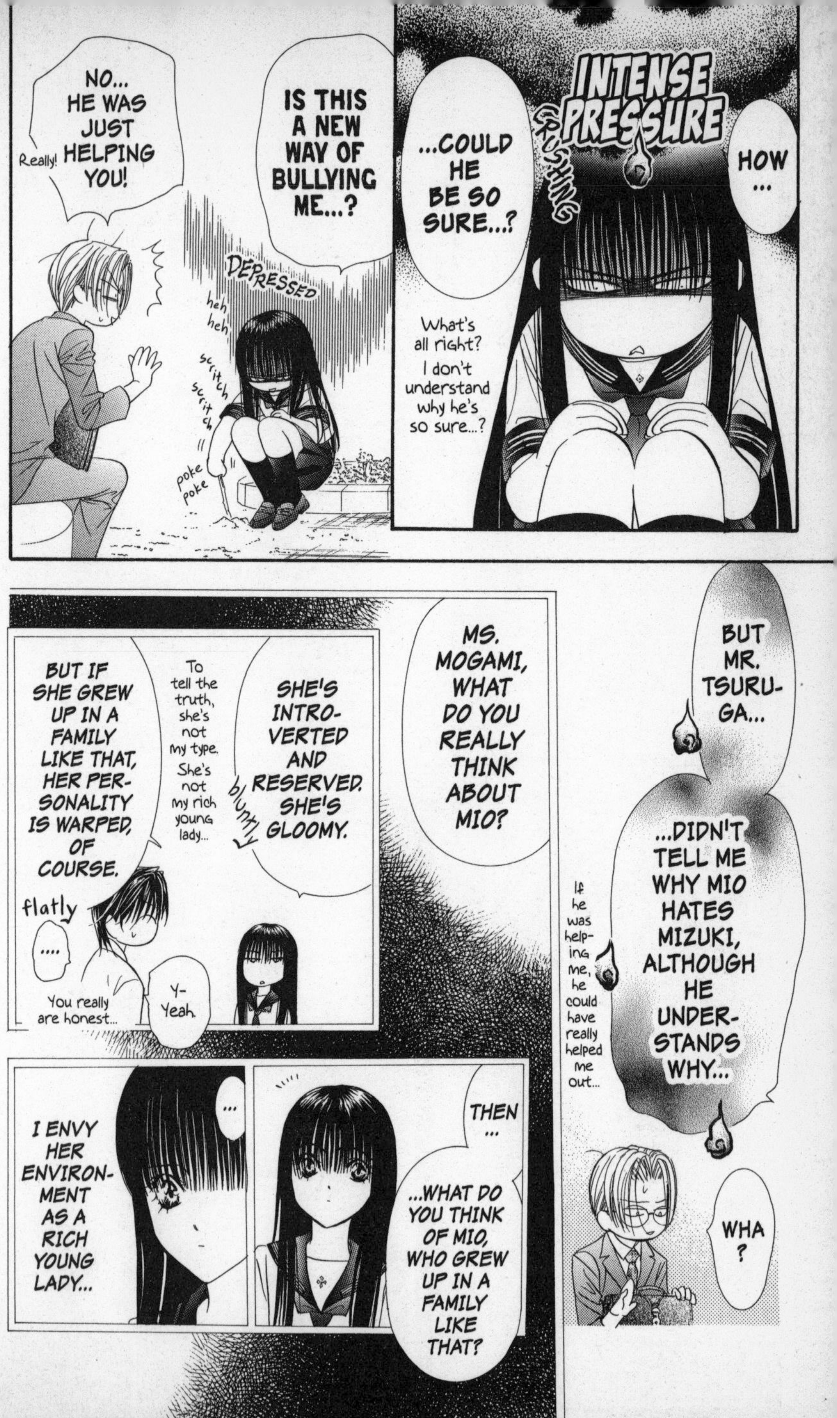
HOW...
INTENSE PRESSURE
CRUSHING
...COULD HE BE SO SURE...?
What's all right? I don't understand why he's so sure...?
IS THIS A NEW WAY OF BULLYING ME...?
DEPRESSED
heh heh
scritch scritch
poke poke
NO... HE WAS JUST HELPING YOU!
Really!
BUT MR. TSURUGA...
...DIDN'T TELL ME WHY MIO HATES MIZUKI, ALTHOUGH HE UNDERSTANDS WHY...
If he was helping me, he could have really helped me out...
WHA?
MS. MOGAMI, WHAT DO YOU REALLY THINK ABOUT MIO?
SHE'S INTROVERTED AND RESERVED. SHE'S GLOOMY.
bluntly
To tell the truth, she's not my type. She's not my rich young lady...
BUT IF SHE GREW UP IN A FAMILY LIKE THAT, HER PERSONALITY IS WARPED, OF COURSE.
flatly
....
Y-Yeah.
You really are honest...
THEN...
...WHAT DO YOU THINK OF MIO, WHO GREW UP IN A FAMILY LIKE THAT?
...
I ENVY HER ENVIRONMENT AS A RICH YOUNG LADY...

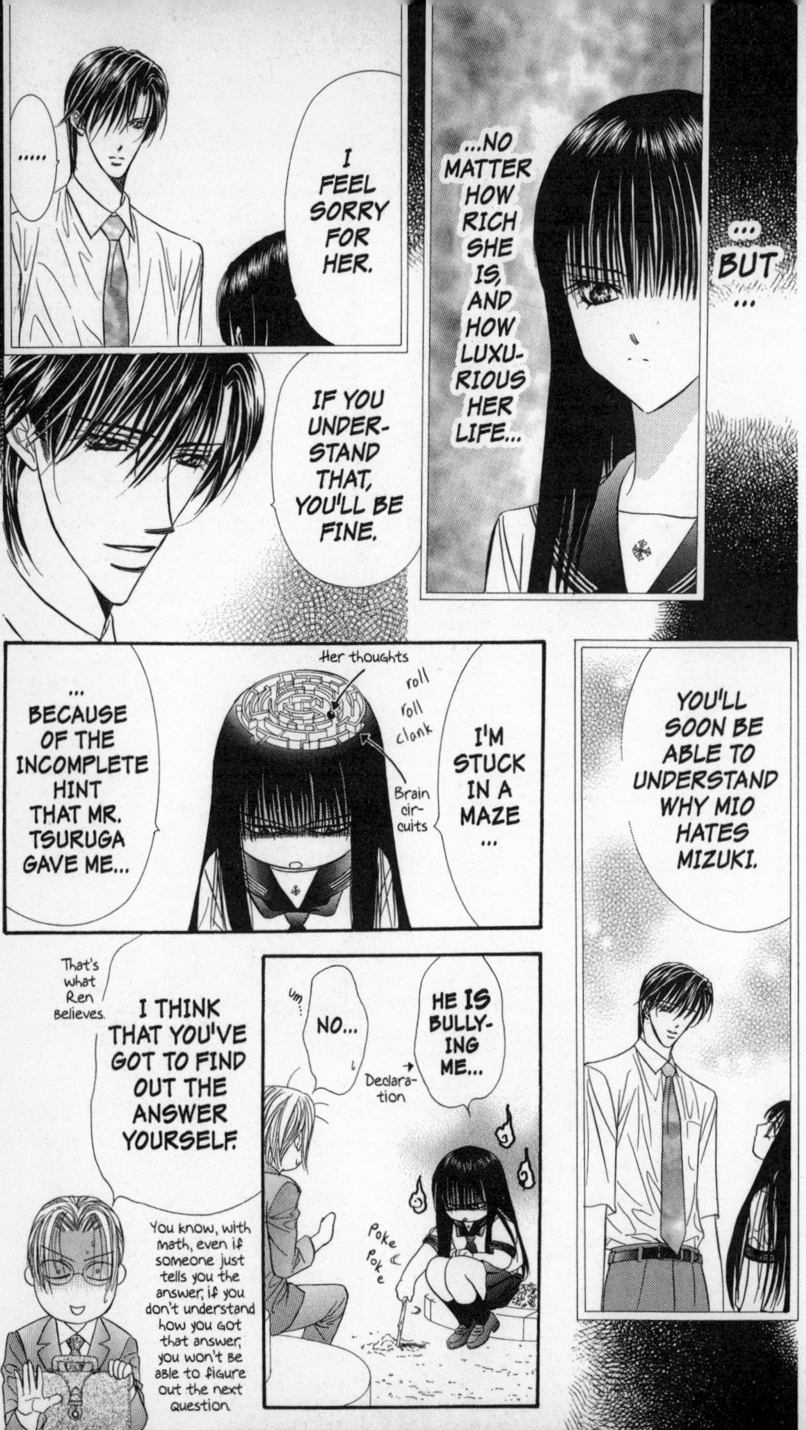
...BUT...
...NO MATTER HOW RICH SHE IS, AND HOW LUXURIOUS HER LIFE...
I FEEL SORRY FOR HER.
.....
IF YOU UNDERSTAND THAT, YOU'LL BE FINE.
YOU'LL SOON BE ABLE TO UNDERSTAND WHY MIO HATES MIZUKI.
I'M STUCK IN A MAZE...
Her thoughts
roll
roll
clank
Brain circuits
...BECAUSE OF THE INCOMPLETE HINT THAT MR. TSURUGA GAVE ME...
HE IS BULLYING ME...
Declaration
NO...
um...
Poke
Poke
I THINK THAT YOU'VE GOT TO FIND OUT THE ANSWER YOURSELF.
That's what Ren Believes.
You know, with math, even if someone just tells you the answer, if you don't understand how you got that answer, you won't be able to figure out the next question.

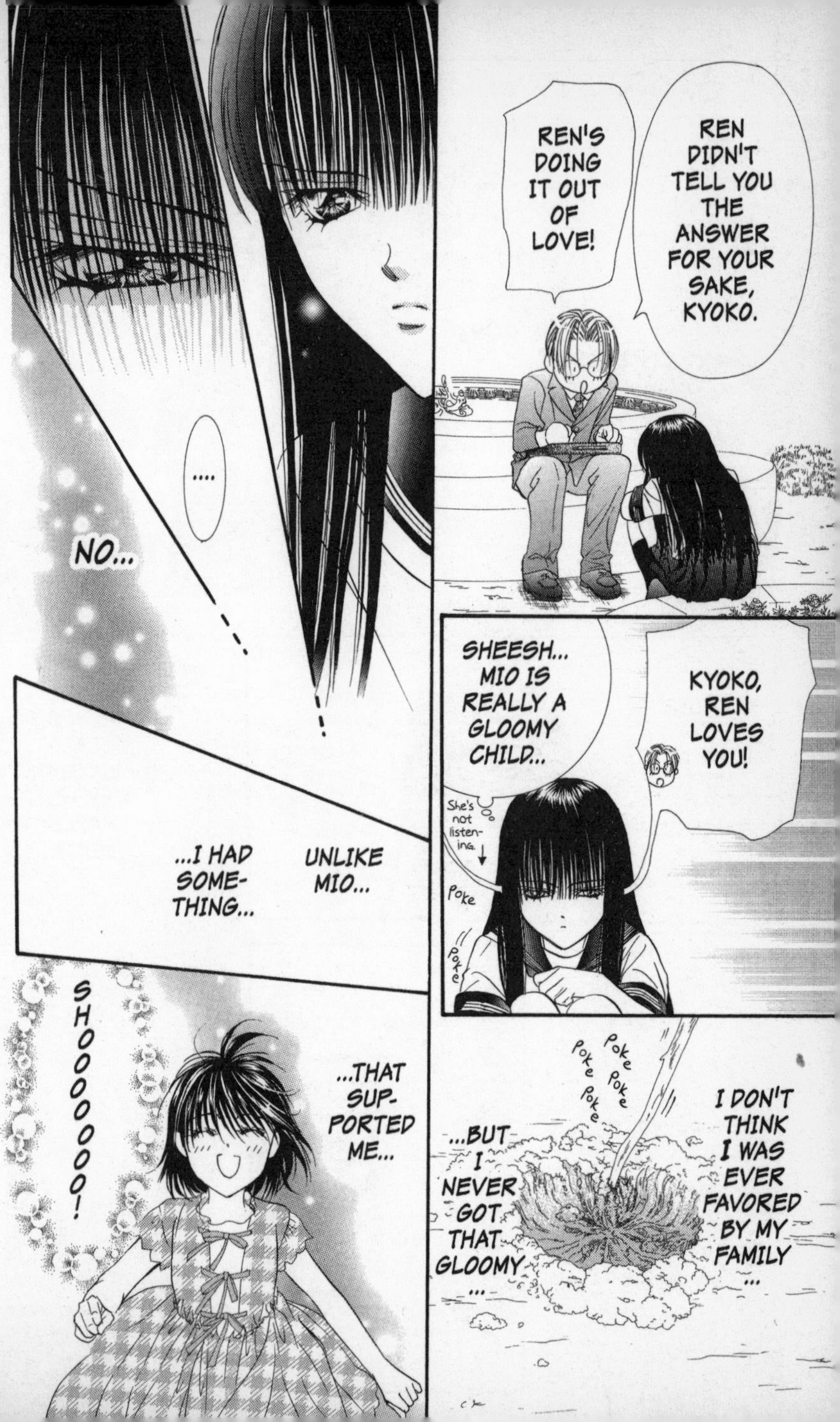

REN DIDN'T TELL YOU THE ANSWER FOR YOUR SAKE, KYOKO.
REN'S DOING IT OUT OF LOVE!
KYOKO, REN LOVES YOU!
SHEESH... MIO IS REALLY A GLOOMY CHILD...
She's not listening.
Poke
Poke
Poke Poke
Poke Poke
I DON'T THINK I WAS EVER FAVORED BY MY FAMILY...
...BUT I NEVER GOT THAT GLOOMY...
....
NO...
UNLIKE MIO...
...I HAD SOMETHING...
SHOOOOOOOO!
...THAT SUPPORTED ME...

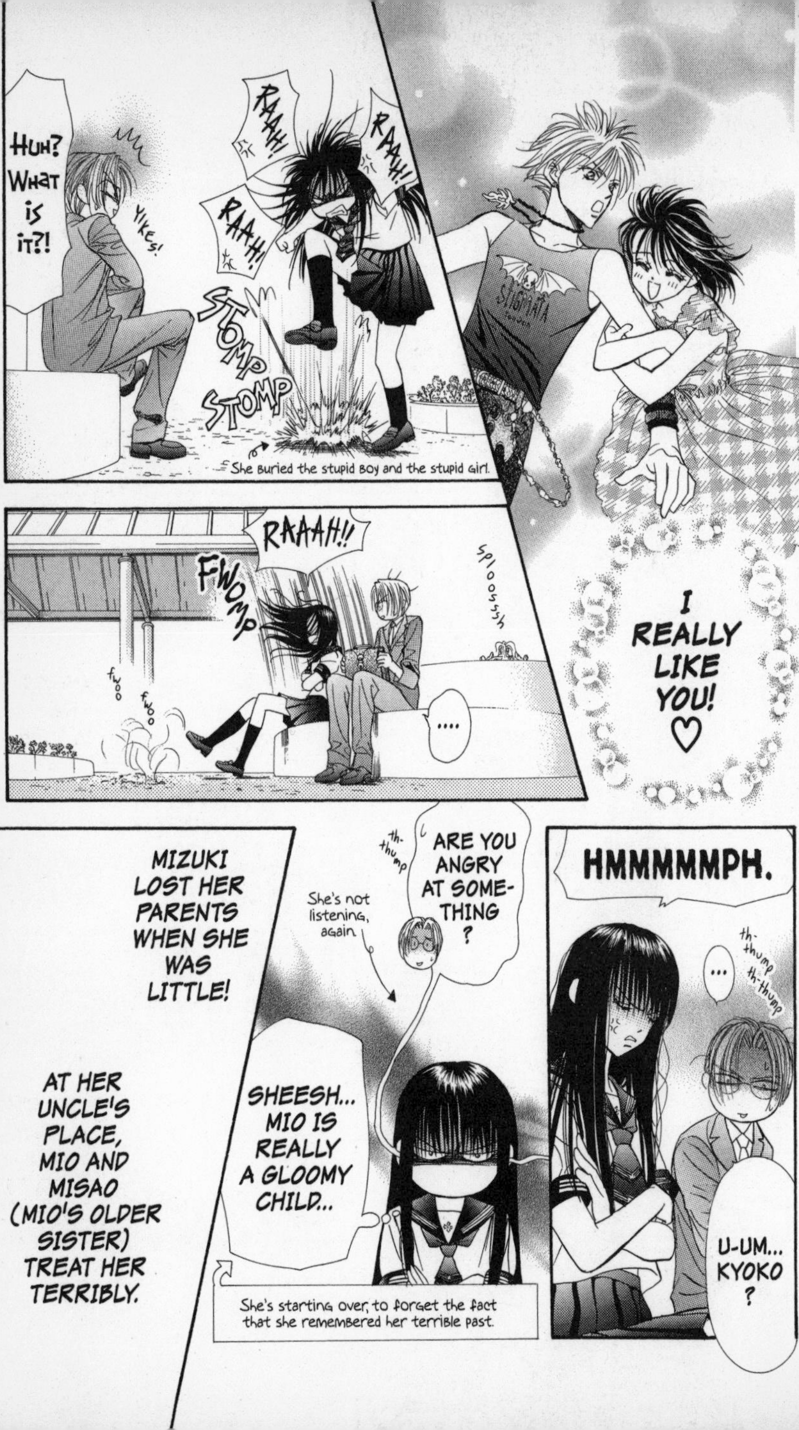
I REALLY LIKE YOU! ♡
RAAAH!
RAAAH!
HUH? WHAT is it?!
YIKES!
RAAH!
STOMP STOMP
She buried the stupid boy and the stupid girl.
RAAAH!!
FWOMP
sploossssh
fwoo
fwoo
....
HMMMMMPH.
th-thump th-thump
...
U-UM... KYOKO?
ARE YOU ANGRY AT SOME-THING?
th-thump
She's not listening, again.
SHEESH... MIO IS REALLY A GLOOMY CHILD...
She's starting over, to forget the fact that she remembered her terrible past.
MIZUKI LOST HER PARENTS WHEN SHE WAS LITTLE!
AT HER UNCLE'S PLACE, MIO AND MISAO (MIO'S OLDER SISTER) TREAT HER TERRIBLY.

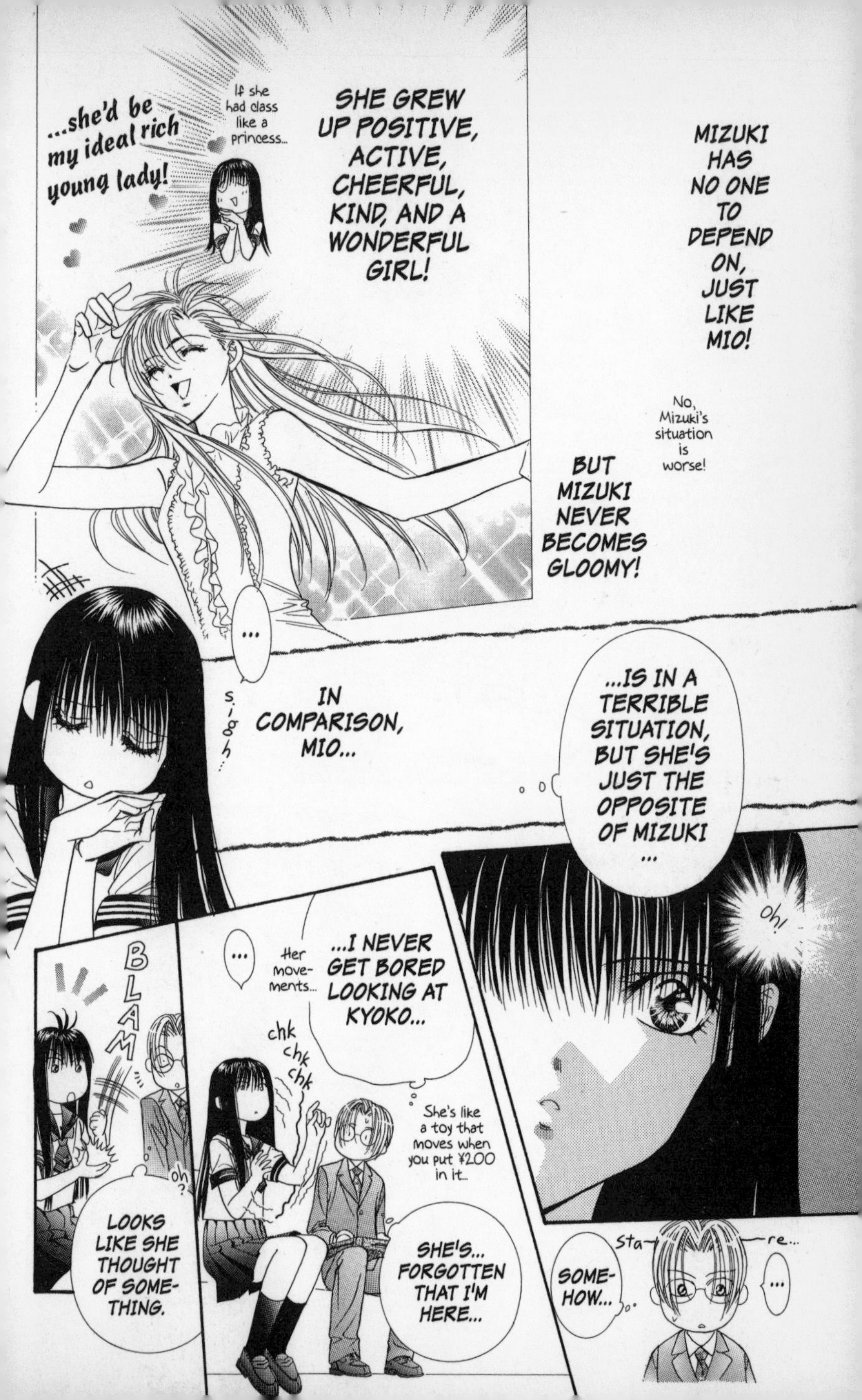
MIZUKI HAS NO ONE TO DEPEND ON, JUST LIKE MIO!
No, Mizuki's situation is worse!
BUT MIZUKI NEVER BECOMES GLOOMY!
SHE GREW UP POSITIVE, ACTIVE, CHEERFUL, KIND, AND A WONDERFUL GIRL!
If she had class like a princess...
...she'd be my ideal rich young lady!
...
sigh...
IN COMPARISON, MIO...
...IS IN A TERRIBLE SITUATION, BUT SHE'S JUST THE OPPOSITE OF MIZUKI...
Oh!
Sta—re...
SOME-HOW...
...
...I NEVER GET BORED LOOKING AT KYOKO...
Her move-ments...
...
chk chk chk
She's like a toy that moves when you put ¥200 in it...
SHE'S... FORGOTTEN THAT I'M HERE...
BLAM
oh?
LOOKS LIKE SHE THOUGHT OF SOME-THING.

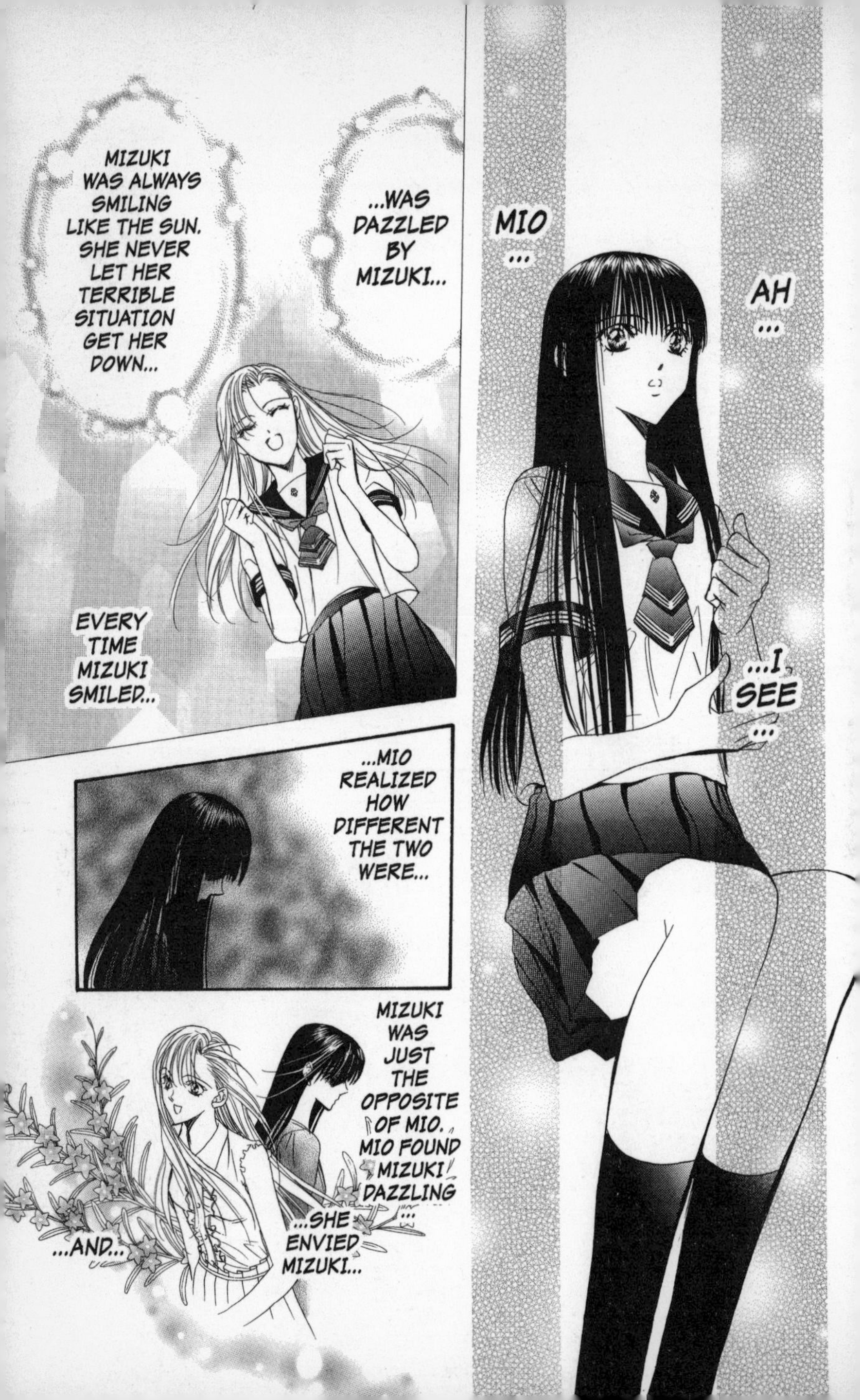
MIO ...
AH ...
...I, SEE ...
...WAS DAZZLED BY MIZUKI...
MIZUKI WAS ALWAYS SMILING LIKE THE SUN. SHE NEVER LET HER TERRIBLE SITUATION GET HER DOWN...
EVERY TIME MIZUKI SMILED...
...MIO REALIZED HOW DIFFERENT THE TWO WERE...
MIZUKI WAS JUST THE OPPOSITE OF MIO. MIO FOUND MIZUKI DAZZLING ...
...SHE ENVIED MIZUKI...
...AND...

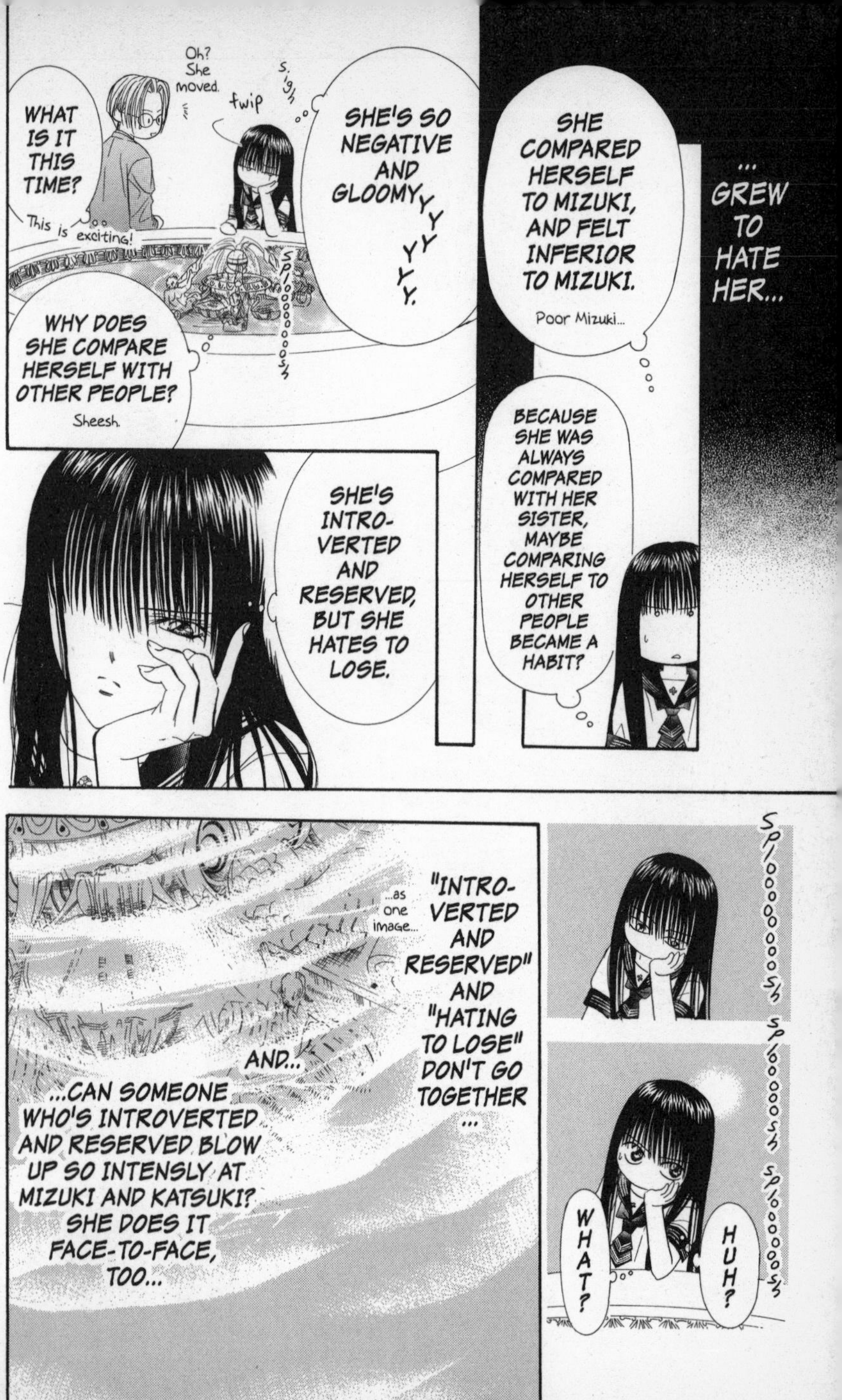

...GREW TO HATE HER...
SHE COMPARED HERSELF TO MIZUKI, AND FELT INFERIOR TO MIZUKI.
Poor Mizuki...
BECAUSE SHE WAS ALWAYS COMPARED WITH HER SISTER, MAYBE COMPARING HERSELF TO OTHER PEOPLE BECAME A HABIT?
sigh
SHE'S SO NEGATIVE AND GLOOMYYYYYYY.
fwip
Oh? She moved.
WHAT IS IT THIS TIME?
This is exciting!
Splooooooooooosh
WHY DOES SHE COMPARE HERSELF WITH OTHER PEOPLE?
Sheesh.
SHE'S INTROVERTED AND RESERVED, BUT SHE HATES TO LOSE.
Splooooooooosh
Splooooosh
Splooooosh
HUH?
WHAT?
"INTROVERTED AND RESERVED" AND "HATING TO LOSE" DON'T GO TOGETHER ...
...as one image...
AND...
...CAN SOMEONE WHO'S INTROVERTED AND RESERVED BLOW UP SO INTENSELY AT MIZUKI AND KATSUKI? SHE DOES IT FACE-TO-FACE, TOO...

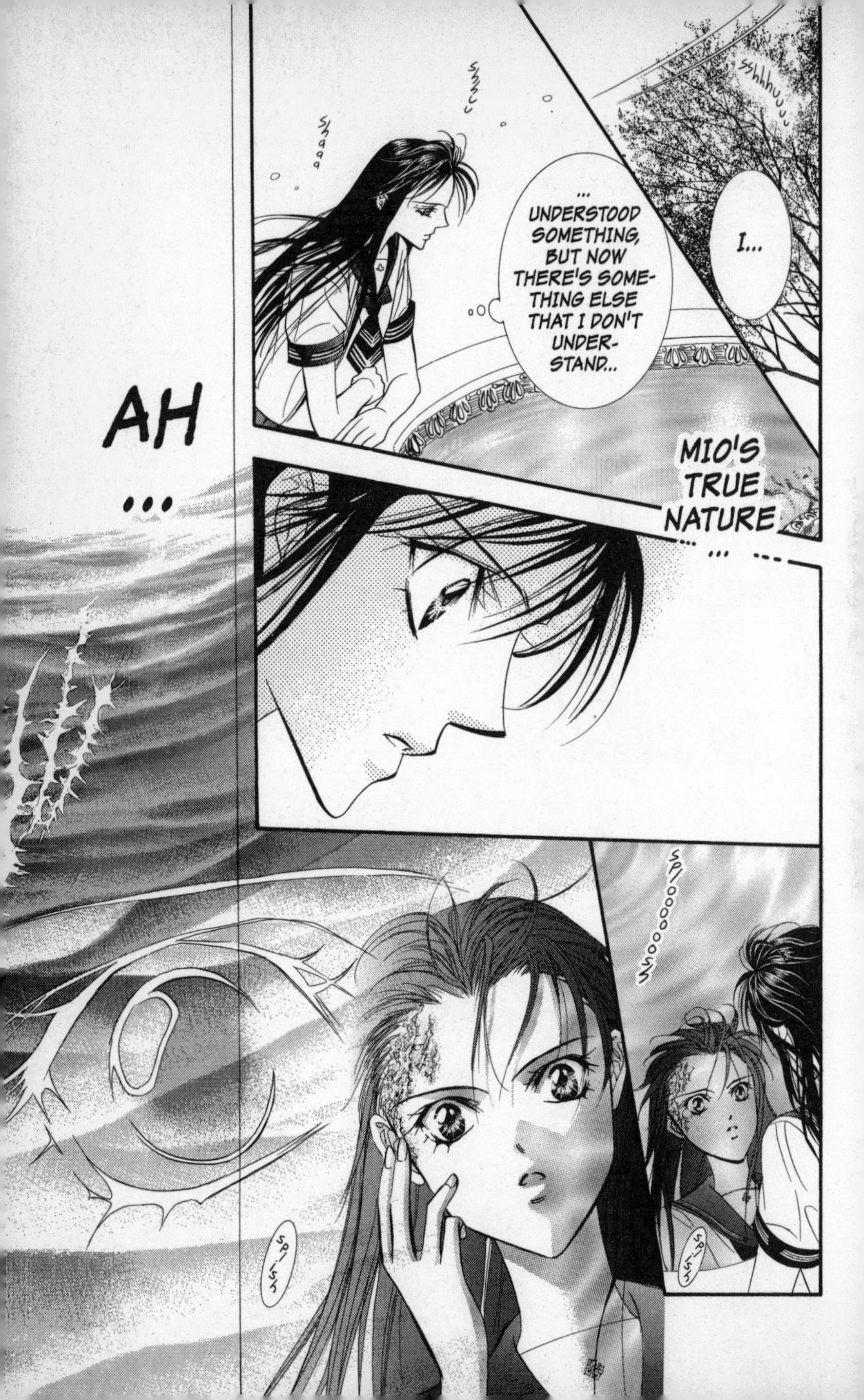
sshhhuuu
I...
... UNDERSTOOD SOMETHING, BUT NOW THERE'S SOME-THING ELSE THAT I DON'T UNDER-STAND...
shaaaa
MIO'S TRUE NATURE
... ...
AH ...
splooooosh
splish
splish

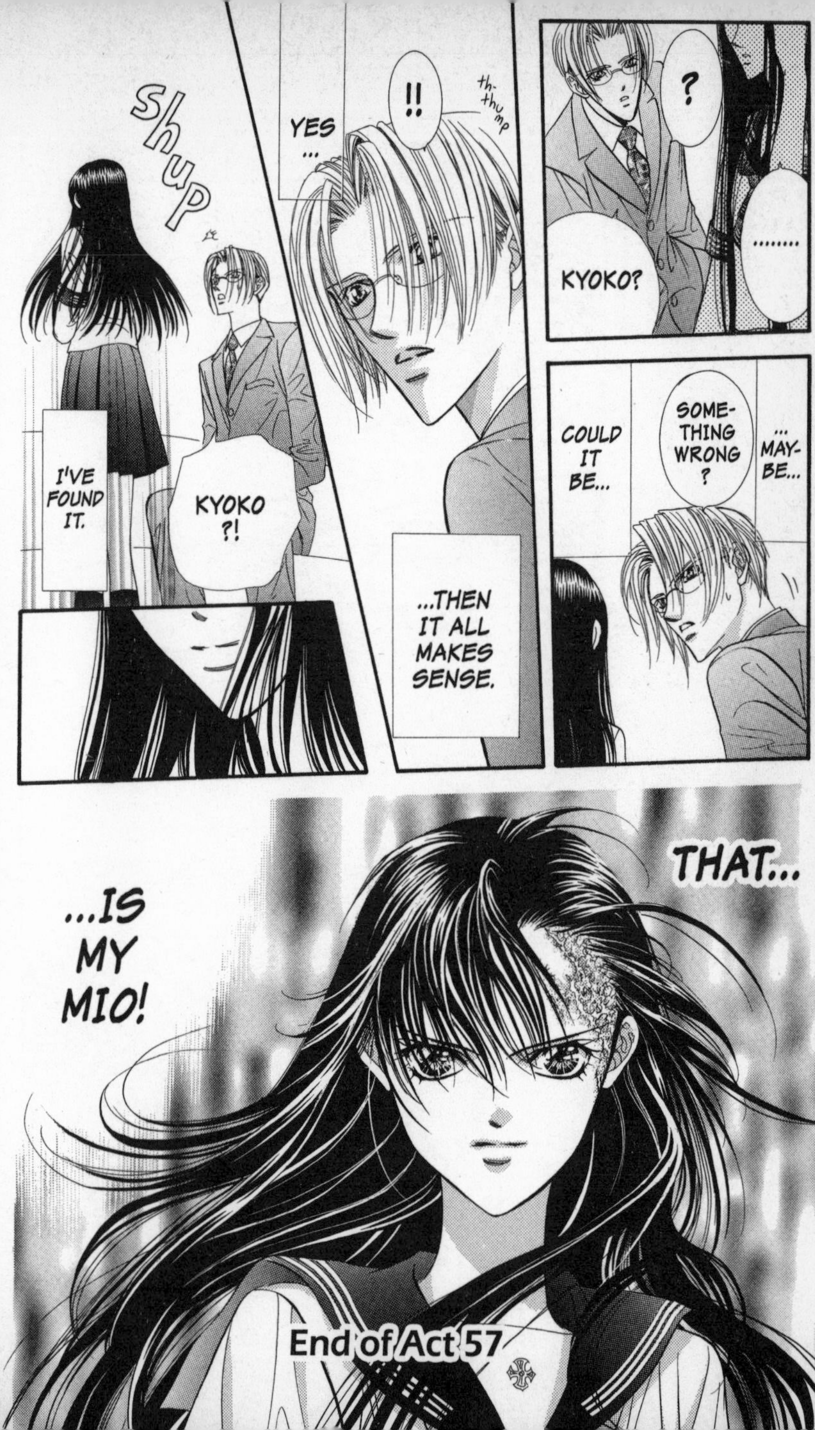
?
....
KYOKO?
...MAY-BE...
SOME-THING WRONG?
COULD IT BE...
!!
th-thump
YES...
...THEN IT ALL MAKES SENSE.
Shup
KYOKO?!
I'VE FOUND IT.
THAT...
...IS MY MIO!
End of Act 57

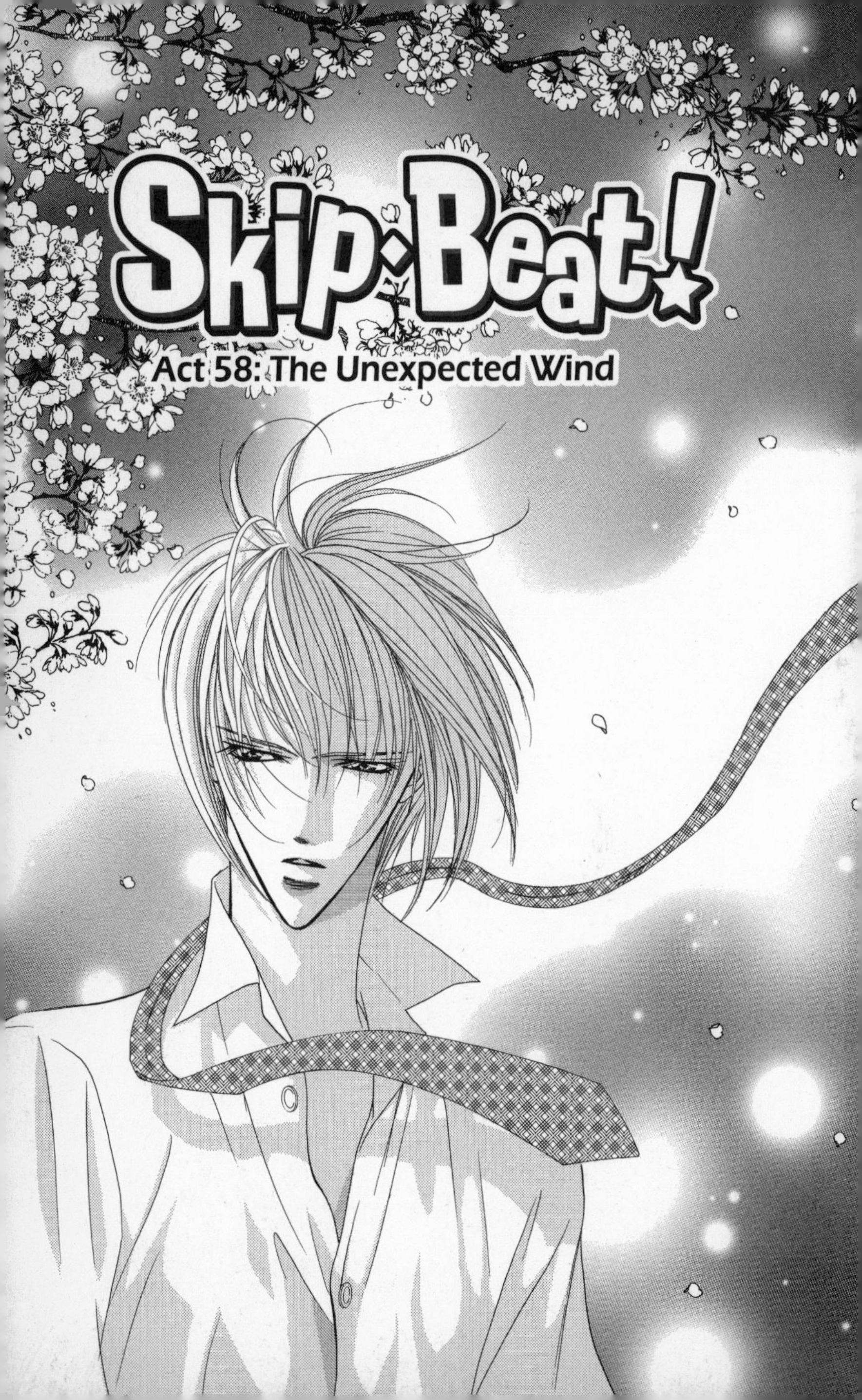
Skip·Beat!
Act 58: The Unexpected Wind

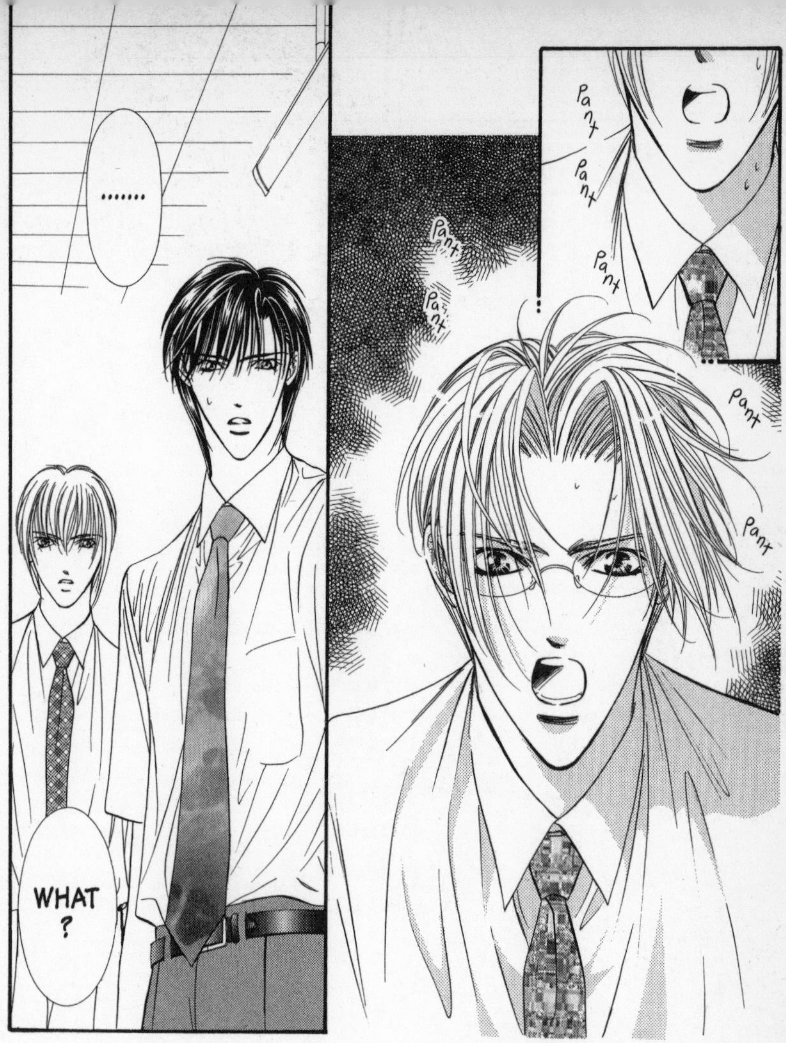
Pant
Pant
Pant
Pant
Pant
pant
Pant
....
WHAT ?

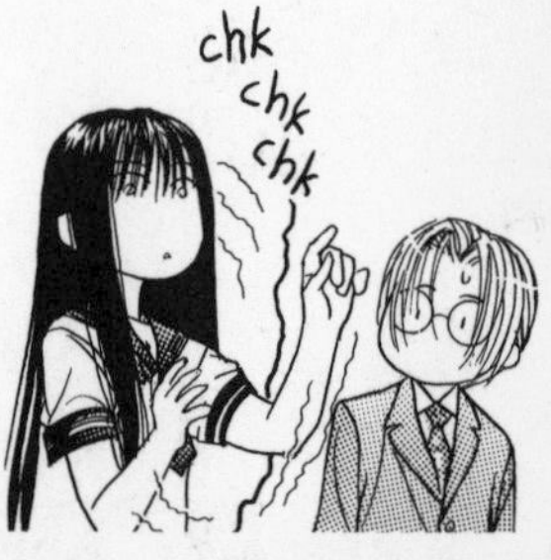
chk chk chk

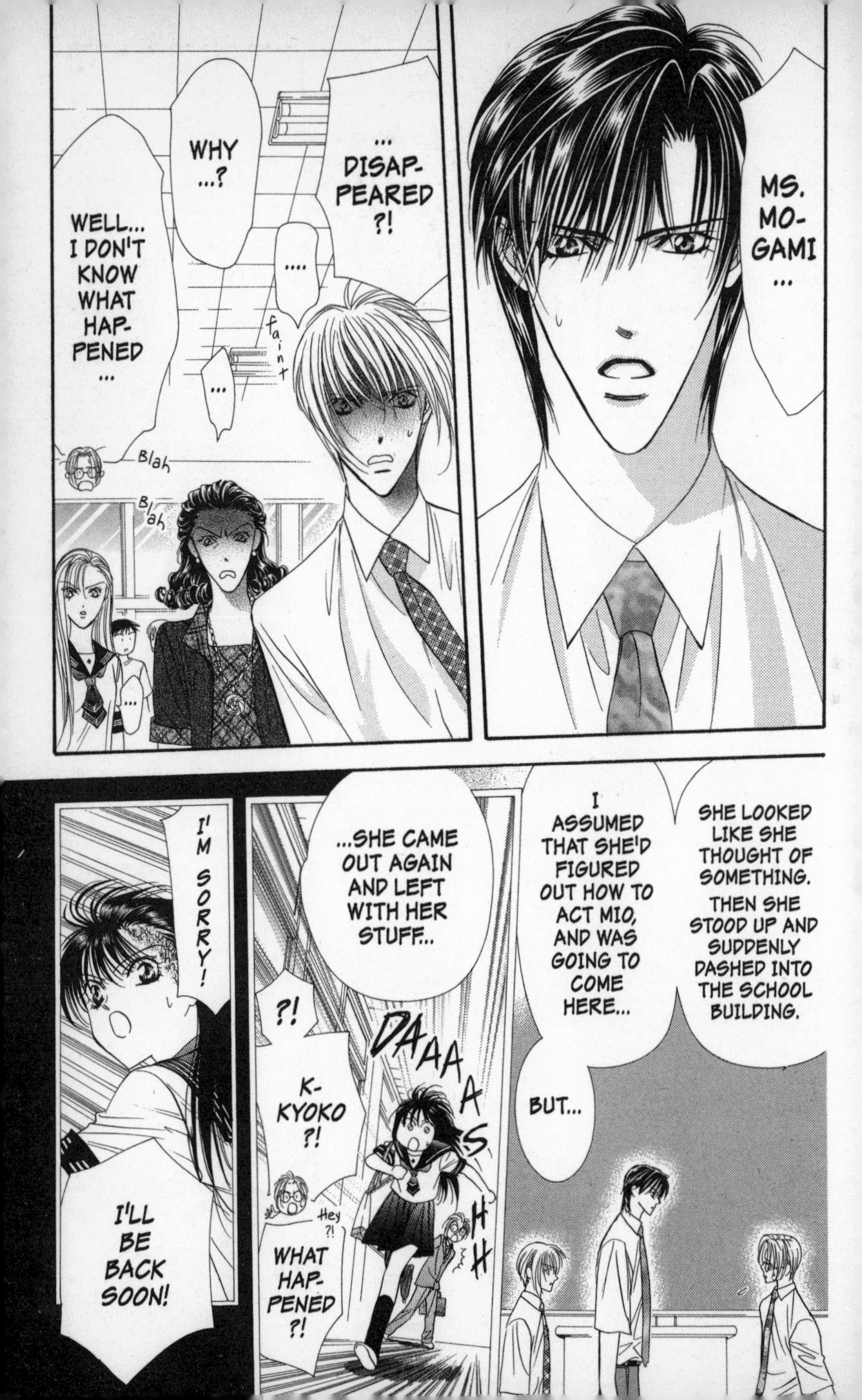
MS. MO-GAMI ...
... DISAP-PEARED ?!
WHY ...?
....
WELL... I DON'T KNOW WHAT HAP-PENED ...
faint
...
Blah
Blah
...
SHE LOOKED LIKE SHE THOUGHT OF SOMETHING.
THEN SHE STOOD UP AND SUDDENLY DASHED INTO THE SCHOOL BUILDING.
I ASSUMED THAT SHE'D FIGURED OUT HOW TO ACT MIO, AND WAS GOING TO COME HERE...
BUT...
...SHE CAME OUT AGAIN AND LEFT WITH HER STUFF...
?!
DAAAASHH
K-KYOKO ?!
Hey ?!
WHAT HAP-PENED ?!
I'M SORRY!
I'LL BE BACK SOON!

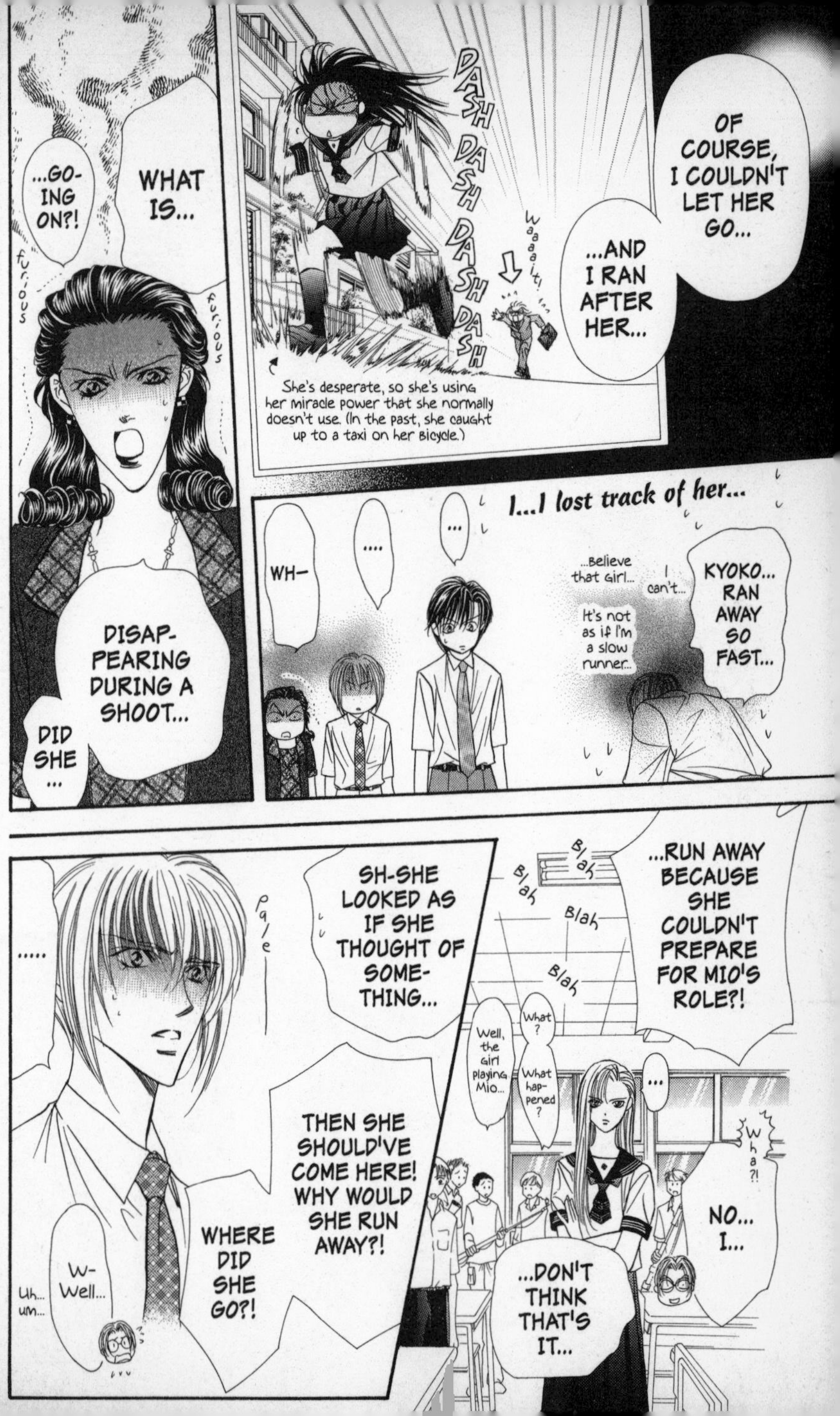
OF COURSE, I COULDN'T LET HER GO...
...AND I RAN AFTER HER...
DASH DASH DASH DASH DASH
Waaaait!
She's desperate, so she's using her miracle power that she normally doesn't use. (In the past, she caught up to a taxi on her bicycle.)
I...I lost track of her...
KYOKO... RAN AWAY SO FAST...
I can't...
...Believe that girl...
It's not as if I'm a slow runner...
...
....
WH-
WHAT IS...
...GO-ING ON?!
furious
furious
DISAP-PEARING DURING A SHOOT...
DID SHE...
...RUN AWAY BECAUSE SHE COULDN'T PREPARE FOR MIO'S ROLE?!
Blah
Blah
Blah
Blah
...
What?
What happened?
Well, the girl playing Mio...
Wha?!
NO... I...
...DON'T THINK THAT'S IT...
SH-SHE LOOKED AS IF SHE THOUGHT OF SOME-THING...
Pale
.....
THEN SHE SHOULD'VE COME HERE! WHY WOULD SHE RUN AWAY?!
WHERE DID SHE GO?!
W-Well...
Uh... um...

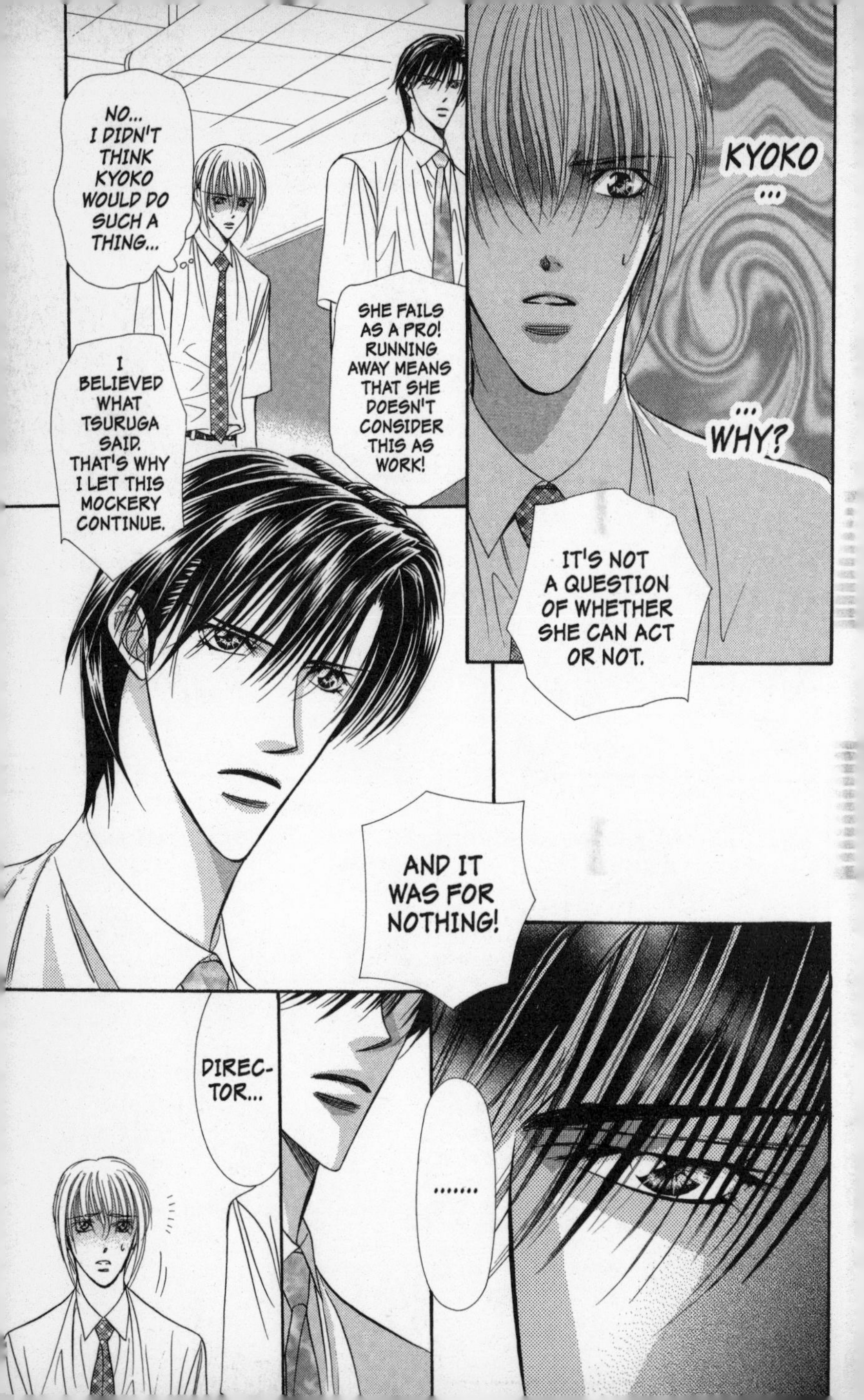
KYOKO ...
... WHY?
NO... I DIDN'T THINK KYOKO WOULD DO SUCH A THING...
SHE FAILS AS A PRO! RUNNING AWAY MEANS THAT SHE DOESN'T CONSIDER THIS AS WORK!
I BELIEVED WHAT TSURUGA SAID. THAT'S WHY I LET THIS MOCKERY CONTINUE.
IT'S NOT A QUESTION OF WHETHER SHE CAN ACT OR NOT.
AND IT WAS FOR NOTHING!
DIREC-TOR...
....

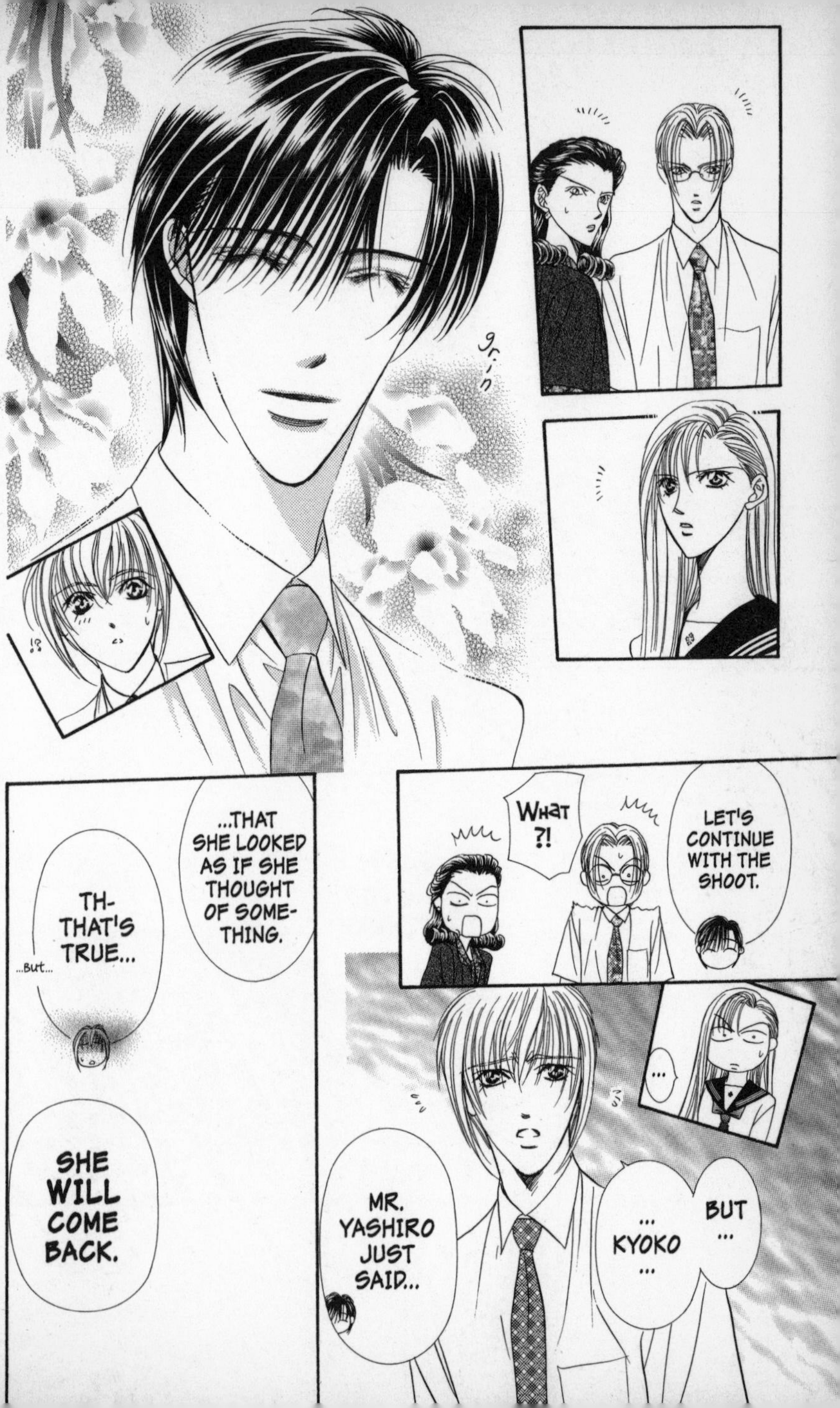

grin
!?
LET'S CONTINUE WITH THE SHOOT.
WHAT ?!
...
BUT ...
... KYOKO ...
MR. YASHIRO JUST SAID...
...THAT SHE LOOKED AS IF SHE THOUGHT OF SOME-THING.
TH-THAT'S TRUE...
...but...
SHE WILL COME BACK.

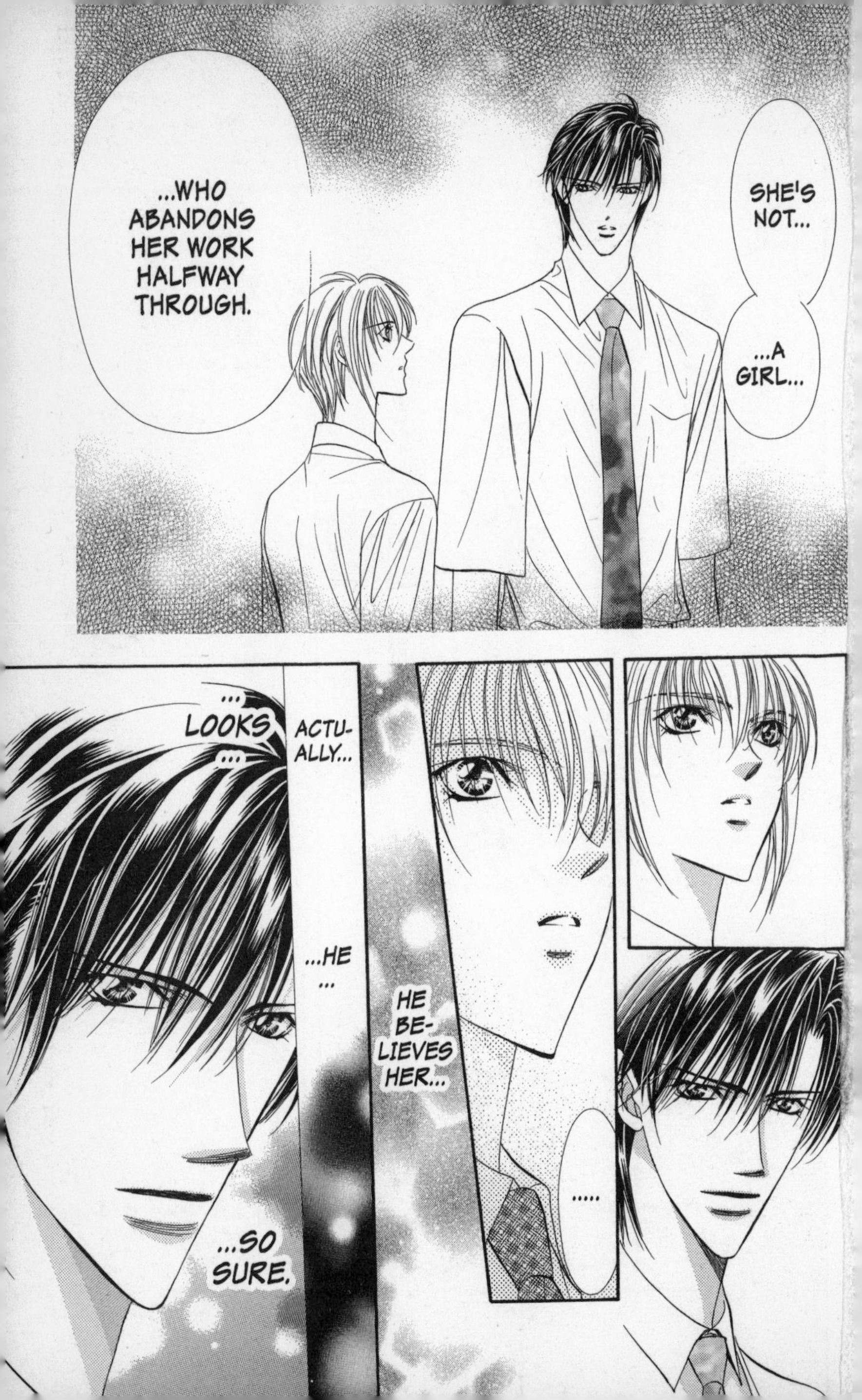
SHE'S NOT...
...A GIRL...
...WHO ABANDONS HER WORK HALFWAY THROUGH.
.....
HE BE-LIEVES HER...
ACTU-ALLY...
...HE ...
... LOOKS ...
...SO SURE.

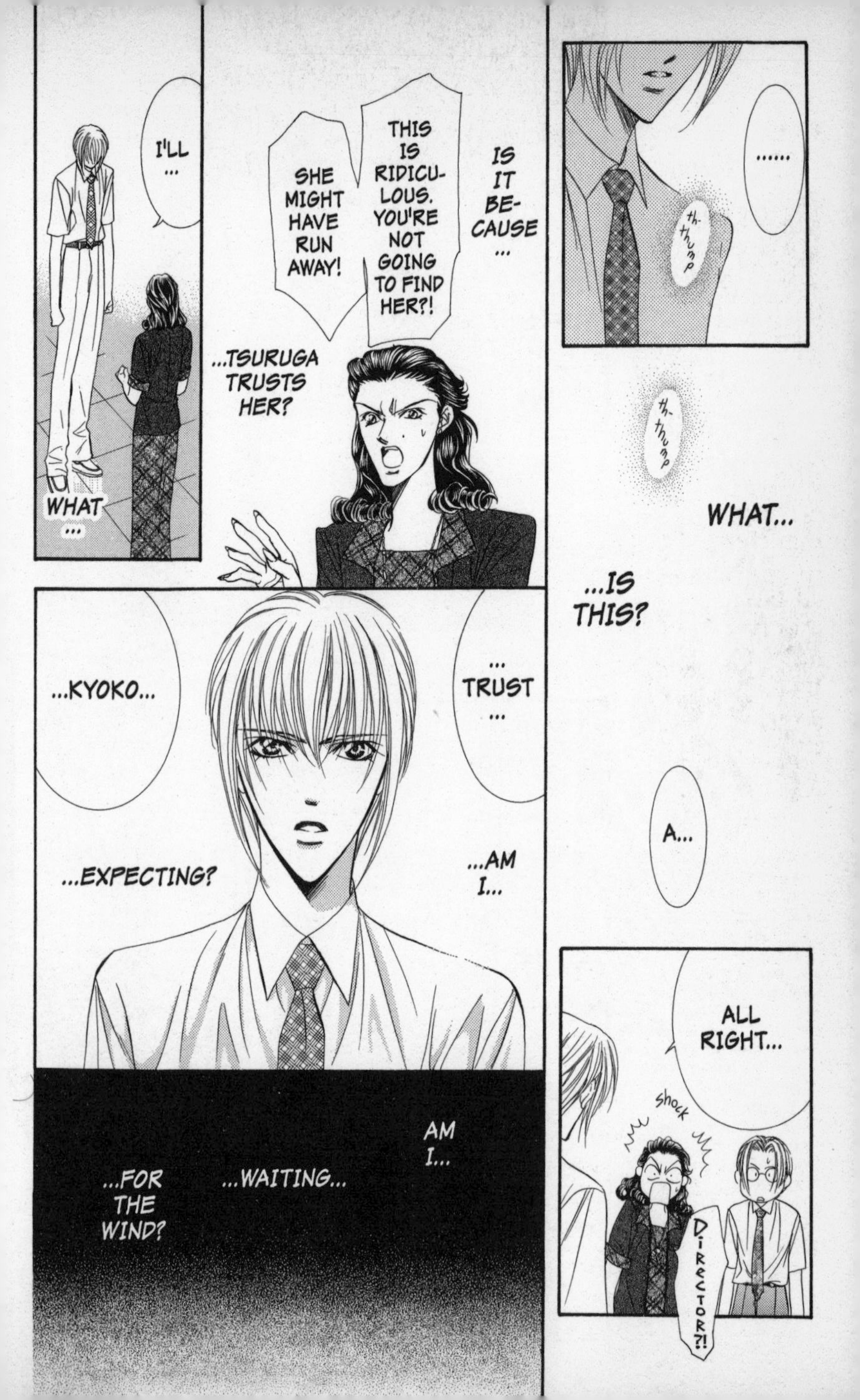
......
th-thump
th-thump
WHAT...
...IS THIS?
A...
ALL RIGHT...
shock
DIRECTOR?!
IS IT BECAUSE ...
THIS IS RIDICULOUS. YOU'RE NOT GOING TO FIND HER?!
SHE MIGHT HAVE RUN AWAY!
...TSURUGA TRUSTS HER?
I'LL ...
WHAT ...
... TRUST ...
...KYOKO...
...AM I...
...EXPECTING?
AM I...
...WAITING...
...FOR THE WIND?

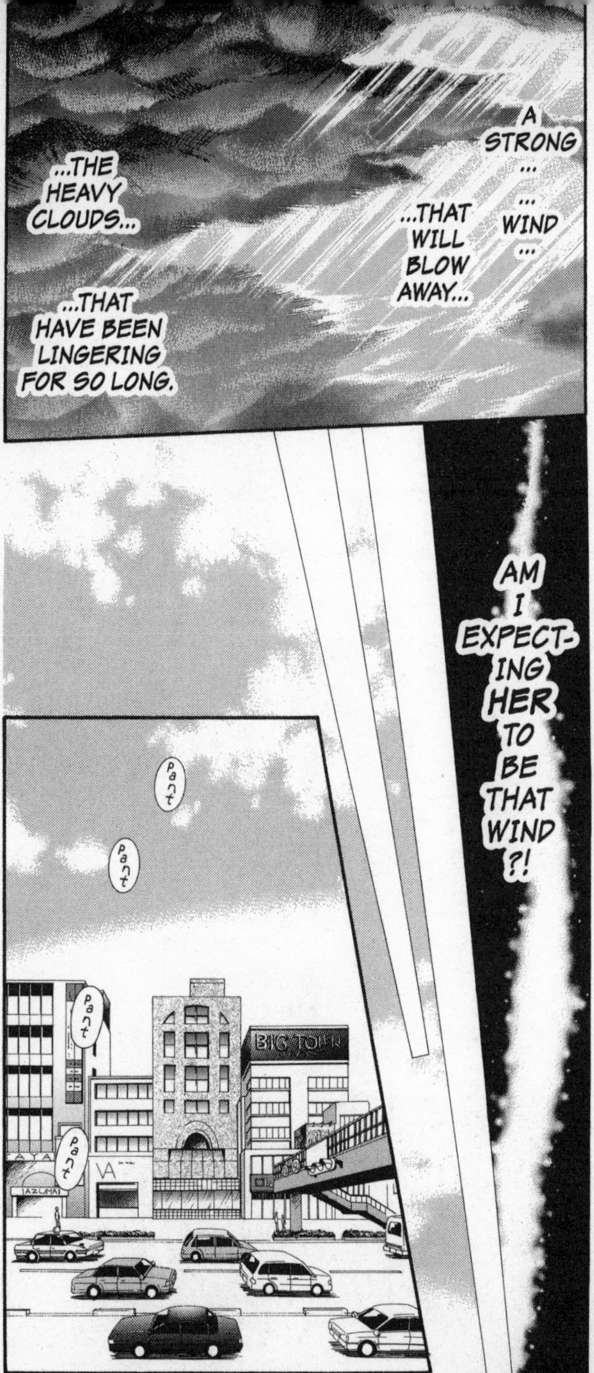
A STRONG ... ... WIND ...
...THAT WILL BLOW AWAY...
...THE HEAVY CLOUDS...
...THAT HAVE BEEN LINGERING FOR SO LONG.
AM I EXPECT-ING HER TO BE THAT WIND ?!
Pant
Pant
Pant
Pant

Mio Hongo

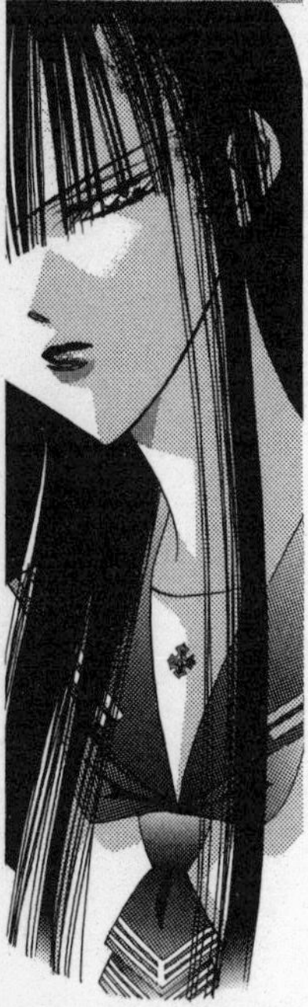

I wrote this in the magazine too, but the long-haired Mio turned out to be like Pochi... But...this was only temporary, until she became the New Mio, and the hairstyle looks fine in this age (Mio's hairstyle when Ms. Iizuka played it wouldn't go well now...) Moreover, the hairstyle had to be something that could hide the scars on her face, and I could only think up this one... ...But...it only appears in the beginning...so...it's all right...and I decided to go ahead with it...

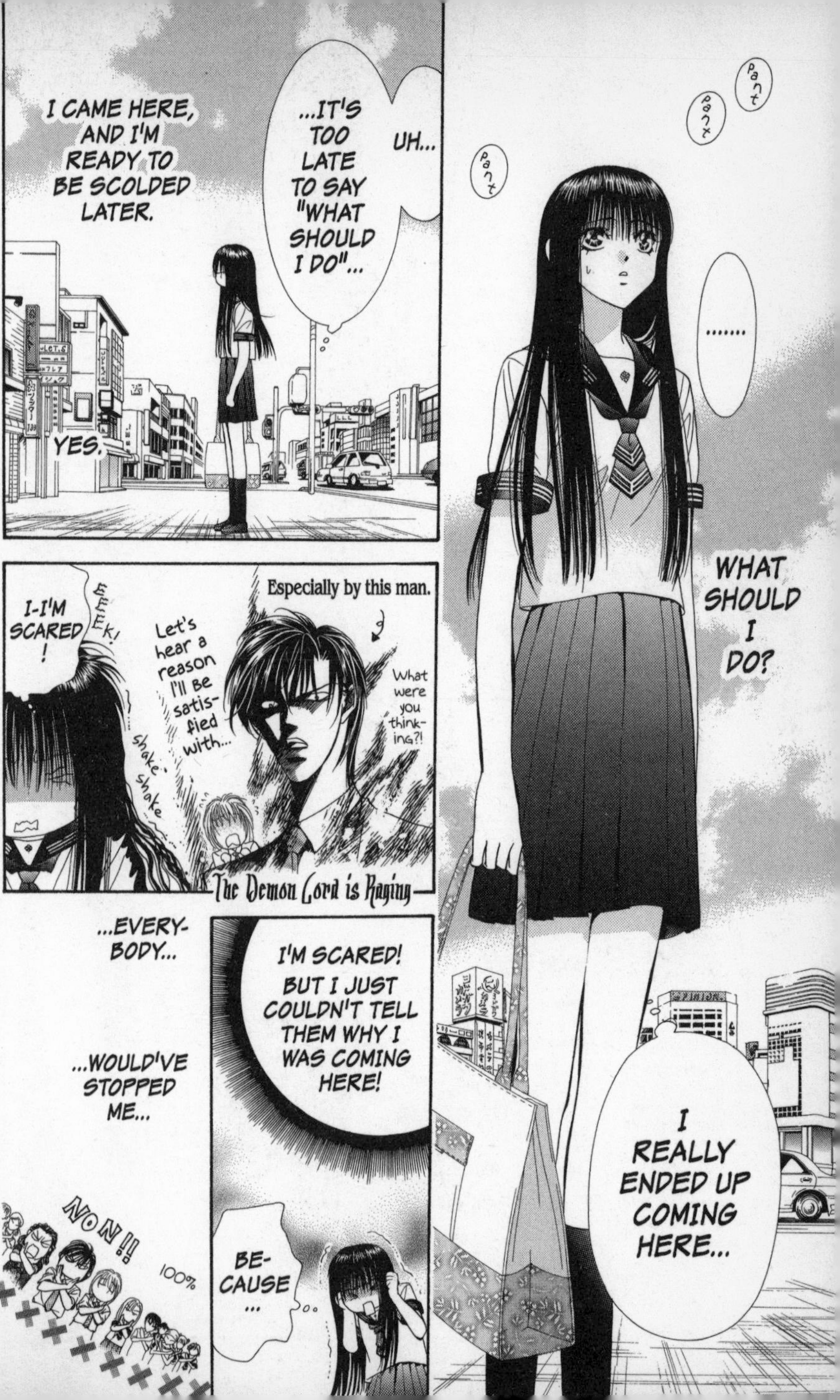
Pant
Pant
Pant
......
WHAT SHOULD I DO?
I REALLY ENDED UP COMING HERE...
UH...
...IT'S TOO LATE TO SAY "WHAT SHOULD I DO"...
I CAME HERE, AND I'M READY TO BE SCOLDED LATER.
YES.
Especially by this man.
What were you thinking?!
Let's hear a reason I'll be satisfied with...
EEEK!
I-I'M SCARED!
shake shake
The Demon Lord is Raging
I'M SCARED! BUT I JUST COULDN'T TELL THEM WHY I WAS COMING HERE!
BE-CAUSE...
...EVERY-BODY...
...WOULD'VE STOPPED ME...
NON!!
100%

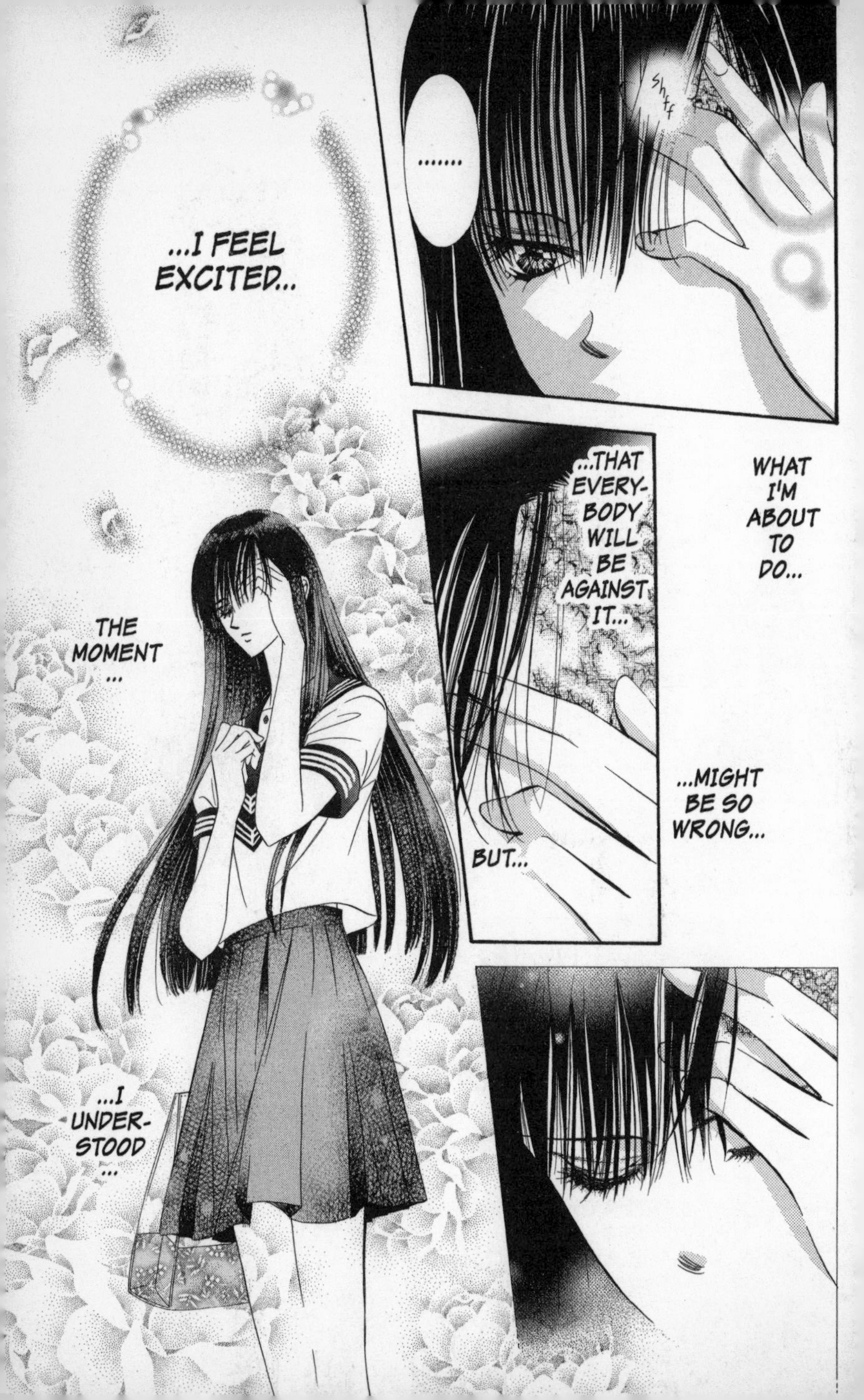

Shfff
......
WHAT I'M ABOUT TO DO...
...MIGHT BE SO WRONG...
...THAT EVERY-BODY WILL BE AGAINST IT...
BUT...
THE MOMENT ...
...I UNDER-STOOD ...
...I FEEL EXCITED...

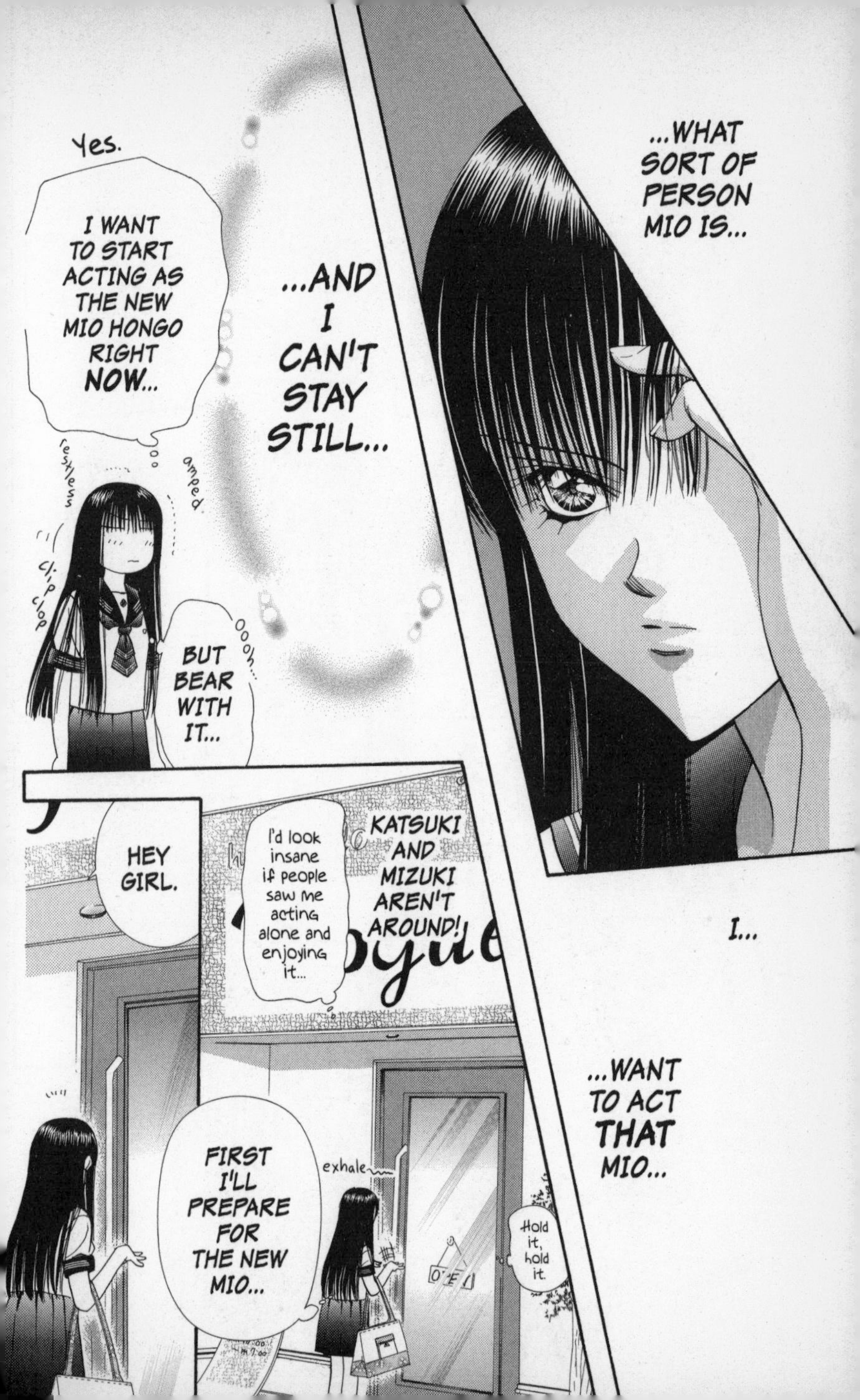
...WHAT SORT OF PERSON MIO IS...
I...
...WANT TO ACT THAT MIO...
...AND I CAN'T STAY STILL...
Yes.
I WANT TO START ACTING AS THE NEW MIO HONGO RIGHT NOW...
restless
amped
clip clop
Oooh...
BUT BEAR WITH IT...
KATSUKI AND MIZUKI AREN'T AROUND!
I'd look insane if people saw me acting alone and enjoying it...
HEY GIRL.
Hold it, hold it.
exhale
FIRST I'LL PREPARE FOR THE NEW MIO...

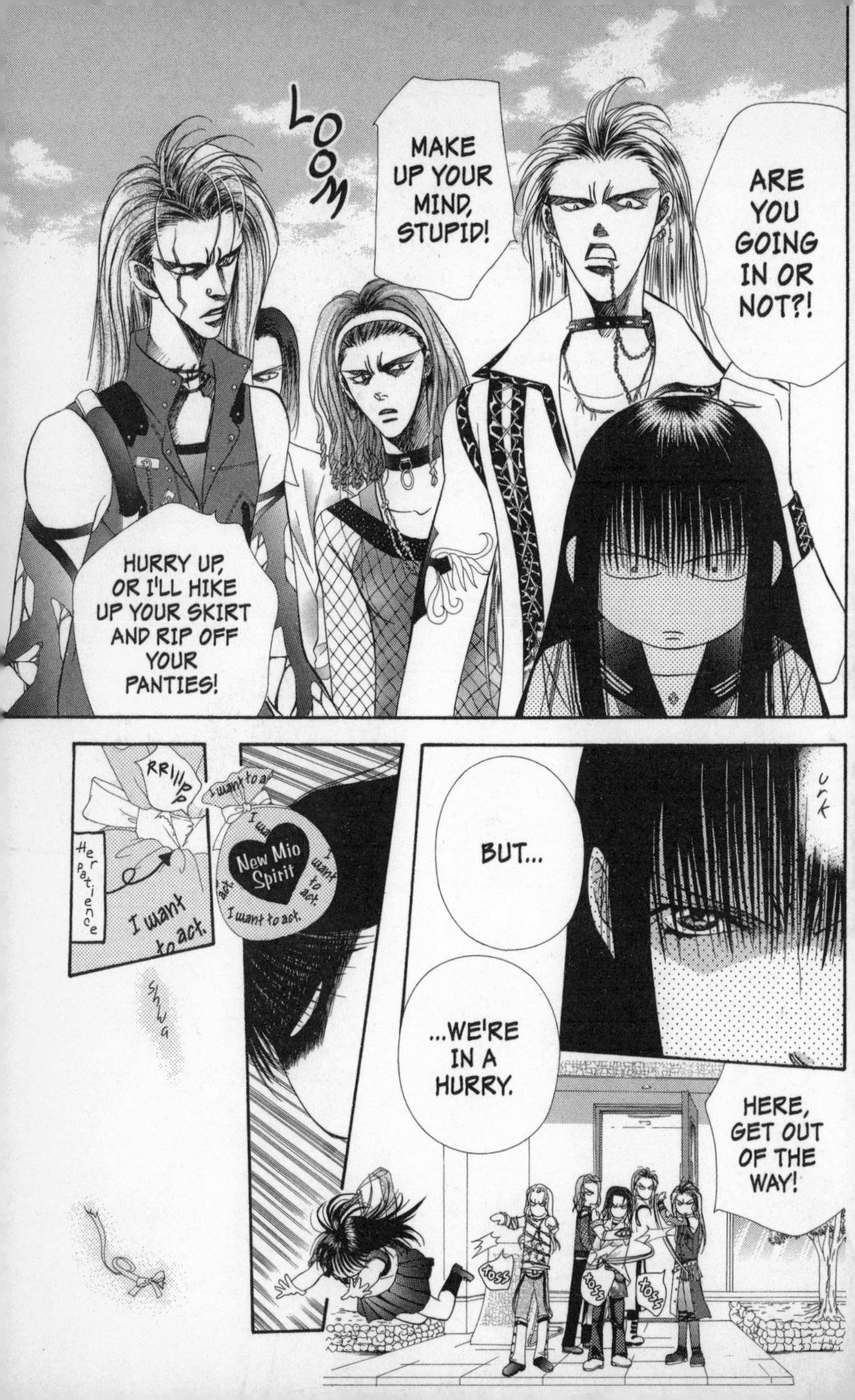
ARE YOU GOING IN OR NOT?!
MAKE UP YOUR MIND, STUPID!
LOOM
HURRY UP, OR I'LL HIKE UP YOUR SKIRT AND RIP OFF YOUR PANTIES!
URK
BUT...
...WE'RE IN A HURRY.
HERE, GET OUT OF THE WAY!
TOSS
TOSS
TOSS
RRIIPP
I want to act.
New Mio Spirit
I want to act.
Her patience
I want to act.
SHWA

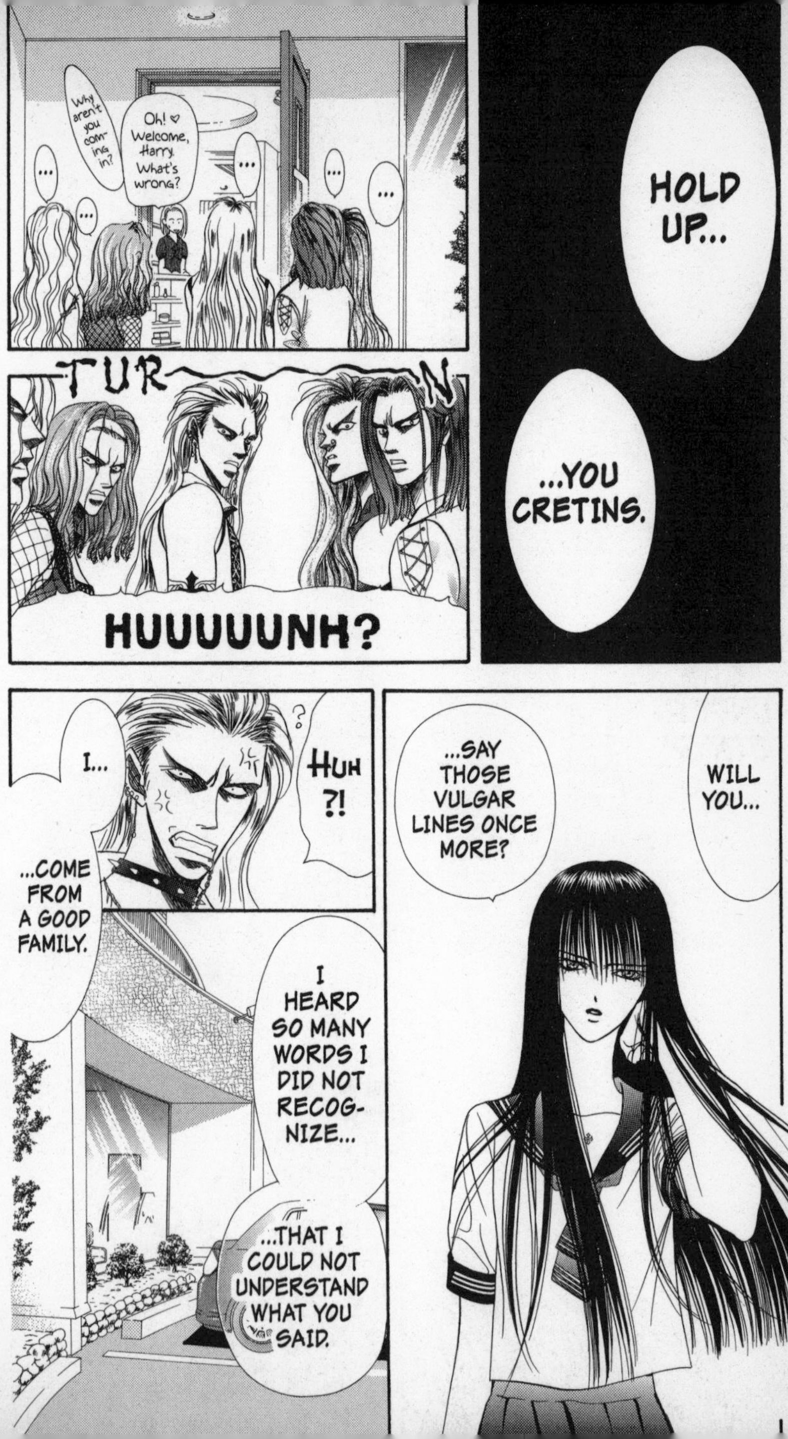
HOLD UP...
...YOU CRETINS.
...
...
...
Oh! ♡ Welcome, Harry. What's wrong?
Why aren't you coming in?
...
...
TUR—N
HUUUUUNH?
WILL YOU...
...SAY THOSE VULGAR LINES ONCE MORE?
?
Huh ?!
I...
...COME FROM A GOOD FAMILY.
I HEARD SO MANY WORDS I DID NOT RECOGNIZE...
...THAT I COULD NOT UNDERSTAND WHAT YOU SAID.

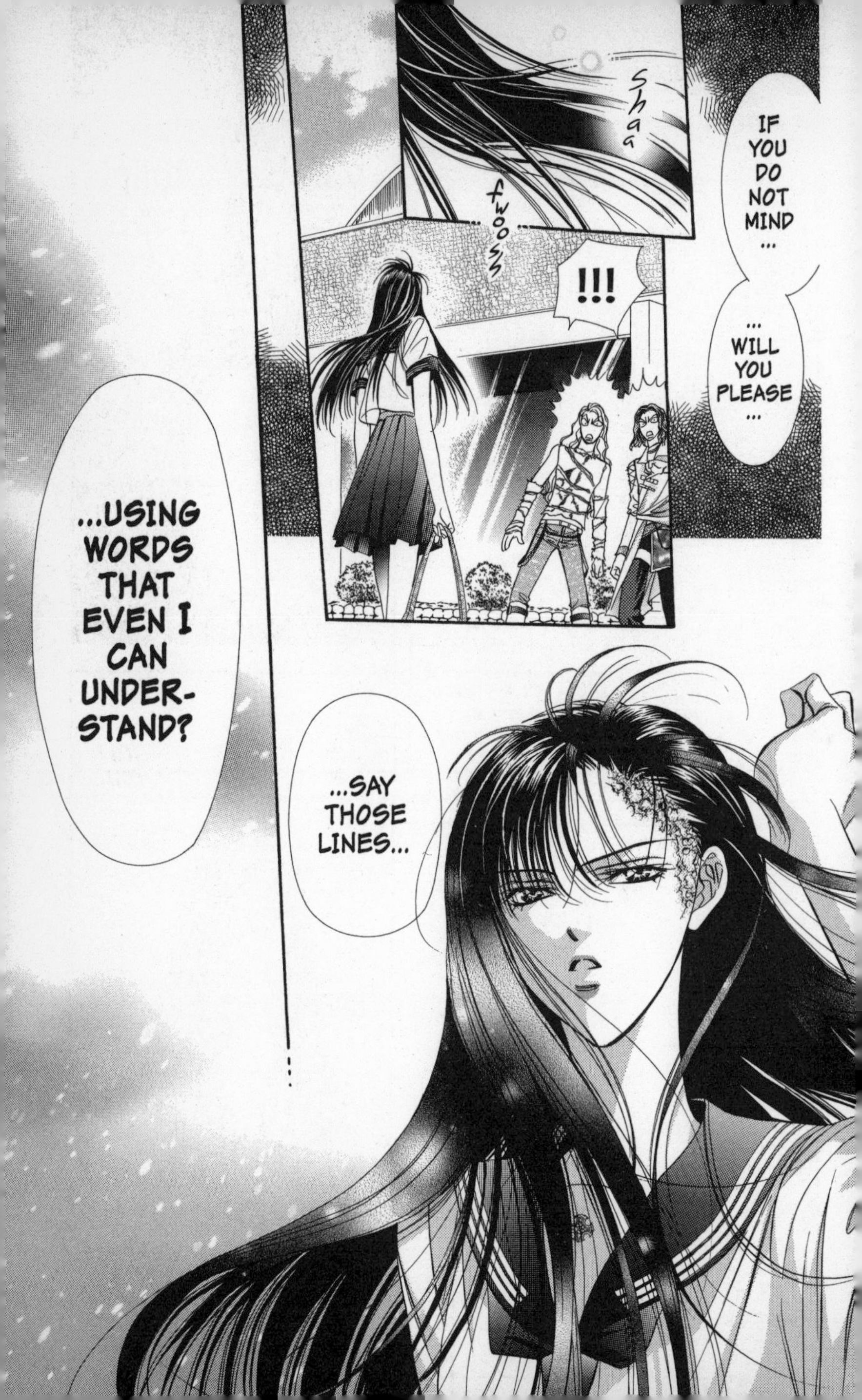
shaa
fwoosh
IF YOU DO NOT MIND...
...WILL YOU PLEASE...
!!!
...SAY THOSE LINES...
...USING WORDS THAT EVEN I CAN UNDERSTAND?

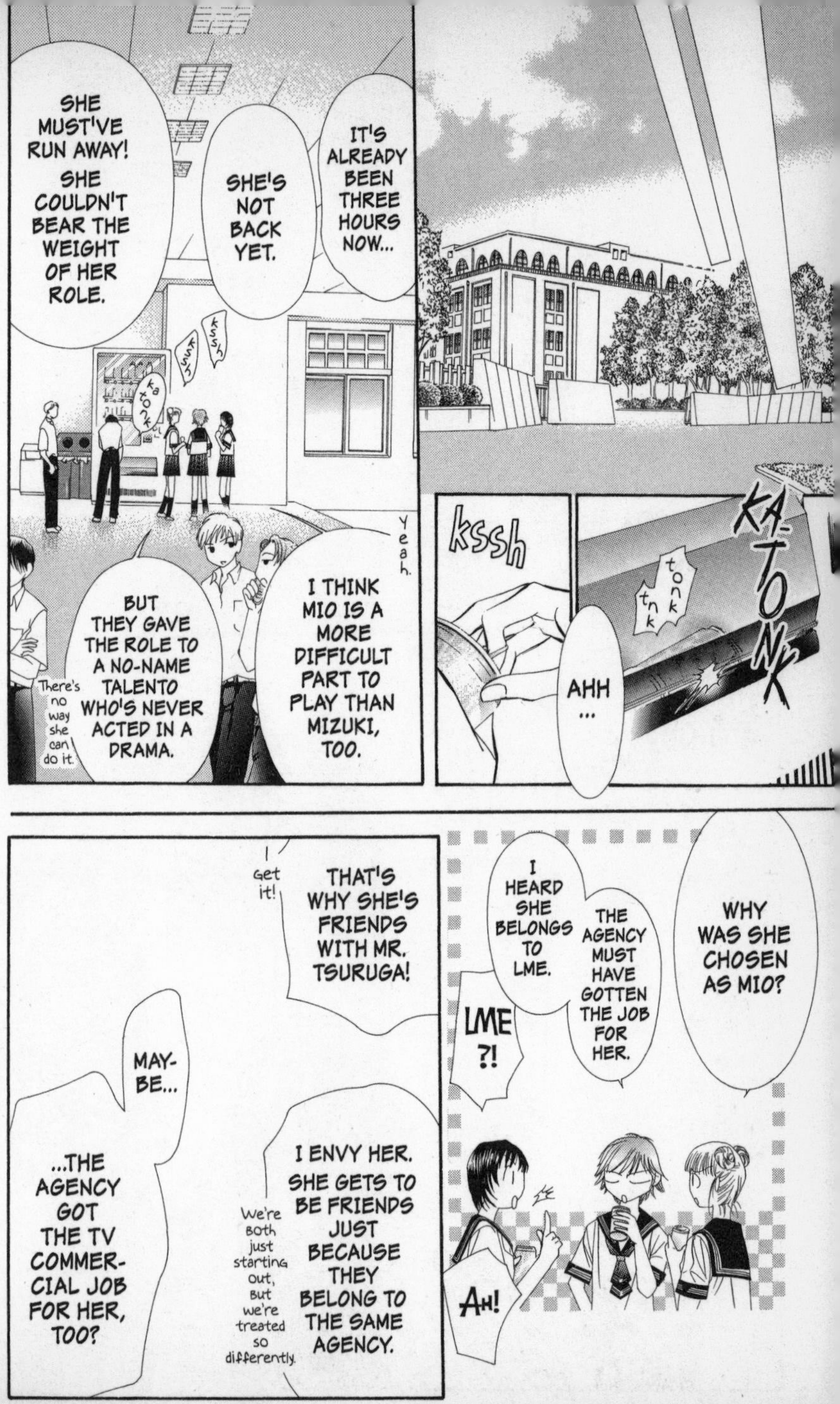
KA-TONK
tonk
tnk
kssh
AHH...
IT'S ALREADY BEEN THREE HOURS NOW...
SHE'S NOT BACK YET.
SHE MUST'VE RUN AWAY! SHE COULDN'T BEAR THE WEIGHT OF HER ROLE.
kssh
kssh
ka tonk
I THINK MIO IS A MORE DIFFICULT PART TO PLAY THAN MIZUKI, TOO.
Yeah.
BUT THEY GAVE THE ROLE TO A NO-NAME TALENTO WHO'S NEVER ACTED IN A DRAMA.
There's no way she can do it.
WHY WAS SHE CHOSEN AS MIO?
I HEARD SHE BELONGS TO LME.
THE AGENCY MUST HAVE GOTTEN THE JOB FOR HER.
LME?!
AH!
THAT'S WHY SHE'S FRIENDS WITH MR. TSURUGA!
I get it!
I ENVY HER. SHE GETS TO BE FRIENDS JUST BECAUSE THEY BELONG TO THE SAME AGENCY.
We're both just starting out, but we're treated so differently.
MAY-BE...
...THE AGENCY GOT THE TV COMMERCIAL JOB FOR HER, TOO?

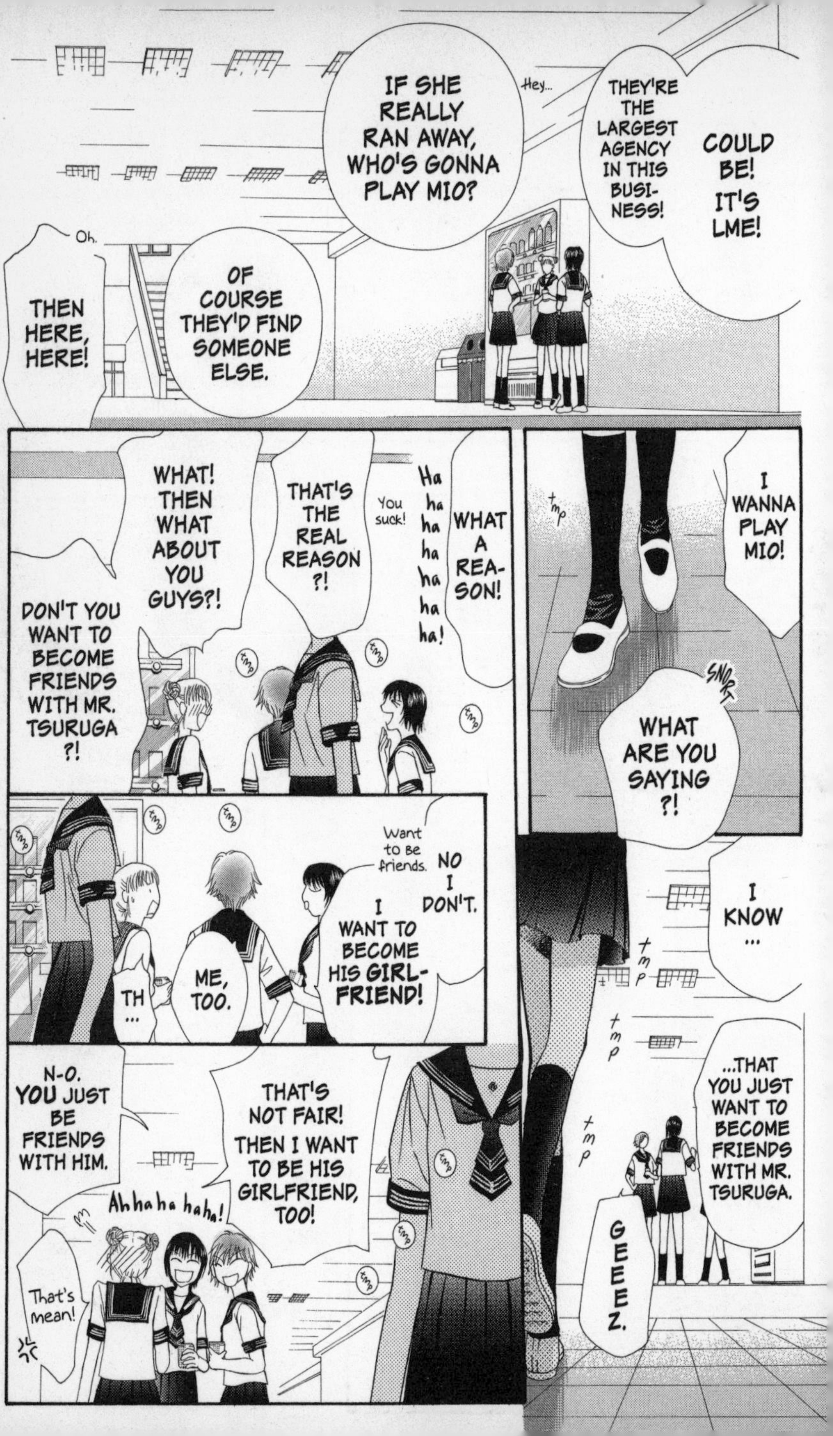
COULD BE! IT'S LME!
THEY'RE THE LARGEST AGENCY IN THIS BUSINESS!
Hey...
IF SHE REALLY RAN AWAY, WHO'S GONNA PLAY MIO?
OF COURSE THEY'D FIND SOMEONE ELSE.
Oh.
THEN HERE, HERE!
I WANNA PLAY MIO!
SNORT
WHAT ARE YOU SAYING?!
DON'T YOU WANT TO BECOME FRIENDS WITH MR. TSURUGA?!
WHAT A REASON!
Ha ha ha ha ha ha ha ha!
You suck!
THAT'S THE REAL REASON?!
WHAT! THEN WHAT ABOUT YOU GUYS?!
NO I DON'T.
Want to be friends.
I WANT TO BECOME HIS GIRLFRIEND!
ME, TOO.
TH...
THAT'S NOT FAIR! THEN I WANT TO BE HIS GIRLFRIEND, TOO!
N-O. YOU JUST BE FRIENDS WITH HIM.
Ahhahahaha!
That's mean!
I KNOW...
...THAT YOU JUST WANT TO BECOME FRIENDS WITH MR. TSURUGA.
GEEEZ.

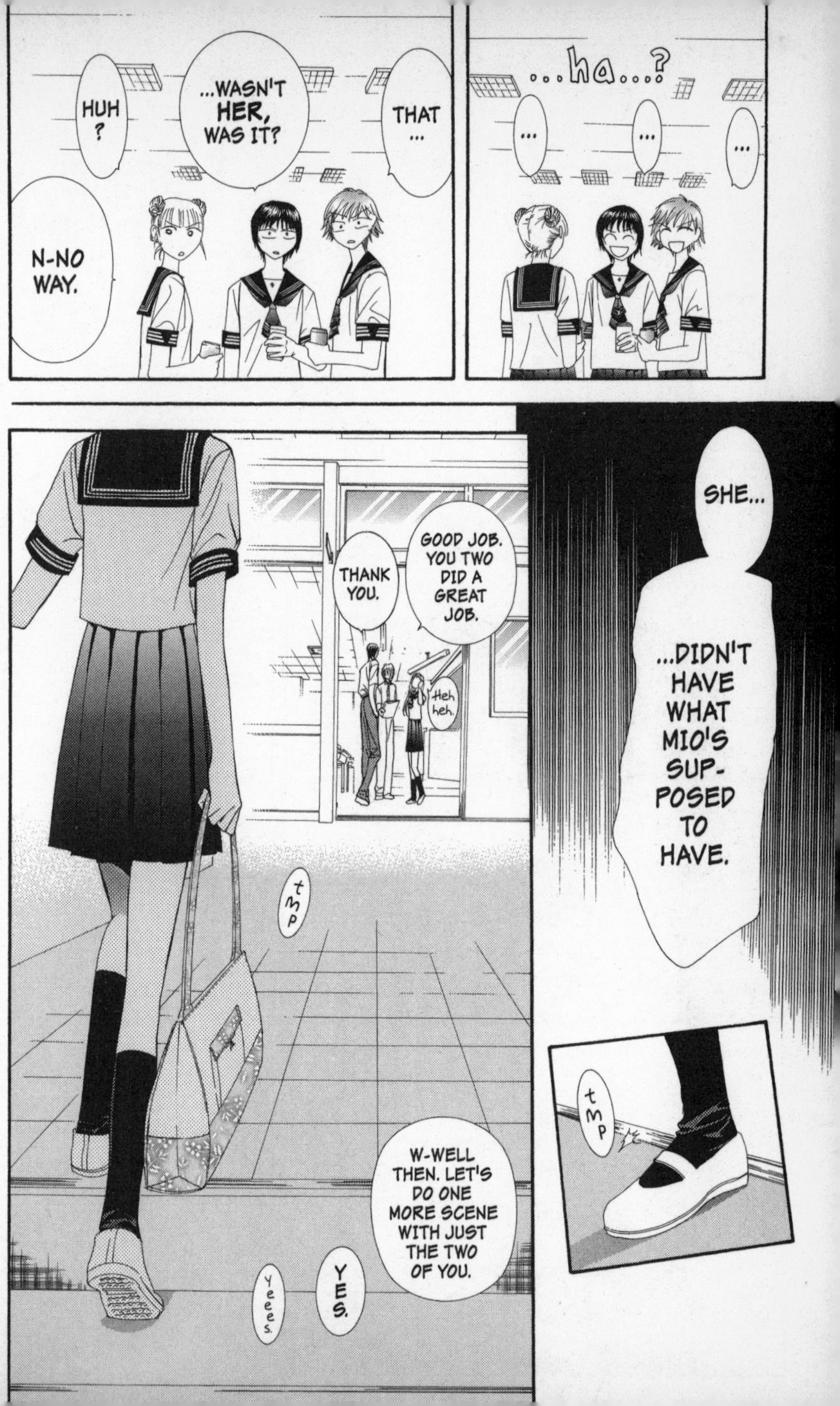
...ha...?
...
...
...
THAT ...
...WASN'T HER, WAS IT?
HUH ?
N-NO WAY.
SHE...
...DIDN'T HAVE WHAT MIO'S SUP-POSED TO HAVE.
tmp
GOOD JOB. YOU TWO DID A GREAT JOB.
THANK YOU.
Heh heh.
tmp
W-WELL THEN. LET'S DO ONE MORE SCENE WITH JUST THE TWO OF YOU.
YES.
Yeees.

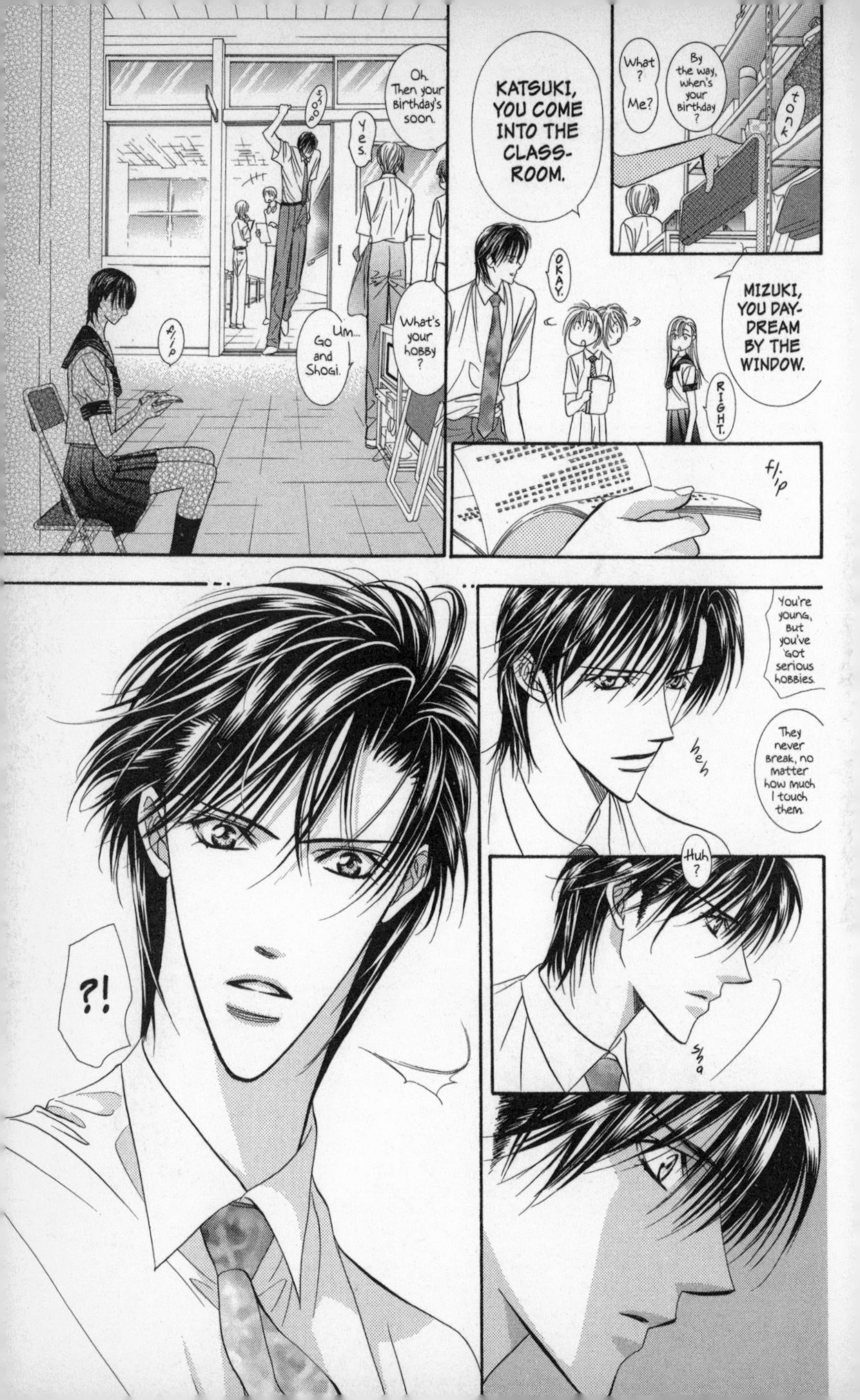
tonk
By the way, when's your birthday?
What? Me?
KATSUKI, YOU COME INTO THE CLASS-ROOM.
OKAY.
MIZUKI, YOU DAY-DREAM BY THE WINDOW.
RIGHT.
flip
Oh. Then your Birthday's soon.
swoop
Yes.
What's your hobby?
Um... Go and Shogi.
flip
You're young, but you've got serious hobbies.
heh
They never break, no matter how much I touch them.
Huh?
sha
?!

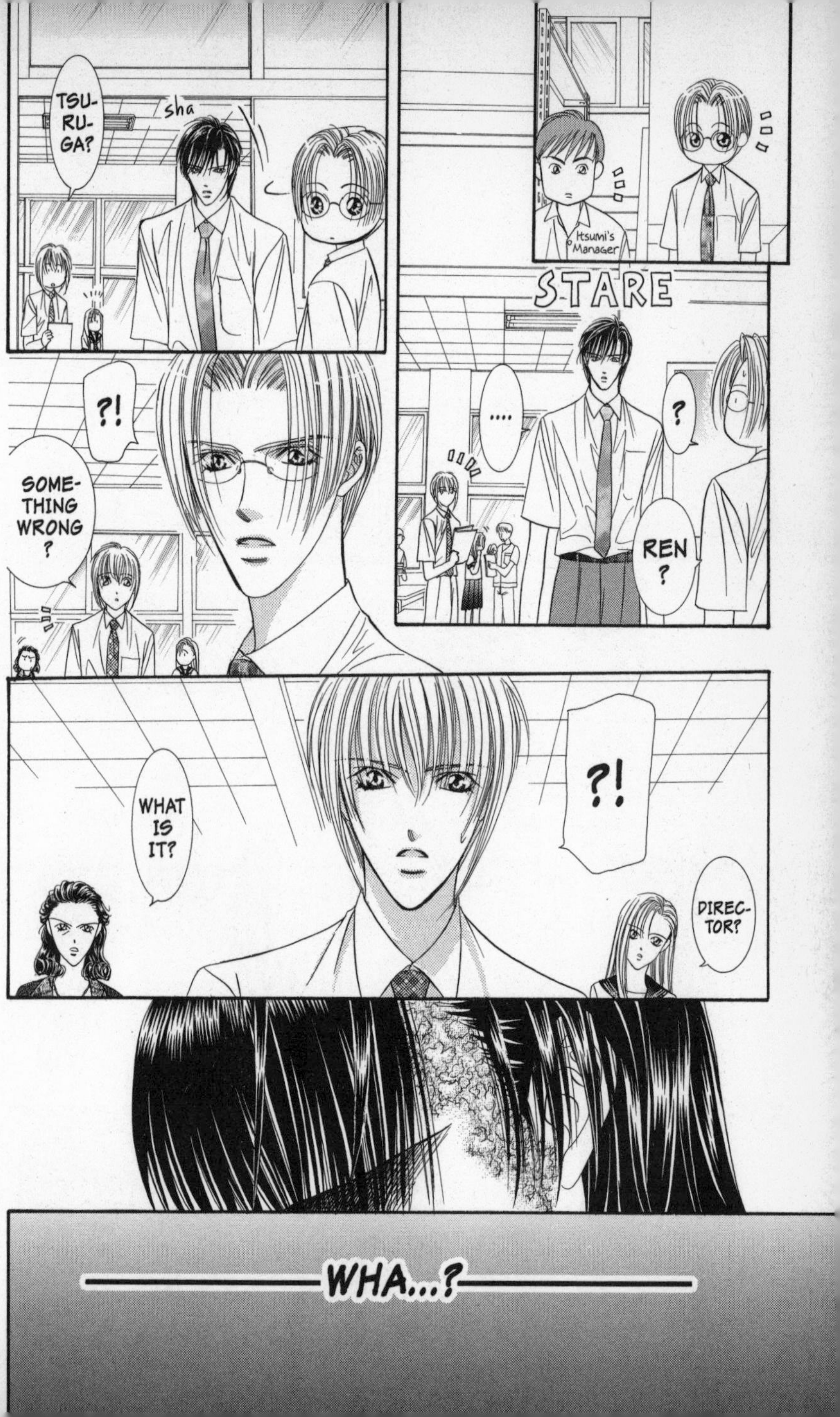
Itsumi's Manager
TSU-RU-GA?
sha
STARE
?
REN ?
....
?!
SOMETHING WRONG ?
?!
DIRECTOR?
WHAT IS IT?
WHA...?

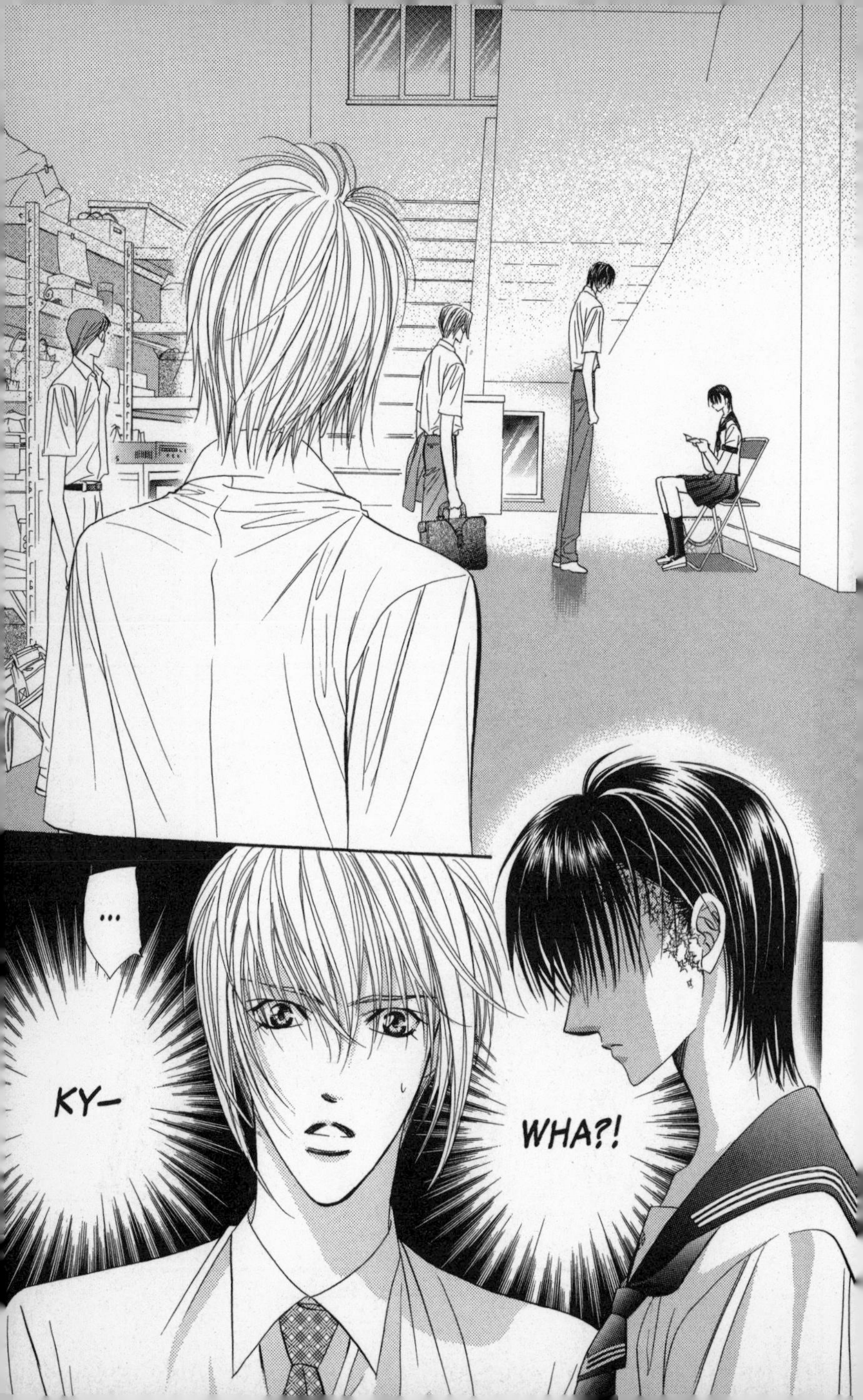
WHA?!
...
KY-

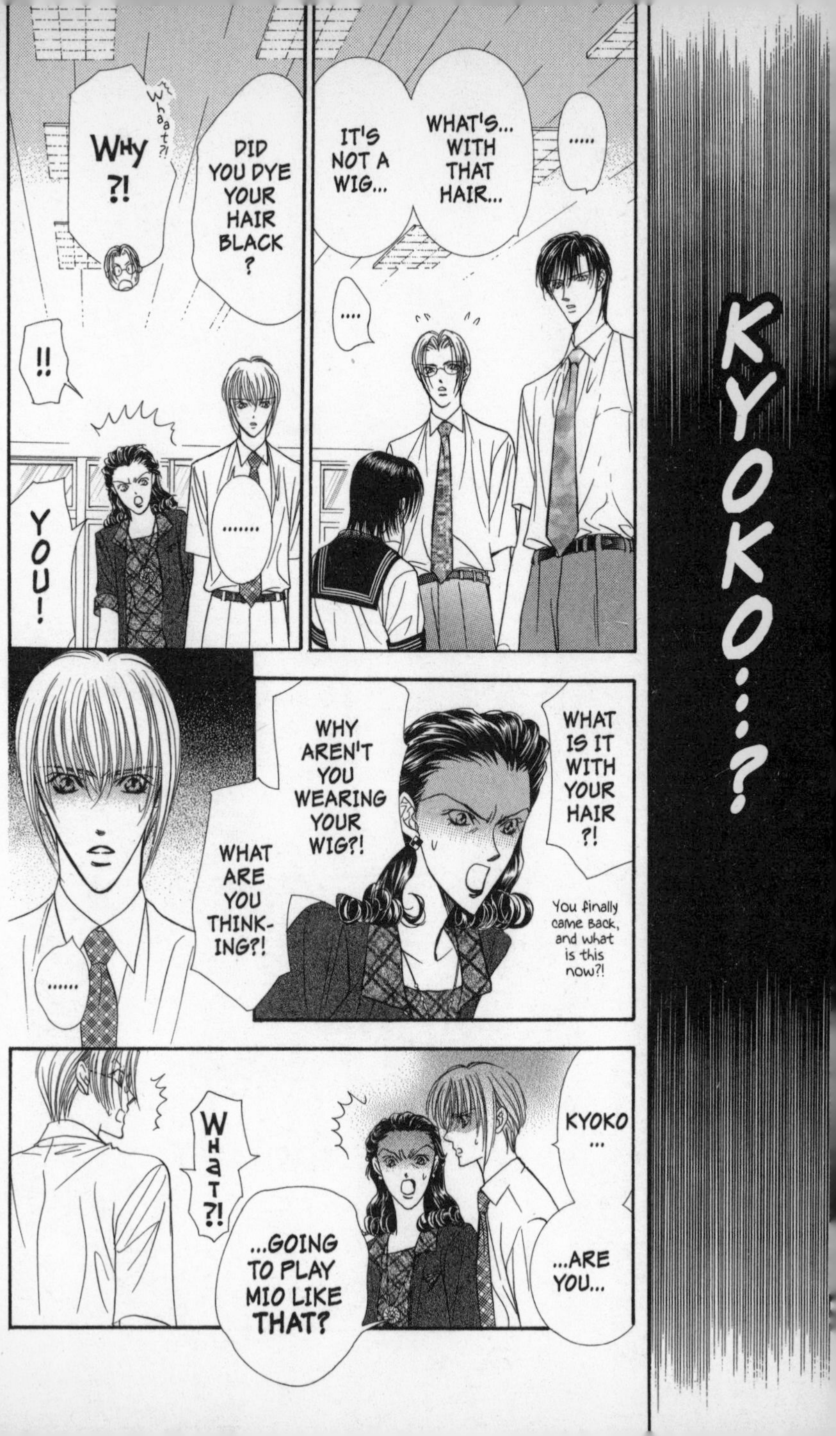
KYOKO...?
.....
WHAT'S... WITH THAT HAIR...
IT'S NOT A WIG...
....
DID YOU DYE YOUR HAIR BLACK?
WHY?!
Whaat?!
!!
YOU!
....
WHAT IS IT WITH YOUR HAIR?!
You finally came back, and what is this now?!
WHY AREN'T YOU WEARING YOUR WIG?!
WHAT ARE YOU THINKING?!
......
KYOKO...
...ARE YOU...
...GOING TO PLAY MIO LIKE THAT?
WHAT?!

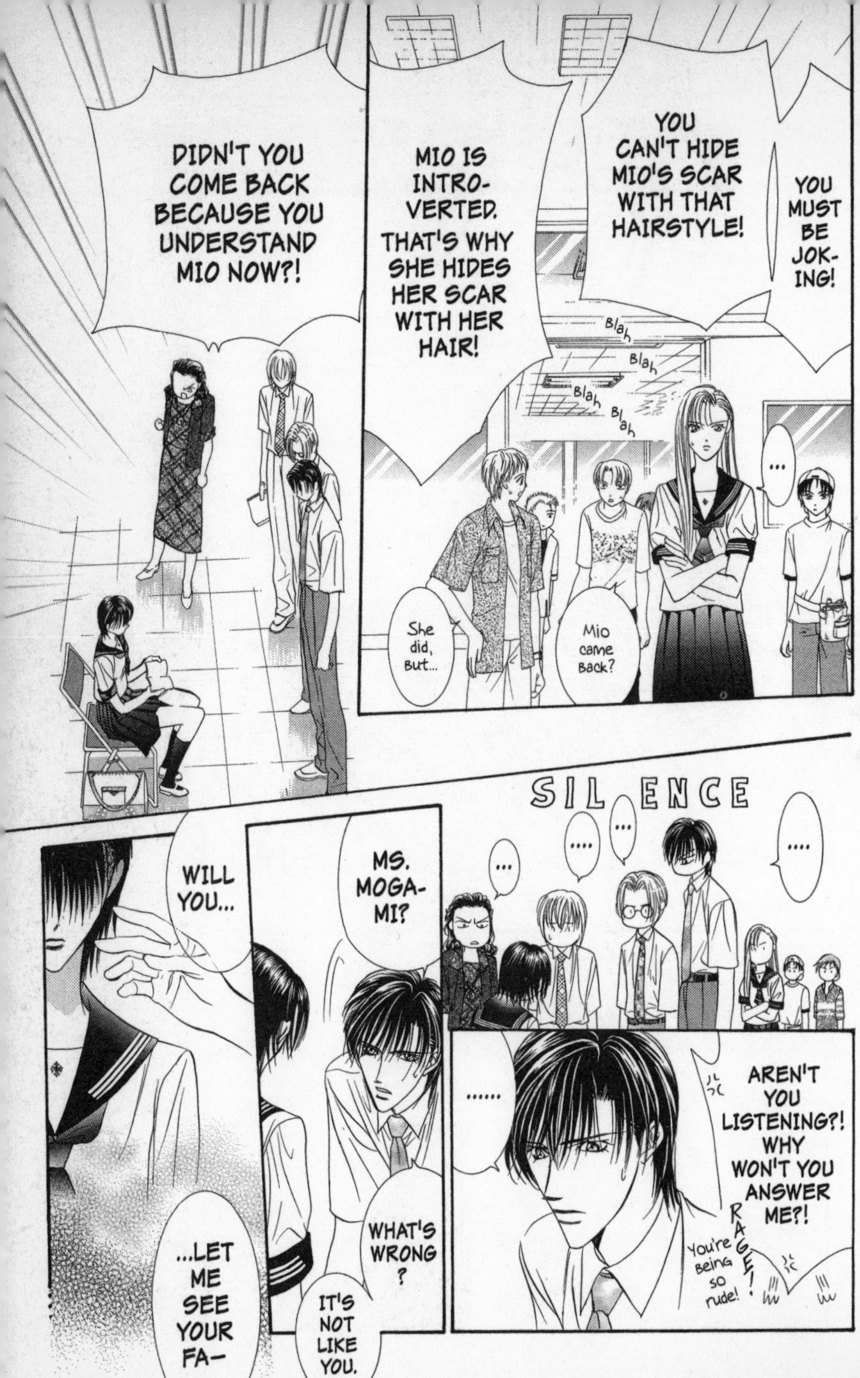
YOU MUST BE JOK-ING!
YOU CAN'T HIDE MIO'S SCAR WITH THAT HAIRSTYLE!
MIO IS INTRO-VERTED. THAT'S WHY SHE HIDES HER SCAR WITH HER HAIR!
Blah Blah Blah Blah
...
Mio came back?
She did, but...
DIDN'T YOU COME BACK BECAUSE YOU UNDERSTAND MIO NOW?!
SIL ENCE
....
....
...
...
ARE'NT YOU LISTENING?! WHY WON'T YOU ANSWER ME?!
......
RAGE!
You're being so rude!
MS. MOGA-MI?
WHAT'S WRONG?
IT'S NOT LIKE YOU.
WILL YOU...
...LET ME SEE YOUR FA-

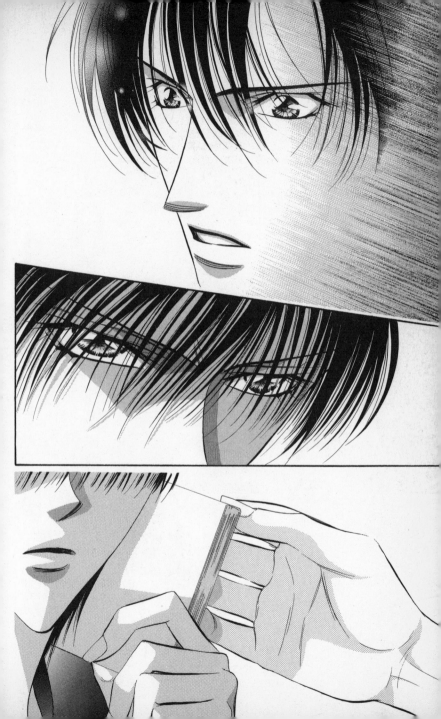

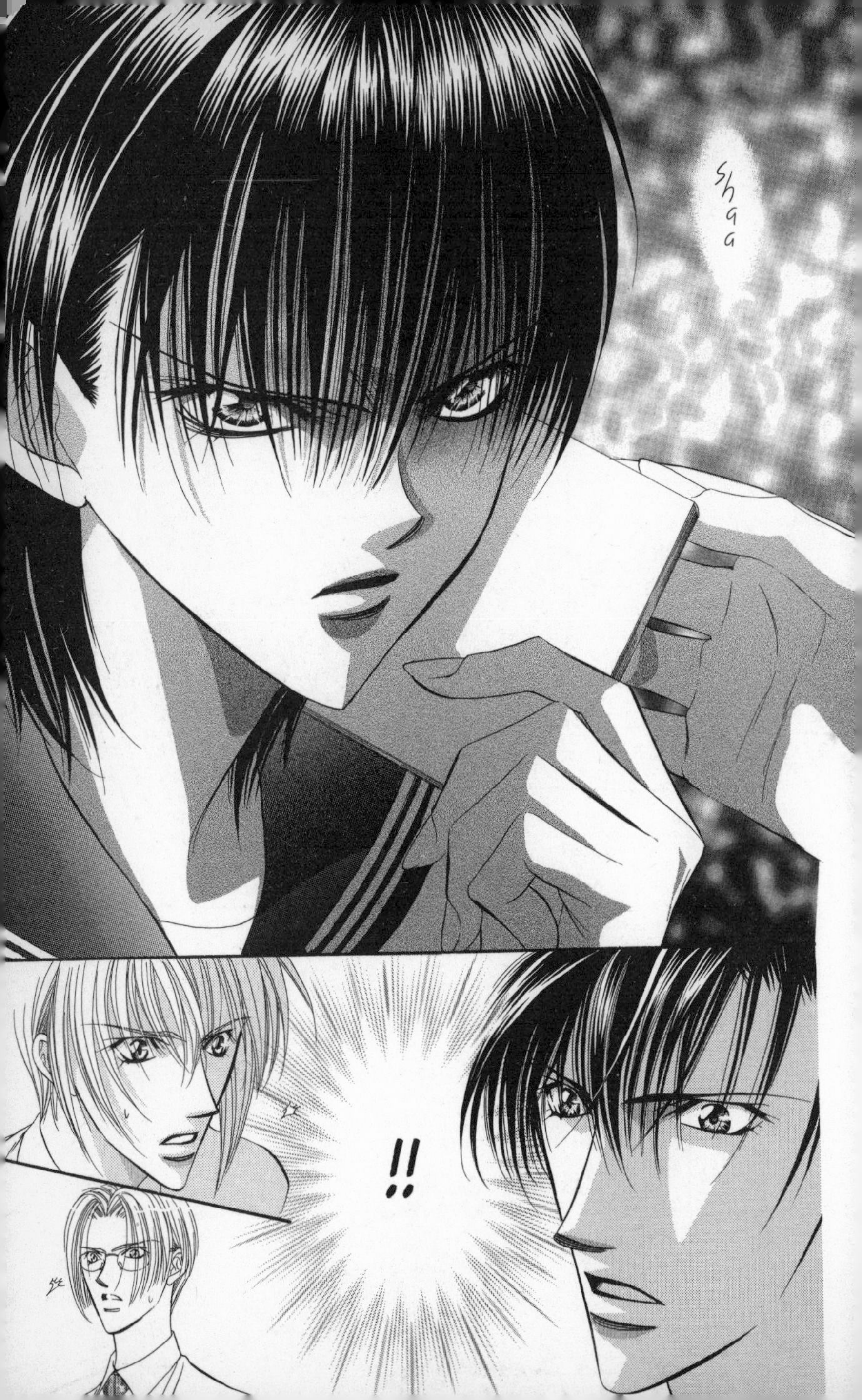
Shaa
!!

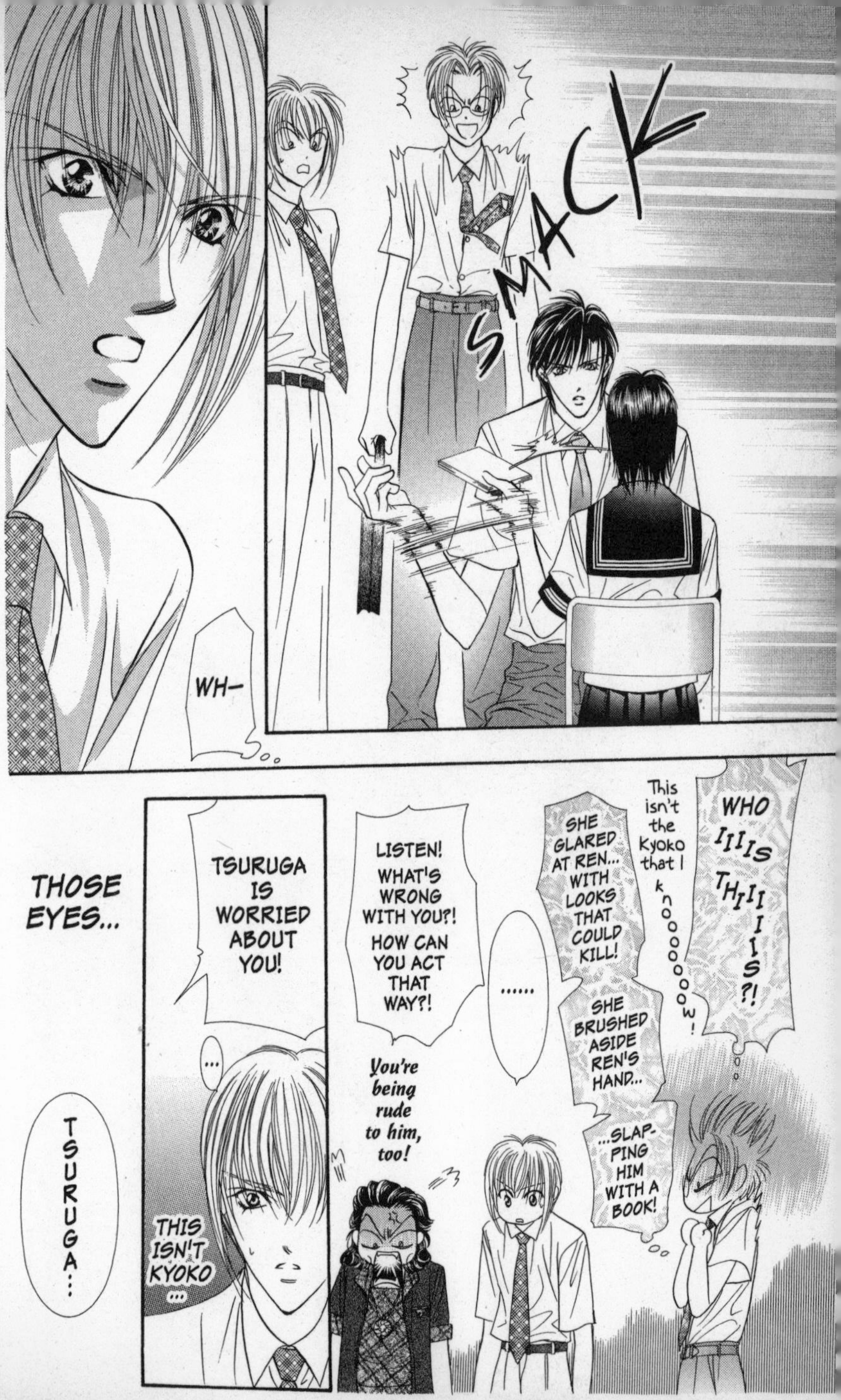
SMACK
WH-
WHO IIIIS THIIIIIS?!
This isn't the Kyoko that I knoooooow!
SHE GLARED AT REN... WITH LOOKS THAT COULD KILL!
SHE BRUSHED ASIDE REN'S HAND...
...SLAPPING HIM WITH A BOOK!
......
LISTEN! WHAT'S WRONG WITH YOU?! HOW CAN YOU ACT THAT WAY?!
You're being rude to him, too!
TSURUGA IS WORRIED ABOUT YOU!
...
THIS ISN'T KYOKO...
THOSE EYES...
TSURUGA...

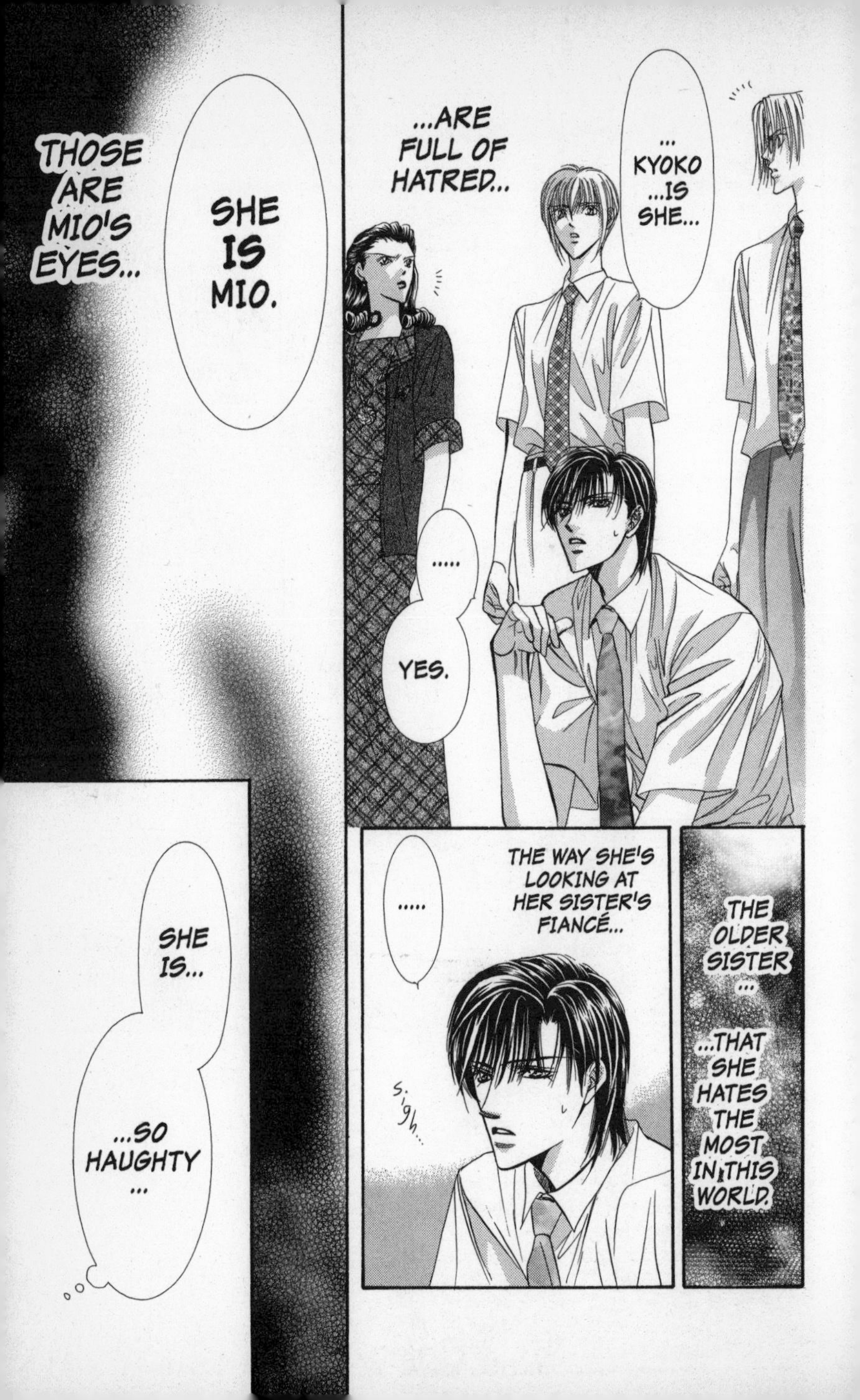
...
KYOKO
...IS
SHE...
...ARE
FULL OF
HATRED...
.....
YES.
THE
OLDER
SISTER
...
...THAT
SHE
HATES
THE
MOST
IN THIS
WORLD.
THE WAY SHE'S
LOOKING AT
HER SISTER'S
FIANCÉ...
.....
sigh...
SHE
IS
MIO.
THOSE
ARE
MIO'S
EYES...
SHE
IS...
...SO
HAUGHTY
...

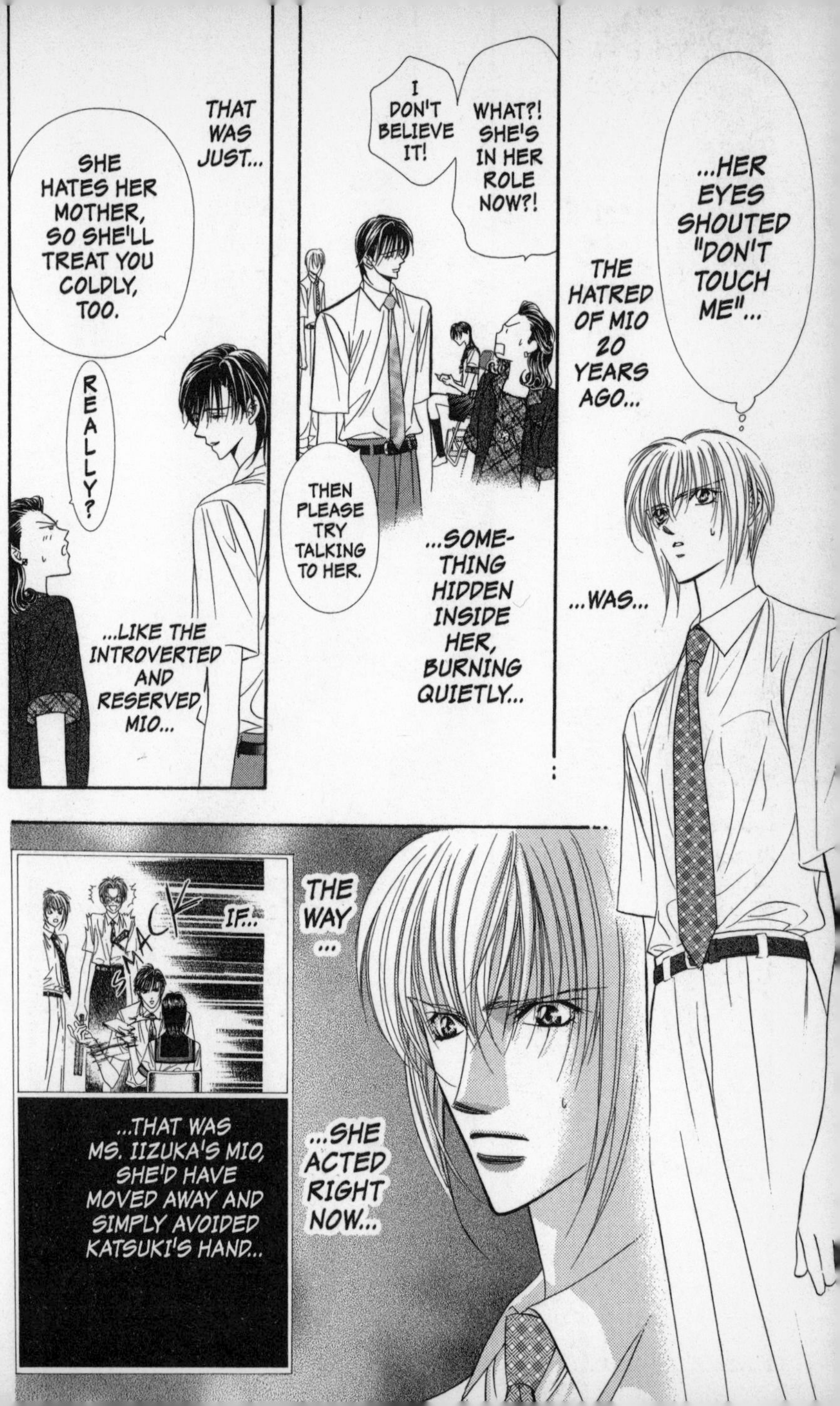
...HER EYES SHOUTED "DON'T TOUCH ME"...
THE HATRED OF MIO 20 YEARS AGO...
...WAS...
WHAT?! SHE'S IN HER ROLE NOW?!
I DON'T BELIEVE IT!
THEN PLEASE TRY TALKING TO HER.
...SOME-THING HIDDEN INSIDE HER, BURNING QUIETLY...
THAT WAS JUST...
SHE HATES HER MOTHER, SO SHE'LL TREAT YOU COLDLY, TOO.
REALLY?
...LIKE THE INTROVERTED AND RESERVED MIO...
THE WAY ...
...SHE ACTED RIGHT NOW...
IF...
SMACK
...THAT WAS MS. IIZUKA'S MIO, SHE'D HAVE MOVED AWAY AND SIMPLY AVOIDED KATSUKI'S HAND...

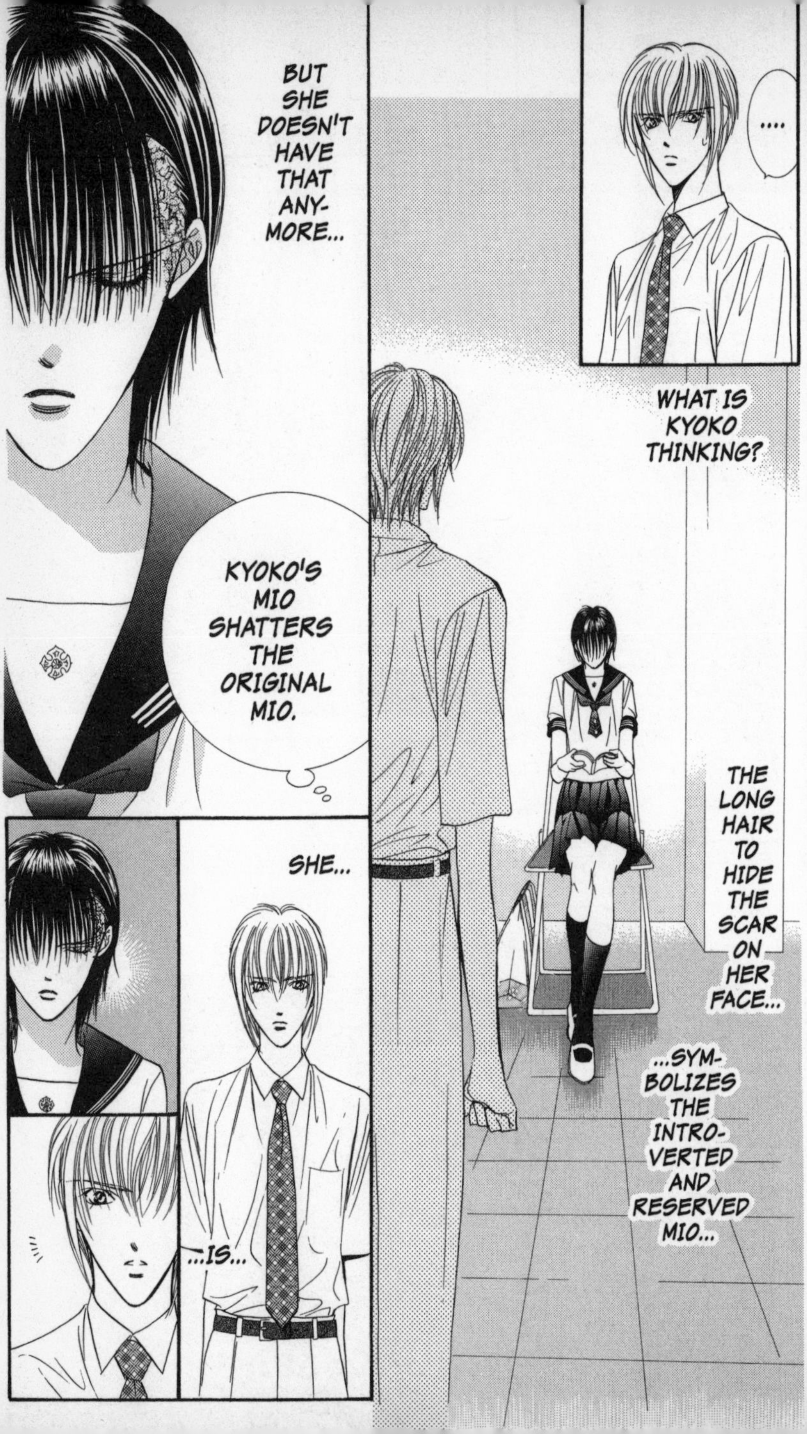
....
WHAT IS KYOKO THINKING?
THE LONG HAIR TO HIDE THE SCAR ON HER FACE...
...SYMBOLIZES THE INTROVERTED AND RESERVED MIO...
BUT SHE DOESN'T HAVE THAT ANYMORE...
KYOKO'S MIO SHATTERS THE ORIGINAL MIO.
SHE...
...IS...

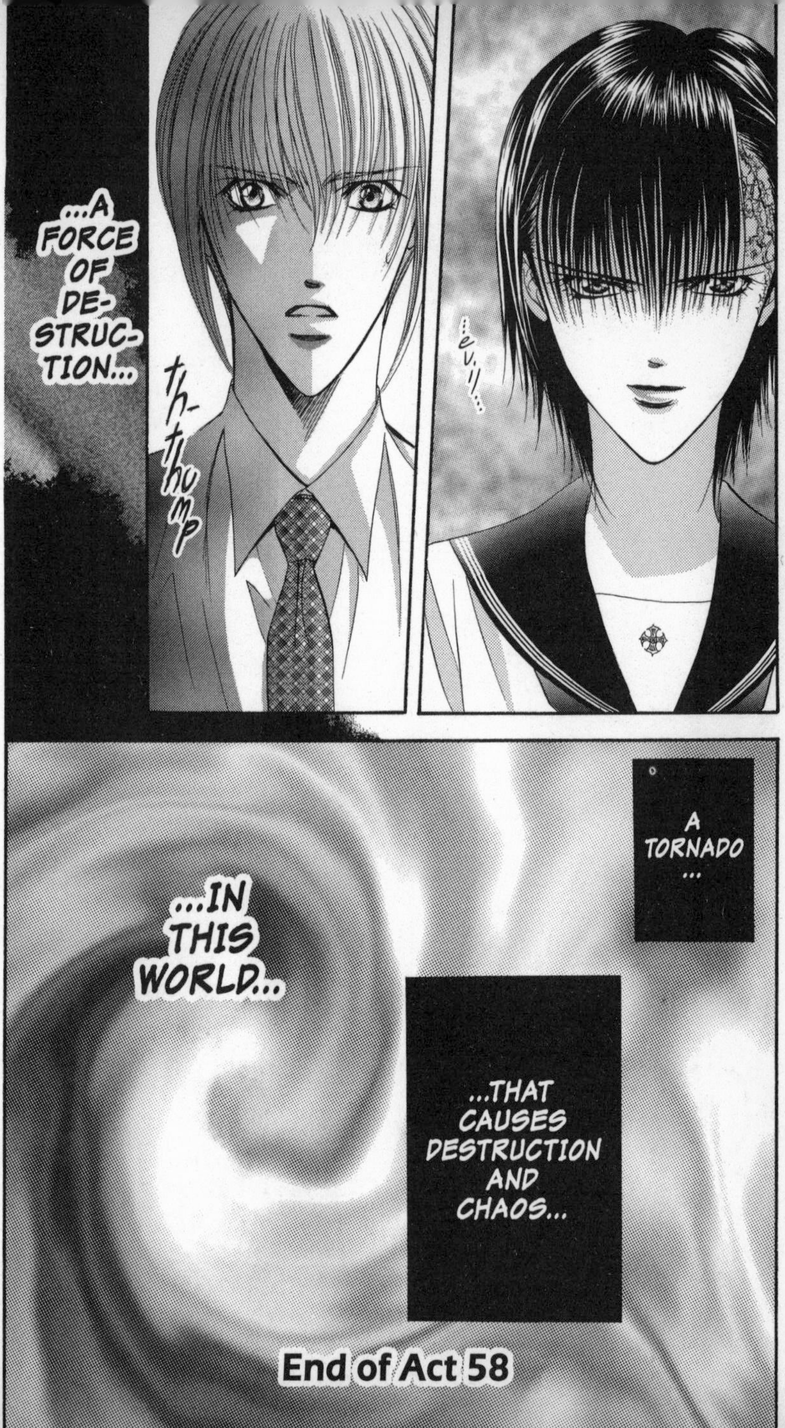
...evil...
th-thump
...A FORCE OF DESTRUCTION...
A TORNADO ...
...IN THIS WORLD...
...THAT CAUSES DESTRUCTION AND CHAOS...
End of Act 58

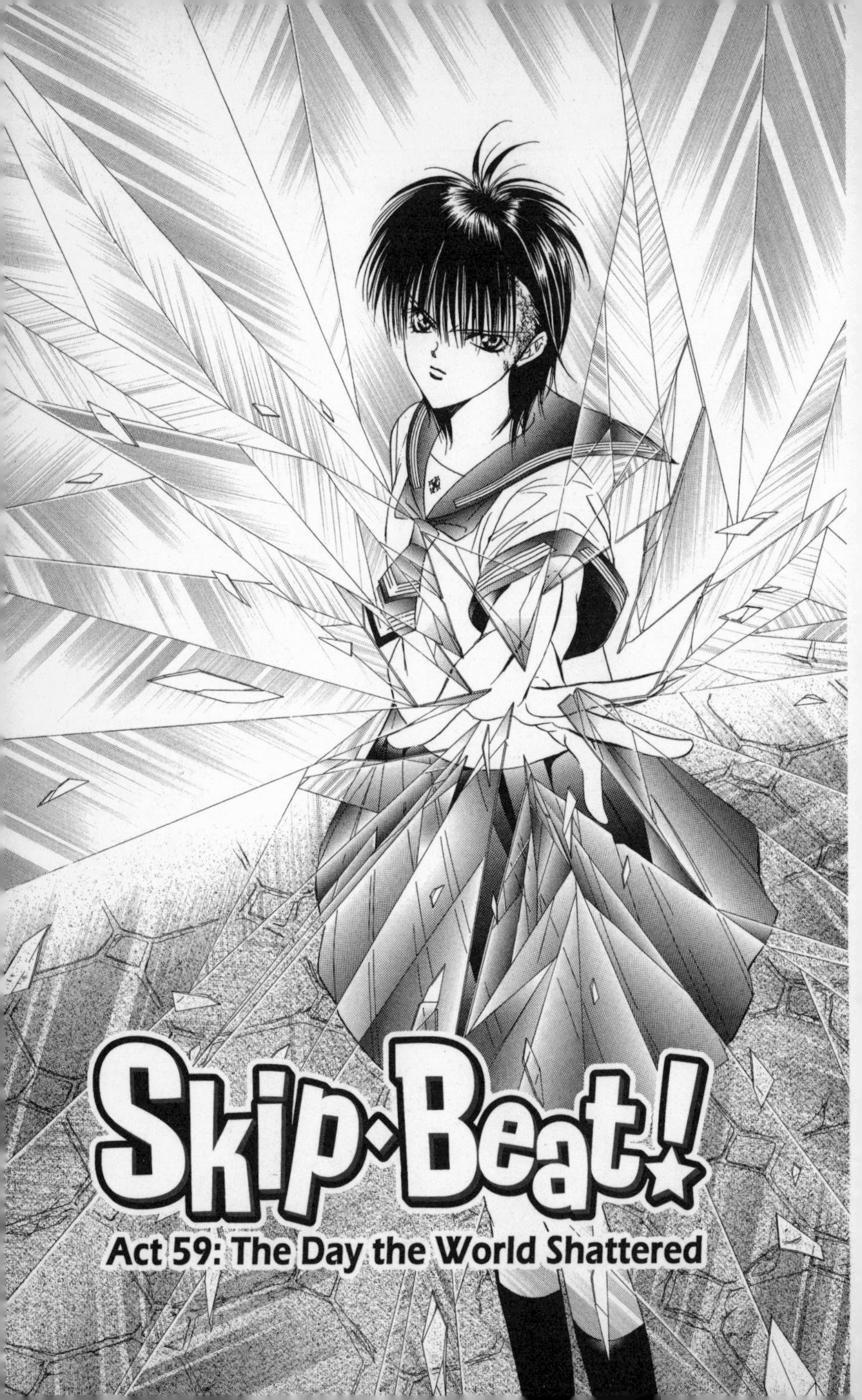
Skip·Beat!
Act 59: The Day the World Shattered

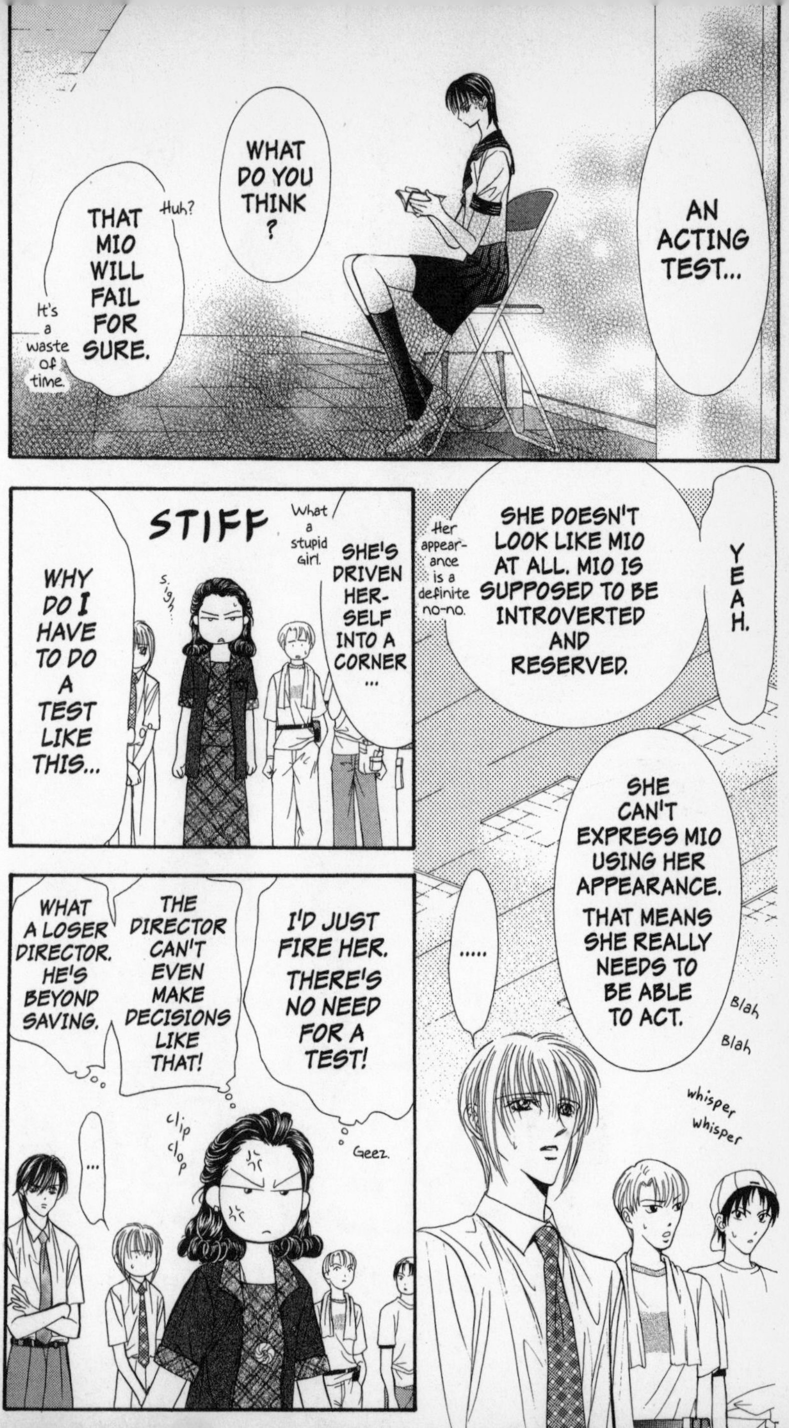
AN ACTING TEST...
WHAT DO YOU THINK?
Huh?
THAT MIO WILL FAIL FOR SURE.
It's a waste of time.
YEAH.
SHE DOESN'T LOOK LIKE MIO AT ALL. MIO IS SUPPOSED TO BE INTROVERTED AND RESERVED.
Her appearance is a definite no-no.
SHE CAN'T EXPRESS MIO USING HER APPEARANCE. THAT MEANS SHE REALLY NEEDS TO BE ABLE TO ACT.
.....
Blah Blah
whisper whisper
What a stupid Girl.
SHE'S DRIVEN HERSELF INTO A CORNER...
STIFF
sigh...
WHY DO I HAVE TO DO A TEST LIKE THIS...
I'D JUST FIRE HER. THERE'S NO NEED FOR A TEST!
THE DIRECTOR CAN'T EVEN MAKE DECISIONS LIKE THAT!
WHAT A LOSER DIRECTOR. HE'S BEYOND SAVING.
Geez.
clip clop
...

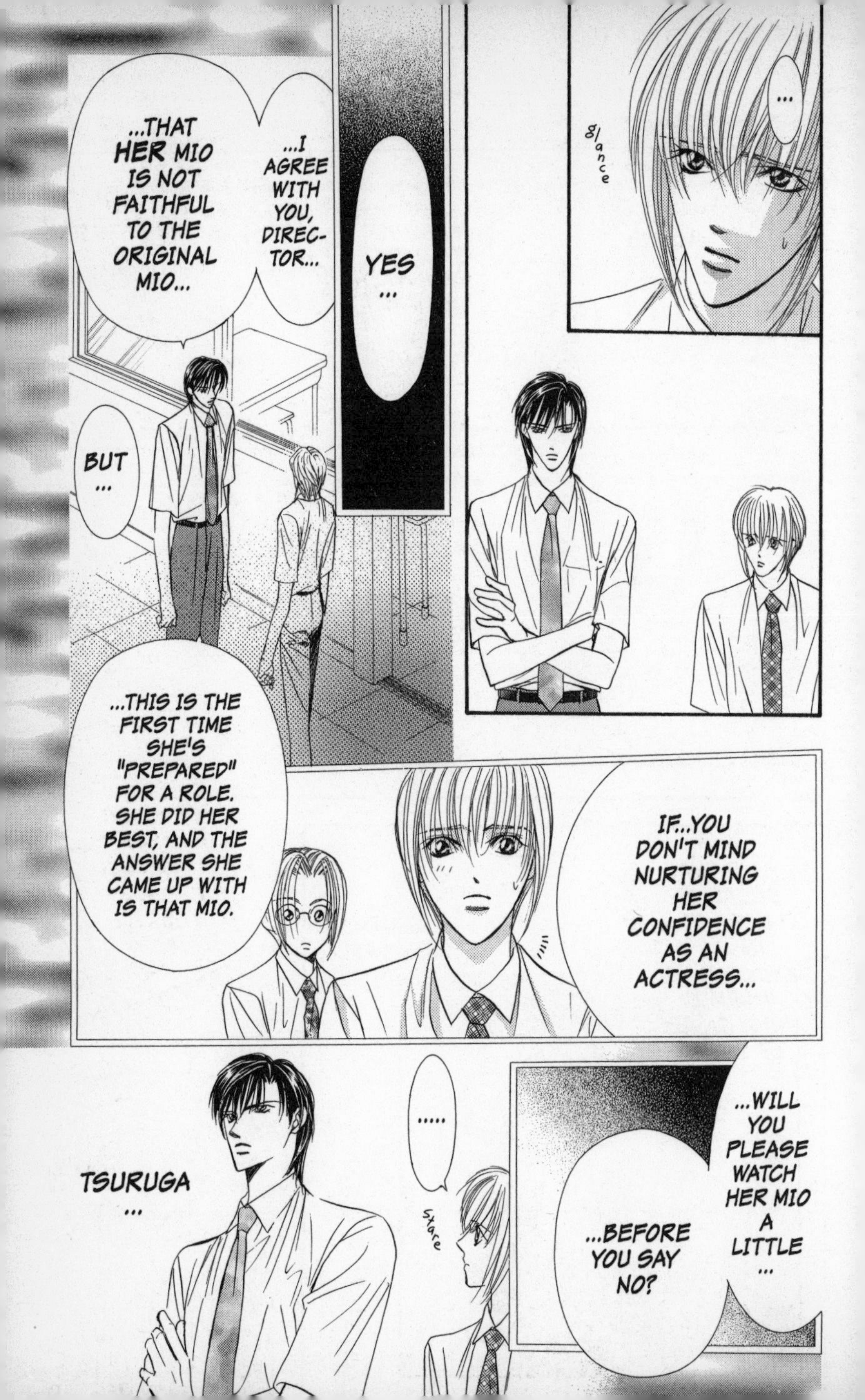
...
glance
YES ...
...I AGREE WITH YOU, DIRECTOR...
...THAT HER MIO IS NOT FAITHFUL TO THE ORIGINAL MIO...
BUT ...
...THIS IS THE FIRST TIME SHE'S "PREPARED" FOR A ROLE. SHE DID HER BEST, AND THE ANSWER SHE CAME UP WITH IS THAT MIO.
IF...YOU DON'T MIND NURTURING HER CONFIDENCE AS AN ACTRESS...
...WILL YOU PLEASE WATCH HER MIO A LITTLE ...
...BEFORE YOU SAY NO?
......
stare
TSURUGA ...

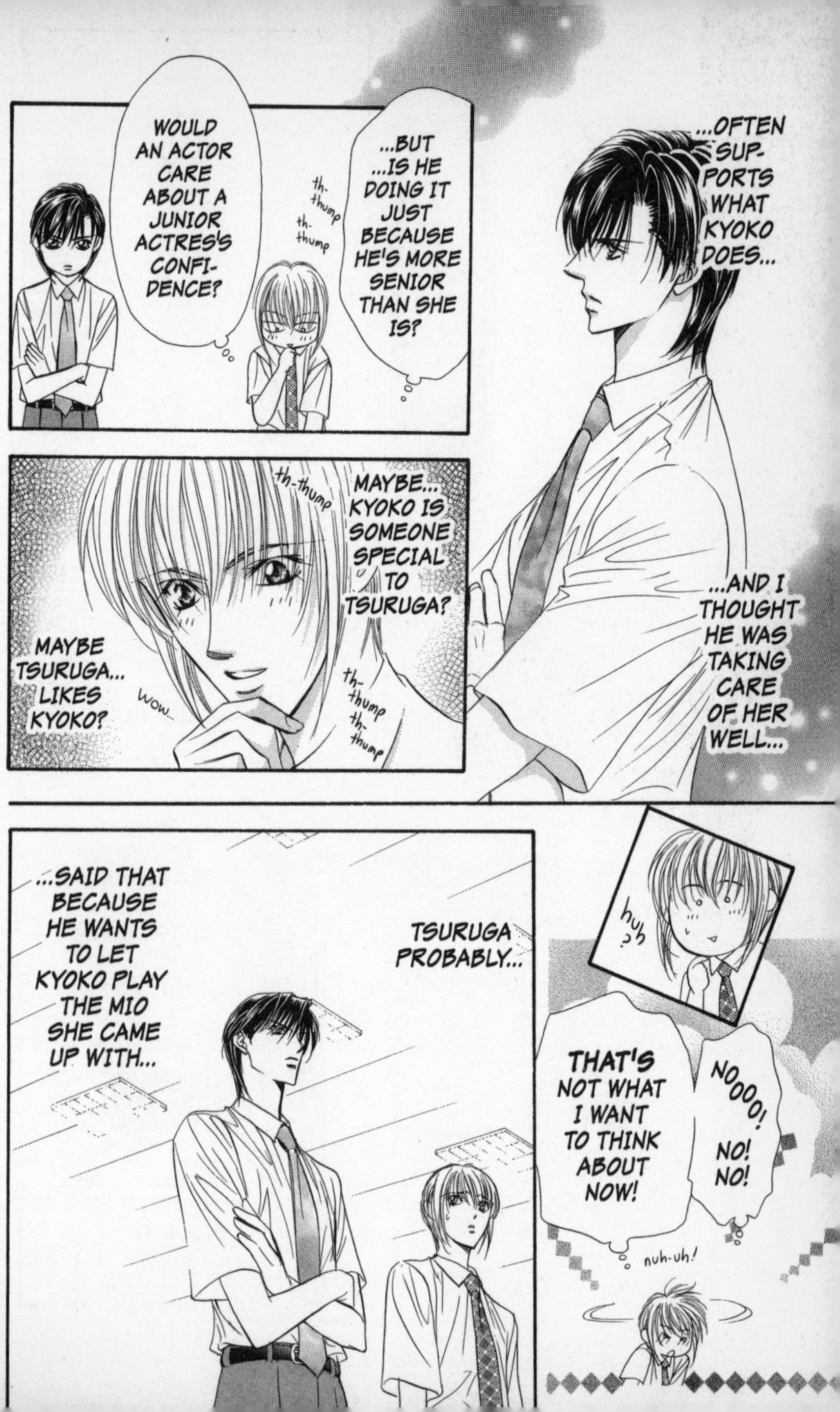
...OFTEN SUP-PORTS WHAT KYOKO DOES...
...AND I THOUGHT HE WAS TAKING CARE OF HER WELL...
...BUT ...IS HE DOING IT JUST BECAUSE HE'S MORE SENIOR THAN SHE IS?
th-thump th-thump
WOULD AN ACTOR CARE ABOUT A JUNIOR ACTRESS'S CONFI-DENCE?
MAYBE... KYOKO IS SOMEONE SPECIAL TO TSURUGA?
th-thump
th-thump th-thump
wow...
MAYBE TSURUGA... LIKES KYOKO?
huh?
NOOOO! NO! NO!
THAT'S NOT WHAT I WANT TO THINK ABOUT NOW!
nuh-uh!
TSURUGA PROBABLY...
...SAID THAT BECAUSE HE WANTS TO LET KYOKO PLAY THE MIO SHE CAME UP WITH...

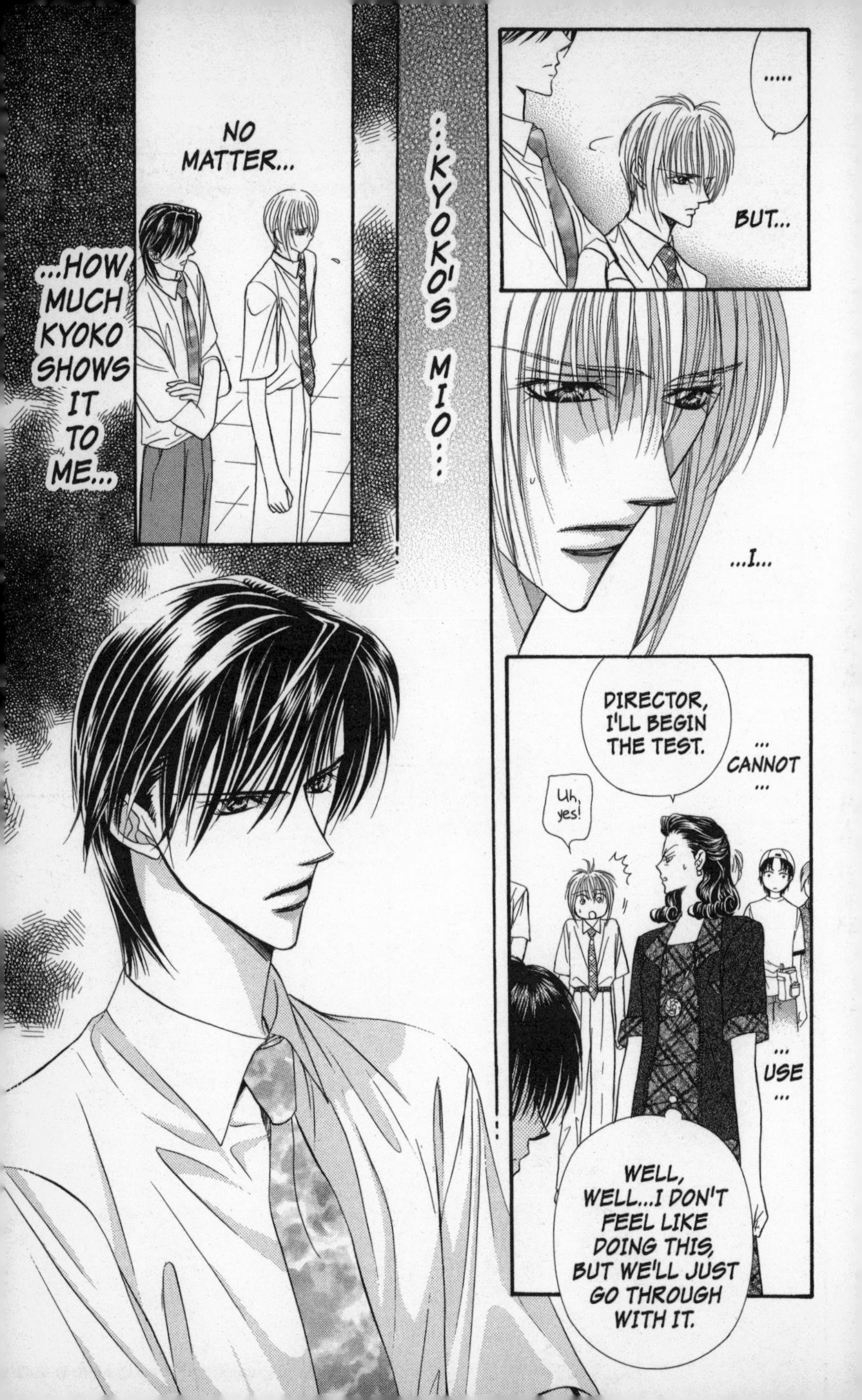
.....
BUT...
...I...
DIRECTOR, I'LL BEGIN THE TEST.
Uh, yes!
...CANNOT...
...USE...
WELL, WELL...I DON'T FEEL LIKE DOING THIS, BUT WE'LL JUST GO THROUGH WITH IT.
NO MATTER...
...HOW MUCH KYOKO SHOWS IT TO ME...
...KYOKO'S MIO...

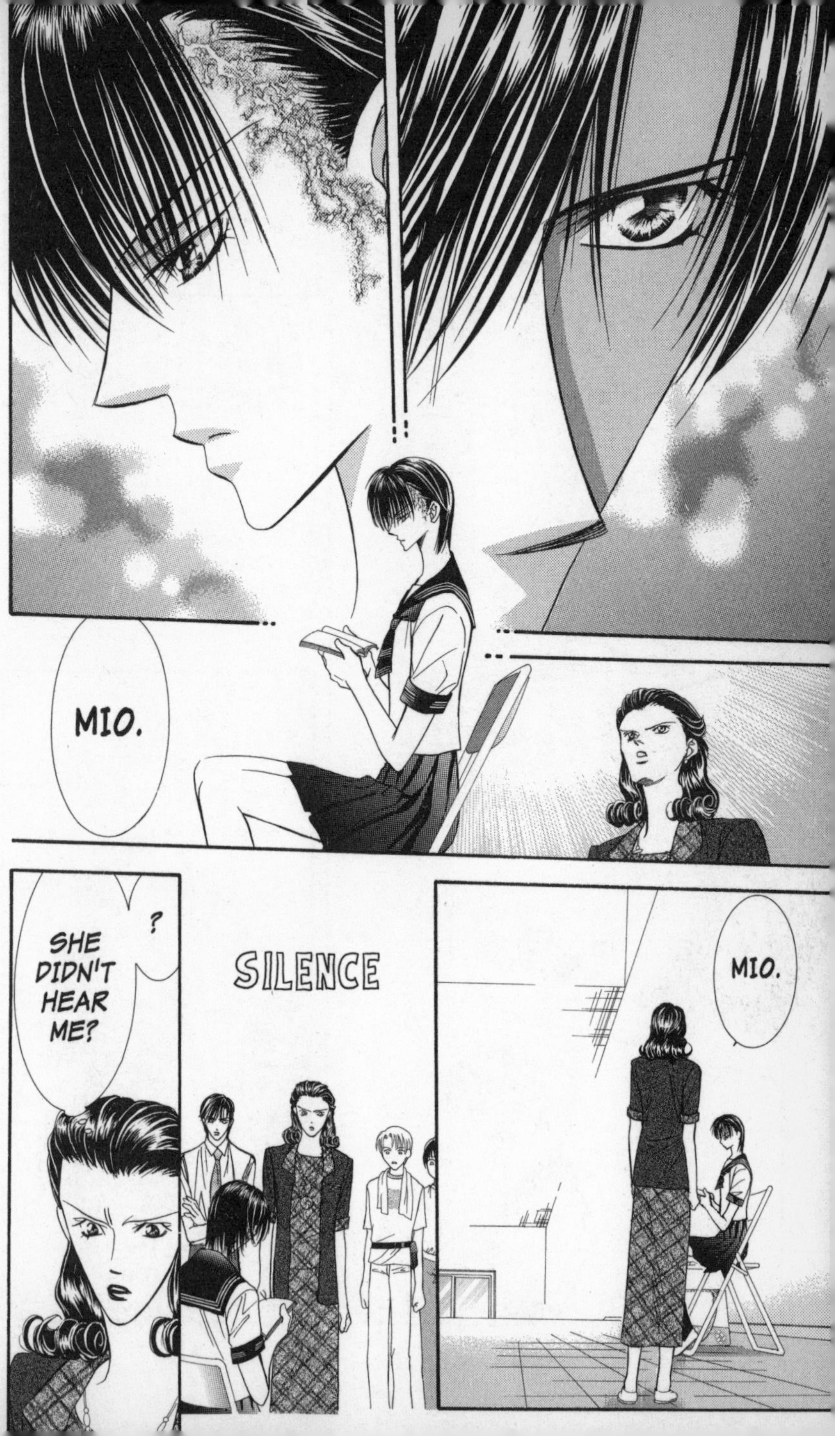
MIO.
MIO.
?
SILENCE
SHE DIDN'T HEAR ME?

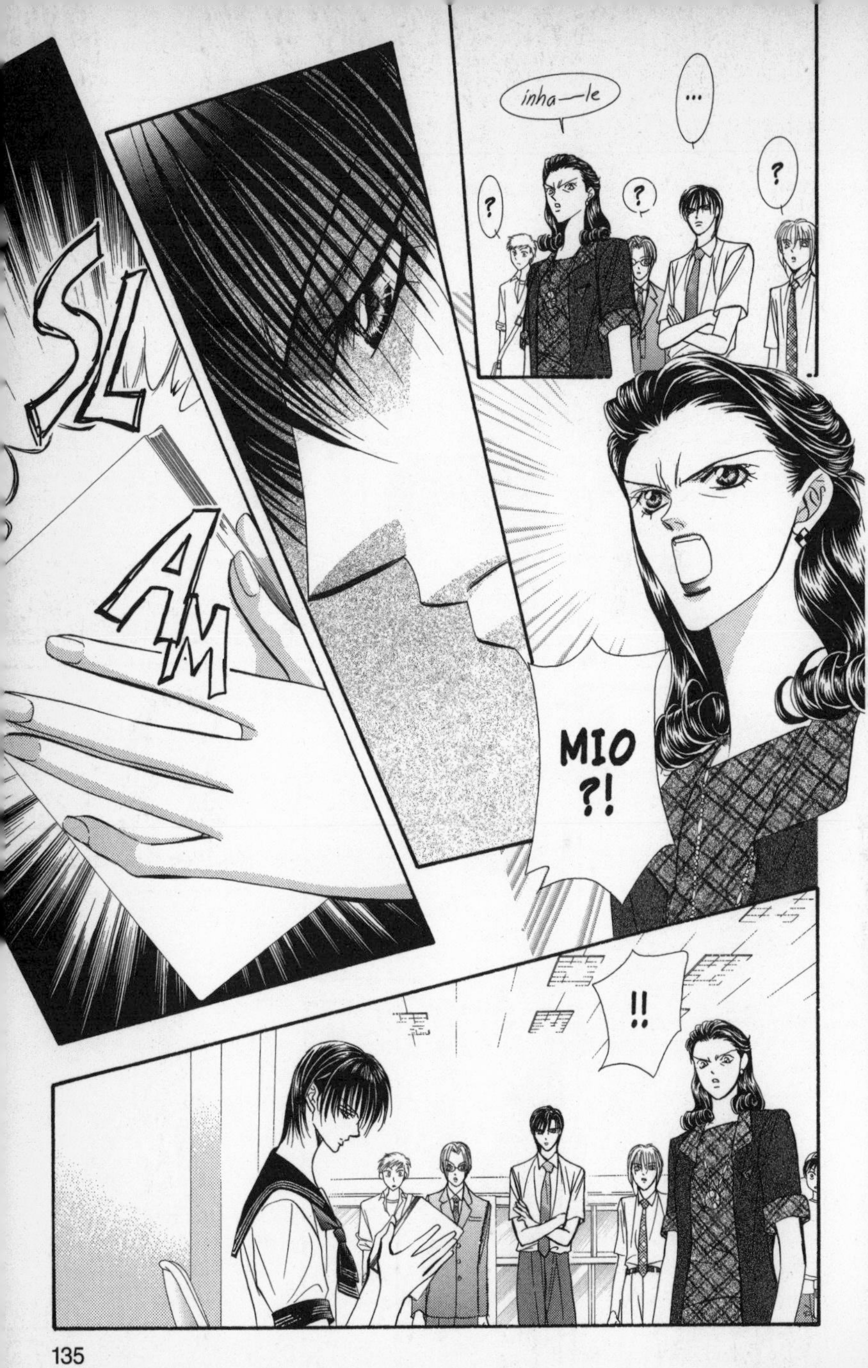

...
inha—le
?
?
?
MIO ?!
SLAM
!!

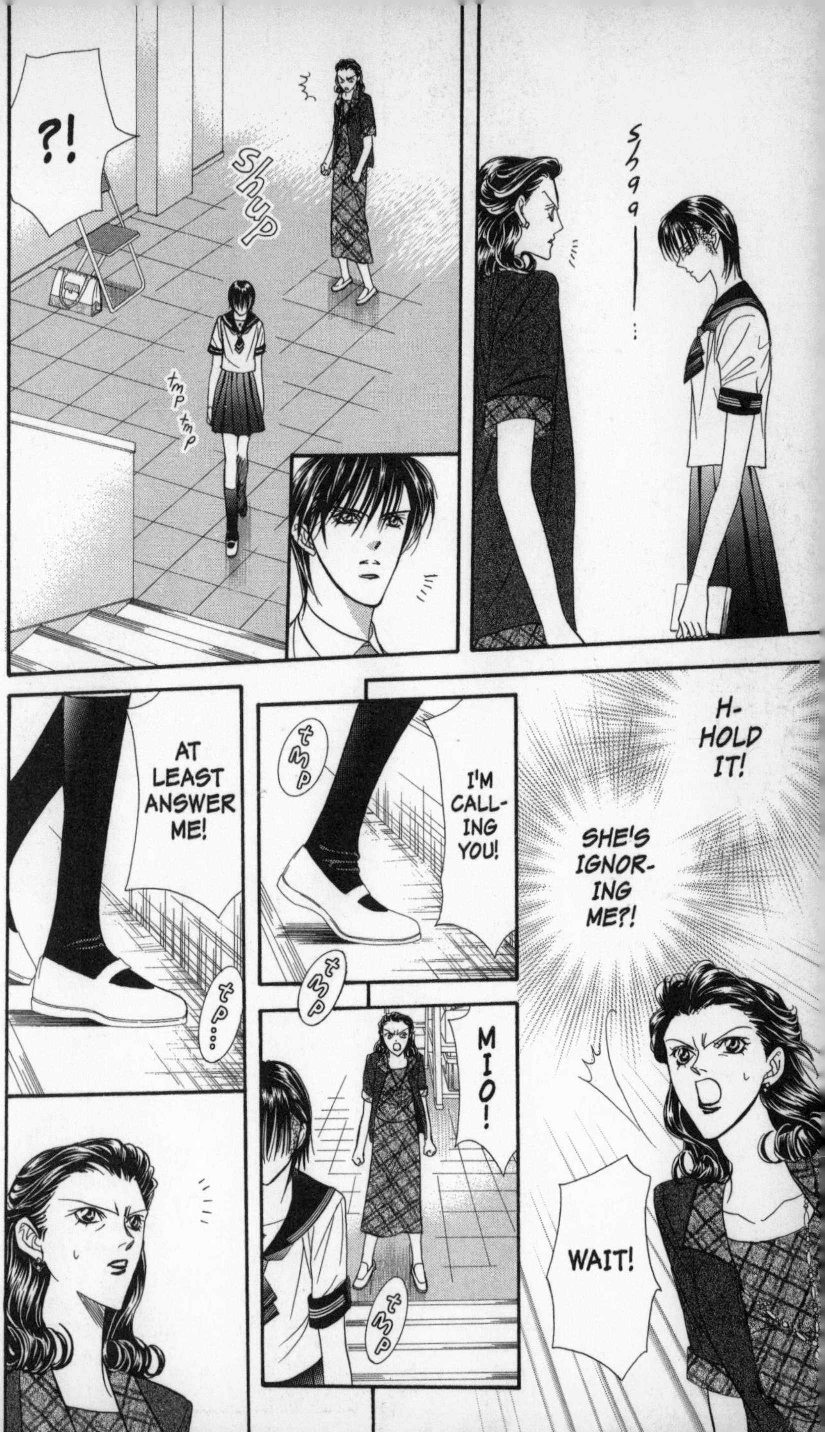
Shaa—...
?!
Shup
xmp xmp
H-HOLD IT!
SHE'S IGNORING ME?!
WAIT!
I'M CALLING YOU!
tmp
tmp
AT LEAST ANSWER ME!
tp...
MIO!
tmp

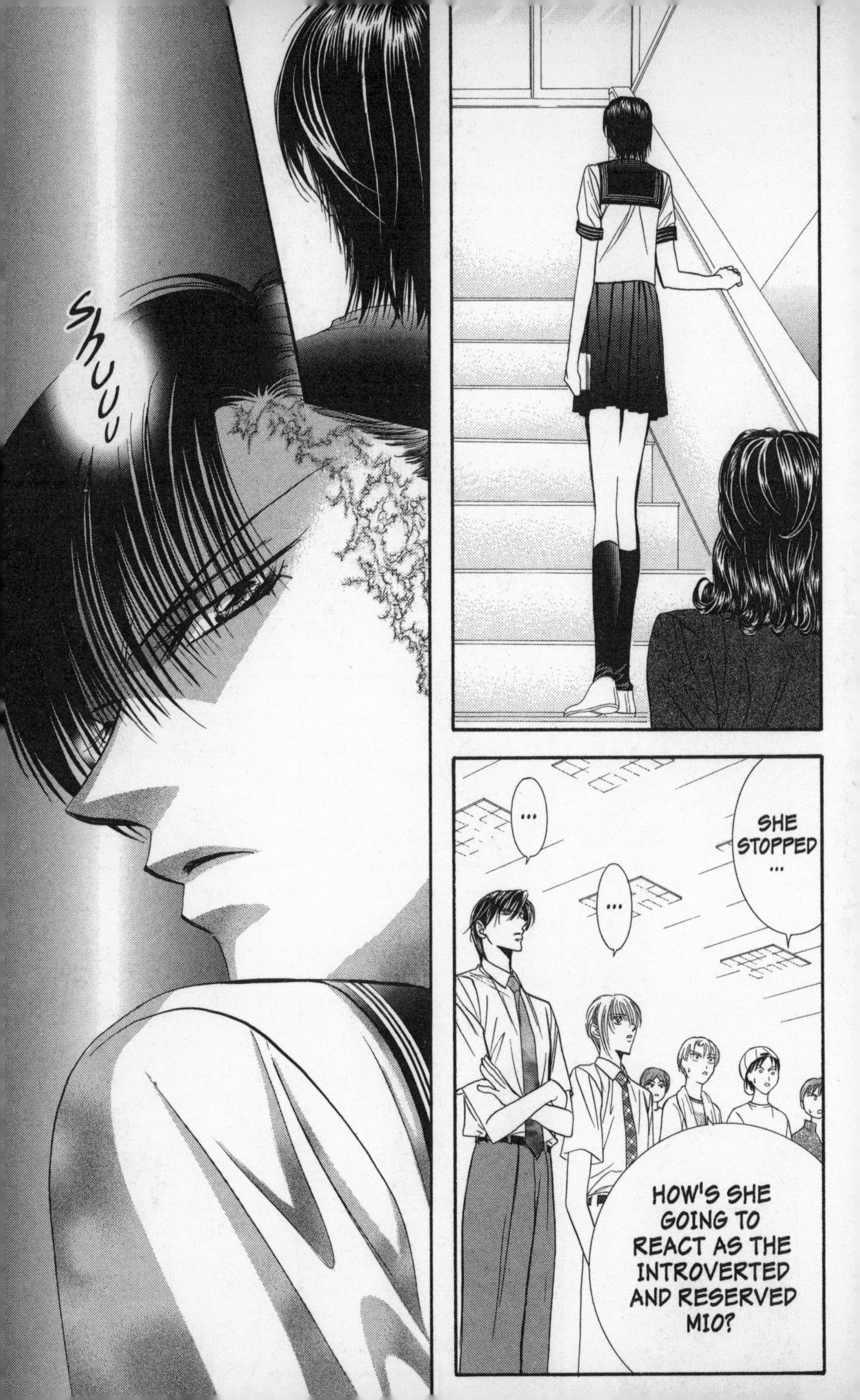
SHE STOPPED ...
...
...
HOW'S SHE GOING TO REACT AS THE INTROVERTED AND RESERVED MIO?
SHUUU

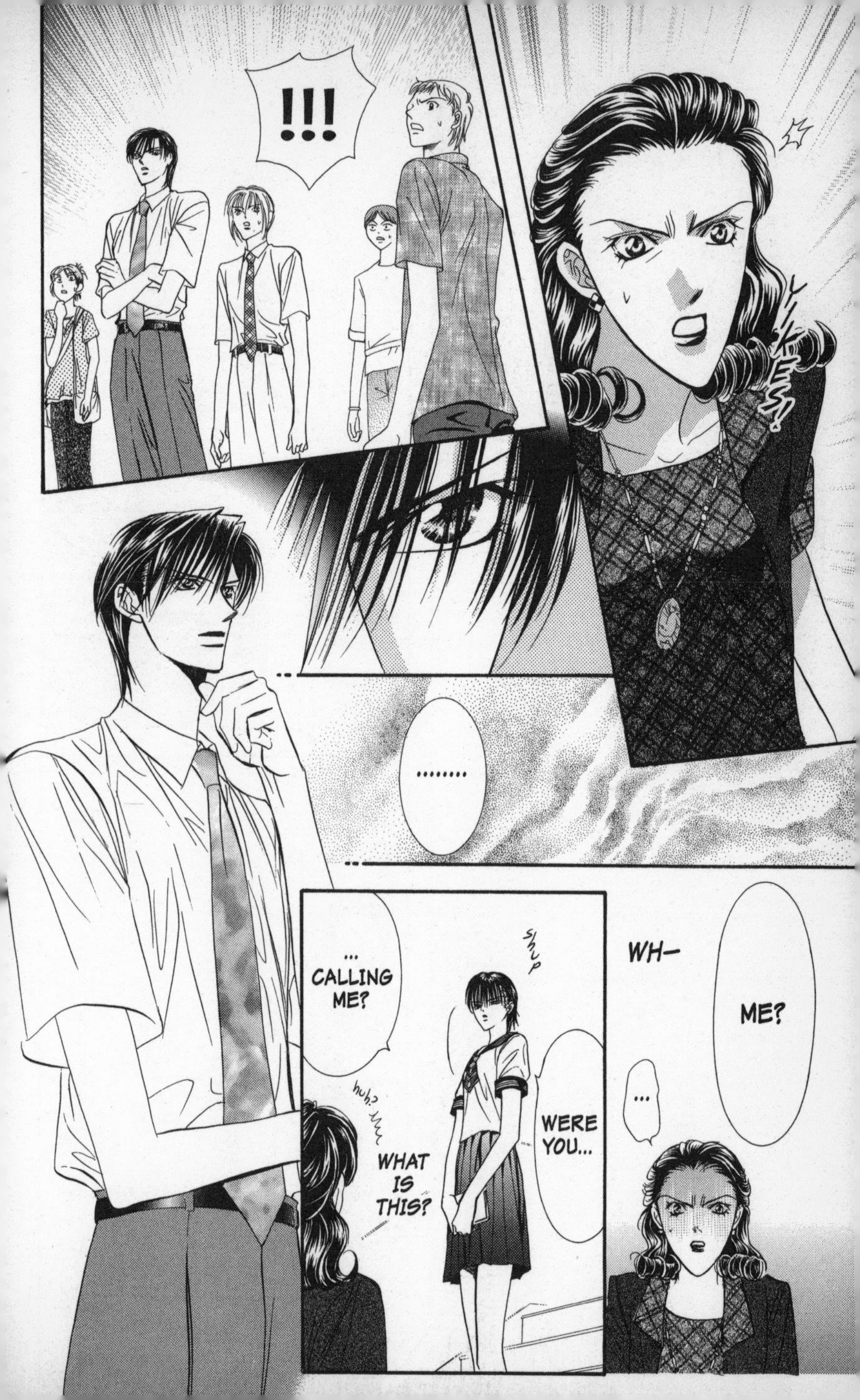
!!!
....
WH—
ME?
...
WERE YOU...
... CALLING ME?
huh?
WHAT IS THIS?

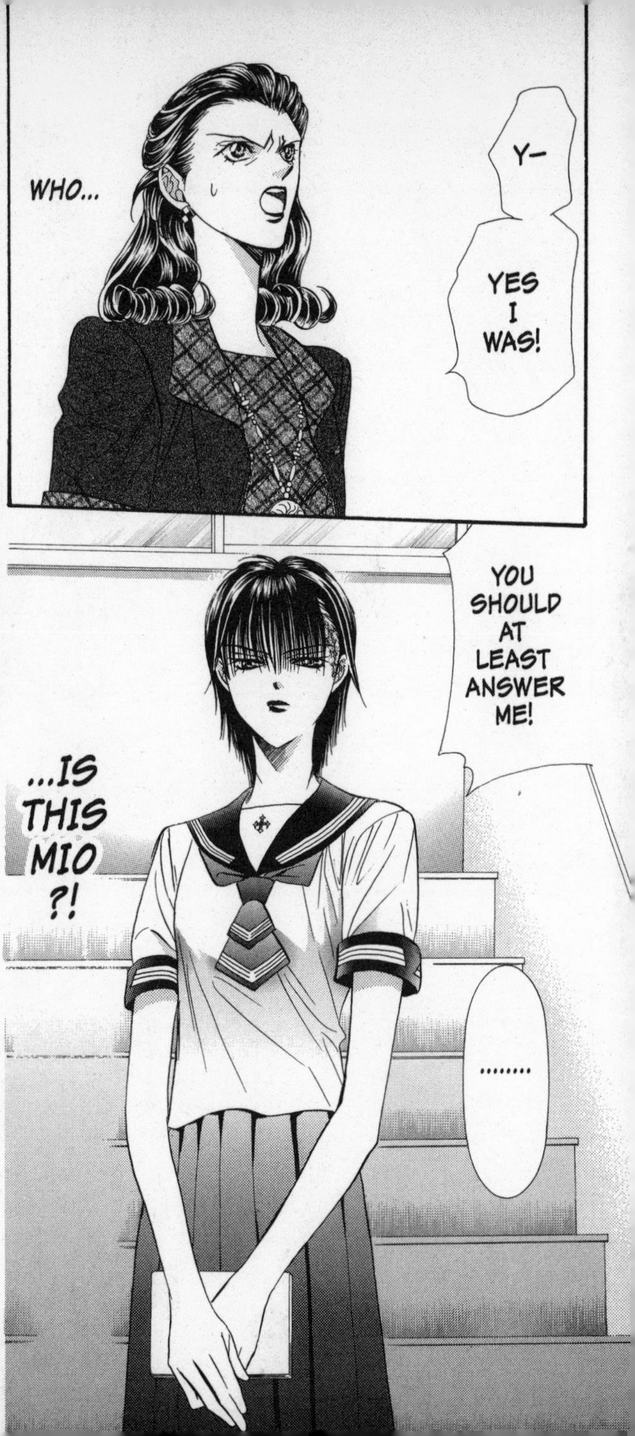
Y—
YES I WAS!
WHO...
YOU SHOULD AT LEAST ANSWER ME!
....
...IS THIS MIO ?!

Hiroko Iizuka

19 years old

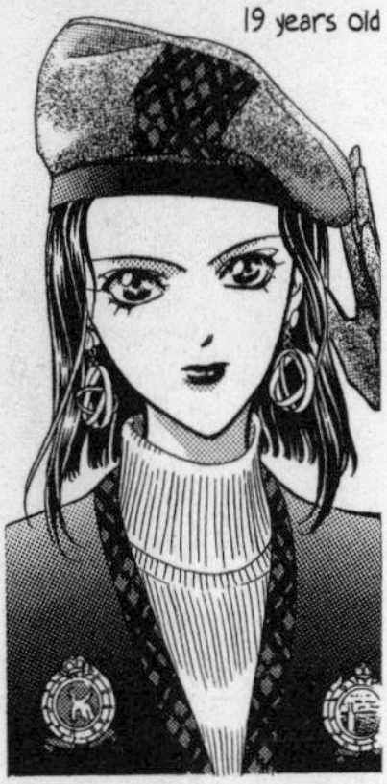

She looked like this when she played Mio. She had talent, but didn't have a chance to appear in a hit drama, and her career was going nowhere. When she found out that Tsukigomori was going to be made into a drama, she boasted, "Only I can play Mio!!" She convinced Director Ogata of her talent and got the role. After she stepped into the limelight with the Mio role, she appeared in hit after hit and became a top-ranked actress right away. Her ferocious hungry spirit brought her luck and her future. She's an actress with guts.

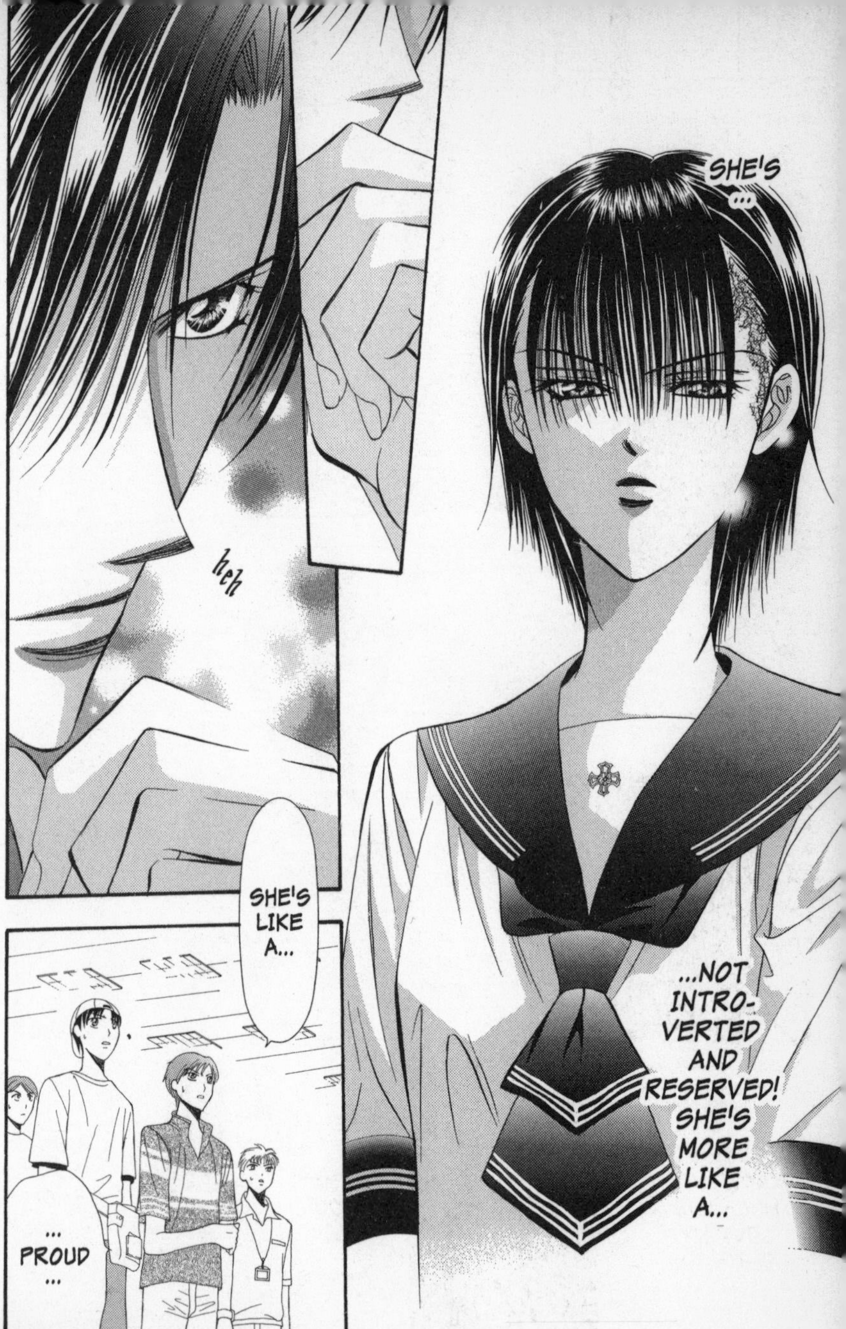
SHE'S ...
...NOT INTRO-VERTED AND RESERVED! SHE'S MORE LIKE A...
heh
SHE'S LIKE A...
... PROUD ...

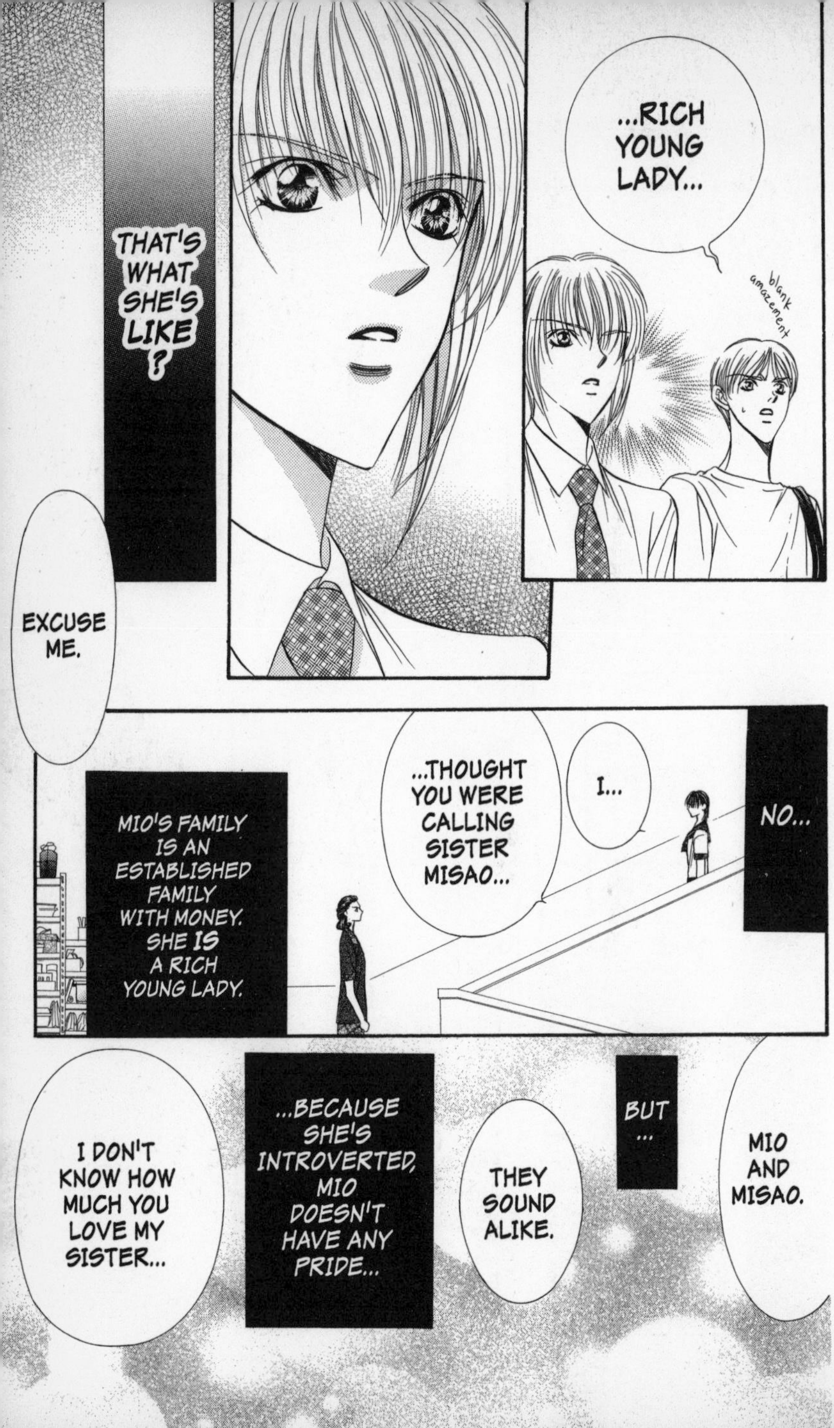
...RICH YOUNG LADY...
blank amazement
THAT'S WHAT SHE'S LIKE?
EXCUSE ME.
NO...
I...
...THOUGHT YOU WERE CALLING SISTER MISAO...
MIO'S FAMILY IS AN ESTABLISHED FAMILY WITH MONEY. SHE IS A RICH YOUNG LADY.
MIO AND MISAO.
BUT ...
THEY SOUND ALIKE.
...BECAUSE SHE'S INTROVERTED, MIO DOESN'T HAVE ANY PRIDE...
I DON'T KNOW HOW MUCH YOU LOVE MY SISTER...

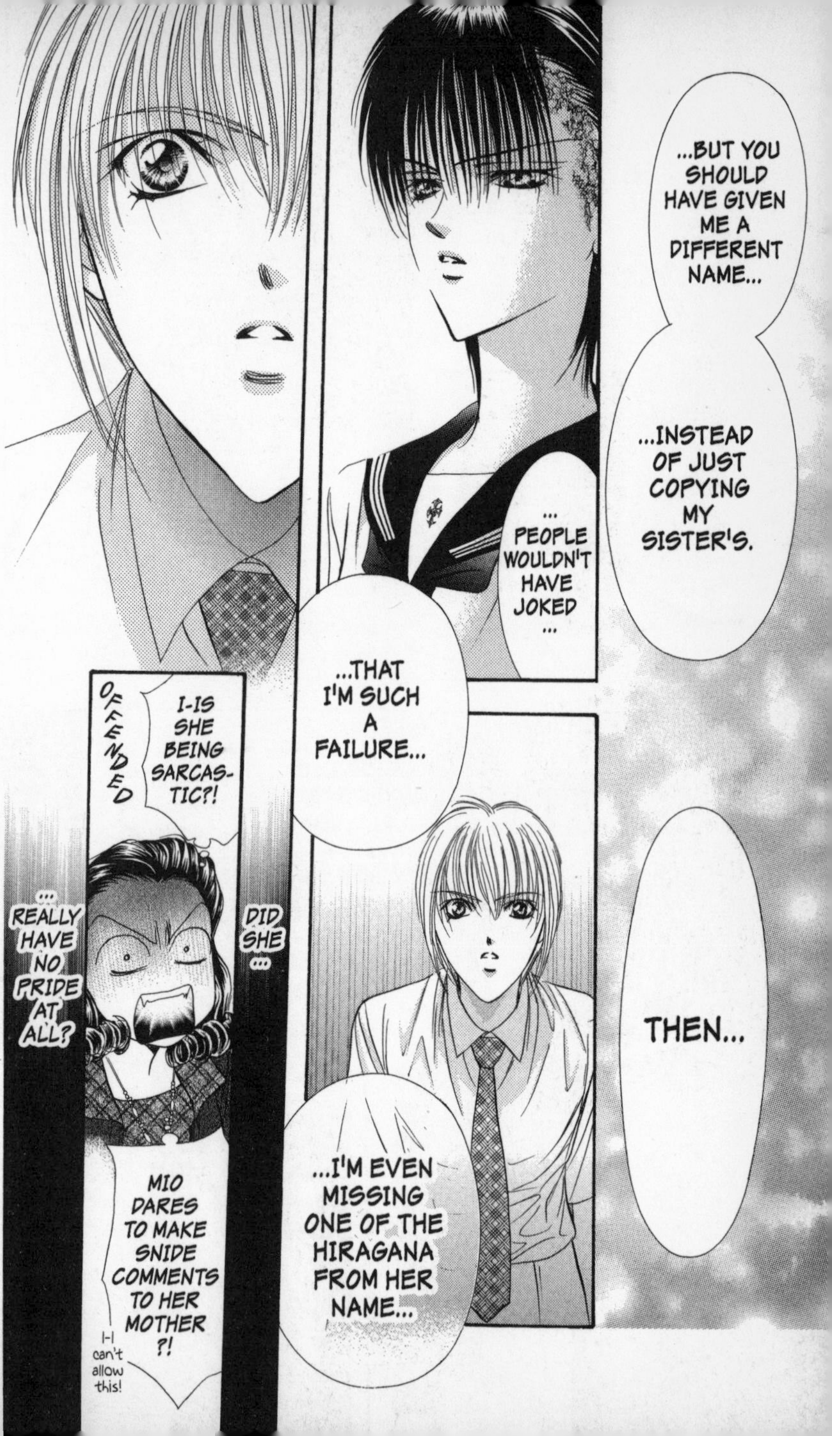
...BUT YOU SHOULD HAVE GIVEN ME A DIFFERENT NAME...
...INSTEAD OF JUST COPYING MY SISTER'S.
...PEOPLE WOULDN'T HAVE JOKED...
...THAT I'M SUCH A FAILURE...
THEN...
...I'M EVEN MISSING ONE OF THE HIRAGANA FROM HER NAME...
OFFENDED
I-IS SHE BEING SARCASTIC?!
DID SHE...
...REALLY HAVE NO PRIDE AT ALL?
MIO DARES TO MAKE SNIDE COMMENTS TO HER MOTHER?!
I-I can't allow this!

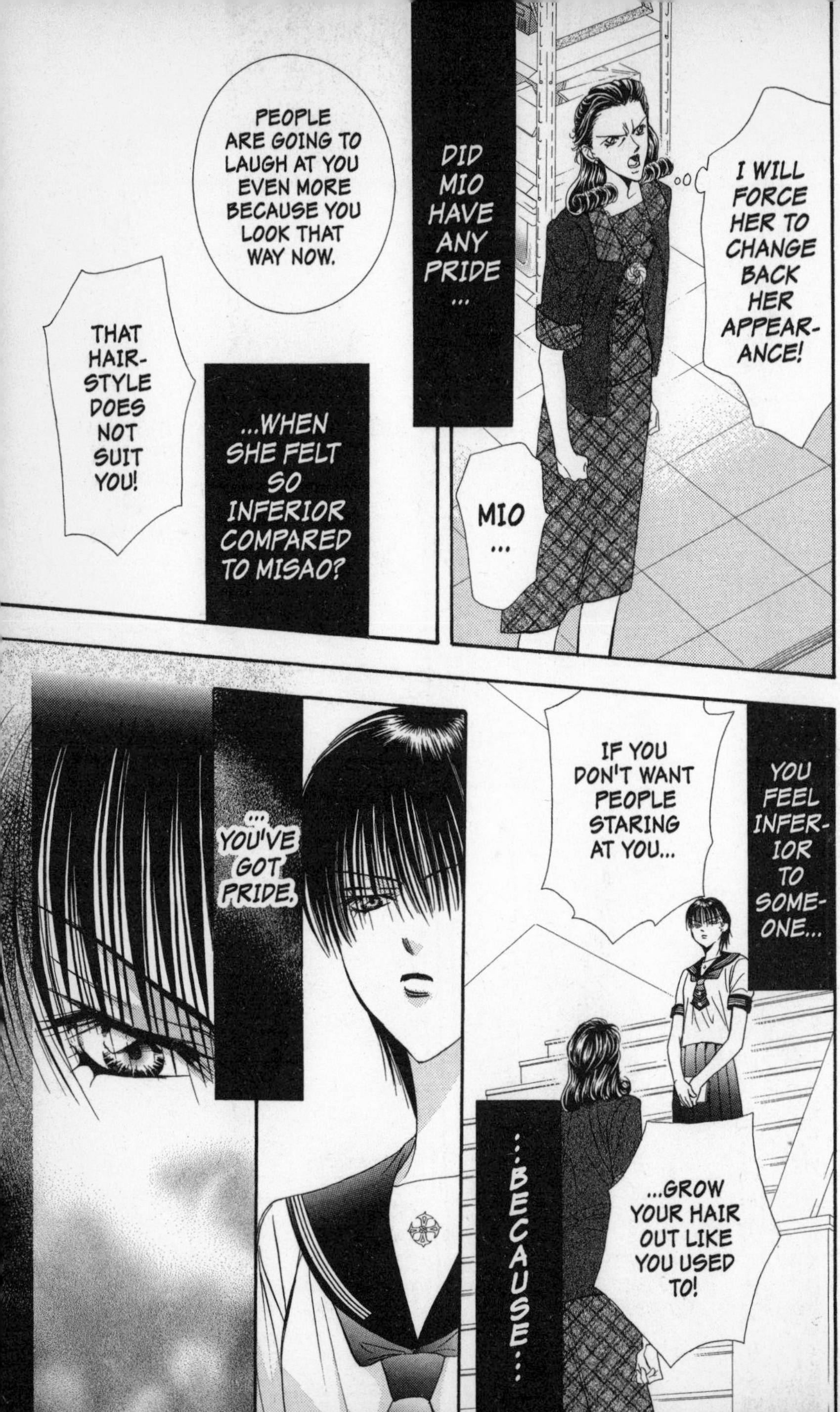
I WILL FORCE HER TO CHANGE BACK HER APPEARANCE!
DID MIO HAVE ANY PRIDE...
MIO...
PEOPLE ARE GOING TO LAUGH AT YOU EVEN MORE BECAUSE YOU LOOK THAT WAY NOW.
...WHEN SHE FELT SO INFERIOR COMPARED TO MISAO?
THAT HAIR-STYLE DOES NOT SUIT YOU!
YOU FEEL INFER-IOR TO SOME-ONE...
IF YOU DON'T WANT PEOPLE STARING AT YOU...
...GROW YOUR HAIR OUT LIKE YOU USED TO!
...BECAUSE...
...YOU'VE GOT PRIDE.

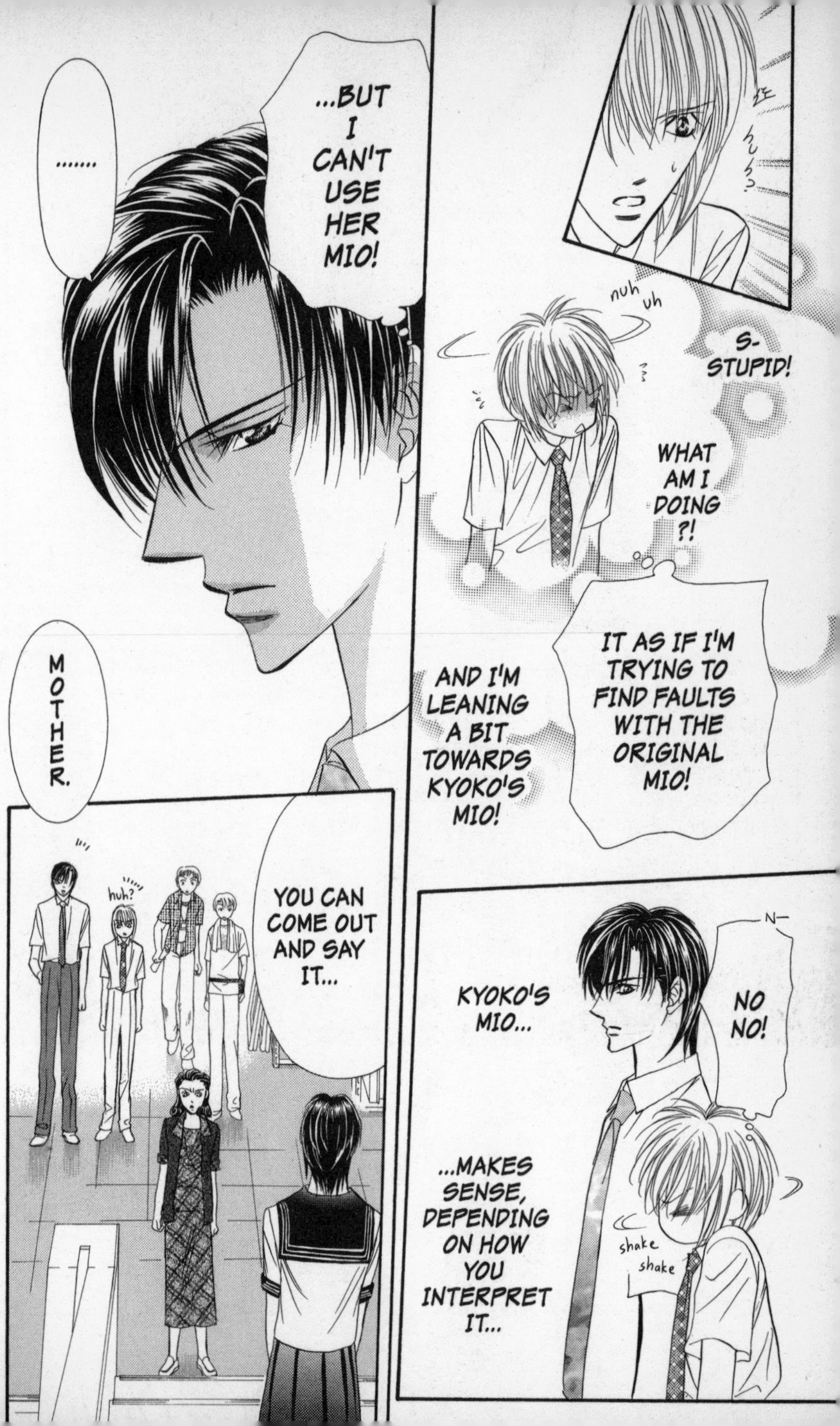
nuh uh
S-STUPID!
WHAT AM I DOING?!
IT AS IF I'M TRYING TO FIND FAULTS WITH THE ORIGINAL MIO!
AND I'M LEANING A BIT TOWARDS KYOKO'S MIO!
...BUT I CAN'T USE HER MIO!
....
MOTHER.
N— NO NO!
KYOKO'S MIO...
...MAKES SENSE, DEPENDING ON HOW YOU INTERPRET IT...
shake shake
YOU CAN COME OUT AND SAY IT...
huh?

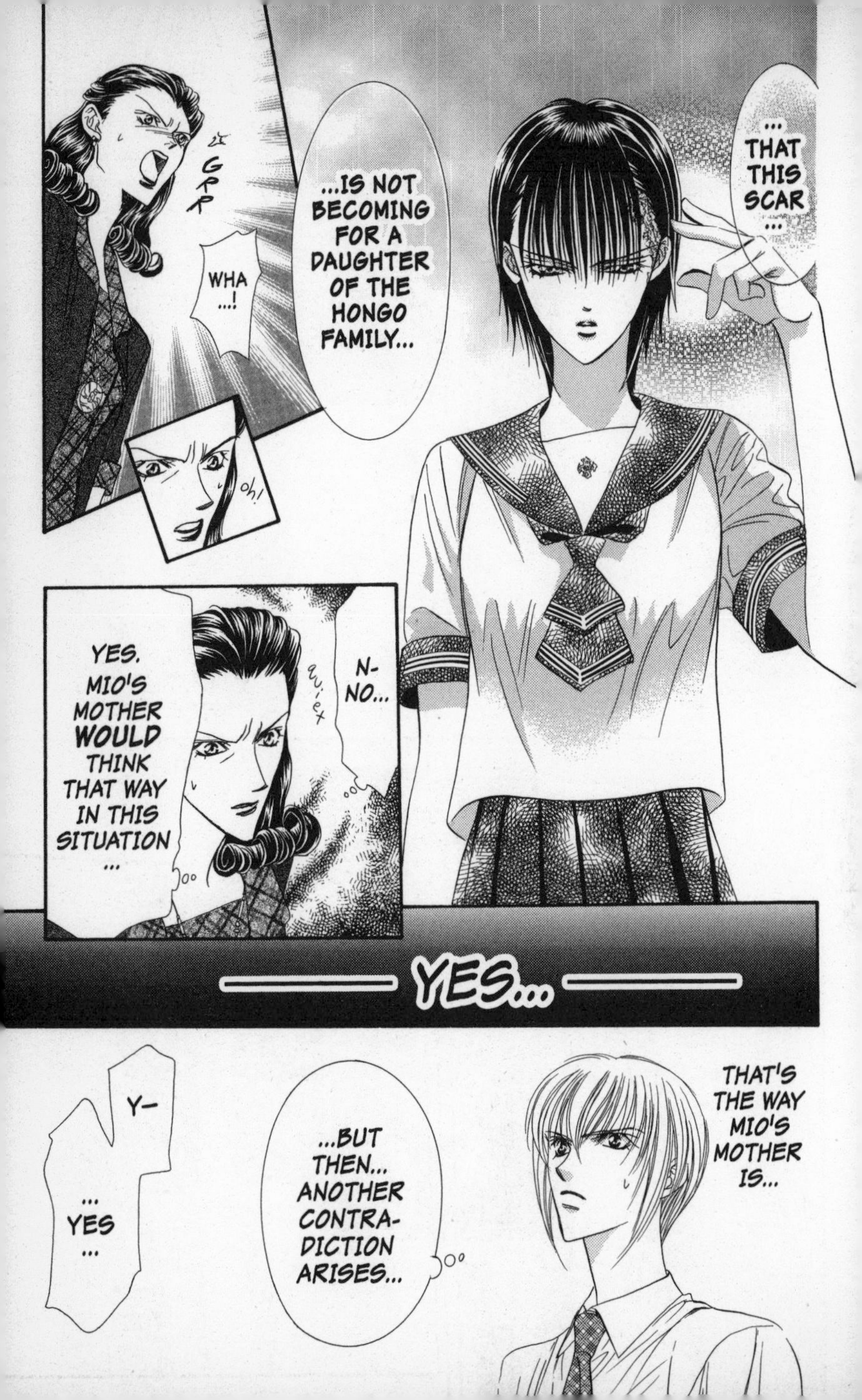
...THAT THIS SCAR...
...IS NOT BECOMING FOR A DAUGHTER OF THE HONGO FAMILY...
GRR
WHA...!
oh!
N-NO...
quiet
YES. MIO'S MOTHER **WOULD** THINK THAT WAY IN THIS SITUATION...
YES...
THAT'S THE WAY MIO'S MOTHER IS...
...BUT THEN... ANOTHER CONTRA-DICTION ARISES...
Y— ...YES...

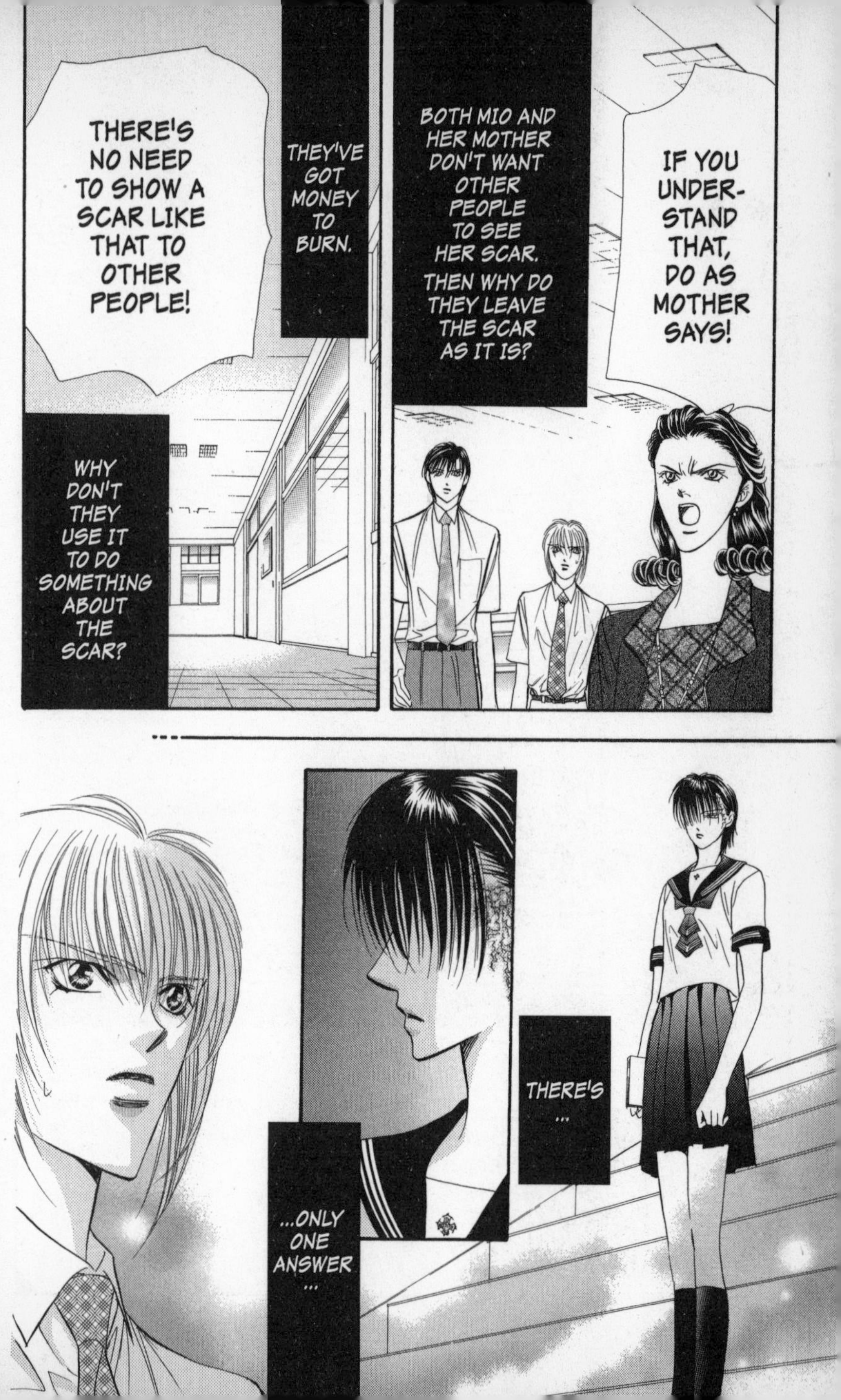
IF YOU UNDERSTAND THAT, DO AS MOTHER SAYS!
BOTH MIO AND HER MOTHER DON'T WANT OTHER PEOPLE TO SEE HER SCAR.
THEN WHY DO THEY LEAVE THE SCAR AS IT IS?
THEY'VE GOT MONEY TO BURN.
THERE'S NO NEED TO SHOW A SCAR LIKE THAT TO OTHER PEOPLE!
WHY DON'T THEY USE IT TO DO SOMETHING ABOUT THE SCAR?

THERE'S ...
...ONLY ONE ANSWER ...

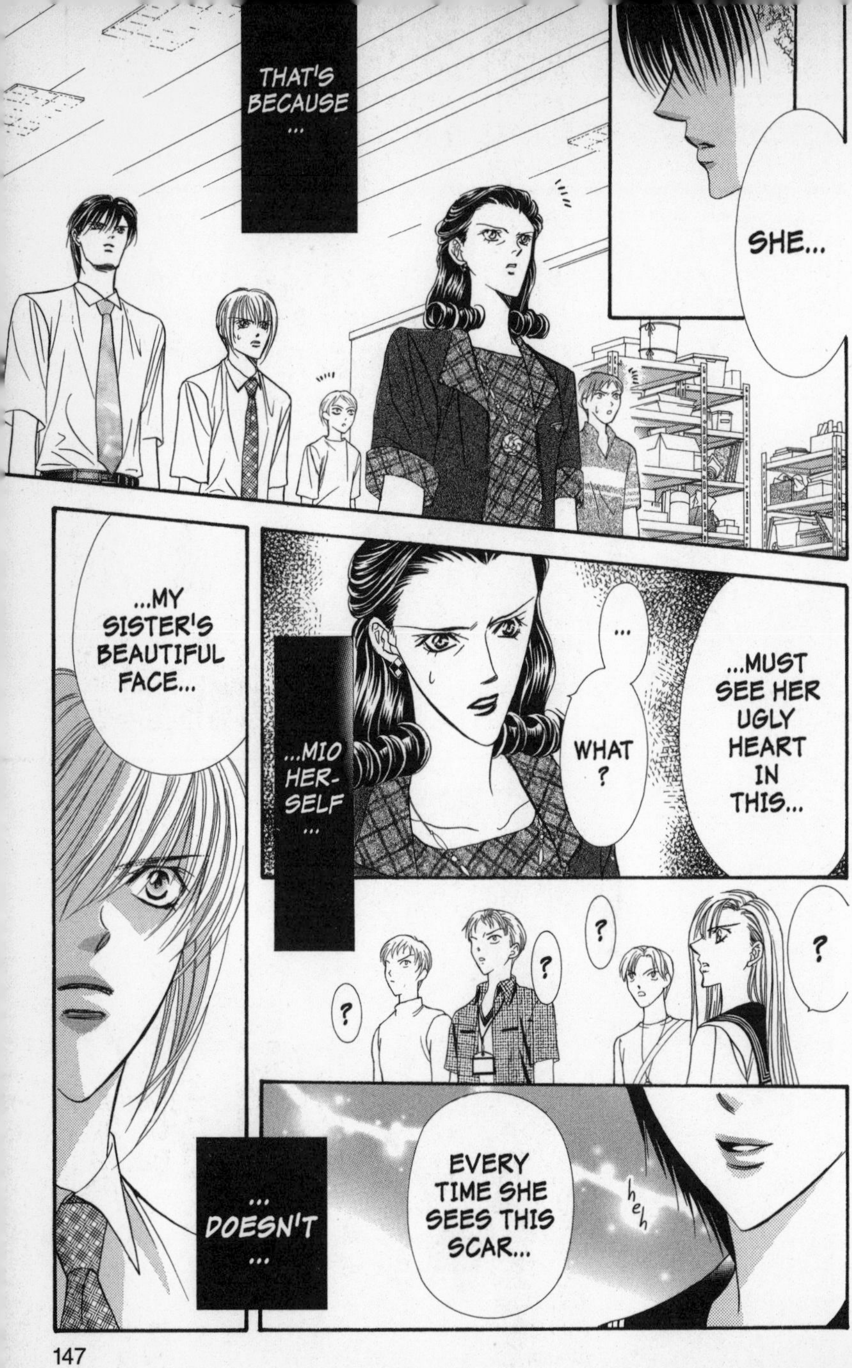
SHE...
THAT'S BECAUSE ...
...MUST SEE HER UGLY HEART IN THIS...
... WHAT?
...MIO HERSELF ...
?
?
?
?
EVERY TIME SHE SEES THIS SCAR...
heh
... DOESN'T ...
...MY SISTER'S BEAUTIFUL FACE...

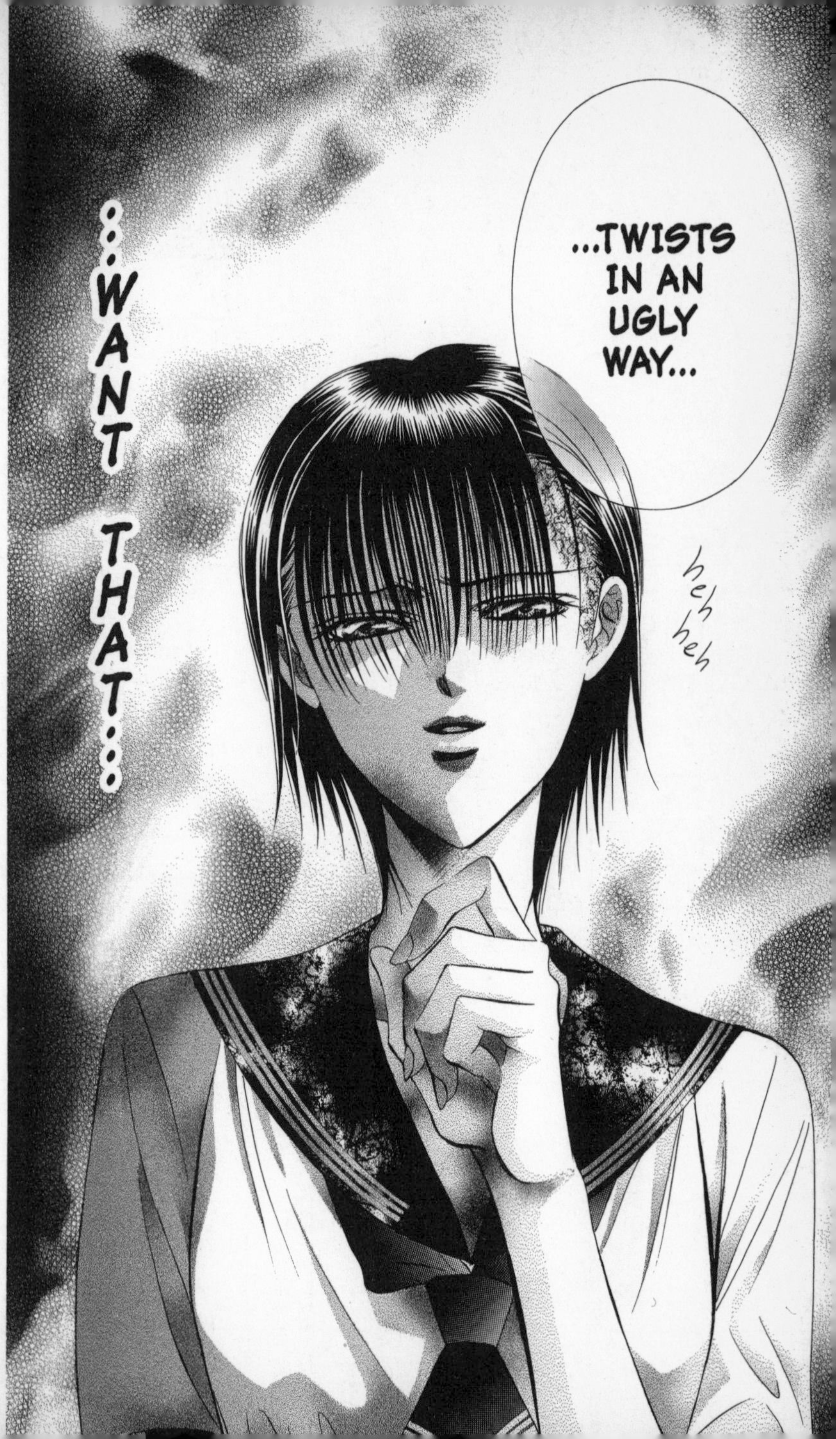
...TWISTS IN AN UGLY WAY...
heh heh
...WANT THAT...

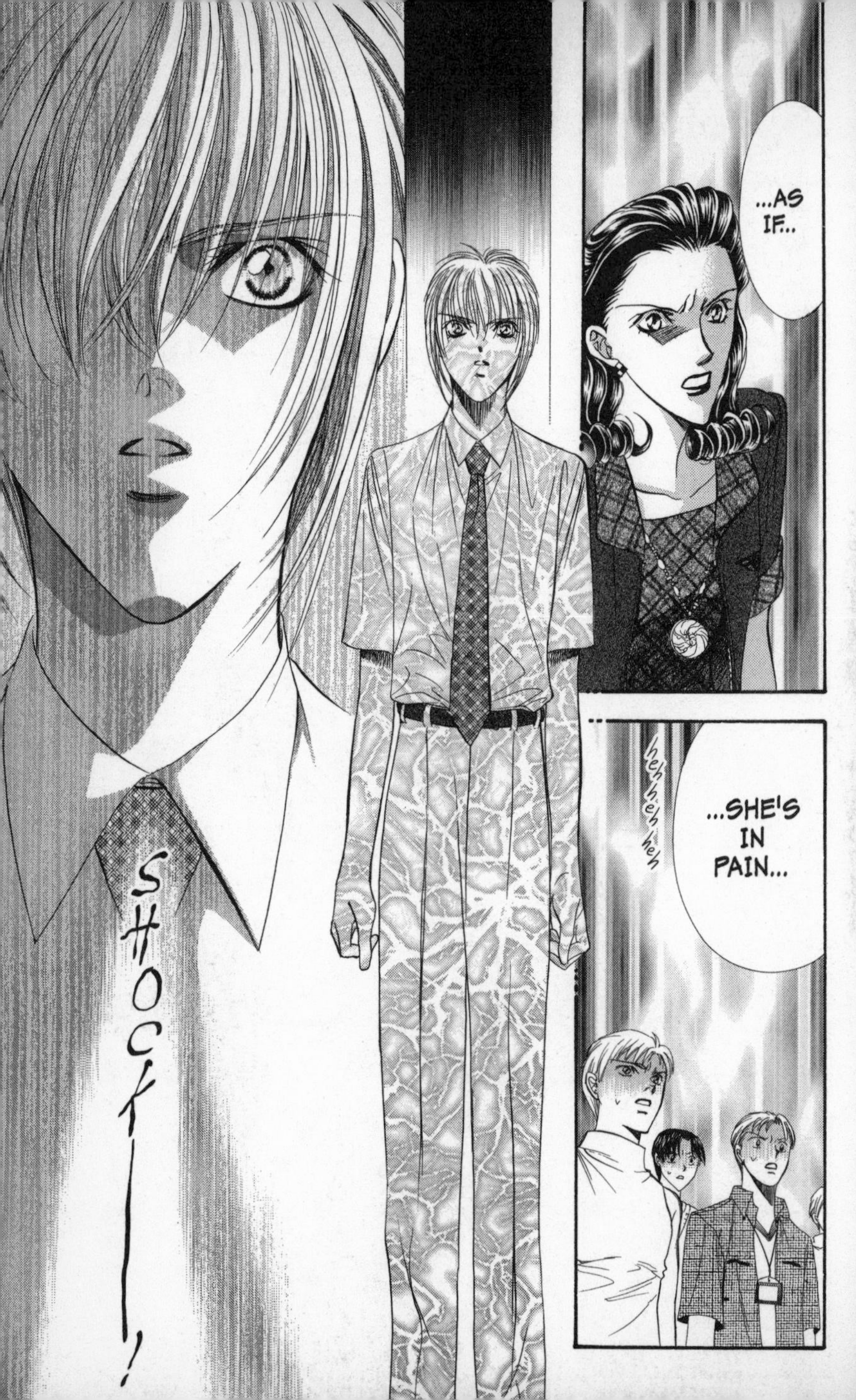
...AS IF...
heh heh heh
...SHE'S IN PAIN...
SHOCK—!

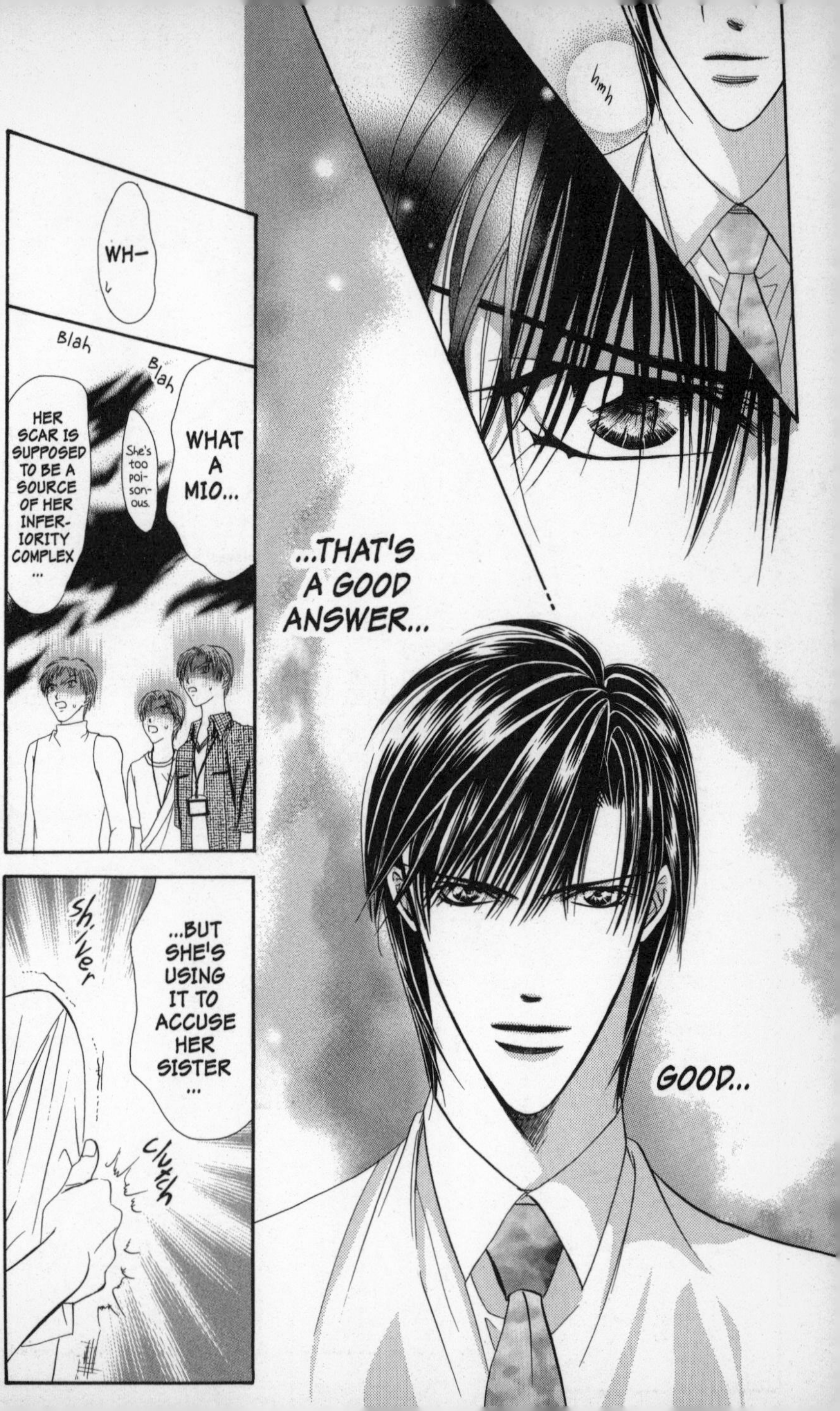
hmh
...THAT'S A GOOD ANSWER...
GOOD...
WH—
Blah
Blah
WHAT A MIO...
She's too poi-son-ous.
HER SCAR IS SUPPOSED TO BE A SOURCE OF HER INFER-IORITY COMPLEX ...
...BUT SHE'S USING IT TO ACCUSE HER SISTER ...
shiver
clutch

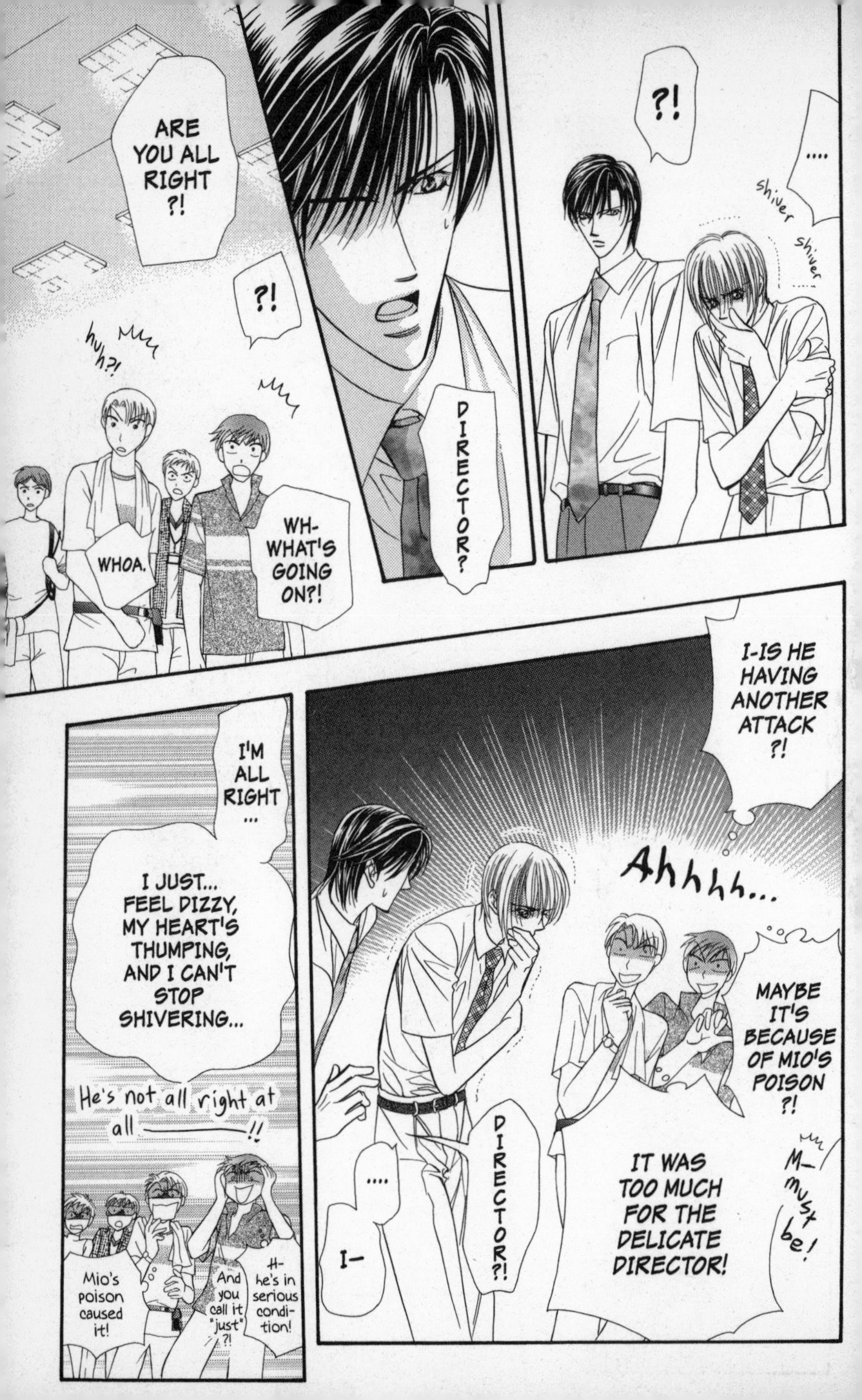
?!
....
shiver shiver
DIRECTOR?
ARE YOU ALL RIGHT ?!
?!
huh?!
WH-WHAT'S GOING ON?!
WHOA.
I-IS HE HAVING ANOTHER ATTACK ?!
Ahhhhh...
MAYBE IT'S BECAUSE OF MIO'S POISON ?!
M-must be!
IT WAS TOO MUCH FOR THE DELICATE DIRECTOR!
DIRECTOR?!
....
I-
I'M ALL RIGHT ...
I JUST... FEEL DIZZY, MY HEART'S THUMPING, AND I CAN'T STOP SHIVERING...
He's not all right at all——!!
H-he's in serious condition!
And you call it "just" ?!
Mio's poison caused it!

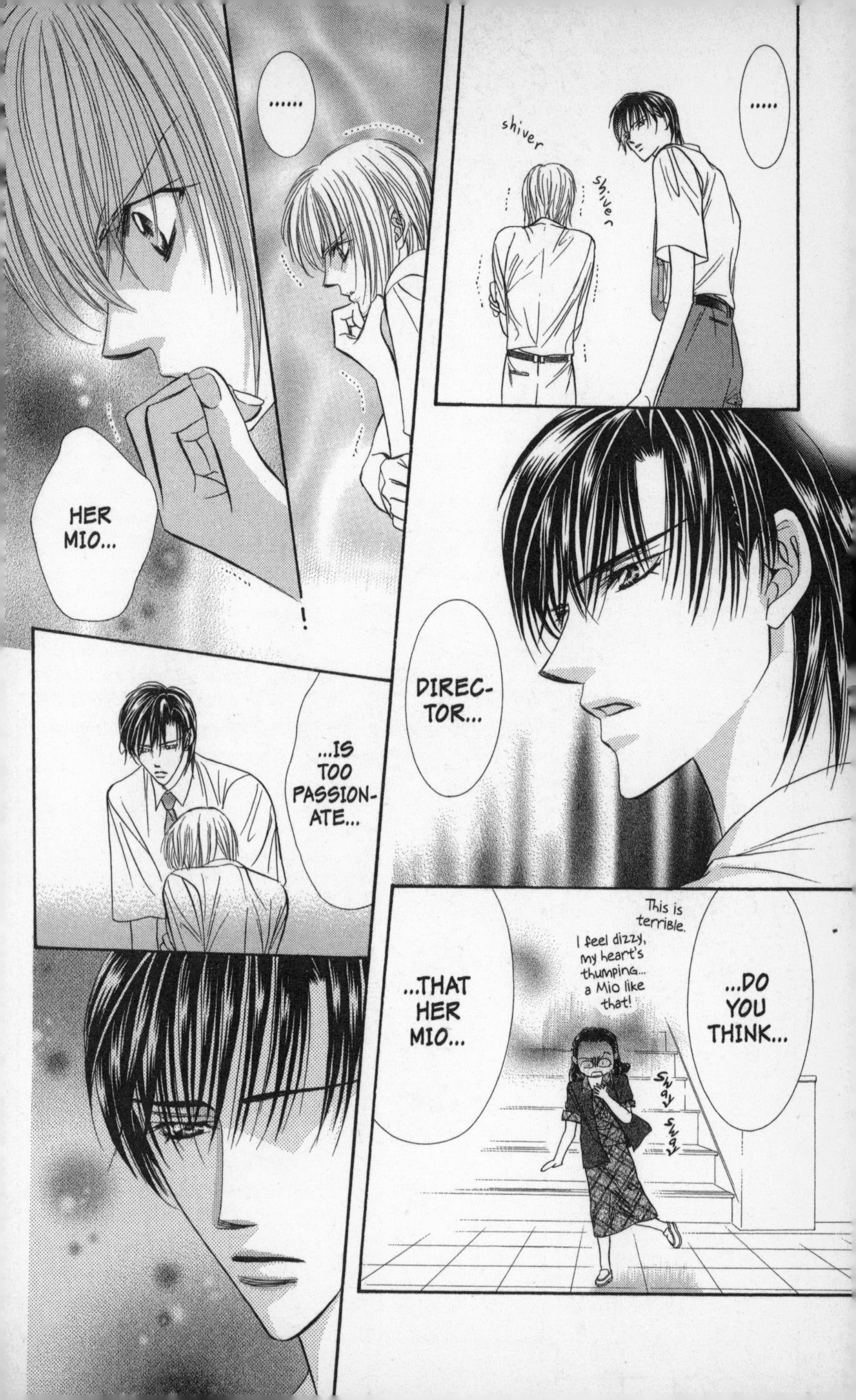

.....
shiver
shiver
......
HER MIO...
!
DIRECTOR...
...IS TOO PASSIONATE...
...DO YOU THINK...
This is terrible.
I feel dizzy, my heart's thumping... a Mio like that!
sway
sway
...THAT HER MIO...

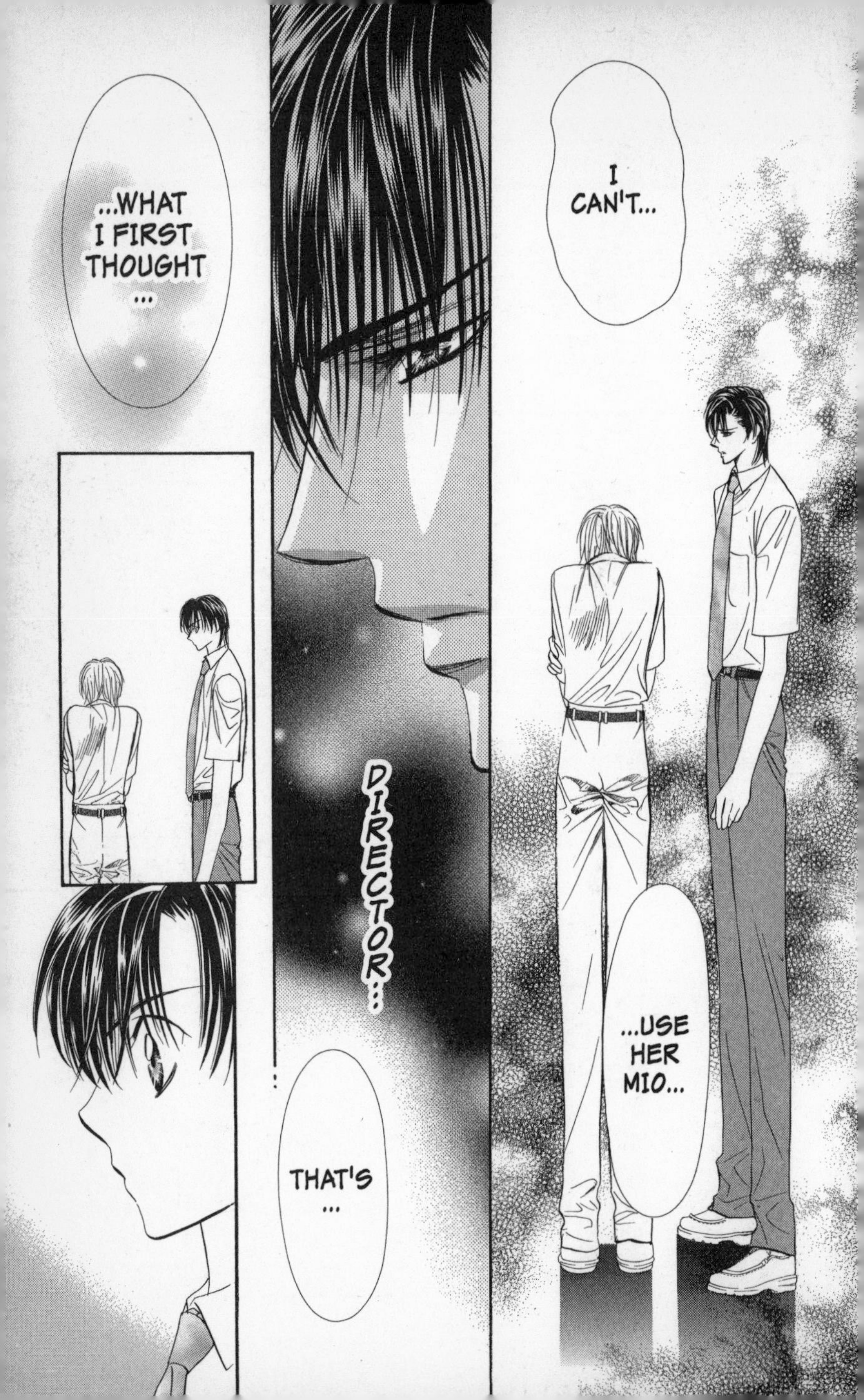
I CAN'T...
...USE HER MIO...
DIRECTOR...
THAT'S ...
...WHAT I FIRST THOUGHT ...

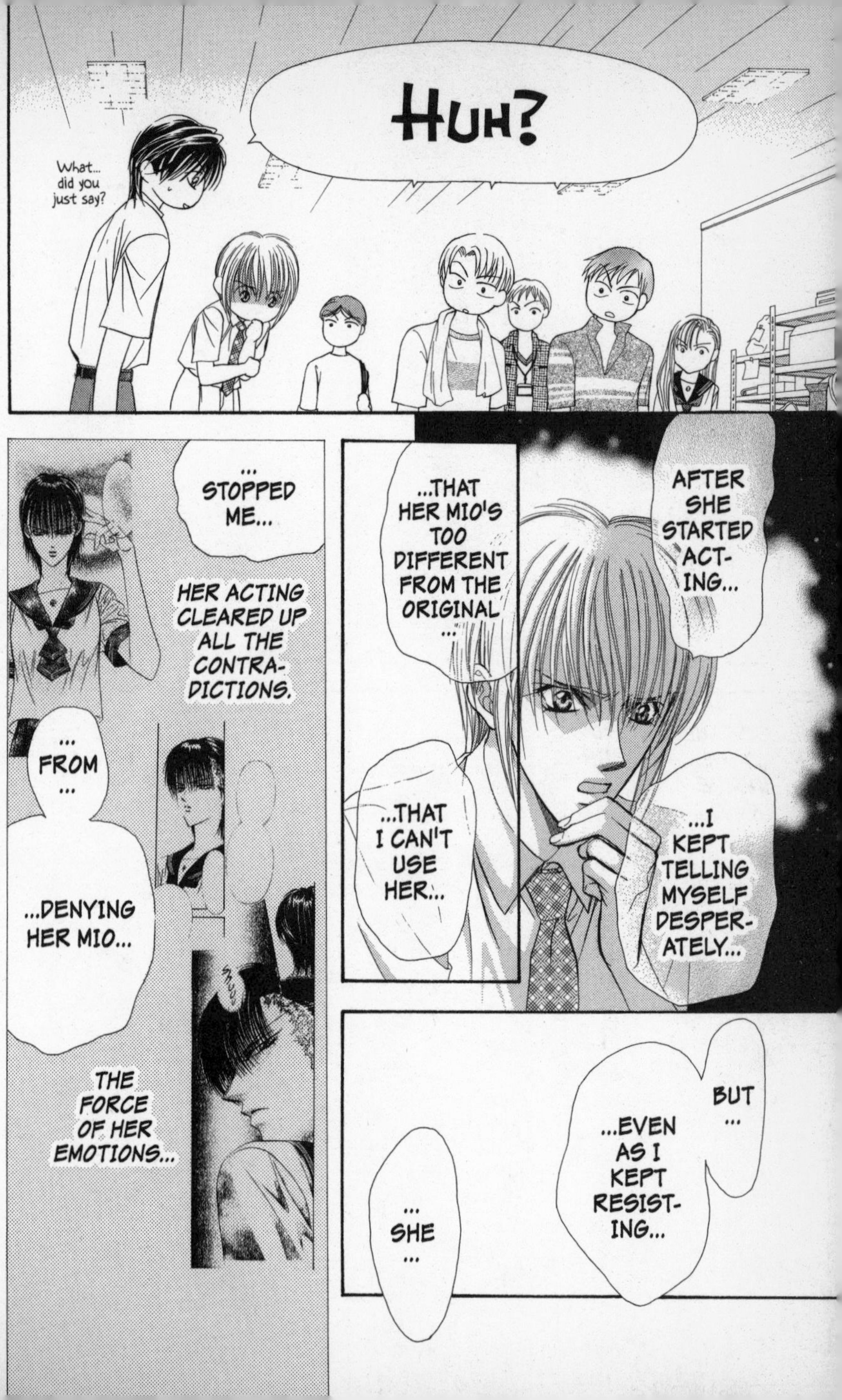

HUH?
What... did you just say?
AFTER SHE STARTED ACT-ING...
...I KEPT TELLING MYSELF DESPER-ATELY...
...THAT HER MIO'S TOO DIFFERENT FROM THE ORIGINAL ...
...THAT I CAN'T USE HER...
BUT ...
...EVEN AS I KEPT RESIST-ING...
... SHE ...
... STOPPED ME...
HER ACTING CLEARED UP ALL THE CONTRA-DICTIONS.
... FROM ...
...DENYING HER MIO...
THE FORCE OF HER EMOTIONS...

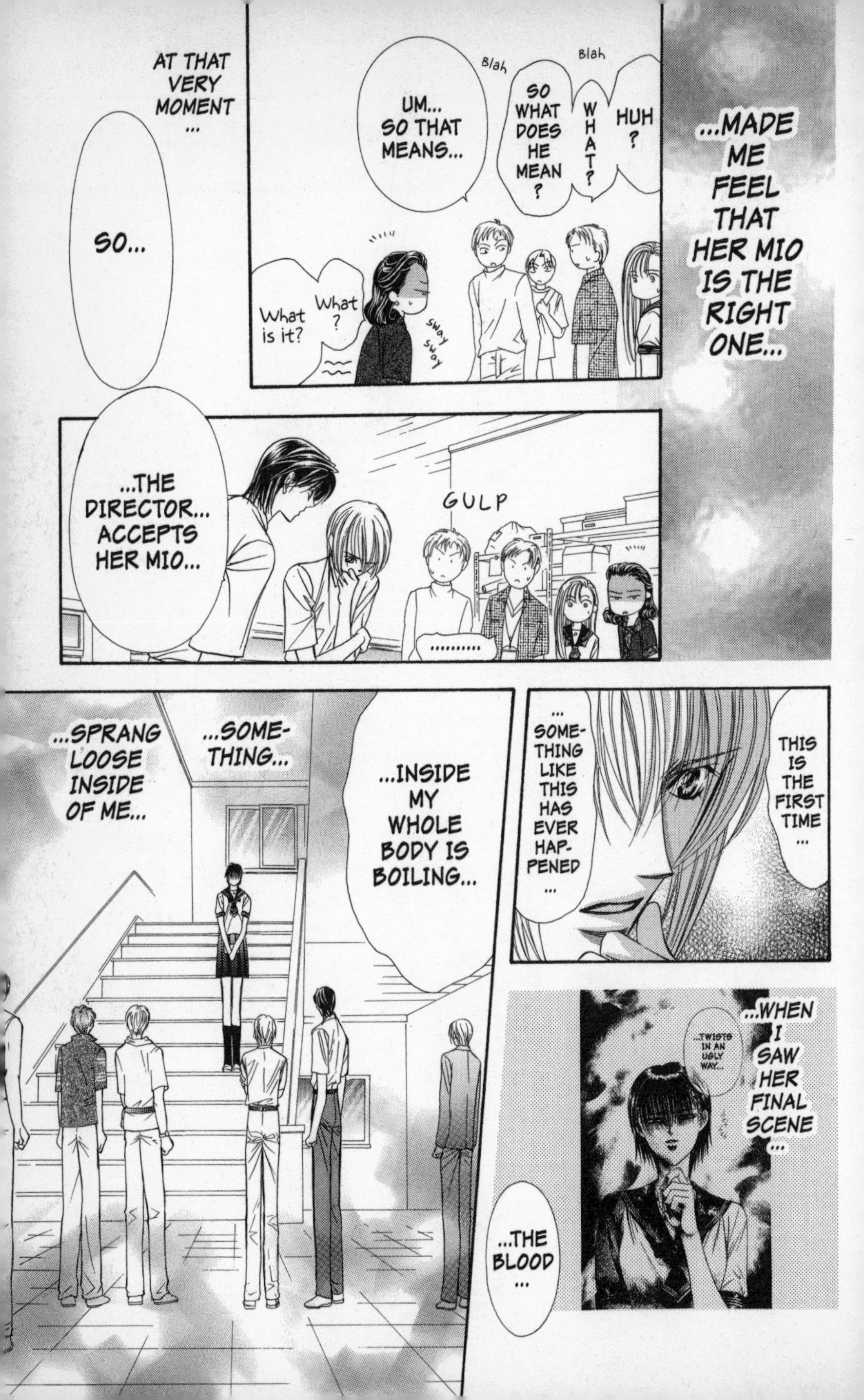
...MADE ME FEEL THAT HER MIO IS THE RIGHT ONE...
Blah
Blah
HUH?
WHAT?
SO WHAT DOES HE MEAN?
UM... SO THAT MEANS...
What?
What is it?
SWAY SWAY
AT THAT VERY MOMENT...
SO...
...THE DIRECTOR... ACCEPTS HER MIO...
GULP
....
THIS IS THE FIRST TIME...
...SOMETHING LIKE THIS HAS EVER HAPPENED...
...WHEN I SAW HER FINAL SCENE...
...THE BLOOD...
...TWISTS IN AN UGLY WAY...
...INSIDE MY WHOLE BODY IS BOILING...
...SOMETHING...
...SPRANG LOOSE INSIDE OF ME...

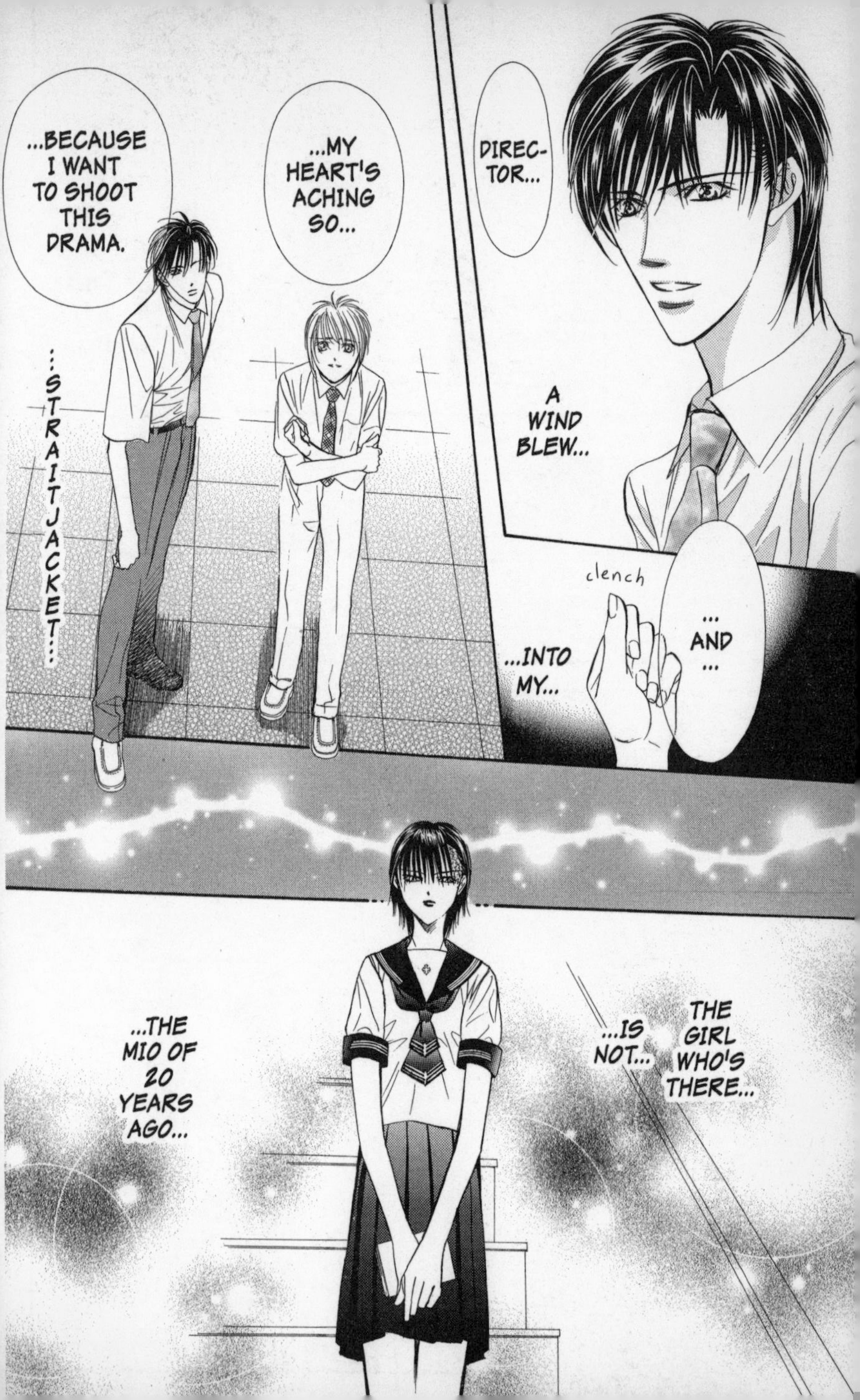
DIRECTOR...
A WIND BLEW...
... AND ...
clench
...INTO MY...
...MY HEART'S ACHING SO...
...BECAUSE I WANT TO SHOOT THIS DRAMA.
...STRAITJACKET...
THE GIRL WHO'S THERE...
...IS NOT...
...THE MIO OF 20 YEARS AGO...

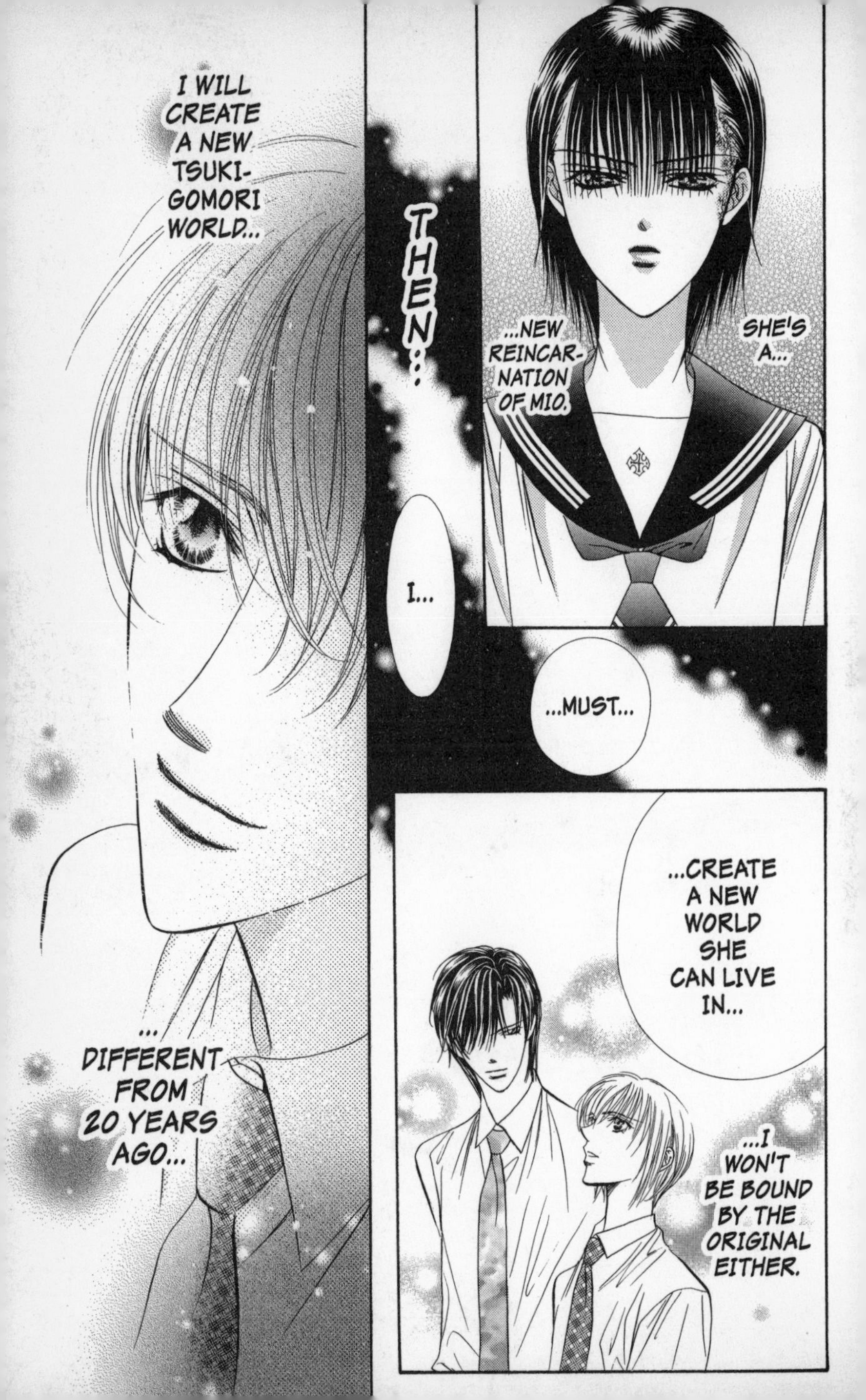
SHE'S A...
...NEW REINCARNATION OF MIO.
THEN...
I...
...MUST...
...CREATE A NEW WORLD SHE CAN LIVE IN...
...I WON'T BE BOUND BY THE ORIGINAL EITHER.
I WILL CREATE A NEW TSUKI-GOMORI WORLD...
...DIFFERENT FROM 20 YEARS AGO...

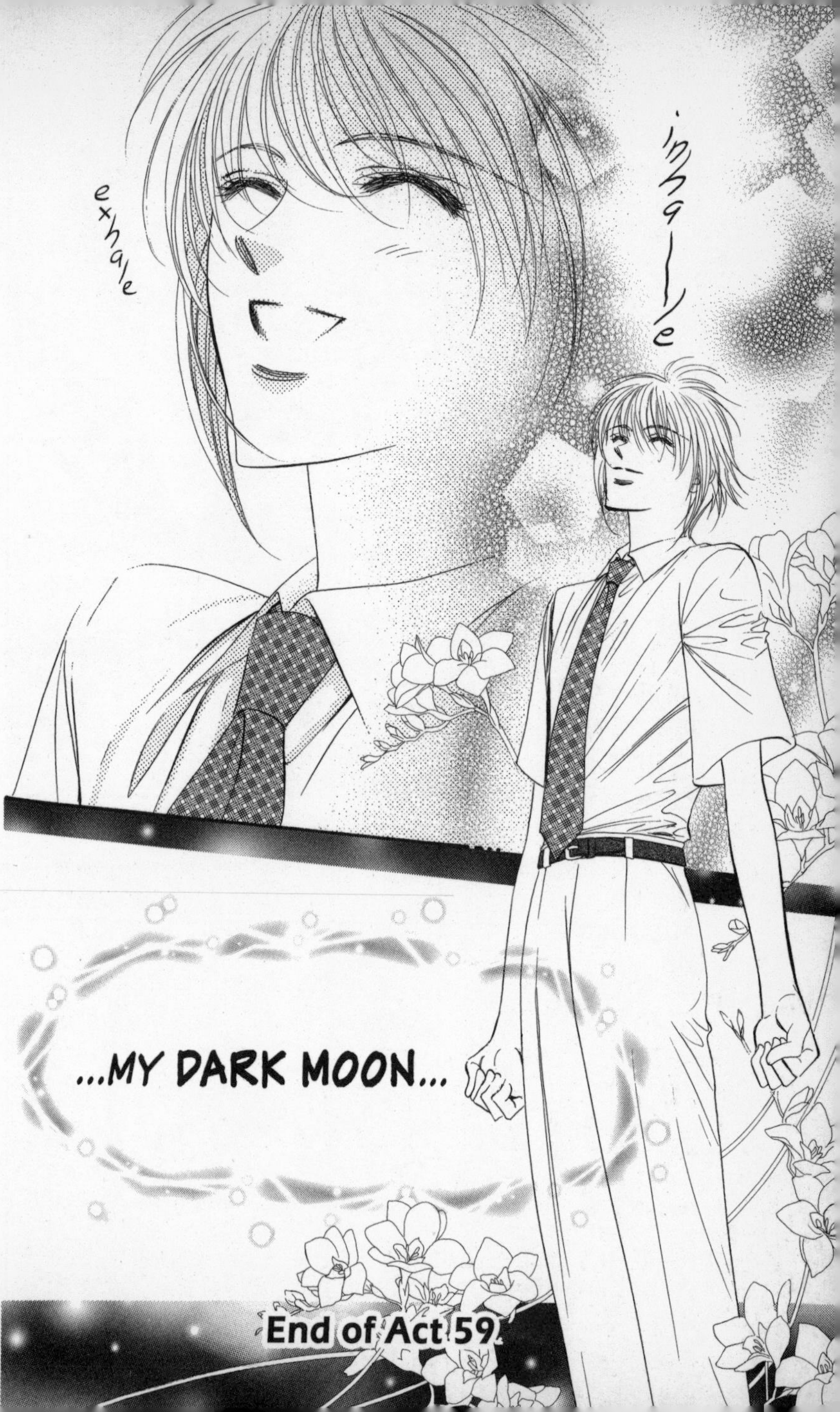
inhale
exhale
...MY DARK MOON...
End of Act 59

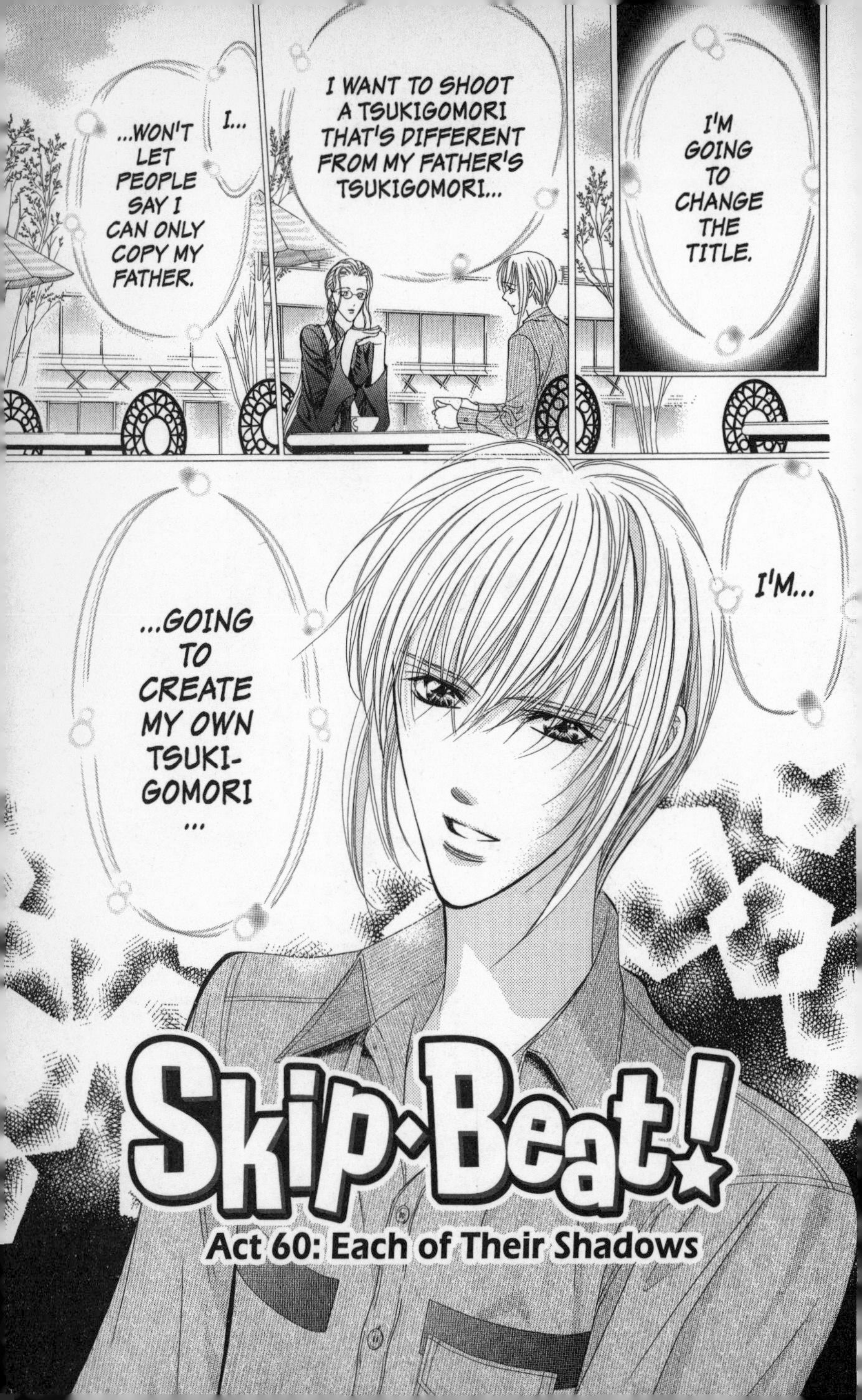
I'M GOING TO CHANGE THE TITLE.
I WANT TO SHOOT A TSUKIGOMORI THAT'S DIFFERENT FROM MY FATHER'S TSUKIGOMORI...
I...
...WON'T LET PEOPLE SAY I CAN ONLY COPY MY FATHER.
I'M...
...GOING TO CREATE MY OWN TSUKI-GOMORI...
Skip·Beat!
Act 60: Each of Their Shadows

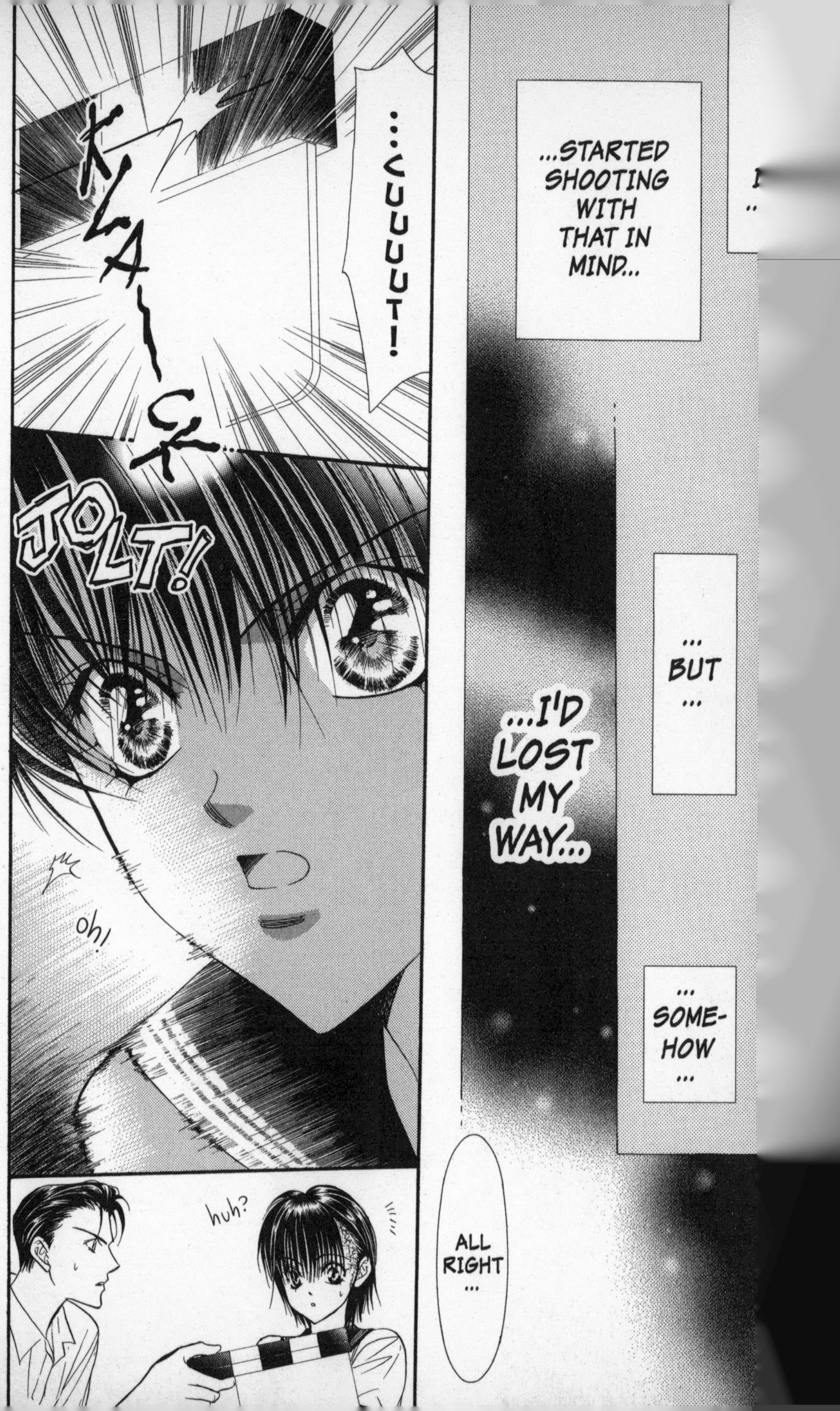
...STARTED SHOOTING WITH THAT IN MIND...
... BUT ...
...I'D LOST MY WAY...
... SOME-HOW ...
ALL RIGHT ...
...CUUUUUT!
KLAAACK...
JOLT!
oh!
huh?

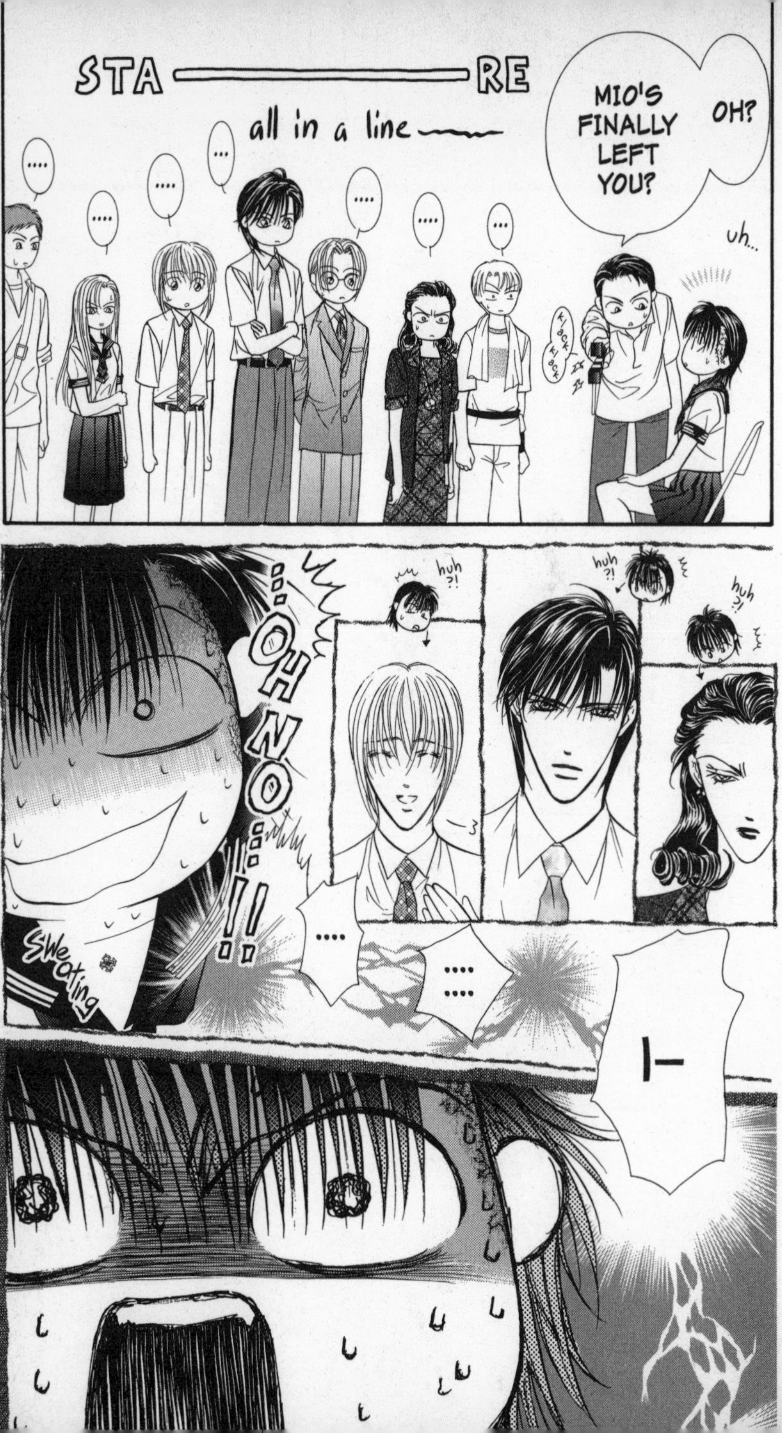
OH?
MIO'S FINALLY LEFT YOU?
uh...
klack klack
STA——RE
all in a line
....
....
....
....
....
....
....
huh ?!
huh ?!
huh ?!
OH NO...!!
Sweating
....
....
....
I—

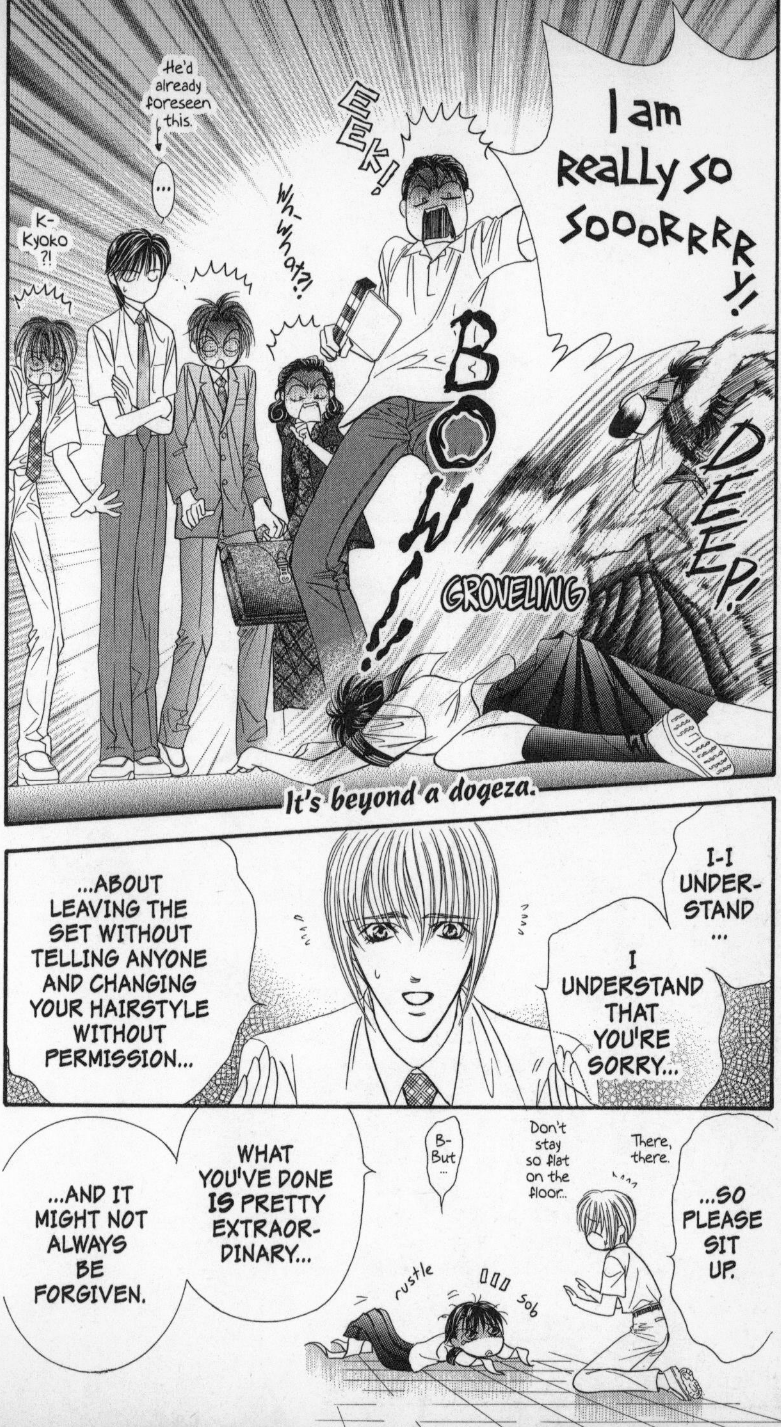
I am really so sooorrrry!!
EEK!
Wh-what?!
He'd already foreseen this.
...
K-Kyoko?!
BOW!!!
DEEP!
GROVELING
It's beyond a dogeza.
I-I UNDERSTAND...
I UNDERSTAND THAT YOU'RE SORRY...
...ABOUT LEAVING THE SET WITHOUT TELLING ANYONE AND CHANGING YOUR HAIRSTYLE WITHOUT PERMISSION...
...SO PLEASE SIT UP.
There, there.
Don't stay so flat on the floor...
B-But...
WHAT YOU'VE DONE IS PRETTY EXTRAORDINARY...
...AND IT MIGHT NOT ALWAYS BE FORGIVEN.
rustle
sob

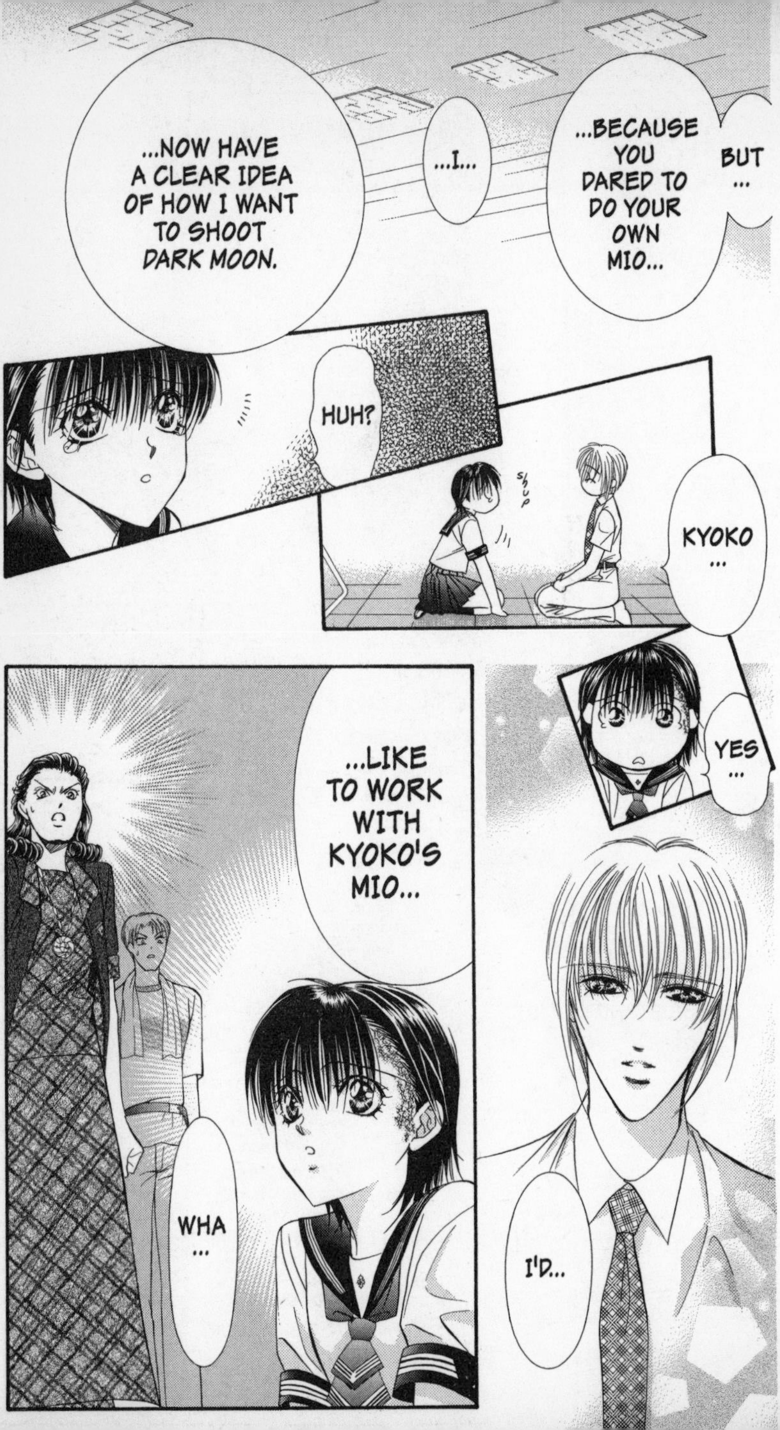
BUT ...
...BECAUSE YOU DARED TO DO YOUR OWN MIO...
...I...
...NOW HAVE A CLEAR IDEA OF HOW I WANT TO SHOOT DARK MOON.
KYOKO ...
SHUP
HUH?
YES ...
I'D...
...LIKE TO WORK WITH KYOKO'S MIO...
WHA ...

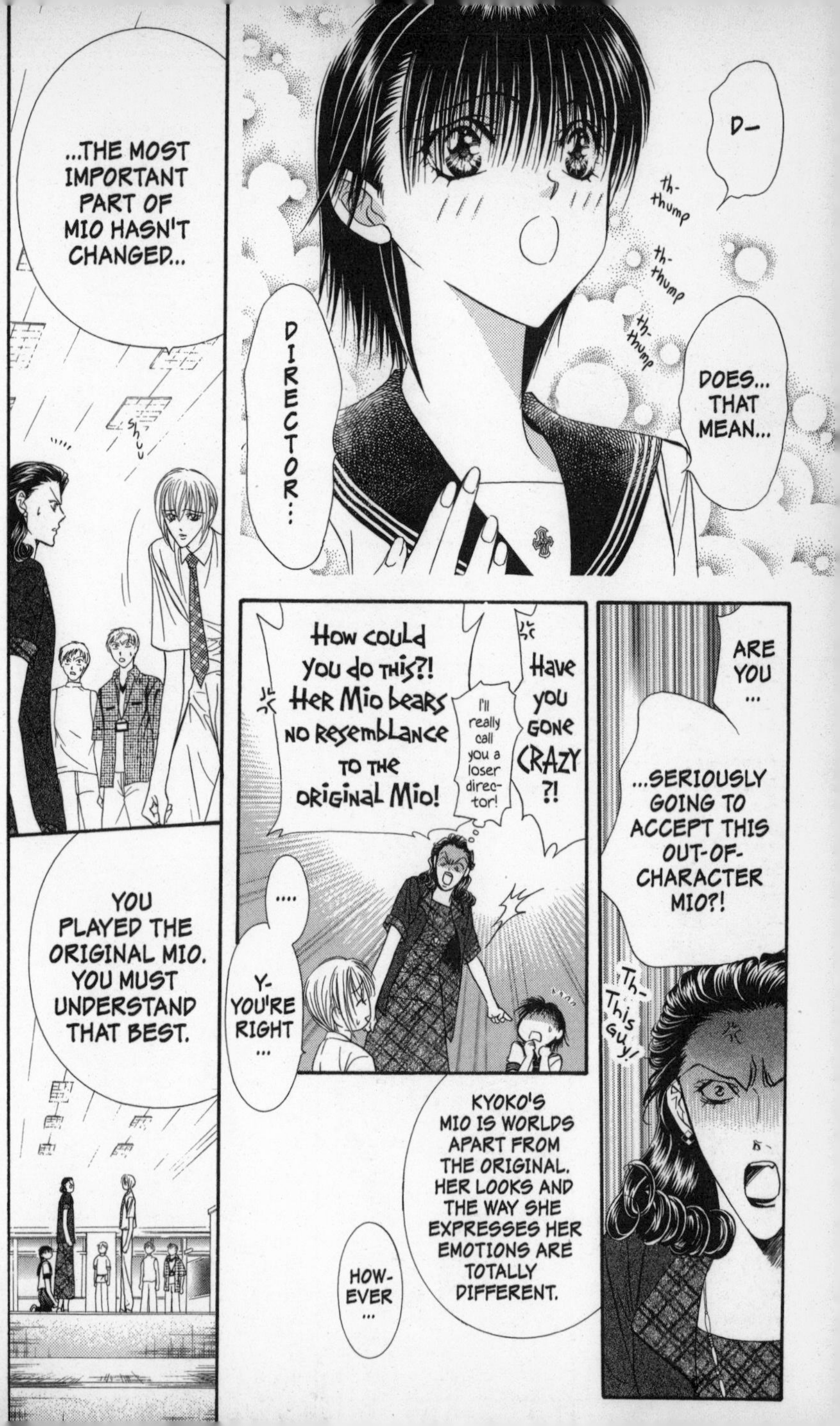
D–
th-thump
th-thump
th-thump
DOES... THAT MEAN...
DIRECTOR...
ARE YOU...
...SERIOUSLY GOING TO ACCEPT THIS OUT-OF-CHARACTER MIO?!
Th-This guy!
Have you gone CRAZY?!
How could you do this?! Her Mio bears no resemblance to the original Mio!
I'll really call you a loser director!
....
Y-YOU'RE RIGHT...
KYOKO'S MIO IS WORLDS APART FROM THE ORIGINAL. HER LOOKS AND THE WAY SHE EXPRESSES HER EMOTIONS ARE TOTALLY DIFFERENT.
HOW-EVER...
...THE MOST IMPORTANT PART OF MIO HASN'T CHANGED...
shuu
YOU PLAYED THE ORIGINAL MIO. YOU MUST UNDERSTAND THAT BEST.

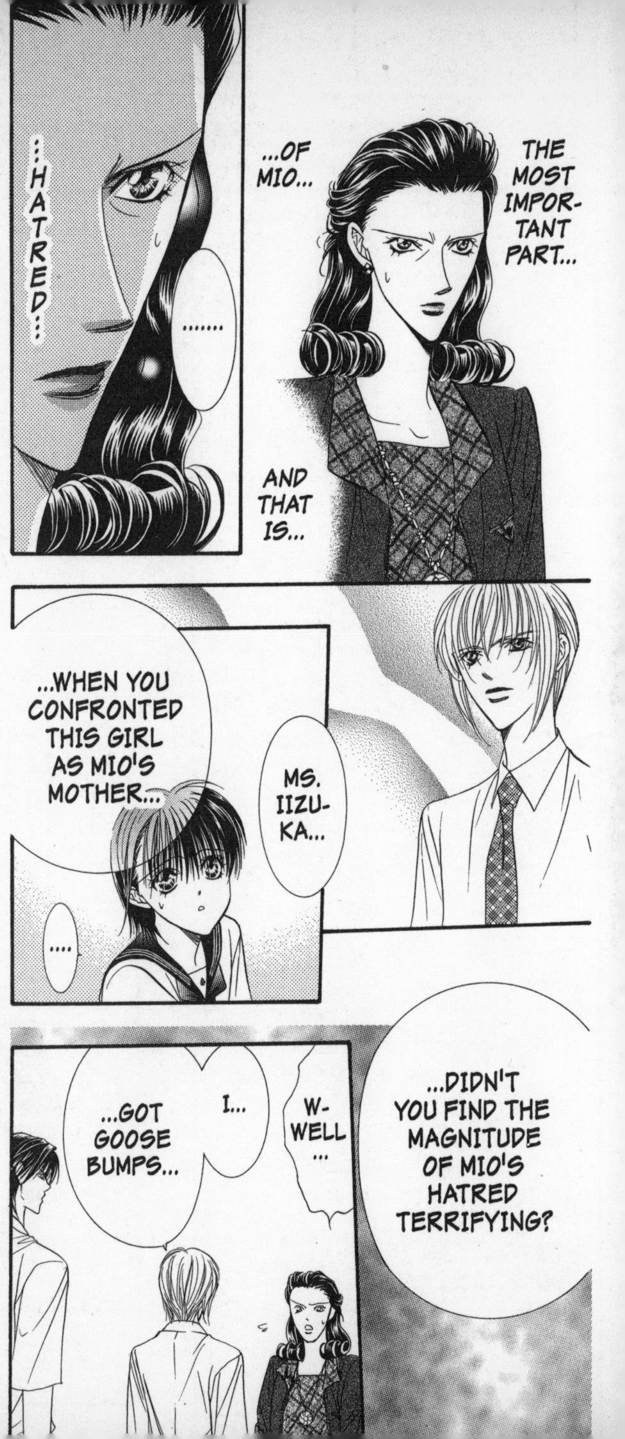
THE MOST IMPORTANT PART...
...OF MIO...
AND THAT IS...
...HATRED...
....
MS. IIZUKA...
...WHEN YOU CONFRONTED THIS GIRL AS MIO'S MOTHER...
....
...DIDN'T YOU FIND THE MAGNITUDE OF MIO'S HATRED TERRIFYING?
W-WELL...
I...
...GOT GOOSE BUMPS...

Harry and the Suspicious-looking Cretins

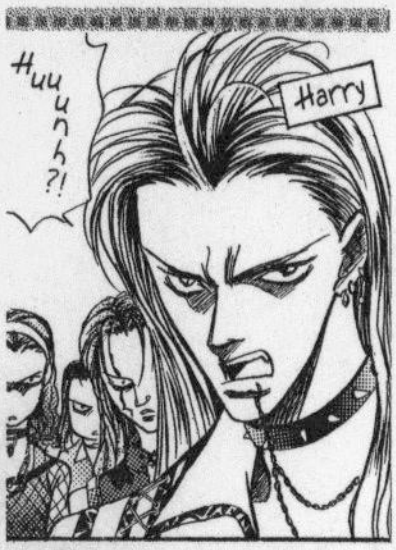
Harry
Huuunh?!

They call themselves a visual-kei band. They unfortunately ran into Kyoko at a hair salon. (I didn't want the readers to figure out what Kyoko was going to do here, so I had the place drawn so you couldn't figure what it was ♭ (By my assistants)). Apparently they were there to have their hair dyed.
↑ Odd colors that you can't buy at a drugstore.
They had a live show that evening, and they were hyper. At the live venue, they must always be playing dangerously, destructively and crazily...

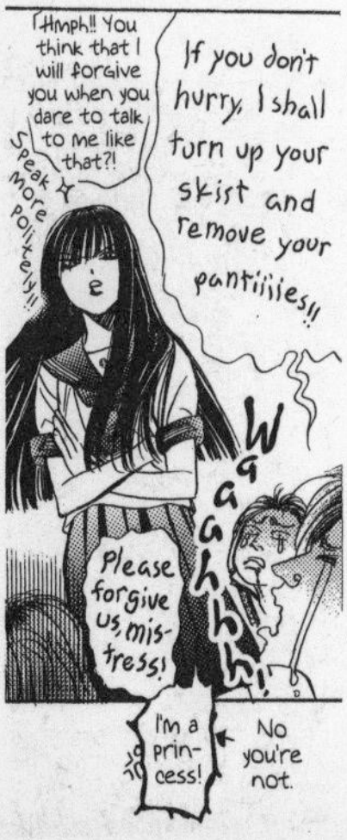
If you don't hurry, I shall turn up your skist and remove your pantiiiies!!
「Hmph!! You think that I will forgive you when you dare to talk to me like that?!
Speak more politely!!
Waaahhh!
Please forgive us, mistress!
No you're not.
I'm a princess!

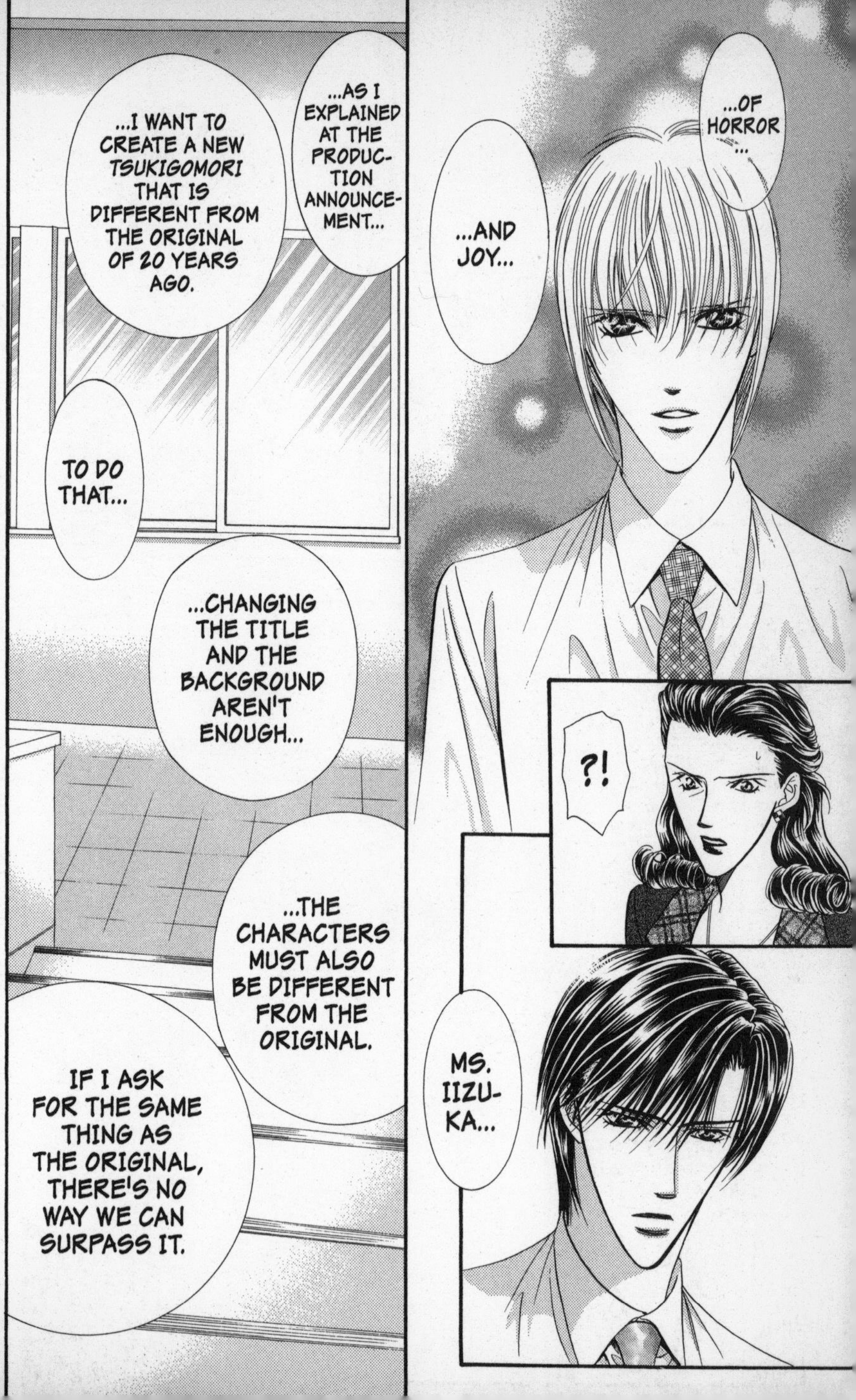
...OF HORROR...
...AND JOY...
?!
MS. IIZUKA...
...AS I EXPLAINED AT THE PRODUCTION ANNOUNCEMENT...
...I WANT TO CREATE A NEW TSUKIGOMORI THAT IS DIFFERENT FROM THE ORIGINAL OF 20 YEARS AGO.
TO DO THAT...
...CHANGING THE TITLE AND THE BACKGROUND AREN'T ENOUGH...
...THE CHARACTERS MUST ALSO BE DIFFERENT FROM THE ORIGINAL.
IF I ASK FOR THE SAME THING AS THE ORIGINAL, THERE'S NO WAY WE CAN SURPASS IT.

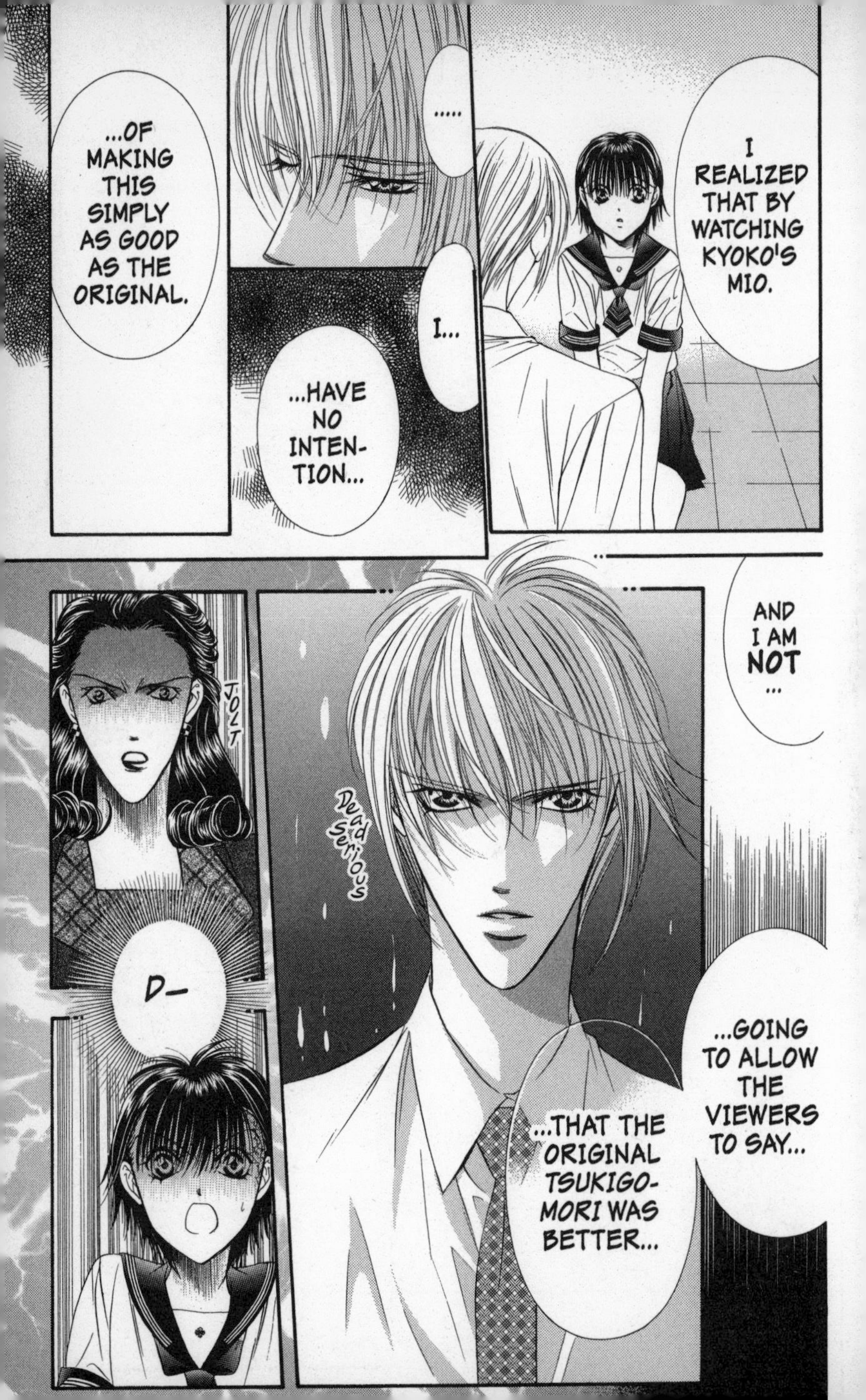
I REALIZED THAT BY WATCHING KYOKO'S MIO.
.....
I...
...HAVE NO INTEN-TION...
...OF MAKING THIS SIMPLY AS GOOD AS THE ORIGINAL.
AND I AM **NOT** ...
...GOING TO ALLOW THE VIEWERS TO SAY...
...THAT THE ORIGINAL TSUKIGO-MORI WAS BETTER...
Dead Serious
JOLT
D_

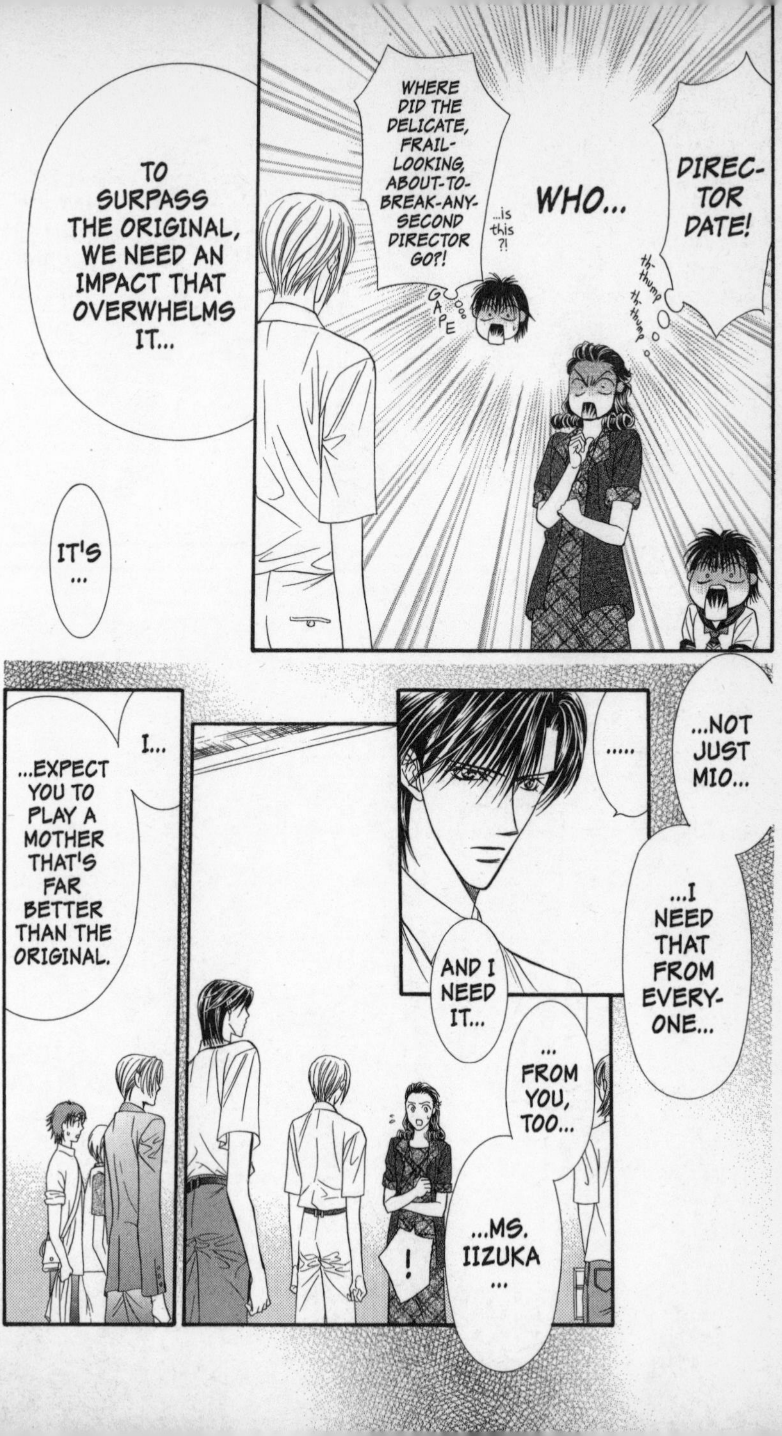
DIRECTOR DATE!
th-thump th-thump
WHO... ...is this?!
WHERE DID THE DELICATE, FRAIL-LOOKING, ABOUT-TO-BREAK-ANY-SECOND DIRECTOR GO?!
GAPE
TO SURPASS THE ORIGINAL, WE NEED AN IMPACT THAT OVERWHELMS IT...
IT'S...
...NOT JUST MIO...
...I NEED THAT FROM EVERYONE...
.....
AND I NEED IT...
...FROM YOU, TOO...
...MS. IIZUKA...
!
I...
...EXPECT YOU TO PLAY A MOTHER THAT'S FAR BETTER THAN THE ORIGINAL.

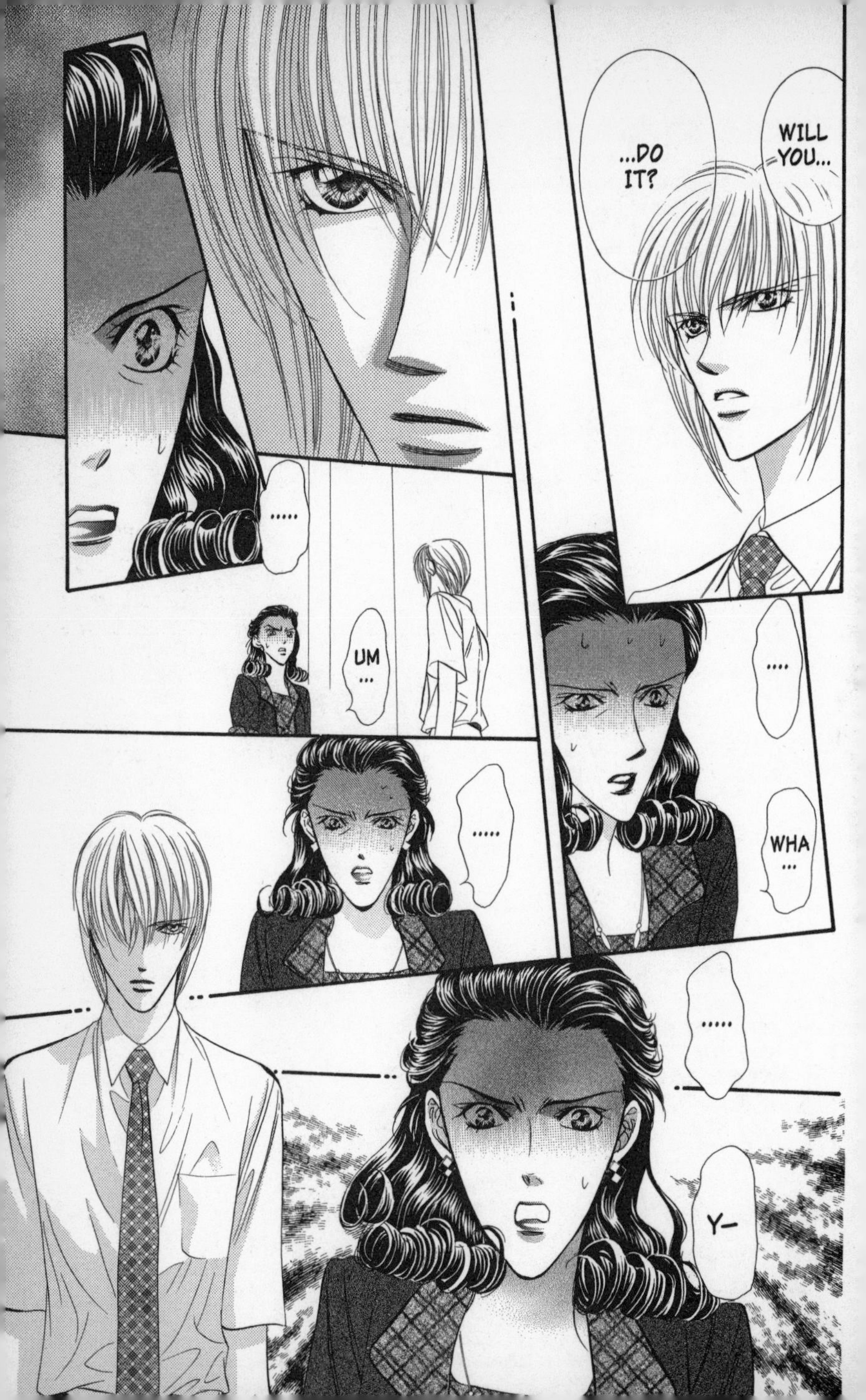
WILL YOU...
...DO IT?
.....
UM ...
....
WHA ...
.....
.....
Y—

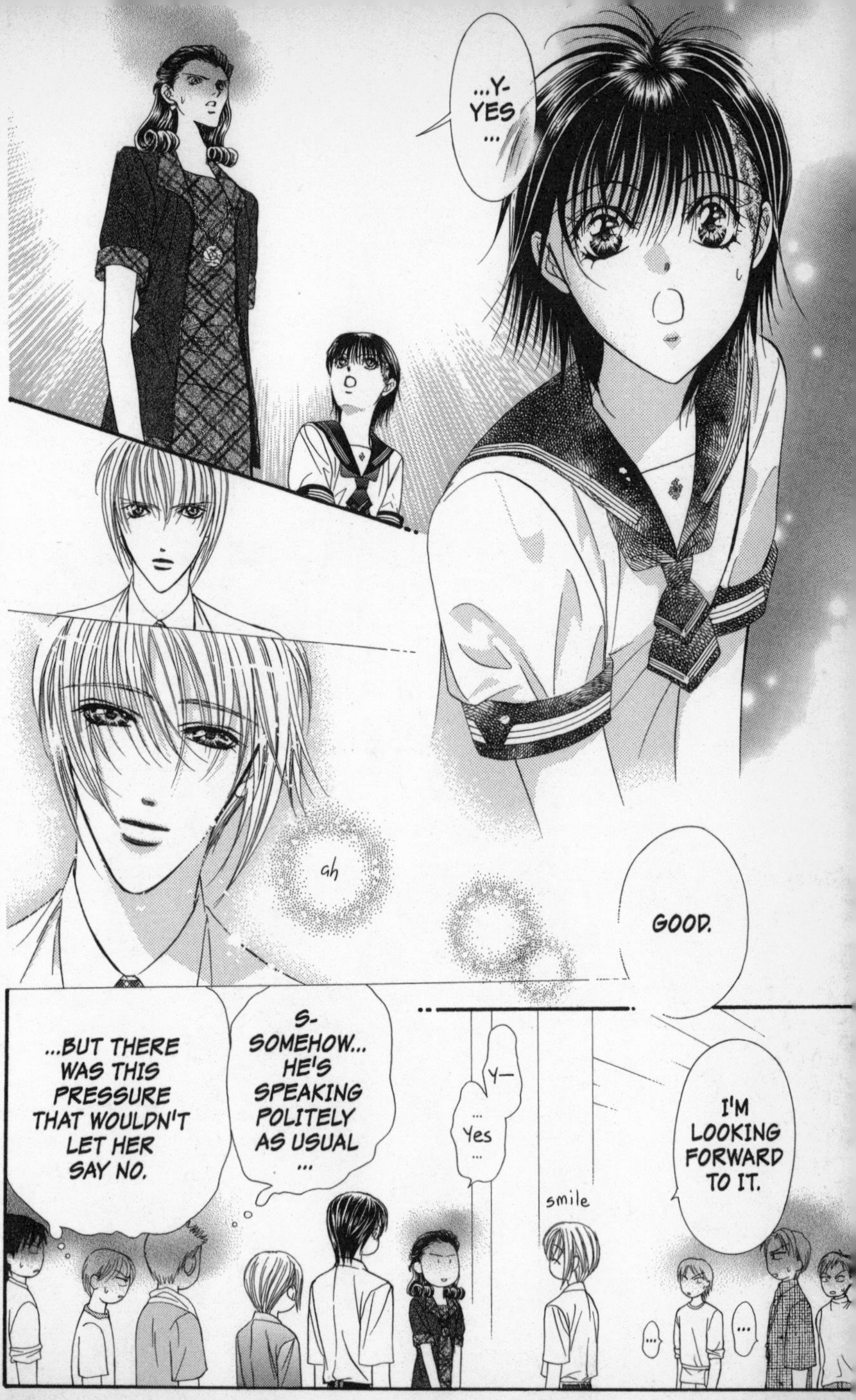
...Y- YES ...
ah
GOOD.
I'M LOOKING FORWARD TO IT.
...
...
smile
Y— ... Yes ...
S- SOMEHOW... HE'S SPEAKING POLITELY AS USUAL ...
...BUT THERE WAS THIS PRESSURE THAT WOULDN'T LET HER SAY NO.

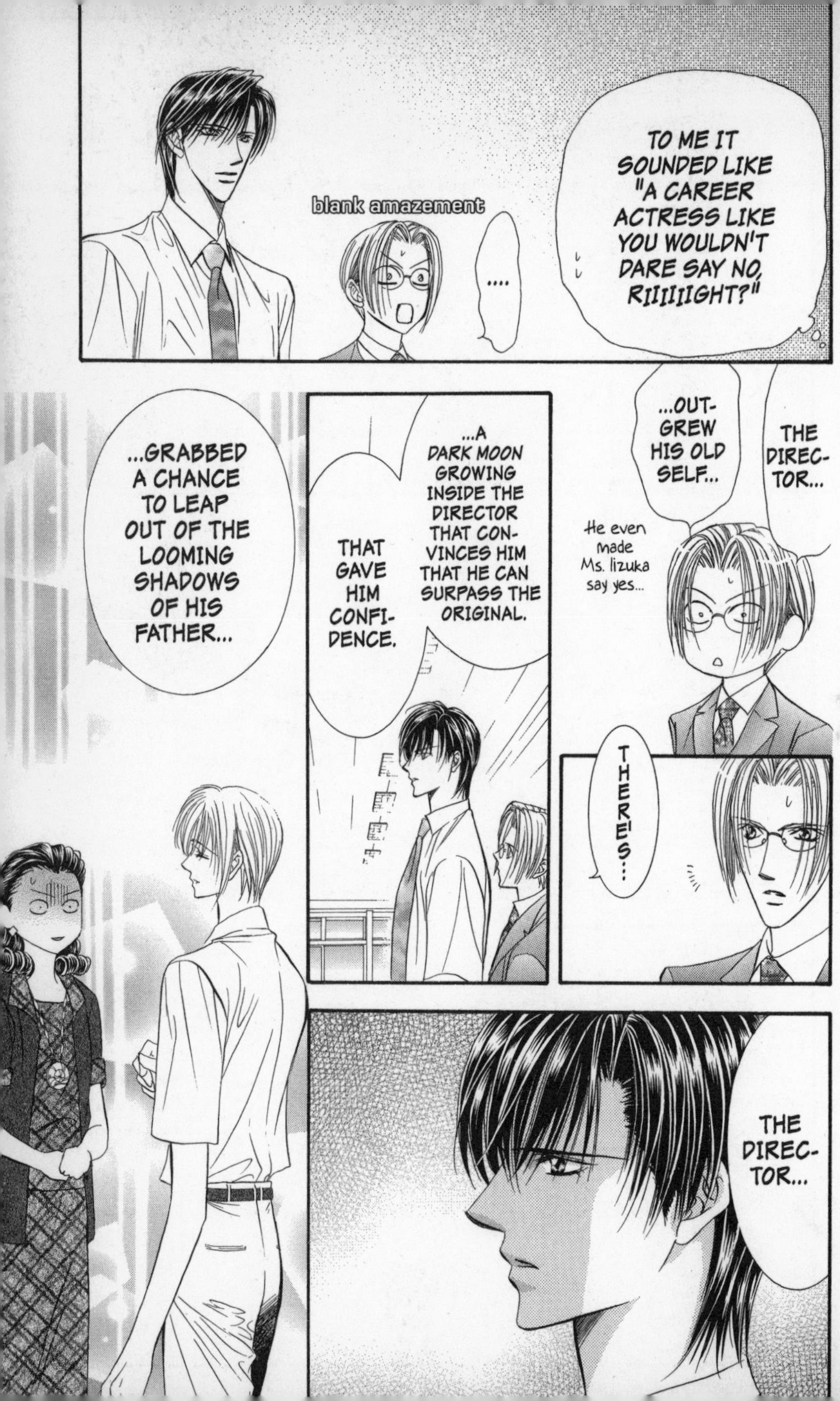
TO ME IT SOUNDED LIKE "A CAREER ACTRESS LIKE YOU WOULDN'T DARE SAY NO, RIIIIIIGHT?"
....
blank amazement
THE DIREC-TOR...
...OUT-GREW HIS OLD SELF...
He even made Ms. Iizuka say yes...
THERE'S...
...A DARK MOON GROWING INSIDE THE DIRECTOR THAT CON-VINCES HIM THAT HE CAN SURPASS THE ORIGINAL.
THAT GAVE HIM CONFI-DENCE.
...GRABBED A CHANCE TO LEAP OUT OF THE LOOMING SHADOWS OF HIS FATHER...
THE DIREC-TOR...

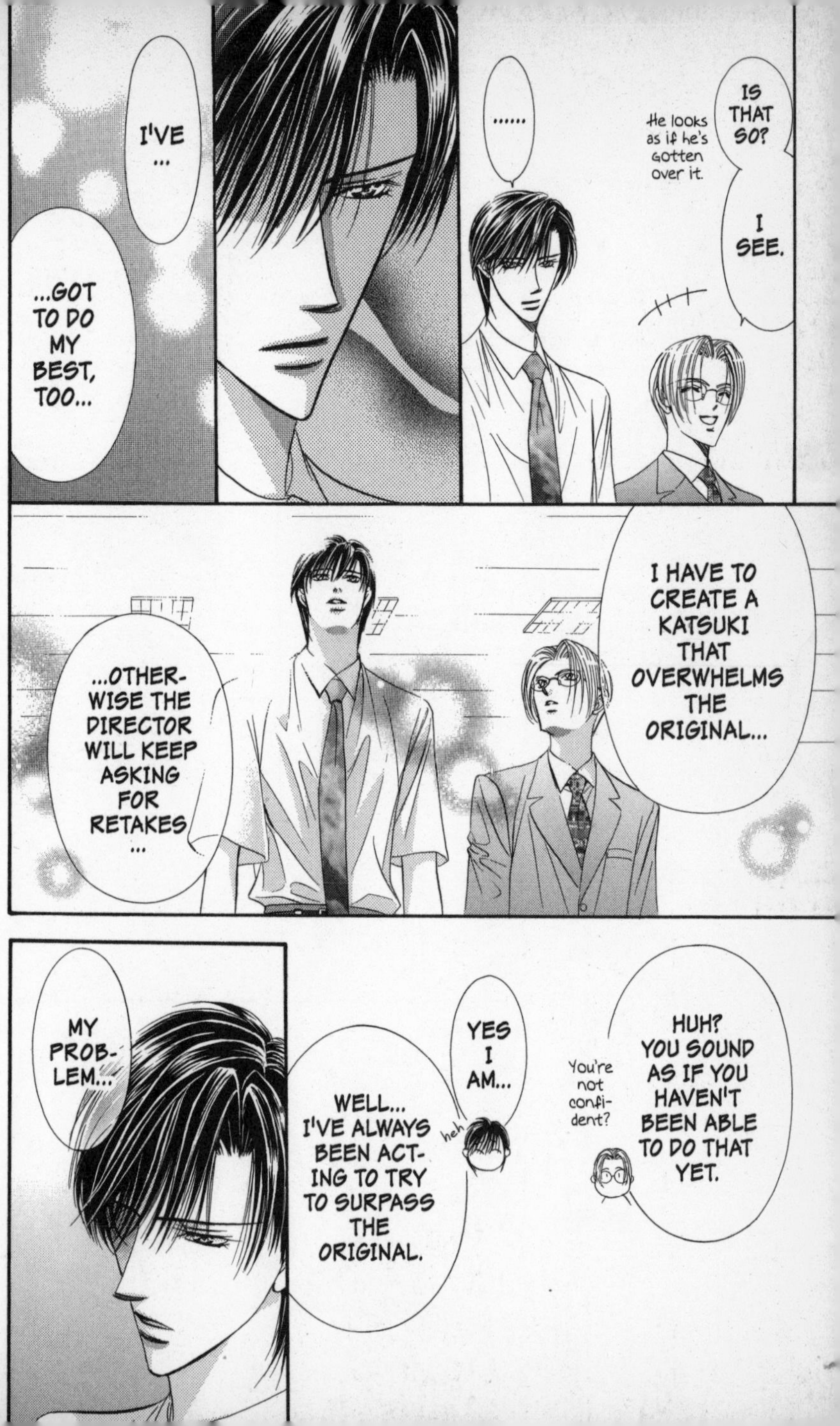
IS THAT SO?
He looks as if he's gotten over it.
I SEE.
......
I'VE ...
...GOT TO DO MY BEST, TOO...
I HAVE TO CREATE A KATSUKI THAT OVERWHELMS THE ORIGINAL...
...OTHERWISE THE DIRECTOR WILL KEEP ASKING FOR RETAKES ...
HUH? YOU SOUND AS IF YOU HAVEN'T BEEN ABLE TO DO THAT YET.
You're not confident?
YES I AM...
heh
WELL... I'VE ALWAYS BEEN ACTING TO TRY TO SURPASS THE ORIGINAL.
MY PROBLEM...

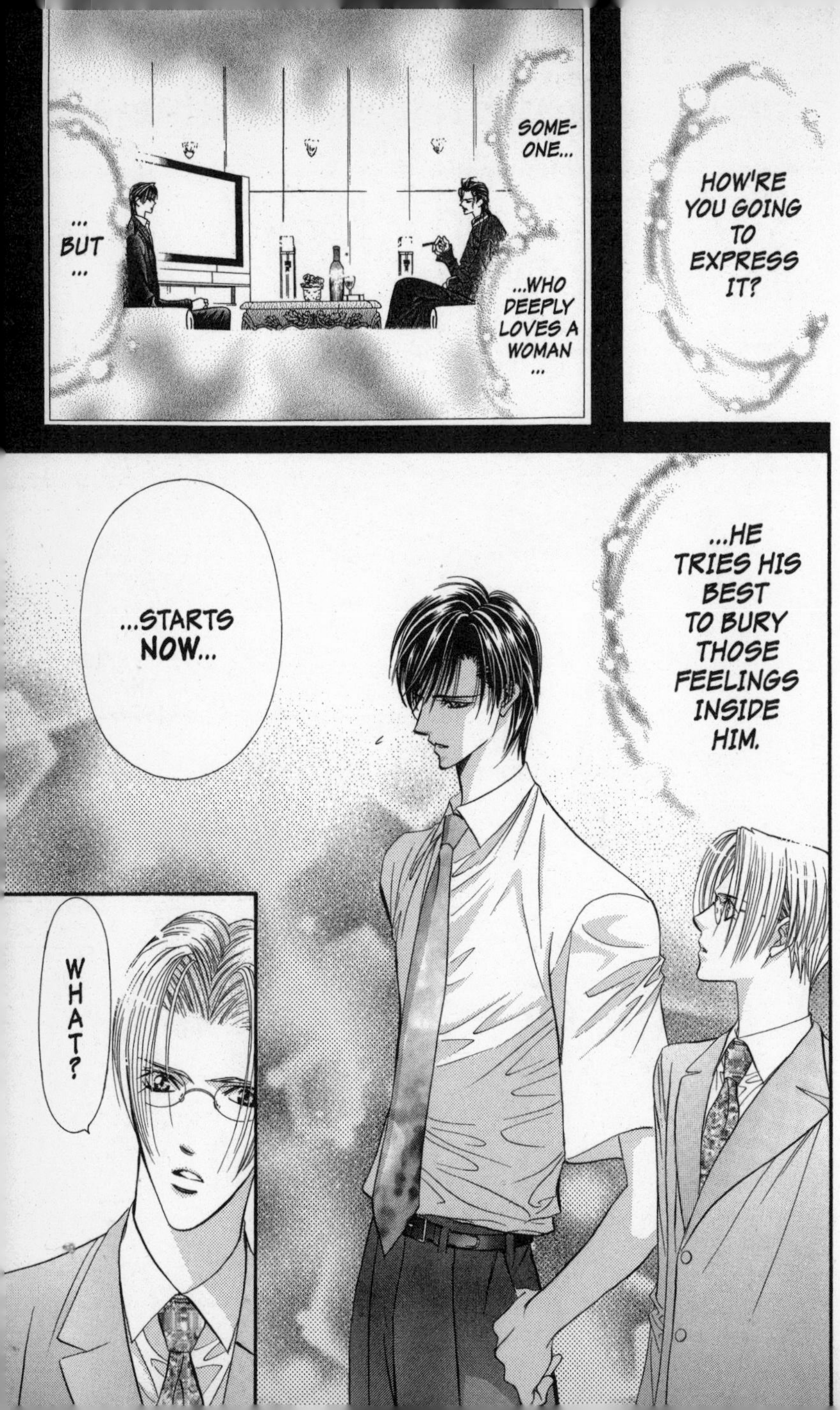
HOW'RE YOU GOING TO EXPRESS IT?
SOME-ONE...
...WHO DEEPLY LOVES A WOMAN ...
... BUT ...
...HE TRIES HIS BEST TO BURY THOSE FEELINGS INSIDE HIM.
...STARTS NOW...
WHAT?

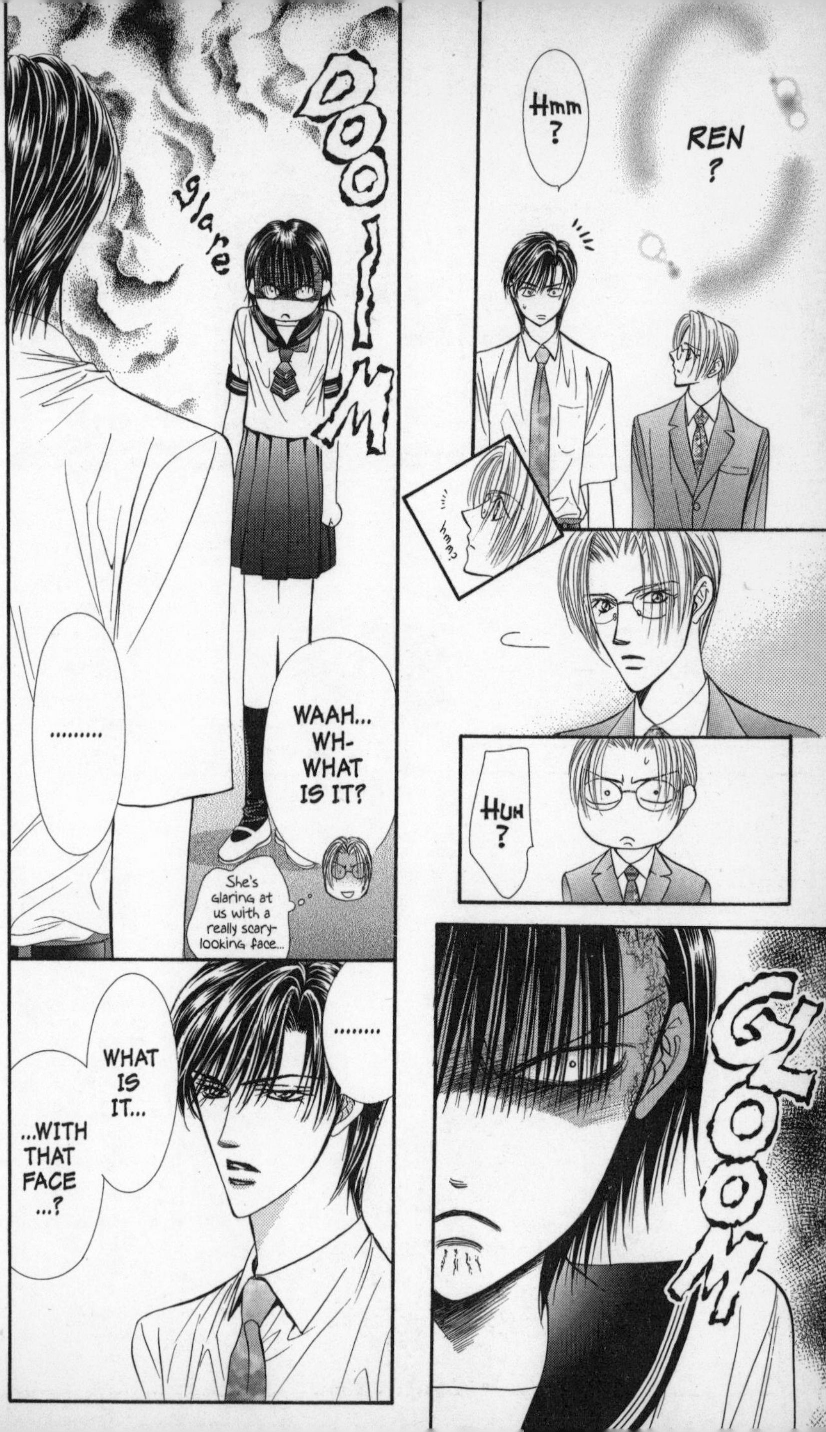
REN?
Hmm?
Hmm?
HUH?
DOOOM
glare
WAAH... WH-WHAT IS IT?
She's glaring at us with a really scary-looking face...
....
GLOOM
....
WHAT IS IT...
...WITH THAT FACE ...?

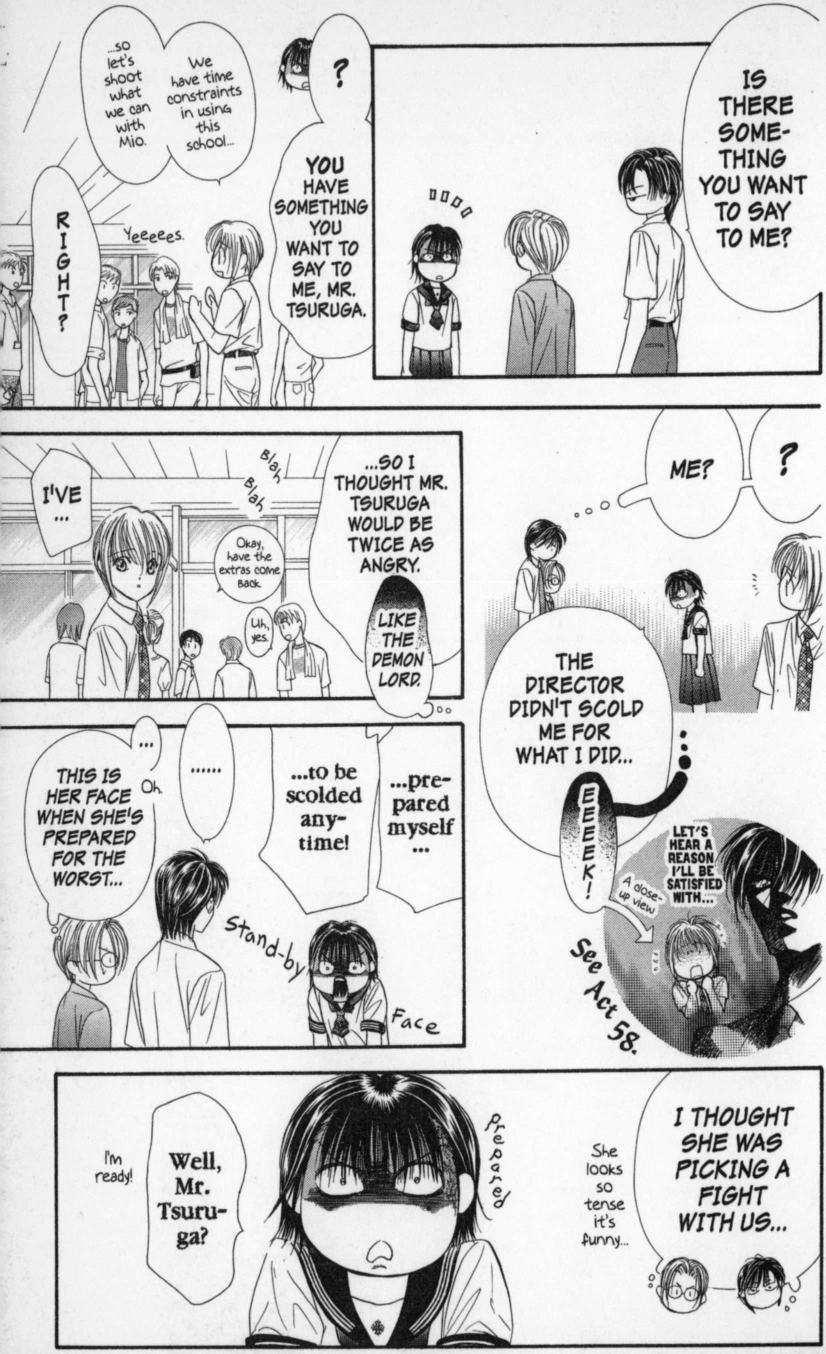
IS THERE SOMETHING YOU WANT TO SAY TO ME?
?
YOU HAVE SOMETHING YOU WANT TO SAY TO ME, MR. TSURUGA.
We have time constraints in using this school...
...so let's shoot what we can with Mio.
RIGHT?
Yeeeees.
?
ME?
THE DIRECTOR DIDN'T SCOLD ME FOR WHAT I DID...
EEEEK!
LET'S HEAR A REASON I'LL BE SATISFIED WITH...
A close-up view
See Act 58.
...SO I THOUGHT MR. TSURUGA WOULD BE TWICE AS ANGRY.
LIKE THE DEMON LORD.
Blah Blah
Okay, have the extras come back.
Uh, yes.
I'VE ...
...prepared myself ...
...to be scolded any-time!
......
...
Oh.
THIS IS HER FACE WHEN SHE'S PREPARED FOR THE WORST...
Stand-by Face
I THOUGHT SHE WAS PICKING A FIGHT WITH US...
She looks so tense it's funny...
Prepared
Well, Mr. Tsuruga?
I'm ready!

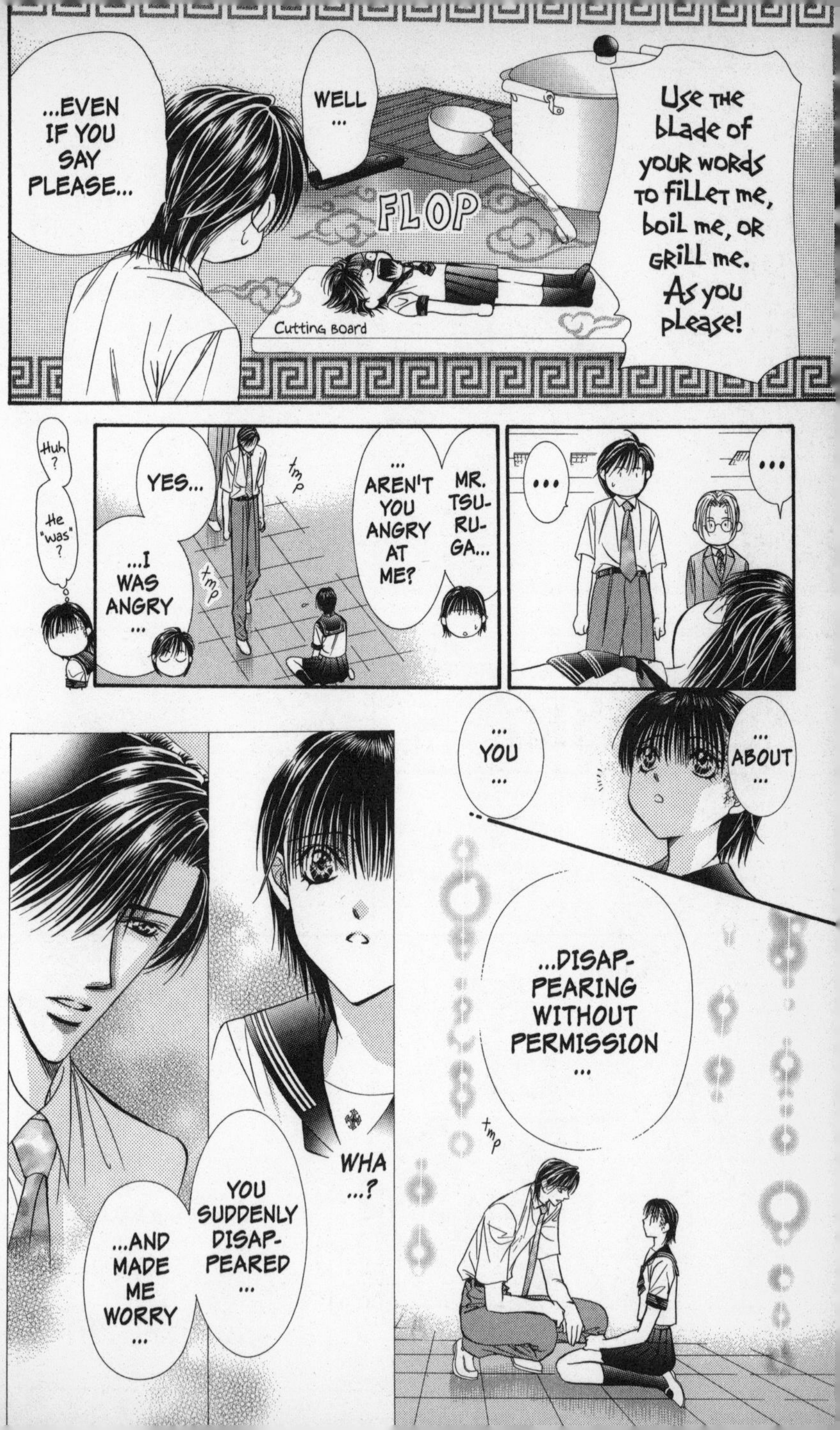
Use the blade of your words to fillet me, boil me, or grill me. As you please!
WELL...
...EVEN IF YOU SAY PLEASE...
FLOP
Cutting board
...
...
MR. TSURUGA...
...AREN'T YOU ANGRY AT ME?
YES...
...I WAS ANGRY...
tmp
tmp
Huh? He "was"?
...ABOUT...
...YOU...
...DISAPPEARING WITHOUT PERMISSION...
tmp
WHA...?
YOU SUDDENLY DISAPPEARED...
...AND MADE ME WORRY...

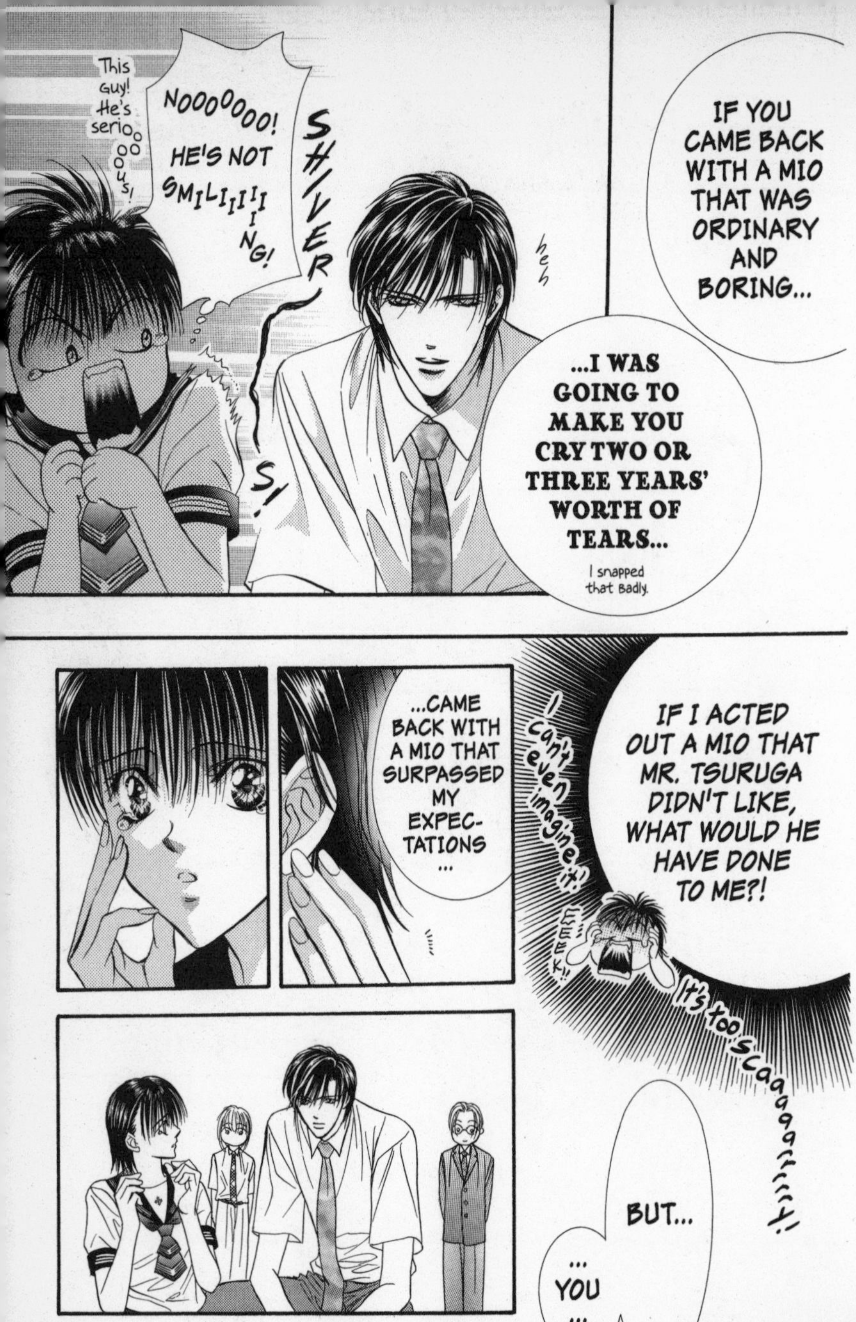
IF YOU CAME BACK WITH A MIO THAT WAS ORDINARY AND BORING...
...I WAS GOING TO MAKE YOU CRY TWO OR THREE YEARS' WORTH OF TEARS...
I snapped that badly.
heh
SHIVERS!
NOOOOOOO! HE'S NOT SMILIIIIIING!
This guy! He's seriooooous!
...CAME BACK WITH A MIO THAT SURPASSED MY EXPECTATIONS ...
IF I ACTED OUT A MIO THAT MR. TSURUGA DIDN'T LIKE, WHAT WOULD HE HAVE DONE TO ME?!
I can't even imagine it!
EEEEK!!
It's too scaaaaarrrry!
BUT...
... YOU ...

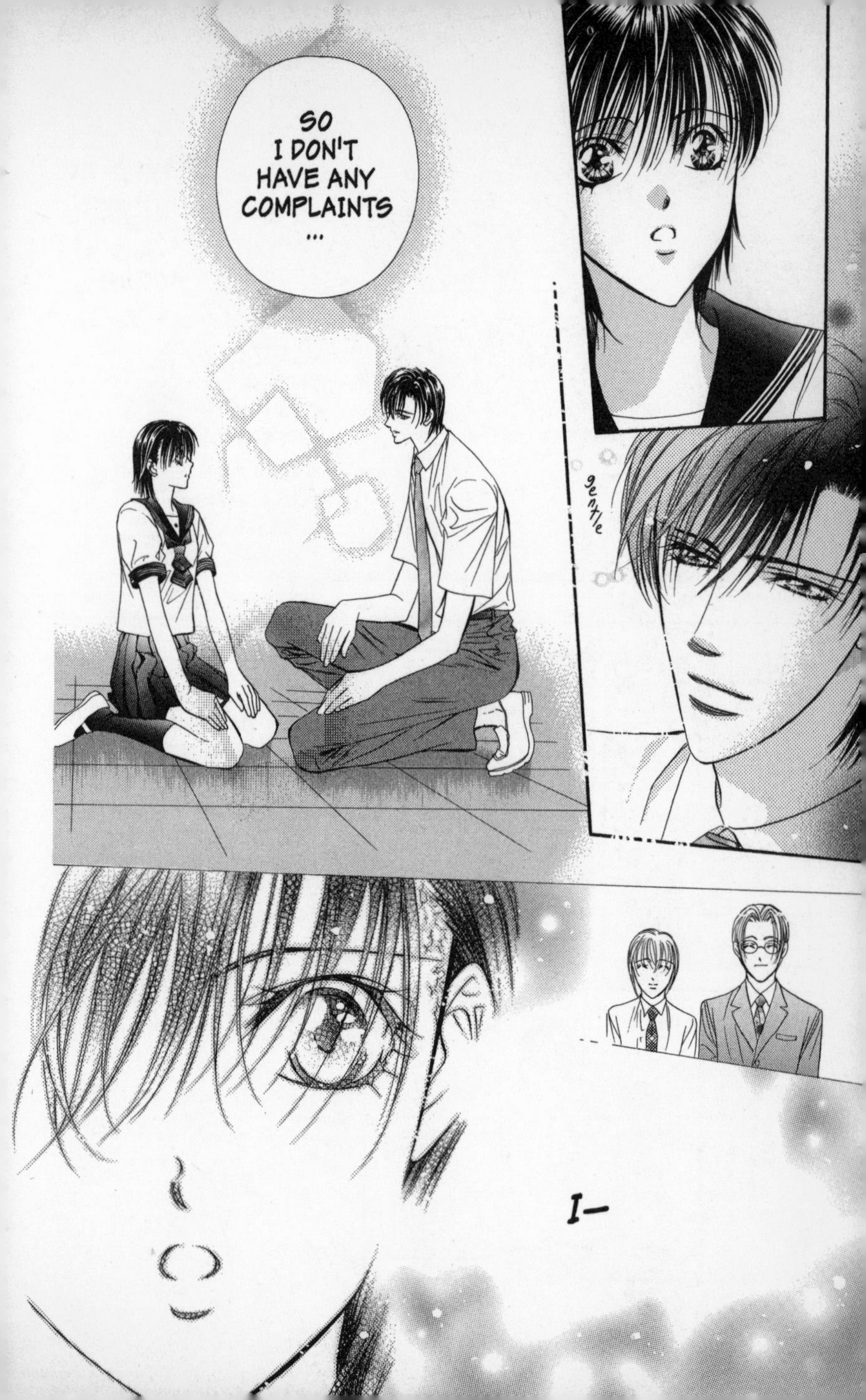
gentle
SO I DON'T HAVE ANY COMPLAINTS ...
I—

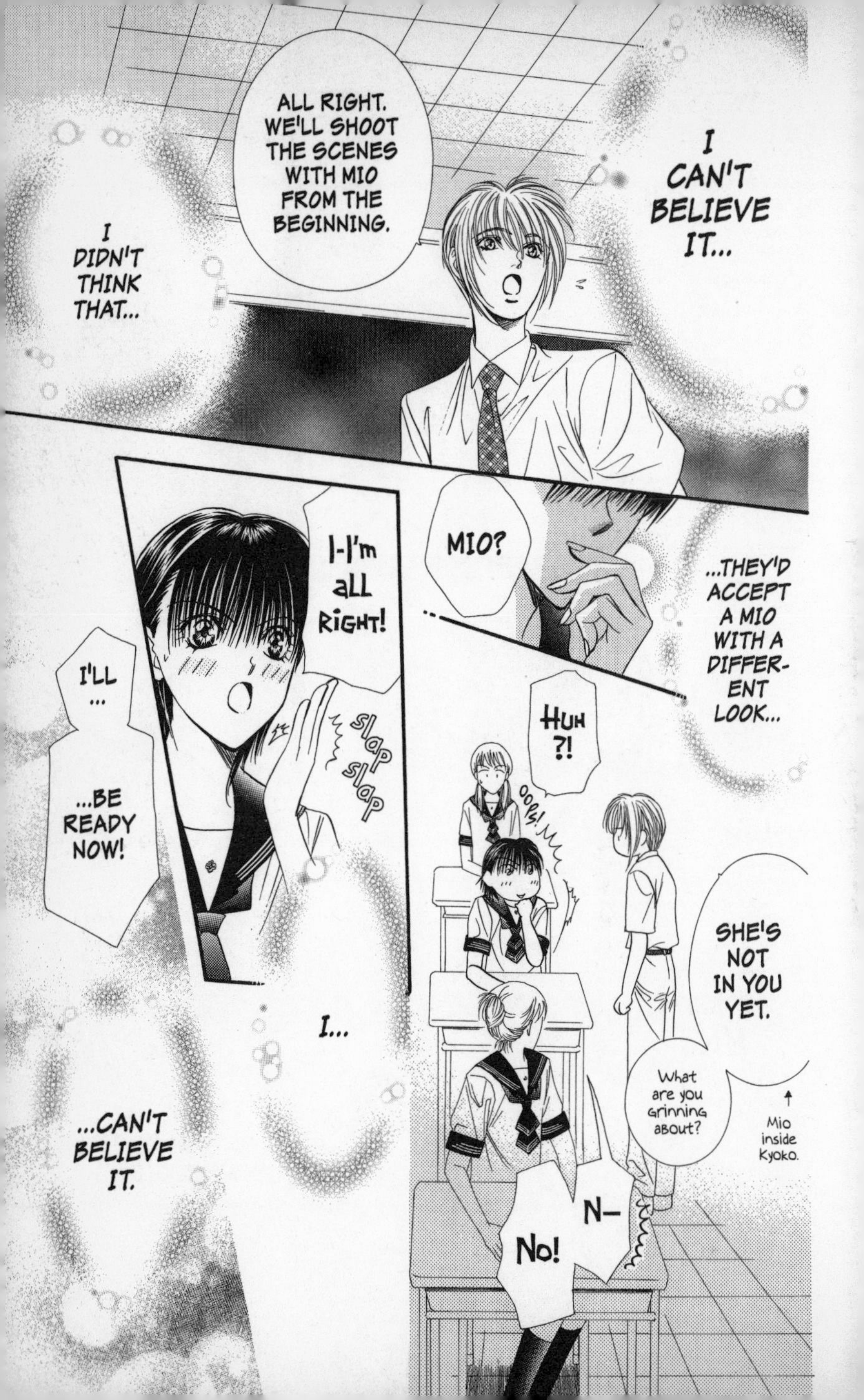
I CAN'T BELIEVE IT...
ALL RIGHT. WE'LL SHOOT THE SCENES WITH MIO FROM THE BEGINNING.
I DIDN'T THINK THAT...
...THEY'D ACCEPT A MIO WITH A DIFFERENT LOOK...
MIO?
I-I'm all RIGHT!
slap slap
I'LL ...
...BE READY NOW!
SHE'S NOT IN YOU YET.
HUH?!
OOPS!
What are you grinning about?
Mio inside Kyoko.
N— No!
I...
...CAN'T BELIEVE IT.

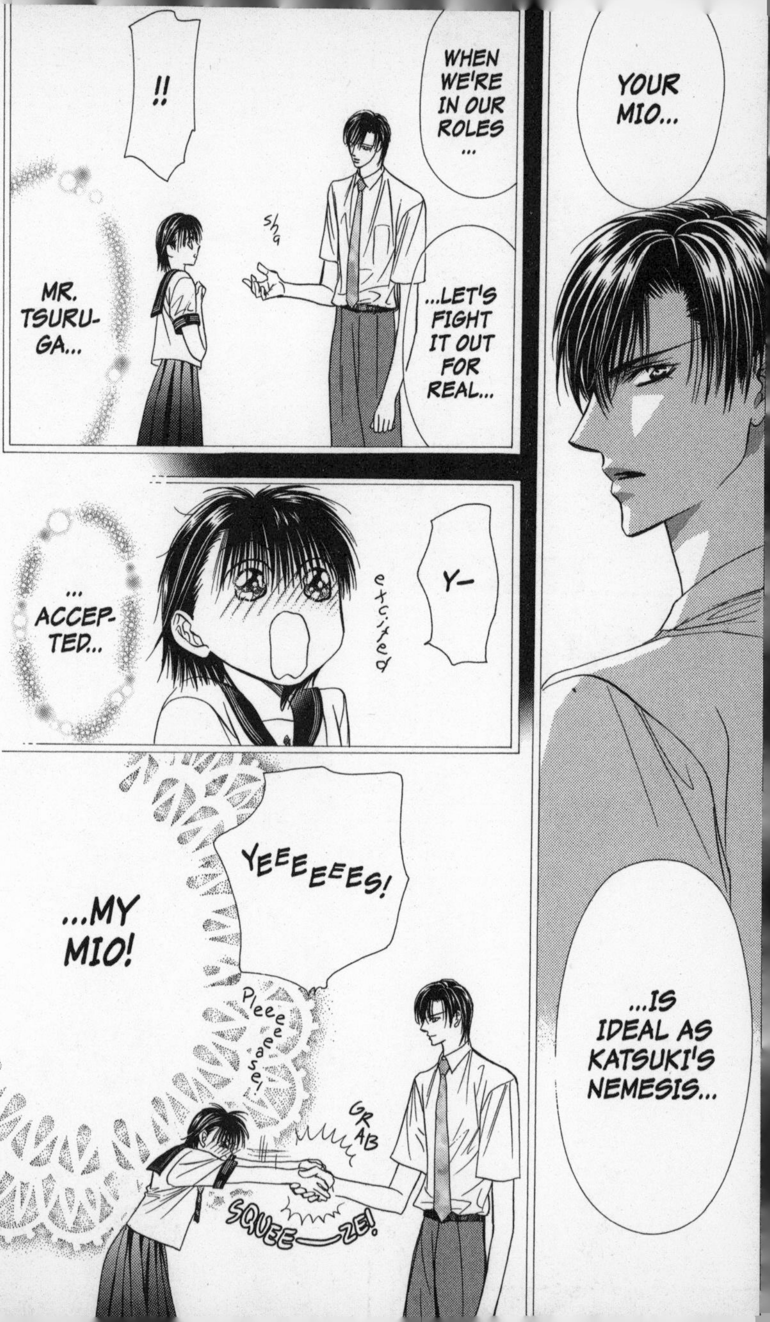
YOUR MIO...
...IS IDEAL AS KATSUKI'S NEMESIS...
WHEN WE'RE IN OUR ROLES...
...LET'S FIGHT IT OUT FOR REAL...
sha
!!
MR. TSURU-GA...
Y-
excited
...ACCEP-TED...
YEEEEEEES!
...MY MIO!
Pleeeeease!
GRAB
SQUEE—ZE!

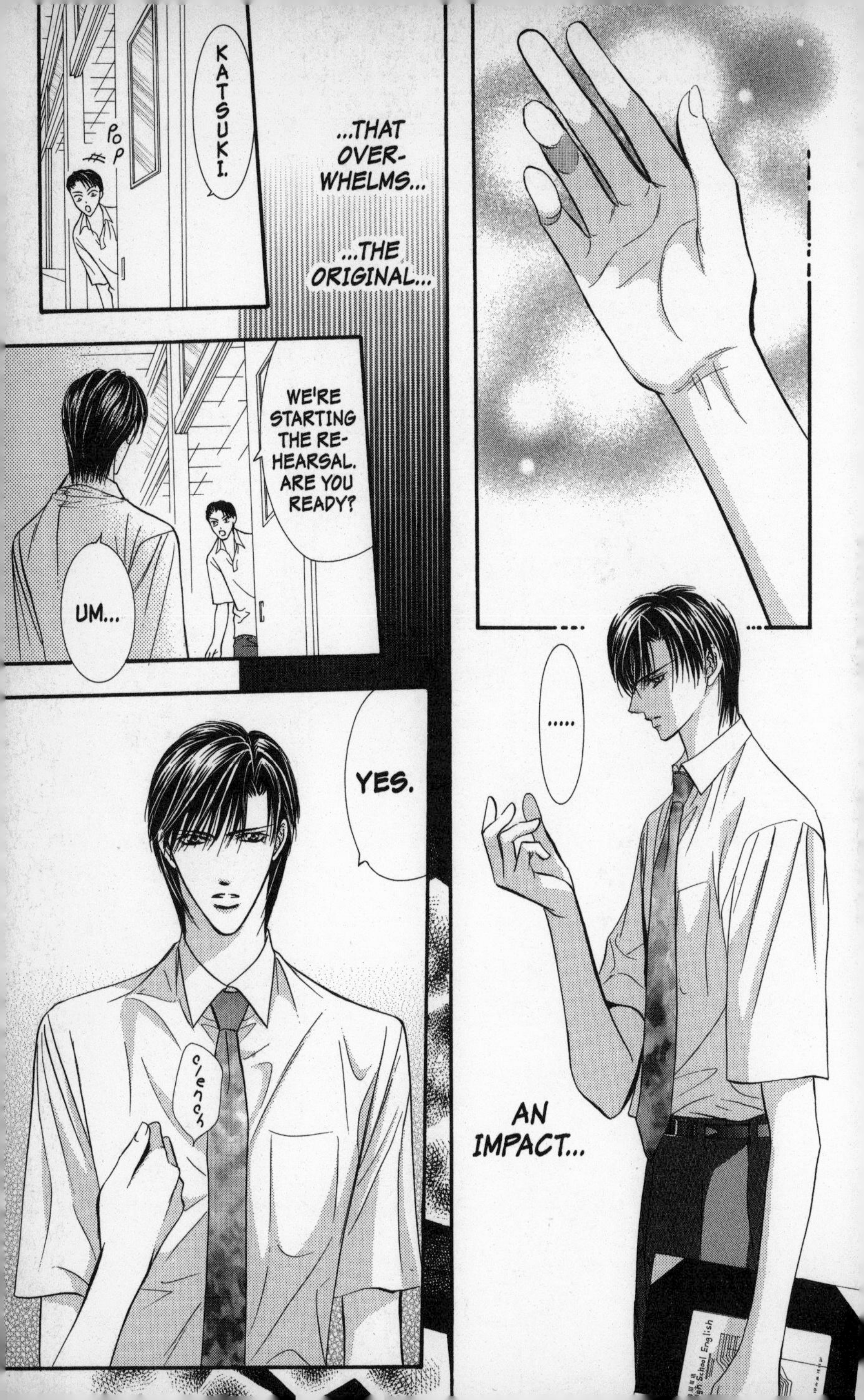
.....
AN IMPACT...
...THAT OVER-WHELMS...
...THE ORIGINAL...
KATSUKI.
POP
WE'RE STARTING THE RE-HEARSAL. ARE YOU READY?
UM...
YES.
clench

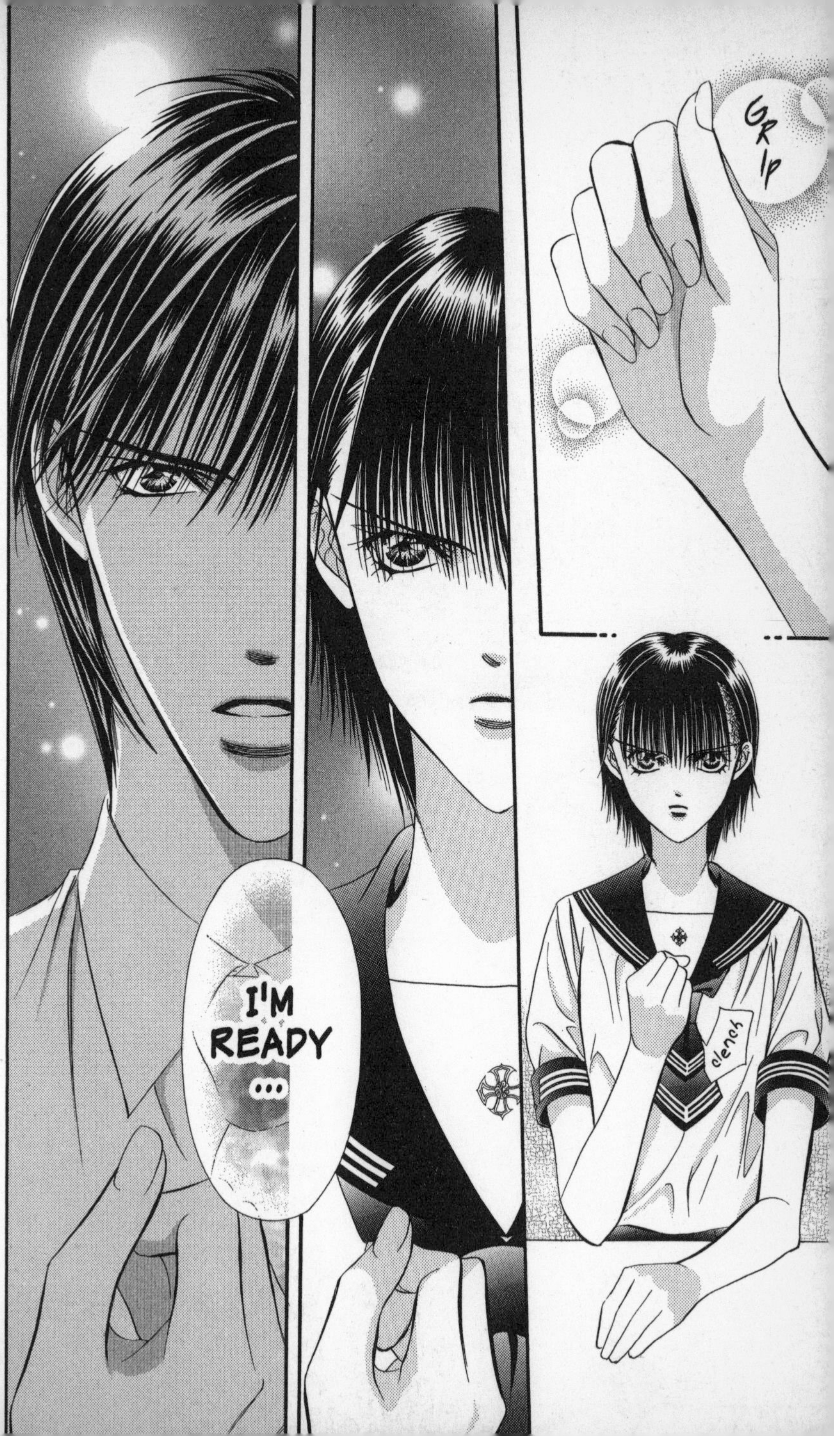
GRIP
clench
I'M READY ...

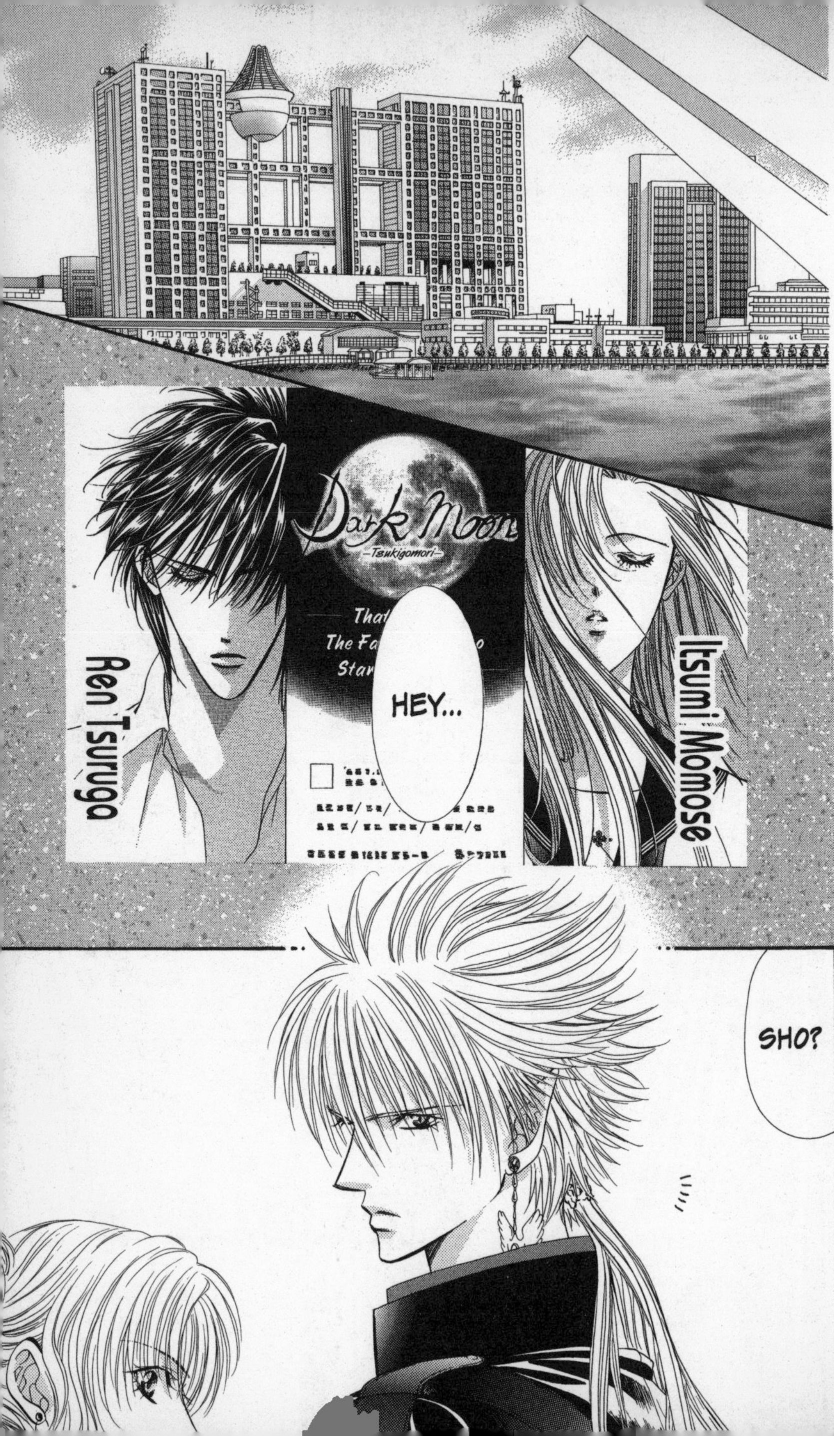
Itsumi Momose
Dark Moon
-Tsukigomori-
Ren Tsuruga
HEY...
SHO?

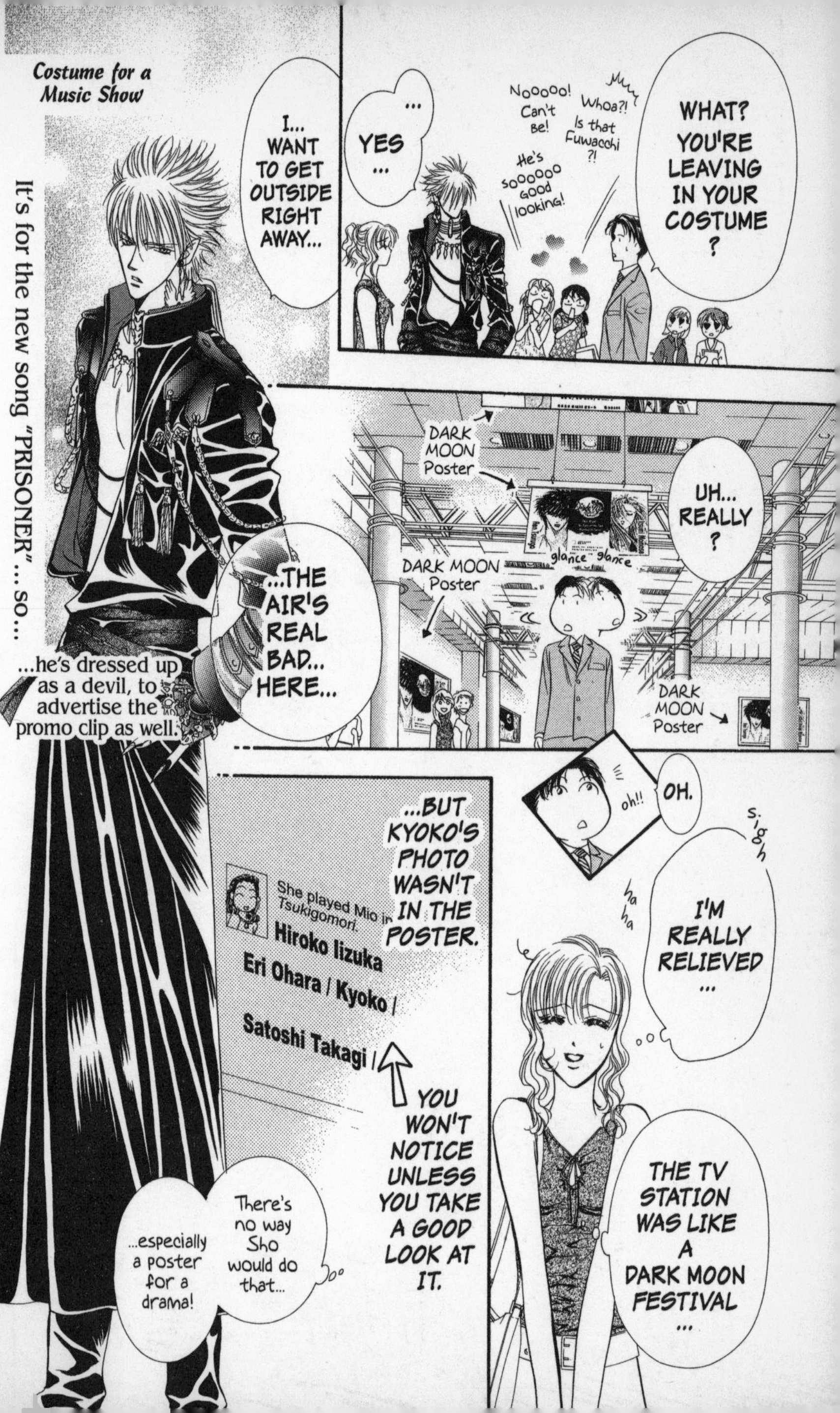
WHAT? YOU'RE LEAVING IN YOUR COSTUME?
Whoa?! Is that Fuwacchi ?!
Nooooo! Can't be!
He's soooooo good looking!
... YES ...
I... WANT TO GET OUTSIDE RIGHT AWAY...
...THE AIR'S REAL BAD... HERE...
UH... REALLY ?
DARK MOON Poster
glance glance
DARK MOON Poster
DARK MOON Poster
OH.
oh!!
sigh
ha ha ha
I'M REALLY RELIEVED ...
THE TV STATION WAS LIKE A DARK MOON FESTIVAL ...
...BUT KYOKO'S PHOTO WASN'T IN THE POSTER.
She played Mio in Tsukigomori.
Hiroko Iizuka
Eri Ohara / Kyoko /
Satoshi Takagi /
YOU WON'T NOTICE UNLESS YOU TAKE A GOOD LOOK AT IT.
There's no way Sho would do that...
...especially a poster for a drama!
Costume for a Music Show
It's for the new song "PRISONER" ... so...
...he's dressed up as a devil, to advertise the promo clip as well.

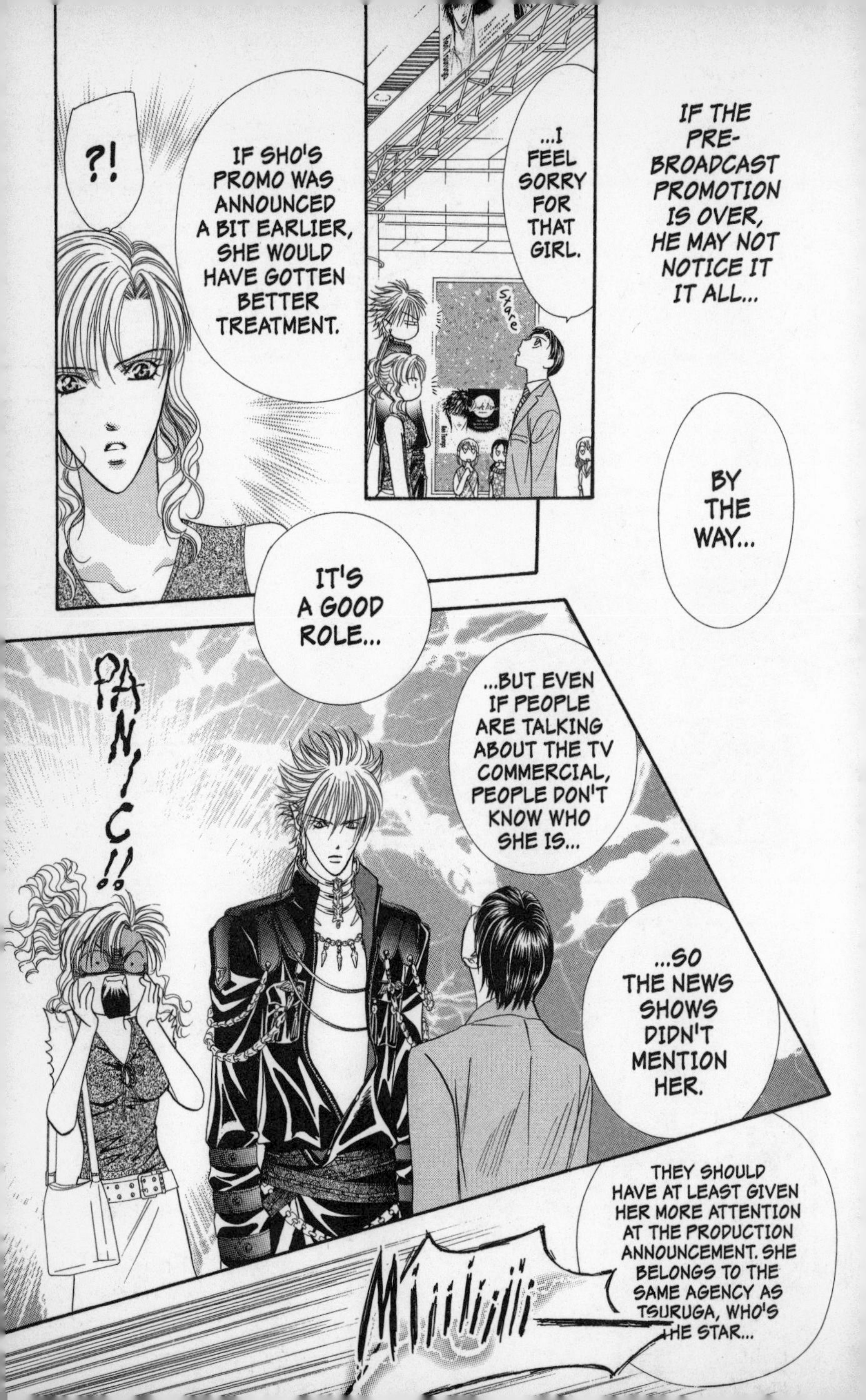
IF THE PRE-BROADCAST PROMOTION IS OVER, HE MAY NOT NOTICE IT IT ALL...
...I FEEL SORRY FOR THAT GIRL.
Stare
IF SHO'S PROMO WAS ANNOUNCED A BIT EARLIER, SHE WOULD HAVE GOTTEN BETTER TREATMENT.
?!
BY THE WAY...
IT'S A GOOD ROLE...
...BUT EVEN IF PEOPLE ARE TALKING ABOUT THE TV COMMERCIAL, PEOPLE DON'T KNOW WHO SHE IS...
...SO THE NEWS SHOWS DIDN'T MENTION HER.
THEY SHOULD HAVE AT LEAST GIVEN HER MORE ATTENTION AT THE PRODUCTION ANNOUNCEMENT. SHE BELONGS TO THE SAME AGENCY AS TSURUGA, WHO'S THE STAR...
Miiiiiiiii
PANIC!!

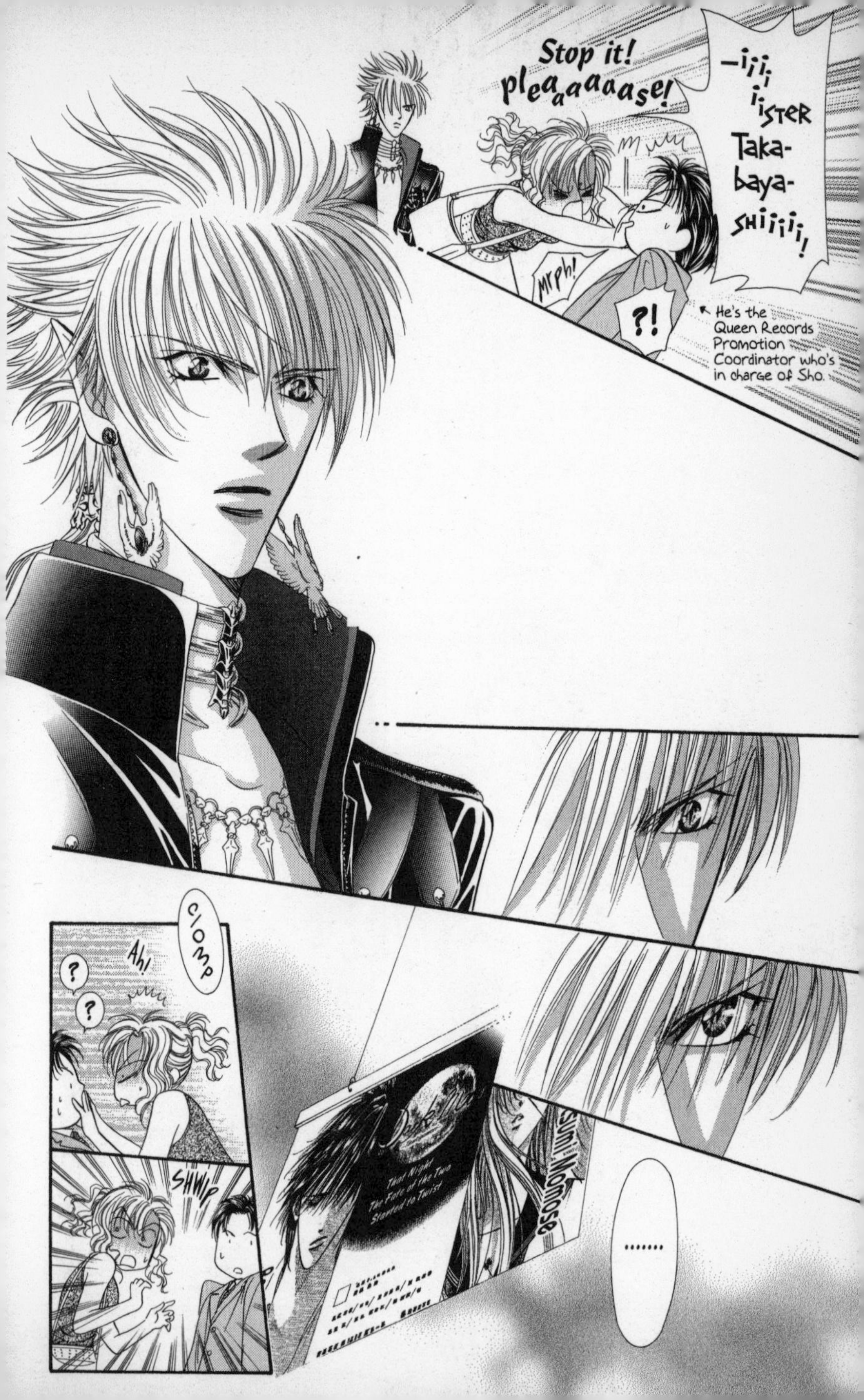

—iiii iiSTER Taka-baya-SHiiiiii!
Stop it! pleaaaaaase!
Mrph!
?!
He's the Queen Records Promotion Coordinator who's in charge of Sho.
....
That Night The Fate of the Two Started to Twist
CLOMP
Ah!
?
?
SHWIP

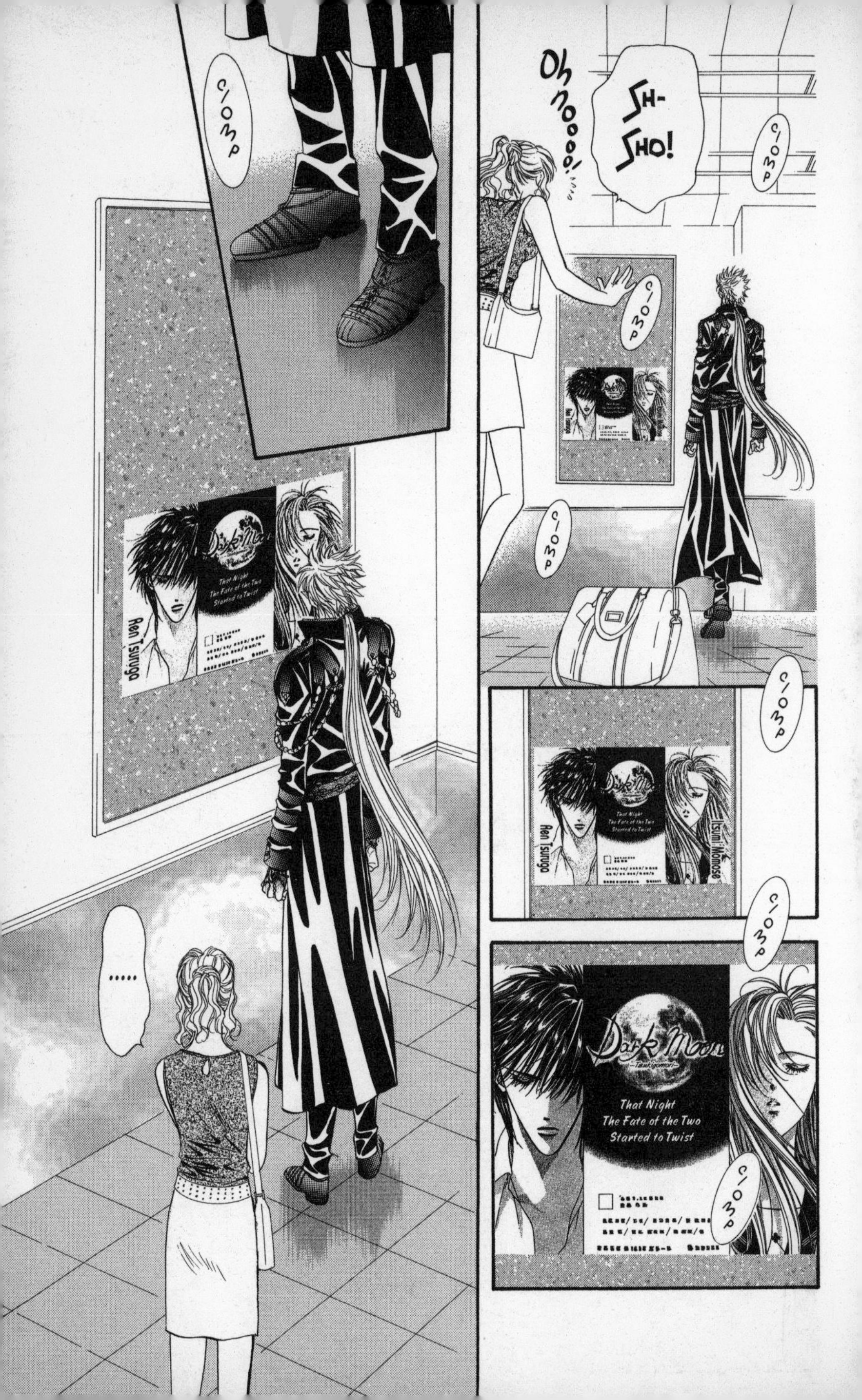
SH-SHO!
Oh nooooo!
CLOMP
CLOMP
CLOMP
CLOMP
Dark Moon
That Night
The Fate of the Two
Started to Twist
Ren Tsuruga
Izumi Momose
CLOMP
Dark Moon
-Tsukigomori-
That Night
The Fate of the Two
Started to Twist
CLOMP
CLOMP
That Night
The Fate of the Two
Started to Twist
Ren Tsuruga
......

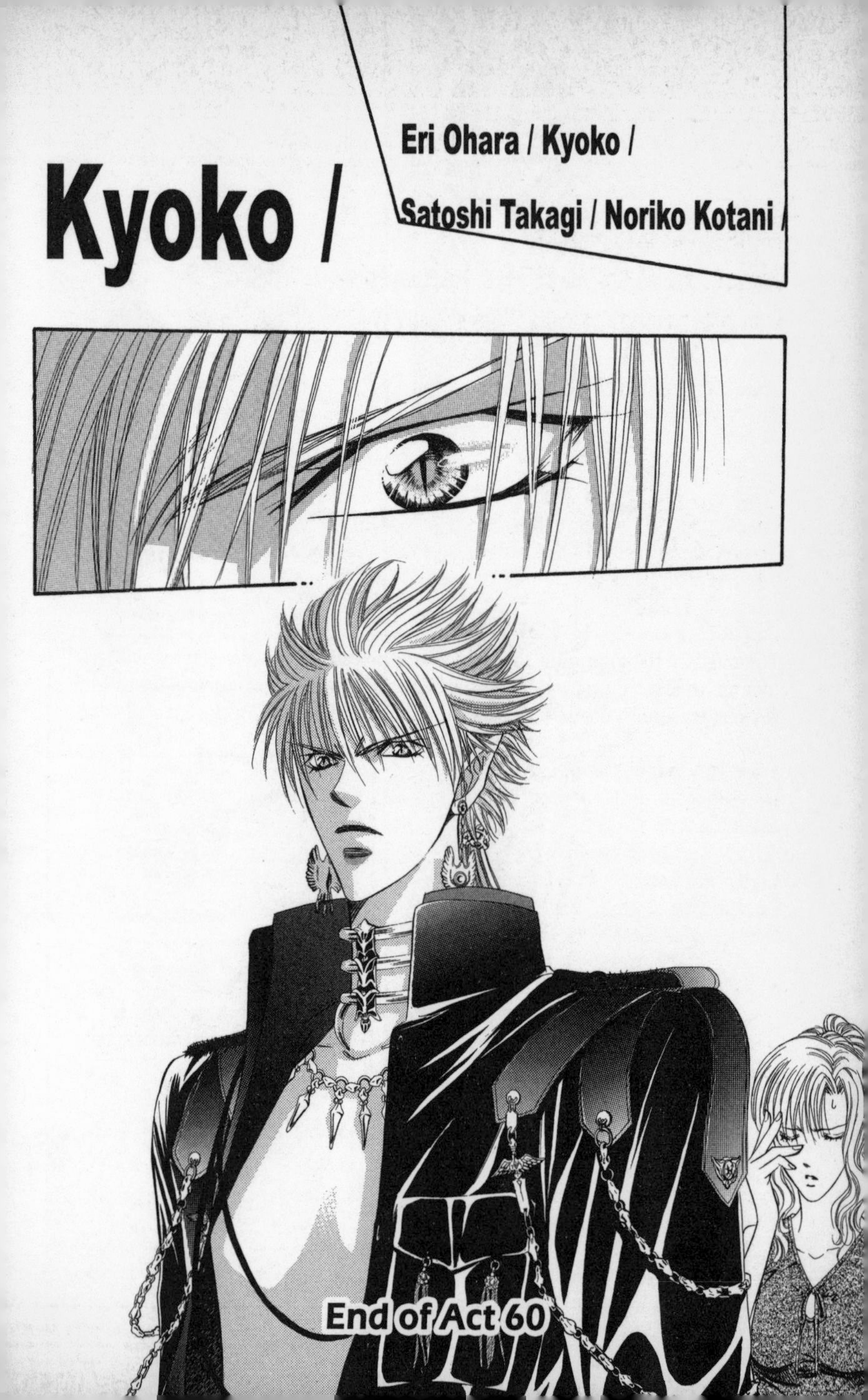
Eri Ohara / Kyoko /
Satoshi Takagi / Noriko Kotani /
Kyoko /
End of Act 60

Skip·Beat! End Notes
Everyone knows how to be a fan, but sometimes cool things
from other cultures need a little help crossing the language barrier.

Page 15, panel 8: N-namu namu
This is the first part of the *daimoku*, a Japanese Buddhist chant that dates back
to 1253.

Page 49, panel 1: Jibakurei
Literally "earthbound spirits." Jibakurei are created through violent deaths,
like accidents or suicide, and are bound to one place and unable to continue
on to the afterworld.

Page 111, panel 5: Her patience
The bag is a visual pun on the phrase *kannin bukuro no o ga kireru*, which
means "to lose you patience/temper." The kanji for *bukuro* means "bag," and
the *o* represents a cord or strap. When the cord breaks, you lose it and snap.

Page 162, panel 1: Dogeza
Bowing from a sitting position and pressing your head against the floor. The
most contrite bow possible.

Page 176, panel 1: Fillet me, etc
In Japanese, "to boil or grill" someone means doing something terrible to
them.

Page 176, panel 1: Kyoko on the cutting board
This is a visual representation of the expression "the carp on the cutting
board," because it is said that once the carp is put on the cutting board, it
gives up its fight.

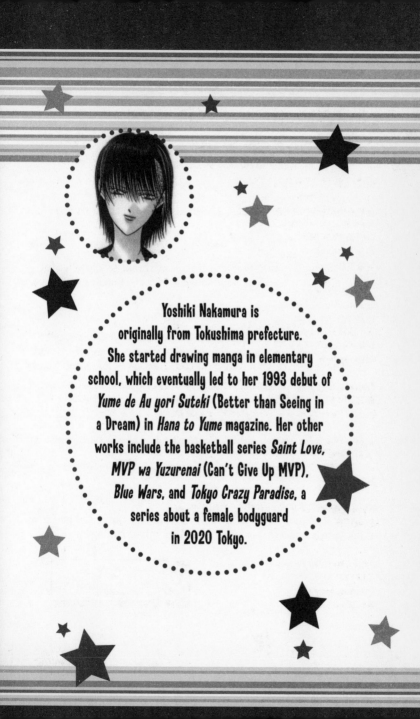

Yoshiki Nakamura is originally from Tokushima prefecture. She started drawing manga in elementary school, which eventually led to her 1993 debut of *Yume de Au yori Suteki* (Better than Seeing in a Dream) in *Hana to Yume* magazine. Her other works include the basketball series *Saint Love*, *MVP wa Yuzurenai* (Can't Give Up MVP), *Blue Wars*, and *Tokyo Crazy Paradise*, a series about a female bodyguard in 2020 Tokyo.

SKIP·BEAT!

Vol. 10

The Shojo Beat Manga Edition

STORY AND ART BY YOSHIKI NAKAMURA

English Translation & Adaptation/Tomo Kimura
Touch-up Art & Lettering/Sabrina Heep
Cover Design/Yukiko Whitley
Interior Design/Izumi Evers
Editor/Pancha Diaz

Editor in Chief, Books/Alvin Lu
Editor in Chief, Magazines/Marc Weidenbaum
VP of Publishing Licensing/Rika Inouye
VP of Sales/Gonzalo Ferreyra
Sr. VP of Marketing/Liza Coppola
Publisher/Hyoe Narita

Printed in Canada

Published by VIZ Media, LLC
P.O. Box 77010
San Francisco, CA 94107

Shojo Beat Manga Edition
10 9 8 7 6 5 4 3 2
First printing, January 2008
Second printing, February 2008

store.viz.com

PARENTAL ADVISORY
SKIP·BEAT! is rated T for Teen and is recommended for ages 13 and up. This volume contains a grudge.

RATED T FOR TEEN

ratings.viz.com

love ★ com
By Aya Nakahara

Class clowns Risa and Ōtani join forces to find love!

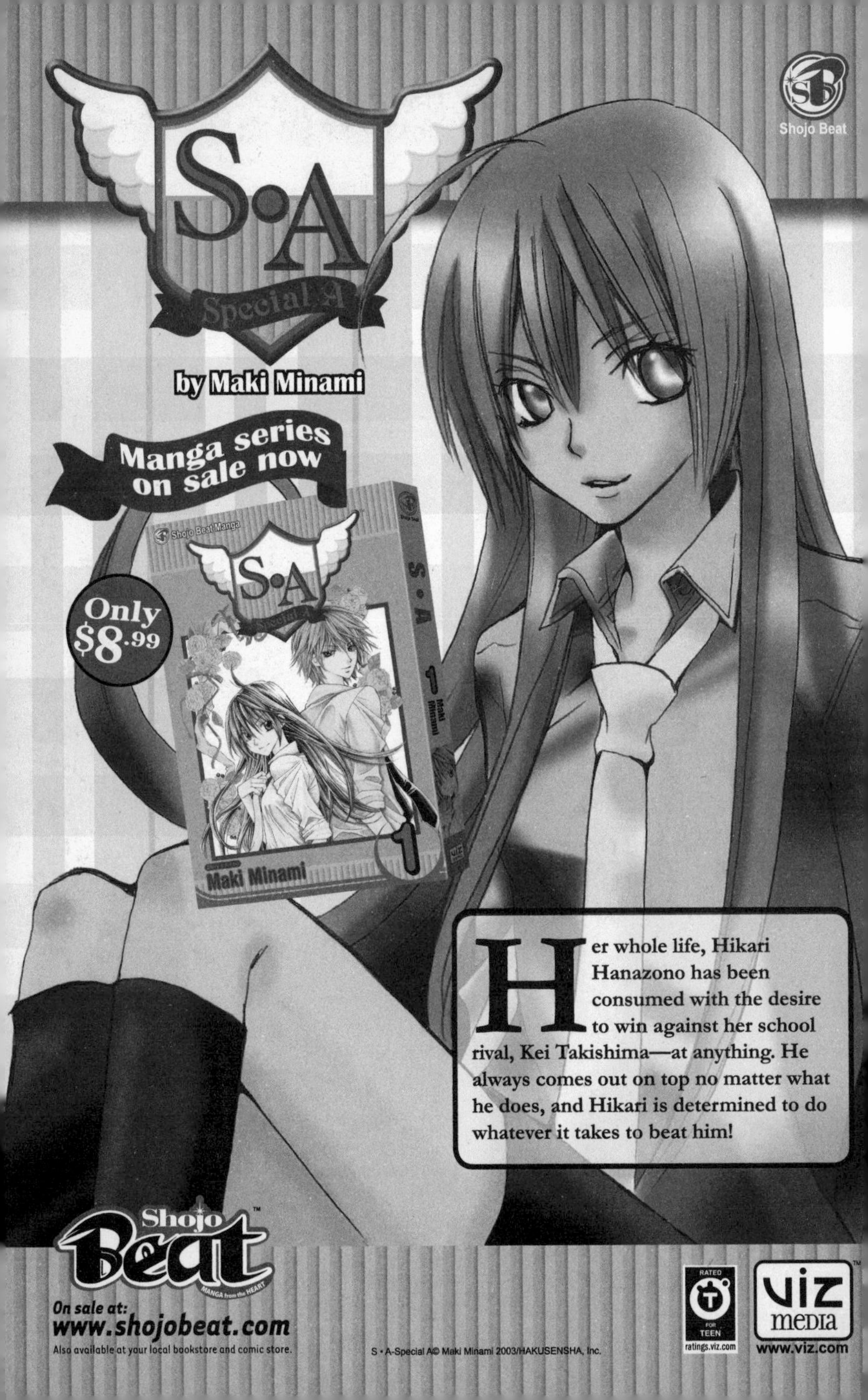
Shojo Beat
S•A
Special A
by Maki Minami
Manga series on sale now
Only $8.99
Shojo Beat Manga
S•A
1
Maki Minami
Her whole life, Hikari Hanazono has been consumed with the desire to win against her school rival, Kei Takishima—at anything. He always comes out on top no matter what he does, and Hikari is determined to do whatever it takes to beat him!
Shojo Beat™
MANGA from the HEART
On sale at:
www.shojobeat.com
Also available at your local bookstore and comic store.
S • A-Special A© Maki Minami 2003/HAKUSENSHA, Inc.
RATED T FOR TEEN
ratings.viz.com
VIZ media
www.viz.com

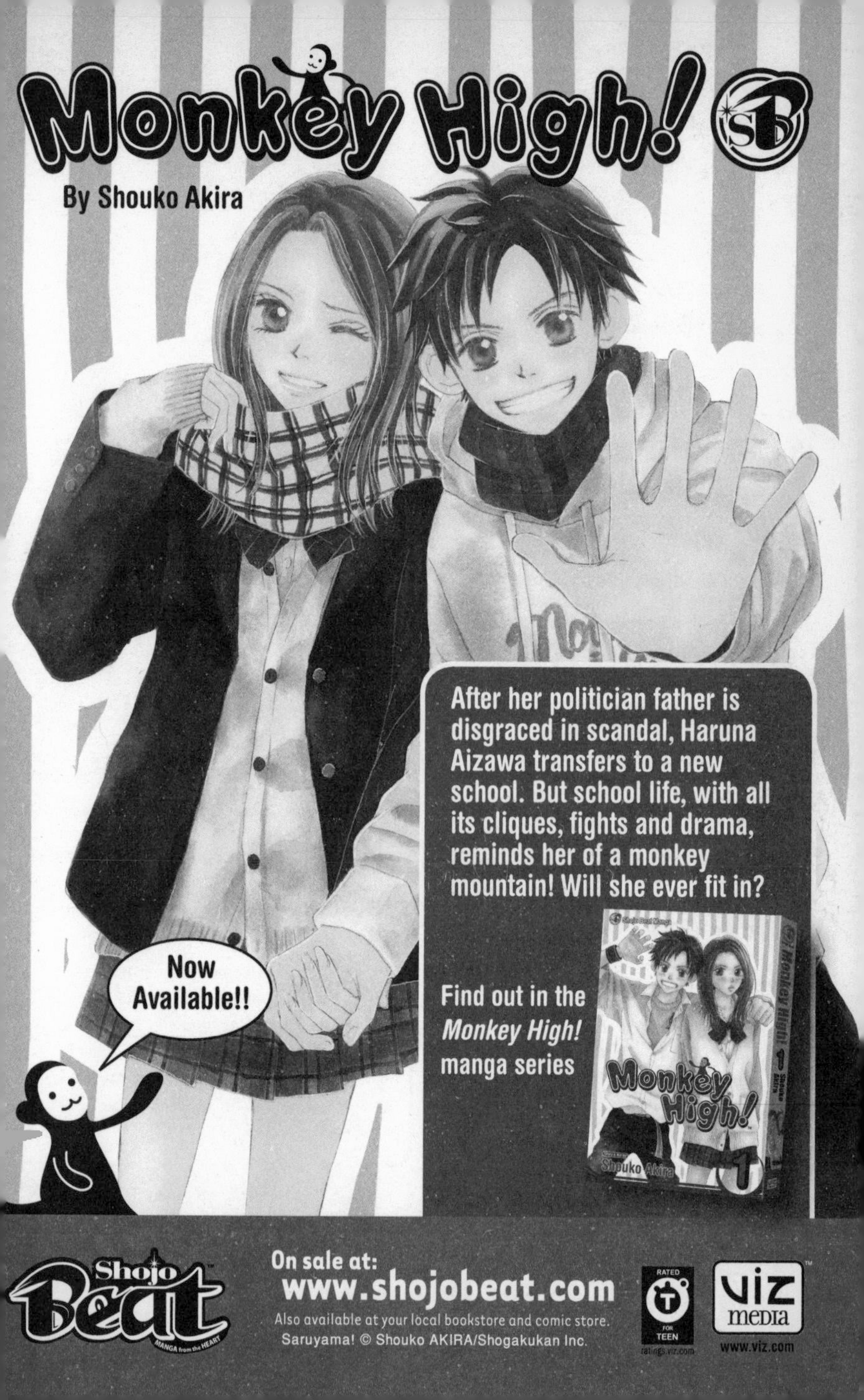
Monkey High!
By Shouko Akira
After her politician father is disgraced in scandal, Haruna Aizawa transfers to a new school. But school life, with all its cliques, fights and drama, reminds her of a monkey mountain! Will she ever fit in?
Now Available!!
Find out in the *Monkey High!* manga series
Shojo Beat
MANGA from the HEART
On sale at:
www.shojobeat.com
Also available at your local bookstore and comic store.
Saruyama! © Shouko AKIRA/Shogakukan Inc.
RATED T FOR TEEN
ratings.viz.com
viz media
www.viz.com

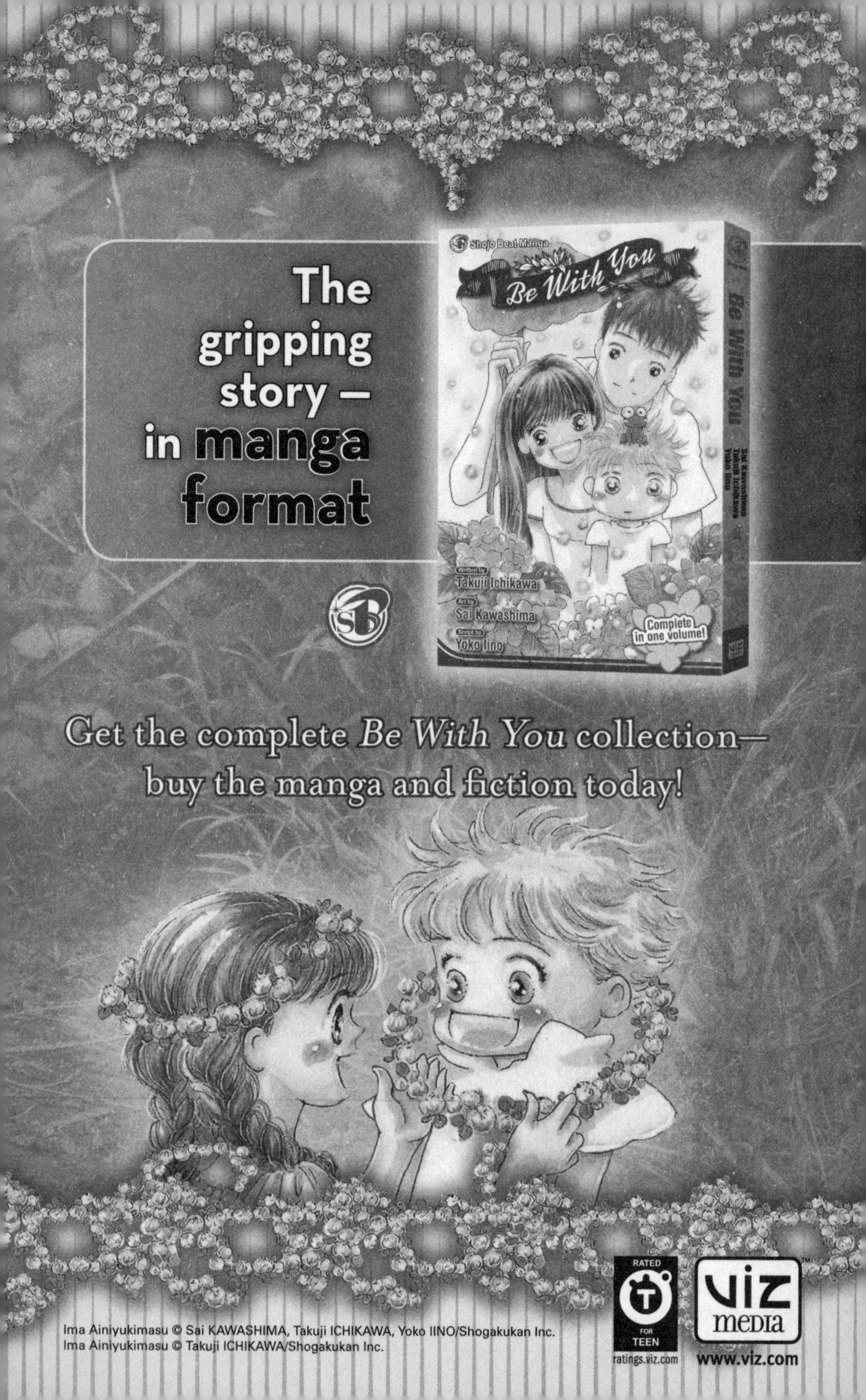
The gripping story — in manga format
Shojo Beat Manga
Be With You
Written by Takuji Ichikawa
Art by Sai Kawashima
Script by Yoko Iino
Complete in one volume!
Get the complete *Be With You* collection—
buy the manga and fiction today!
Ima Ainiyukimasu © Sai KAWASHIMA, Takuji ICHIKAWA, Yoko IINO/Shogakukan Inc.
Ima Ainiyukimasu © Takuji ICHIKAWA/Shogakukan Inc.
RATED T FOR TEEN
ratings.viz.com
VIZ media
www.viz.com

Tell us what about Shojo Beat Manga!

Help us make our product offerings better!

THE REAL DRAMA BEGINS IN...

NOV 09   CH